Exhibitions, Music and the British Empire

Music in Britain, 1600–2000

ISSN 2053-3217

Series Editors:
BYRON ADAMS, RACHEL COWGILL AND PETER HOLMAN

This series provides a forum for the best new work in the field of British music studies, placing music from the early seventeenth to the late twentieth centuries in its social, cultural, and historical contexts. Its approach is deliberately inclusive, covering immigrants and emigrants as well as native musicians, and explores Britain's musical links both within and beyond Europe. The series celebrates the vitality and diversity of music-making across Britain in whatever form it took and wherever it was found, exploring its aesthetic dimensions alongside its meaning for contemporaries, its place in the global market, and its use in the promotion of political and social agendas.

Proposals or queries should be sent in the first instance to Professors Byron Adams, Rachel Cowgill, Peter Holman or Boydell & Brewer at the addresses shown below. All submissions will receive prompt and informed consideration.

Professor Byron Adams,
Department of Music – 061, University of California, Riverside, CA 92521–0325
email: byronadams@earthlink.net

Professor Rachel Cowgill,
Department of Music, University of York
Heslington, York, YO10 5DD
email: rachel.cowgill@york.ac.uk

Emeritus Professor Peter Holman MBE,
119 Maldon Road, Colchester, Essex, CO3 3AX
email: peter@parley.org.uk

Boydell & Brewer, PO Box 9, Woodbridge, Suffolk, IP12 3DF
email: editorial@boydell.co.uk

Previously published volumes in this series are listed at the back of this volume.

Exhibitions, Music and the British Empire

Sarah Kirby

THE BOYDELL PRESS

© Sarah Kirby 2022

All rights reserved. Except as permitted under current legislation
no part of this work may be photocopied, stored in a retrieval system,
published, performed in public, adapted, broadcast,
transmitted, recorded or reproduced in any form or by any means,
without the prior permission of the copyright owner

The right of Sarah Kirby to be identified as
the author of this work has been asserted in accordance with
sections 77 and 78 of the Copyright, Designs and Patents Act 1988

First published 2022
The Boydell Press, Woodbridge

ISBN 978 1 78327 673 8

The Boydell Press is an imprint of Boydell & Brewer Ltd
PO Box 9, Woodbridge, Suffolk IP12 3DF, UK
and of Boydell & Brewer Inc.
668 Mt Hope Avenue, Rochester, NY 14620–2731, USA
website: www.boydellandbrewer.com

The publisher has no responsibility for the continued existence or accuracy of URLs for
external or third-party internet websites referred to in this book, and does not guarantee
that any content on such websites is, or will remain, accurate or appropriate

A CIP catalogue record for this book is available
from the British Library

This publication is printed on acid-free paper

Contents

	List of Illustrations	vii
	Acknowledgements	xi
	List of Abbreviations	xiii
	Introduction	1
1	Exhibiting Music	27
2	The Musical Object	49
3	Sounding Instruments	72
4	Museums and the History of Music	84
5	Performance, Rational Recreation, and Music for 'Progress'	109
6	Music for Leisure and Entertainment	128
7	Nationalism and Music	151
8	Curating Non-Western Musics	170
9	Performing Non-Western Musics	186
	Conclusion: Exhibitions and Their Musical Legacies	209
	Bibliography	215
	Index	237

Illustrations

❦ *Figures*

1. 'Healtheries v. The Theateries', *Punch*, 26 Jul. 1884, p. 33. — 4
2. 'Madame Inventories. Her Last Appearance This Season', *Punch*, 14 Nov. 1885, p. 231. — 5
3. Australian International Exhibition, Sydney, 1879–80 at the Garden Palace [no date]. — 15
4. 'Ground Plan of the International Inventions Exhibition, London, 1885', *Metropolitan Railway and International Inventions Exhibition Guide, South Kensington, 1885* (London, 1885). — 19
5. 'Tobogganing at the Liverpool Exhibition 1886', *The Queen: The Lady's Newspaper*, 20 Nov. 1886, p. 596. — 23
6. 'Melbourne Centennial Exhibition of 1888: Bird's-Eye View of the Buildings', *Australasian Sketcher with Pen and Pencil*, 9 Aug. 1888. — 25
7. Location of the London exhibition buildings in the 1870s and '80s. *International Health Exhibition: Official Guide* (London, 1884), [title page]. — 30
8. 'Érard's Pianoforte and Harps', *The Crystal Palace and its Contents, being an Illustrated Cyclopaedia of the Great Exhibition of 1851* (London, 1852), p. 200. — 43
9. Interior of the Glasgow Exhibition building, 1888. 'The Glasgow Exhibition: The Main Avenue', *Illustrated London News*, 25 Aug. 1888, p. 221. — 54
10. French Court, Great Hall, Melbourne Exhibition Building, 1880–1. — 61
11. 'A Colonial-Made Pianoforte – Mr. Ezold's Exhibit in the New South Wales Gallery', *Illustrated Sydney News*, 20 Dec. 1879, p. 5. — 66
12. 'A Recital on Messrs Nicholson & Ascherberg's Pianofortes', *Illustrated Sydney News and New South Wales Agriculturalist and Grazier*, 29 Nov. 1879, p. 12. — 79

viii   ILLUSTRATIONS

13 'Pianoforte Recitals – Messrs. John Brinsmead and Sons' Stand, in the Nave', *Illustrated Sydney News and New South Wales Agriculturalist and Grazier*, 1 Nov. 1879, p. 5.   82

14 John Dinsdale, 'Old Musical Instruments in Gallery of Albert Hall', *Sketches at the Inventories* (London, 1885).   88

15 'The English Eighteenth-Century Music Room', in 'Music at the Inventions Exhibition, 1885', *Art Journal*, 47 (Aug. 1885), 229–32, at p. 231.   97

16 'A Sixteenth-Century Room', in 'Music at the Inventions Exhibition, 1885', *Art Journal* 47 (Nov. 1885), 349–52, at p.351.   98

17 'The Louis XVI Music Room', in 'Music at the Inventions Exhibition, 1885', *Art Journal*, 47 (Oct. 1885), 305–8, at p. 307.   99

18 'The Opening of the Centennial Exhibition – The Choir Rendering the Cantata', *The Illustrated Australian News*, 399 (15 Aug. 1888), p. 145.   122

19 Illustration of the illuminated fountain in the gardens at night at London 1885 in John Dinsdale, *Sketches at the Inventories* (London, 1885).   131

20 'The Eastern Kiosk', in John Dinsdale, *Sketches at the Inventories* (London, 1885).   132

21 'Evening Fete: Music in the Gardens', *Illustrated London News*, 2 Aug. 1884, p. 97.   133

22 John Lavery, *The Blue Hungarians* (1888).   136

23 'The Great Organ at the Melbourne Exhibition', *Australasian Sketcher*, 28 Aug. 1880, p. 137.   147

24 'Musical Recollections', John Dinsdale, *Sketches at the Inventories* (London, 1885).   160

25 'The Viennese Lady Orchestra', *Magazine of Music*, 4:38 (May 1887), p. 26.   165

26. 'The Indian Annex', in 'The Calcutta Exhibition', *Art Journal*, 46 (Apr. 1884), p. 97.   173

27 'The Chinese Court', *Illustrated London News*, 2 Aug. 1884, p. 96.   197

28 'A Few Bars of "Rule Britannia"', in 'Chinese Music at the Exhibition', *Pall Mall Gazette*, 10 Jul. 1884, p. 6.   201

29   'A Few Bars of "Rule, Britannia"', transcribed from the *Pall Mall Gazette* by François Picard (Apr. 2017).   201

Full credit details are provided in the captions to the images in the text. The author and publisher are grateful to all the institutions and individuals for permission to reproduce the materials in which they hold copyright. Every effort has been made to trace the copyright holders; apologies are offered for any omission, and the publisher will be pleased to add any necessary acknowledgement in subsequent editions.

৬ Tables

1	Daily Orchestral Concerts, Royal Albert Hall, Opening Week 14–18 Apr. 1873	38
2	Classification of Musical Instruments at International Exhibitions in the British Empire, 1851–90	59
3	Round, Catch, and Canon Club, International Inventions Exhibition, 26 Jun. 1885	100
4	Members of the Conservatoire Royal, Brussels, International Inventions Exhibition, 1, 2, and 4 Jul. 1885	101
5	Bristol Madrigal Society, International Inventions Exhibition, 8 Jul. 1885	102
6	Concert of Sacred Music, International Inventions Exhibition, 14 Jul. 1885	102
7	Concert of Ancient Netherlandish Music, International Inventions Exhibition, 15 Jul. 1885	103
8	Grenadier Guards, International Inventions Exhibition, 5 May 1885	138
9	The Band of the 2nd Battalion, U.R., Melbourne International Exhibition, 14 Nov. 1888	138
10	Royal Horse Guards (Blues), Edinburgh International Exhibition, 13 Sep. 1890	139
11	Selected Programmes, Strauss Orchestra, International Inventions Exhibition, 1885	158
12	Austrian Strauss Band, Melbourne International Exhibition, 15 Oct. 1880	162

13   Caron's Australian Band, Melbourne International Exhibition,
     16 Oct. 1880   163

Acknowledgements

Research for this project began at the end of 2015, spanning a couple of continents and dozens of archives. I have had an enormous amount of fun throughout the entire process of researching and writing this book, not least because I have spent the whole thing surrounded by brilliant, funny, caring, intelligent people who have shared their time, expertise, and friendship with me.

My first thanks go to Kerry Murphy who, as a mentor, has provided so much encouragement, generosity, and guidance. Her enthusiasm for musicology in Melbourne is so utterly inspiring and I can't possibly thank her enough. Similarly, I owe a great deal to David Irving for his advice, patience, and kindness, as well as his boundless energy and enthusiasm.

I am extremely grateful for the help of librarians and archivists across Australia and the UK, who have assisted in sourcing materials throughout this project. These include the staff at the Louise Hanson-Dyer Music Library and Baillieu Library at the University of Melbourne, the State Libraries of Victoria and New South Wales, the National Library of Australia, the British Library, National Art Library (London), Victoria & Albert Museum Archives, Royal Albert Hall Archives, Senate House Library at the University of London, the UK National Archives, Surrey History Centre, National Library of Scotland, Mitchell Library in Glasgow, Angela Kenny at the archive Royal Commission for the Exhibition of 1851, and the libraries and archives at the Universities of Cambridge, Oxford, Glasgow, and Edinburgh, and at the Royal College of Music.

I am equally grateful for the feedback I've received at various conferences where parts of this work have been presented, and would like to thank the organisers and participants of countless national and chapter conferences of the Musicological Society of Australia, conferences hosted by the American Musicological Society, North American British Music Studies Association, both the North American and Australian Victorian Studies Associations, and the British Association of Victorian Studies, as well as two Biennial International Conferences on Nineteenth-Century Music, the Sibelius Academy's Music History Symposia, Music in Nineteenth Century Britain, and the 2017 conference on 'Music and the Middlebrow' hosted by the University of Notre Dame.

I have received so much help from so many amazing scholars, who have been so generous with their time and expertise, sharing conversations, ideas, fact and translation checking, and even occasionally jumping into distant archives for me when the pandemic made doing it myself impossible. I'd particularly like to thank Stephen Banfield, Suzanne Cole, Rachel Cowgill, Katharine Ellis, Jennifer Hill, Linda Kouvaras, Rachel McCarthy, Marten Noorduin, Inge van Rij, Madeline Roycroft, Peter Tregear, and Paul Watt.

I'd also like to thank the series editors of Music in Britain 1600–2000 and Lizzie Howard, Michael Middeke, Julia Cook, and all the team at Boydell & Brewer for their help and encouragement. I'd particularly like to thank Laurence Cole for copy editing this book with such care.

Quotations from the music criticism of George Bernard Shaw are reproduced with permission of the Society of Authors, on behalf of the Bernard Shaw Estate.

Parts of Chapter One of this book also appear in the forthcoming volume *Music and Institutionalization* edited by Derek Scott and Saijaleena Rantanen, while parts of Chapters Four and Eight appear as 'Prisms of the Musical Past: British International Exhibitions and "Ancient Instruments", 1885–1890' in volume 47, no. 3 (2019) of the journal *Early Music*.

The research for this project was supported by an Australian Federal Government Endeavour Research Fellowship, as well as a number of grants from the Melbourne Conservatorium of Music.

The publication of this book is supported by the Australian Academy of the Humanities publication subsidy scheme.

I am so grateful for all my friends – musicologists and non-musicologists alike – who have been so kind and supportive over so many years, read chapters and sections, and also humoured my constant talking about ridiculous Victorian stuff. These include Peter Campbell, Tim Daly, Andrew Frampton, Jacob Heywood, Shelley Hogan, Nathan Juriansz, Fred Kiernan, Rachel Landgren, Elly Langford, Thalia Laughlin, Belinda Liew, Michelle Meinhart, Rachel Orzech, Madeline Roycroft (again), Hannah Spracklan-Holl, David Tieri, Alejandro Alberto Téllez Vargas, Louisa Wilson, and Maurice Windleburn. I would also like to thank my family for putting up with me throughout this whole process, and particularly my mother, Anne Merrick, who has read so, so many drafts, and used her genealogical expertise to help me trace many of the little-known composers and performers mentioned throughout. Finally, to my partner, Juho Mäkinen, thank you for just being there, wherever there happened to be.

Abbreviations

B	British Library
NLA	National Library of Australia
RC/A/1851	Royal Commission for the Exhibition of 1851 Archive, Imperial College, London
SLV	State Library of Victoria
V&A	Victoria and Albert Museum

Introduction

'The king is dead, long live the king!' Thus Henry B. Wheatley described the opening of yet another international exhibition in London. 'No sooner', he wrote in 1885, were the doors of one exhibition closed, than 'preparations were made for the reopening of these doors'; just as the exhibits of one show were removed, those of the next were installed.[1] Wheatley referred only to London, which held four exhibitions in quick succession throughout the 1880s, but his observations could be applied to exhibitions in many parts of the British Empire. During this decade, there was barely a year without an international exhibition, in continuation of a fairly recent tradition that had begun with the Great Exhibition in 1851. Arguably some of the most significant cultural phenomena of the nineteenth century, international exhibitions used comparative and competitive displays to reflect – their organisers claimed – the totality of human endeavour, from industry and manufacturing, to art and design. Moreover, they influenced the social, cultural, economic, and political lives of the cities that hosted them. Usually six months long and held in enormous purpose-built edifices packed full of objects, exhibitions were a massive and literal manifestation of the Victorian obsession with collecting, ordering, and classifying the world. But exhibitions were not just a physical and visual display; sound, and particularly music, was integral to their experience.

This book interrogates the role of music at international exhibitions in the British Empire throughout the 1880s. At these events, music was codified, ordered, and all-round 'exhibited' in multiple and changing ways. Sometimes it was represented through physical objects, sometimes through performance. It was used to fulfil the educational remit of the exhibitions, as a rarefied symbol of the highest human achievements in art, and its 'enlightening' qualities employed to edify the public both morally and culturally. At other times, it was engaged for commercial ends, as a tool for instrument manufacturers to advertise their wares, or as a commodified entertainment that could draw a paying crowd. Music was used as a vehicle for nationalist sentiments, or invoked as a marker of universalism. It could represent local talents, or appear so foreign that it challenged the very idea of what music was.

Critics of the time considered exhibitions to provide a snapshot of society: as *The Times* described the Great Exhibition, it provided 'a Daguerreotype likeness, struck off in one moment' of the 'true *organization de* [sic] *travail*'.[2]

---

[1] Henry B. Wheatley, 'Decorative Art in London', *The Decorator and Furnisher*, 5:5 (Feb. 1885), p. 166.

[2] 'The Great Exhibition', *The Times*, 17 Mar. 1851, p. 8; quoted in Paul Young, *Globalization and the Great Exhibition: The Victorian New World Order* (Basingstoke, 2009), p. 3.

Yet, despite any claims to neutral or objective representation, or of any single, intended hegemonic meaning, modern scholarship interprets exhibitions as self-consciously constructed, with multiple and sometimes conflicting meanings.[3] As Peter H. Hoffenberg has pointed out, they are 'reflections, mechanisms, or indices' for the societies that produced them, demonstrating not an impartial representation of the world, but social and cultural life as a contested process.[4] In this way, the nineteenth-century discourses that emerged around music at exhibitions can be revealing. This book argues, through an exploration of the role of music within these events, that exhibitions can demonstrate in microcosm many of the broader musical traditions, purposes, arguments, and anxieties of the day. In doing so, it intends to shed new light on the musical landscape of the societies in which they were held. Considering the exhibitions of the British Empire as part of a network crossing both cultural and social borders, this book examines how these exhibitions highlighted many contested processes in relation to the role of music in British and colonial society, institutions, and thought.

This study examines the exhibitions held in the British Empire throughout the 1880s, but also includes the first Australian exhibition, which was held in Sydney in 1879 and possessed many of the same characteristics. It considers a number of events across the Australian colonies, as well as India, England, and Scotland, concluding with the last nineteenth-century Scottish exhibition held in Edinburgh in 1890. While the exhibition tradition – with its roots in the artistic and agricultural exhibitions of early nineteenth-century Europe – is often said to begin in 1851 at the 'apex of Britain's industrial and commercial supremacy', in many ways, later exhibitions can provide a better insight into national concerns and ideas.[5] These exhibitions were held during a pivotal period in the conscious construction of national and cultural identity, where the British colonies – particularly those in Australia – began to agitate for self-governance. Equally, British imperial propaganda grew with renewed urgency 'in an inverse ratio with the decline of British power'.[6] This decade was, too, an exciting period of new ideas and technologies, spurred into existence by the Second Industrial Revolution. It was also significant in the history of music and musicology. In Britain, interest in the outside world, its cultures, and peoples reached a new peak. Bruno Nettl describes the major intellectual themes of the 1880s as 'taking on the world and doing the impossible; collecting and utilizing one's own national heritage; and seeing what the world was made

---

[3] Peter H. Hoffenberg, *An Empire on Display: English, Indian, and Australian Exhibitions from the Crystal Palace to the Great War* (Berkeley, 2001), p. xviii.
[4] *Ibid*, p. 246.
[5] John M. MacKenzie, *Propaganda and Empire: The Manipulation of British Public Opinion, 1880–1960* (Manchester, 1984), p. 97.
[6] Paul Greenhalgh, *Ephemeral Vistas: The Expositions Universelles, Great Exhibitions and World's Fairs, 1851–1939* (Manchester, 1988), p. 120.

of, how one could make use of it, and how it came to be'.[7] These were also the major themes of the international exhibitions.

Music and International Exhibitions

In 1884 and 1885, *Punch* published two cartoons depicting a personified exhibition – Miss South Kensington – explicitly referencing the musical relevance of these events. South Kensington was the centre of British exhibitions in the latter half of the nineteenth century. The Great Exhibition, held in Hyde Park, was followed by over a dozen exhibitions on a site between Kensington Gore and Cromwell Road. During the 1880s, a series of themed exhibitions were held here, including the 1883 Fisheries, 1884 Health, 1885 Inventions, and 1886 Colonial and Indian Exhibitions. One of the main attractions of all these events was the gardens of the Royal Horticultural Society, where entertainment including regular music by bands and various other carnival attractions could be enjoyed every afternoon and evening.

The music and gardens at South Kensington were so popular that some began to wonder if the exhibitions were having a detrimental effect on London's cultural life, drawing the public away from the usual concert season. It is this anxiety that the *Punch* illustrations depict, while illuminating several other ideas that characterise the reception of music at the exhibitions. In the first (Figure 1), Miss South Kensington – as the 1884 Health Exhibition – looms large over a garden, strung with the Exhibition's iconic electric lighting, and draped in musical notation. Drawing an audience with a large magnet that reads 'Healtheries' (the Exhibition's nickname, playing on 1883's Fisheries), she sits atop a cobweb-covered theatre, while a music hall proprietor slumps despondently below. Amongst other theatre and music hall references, the actor Henry Irving (1838–1905) – in Malvolio's cross-gartered stockings – skulks off in the bottom corner, while a worried-looking J.L. Toole (1830–1906) wears a 'Paw Claw' hat referencing *Paw Claudian*, a burlesque by F.C. Burnand (1836–1917, perhaps not incidentally, *Punch*'s editor) on the popular drama *Claudian*. The 'Chorus of Theatrical Managers' cry 'What's Healtheries to you is Death to Us!', to which Miss South Kensington replies, 'Shut up!' In the following year, Miss South Kensington returns as 'Madame Inventories' of the Inventions Exhibition (Figure 2). Wearing electric lights in her hair, and representations of the Exhibition's themes – inventions and music, depicted by a scroll and lute – Madame Inventories waves goodbye, holding a prize medal marking her *mater necessitas*. To the left are two of the Exhibition's organisers: Phillip Cunliffe Owen (1828–94), an executive commissioner and 'really the acting manager of the whole business', rubs his hands, while John Somers Vine (1847–1929), the City agent to the executive (sometimes described as Owen's 'right-hand man'), cheers on in the background.[8] On the right, theatre managers and music hall

---

[7] Bruno Nettl, *Nettl's Elephant: On the History of Ethnomusicology* (Urbana, 2010), p. 8.
[8] 'The Health Exhibition', *Daily News*, 8 May 1884, p. 6; 'Our London Letter', *Penny Illustrated Paper and Illustrated Times*, 10 May 1884, p. 290.

4   EXHIBITIONS, MUSIC AND THE BRITISH EMPIRE

Figure 1. 'Healtheries v. The Theateries', *Punch*, 26 Jul. 1884, p. 33. Periodicals Collection, SLV.

proprietors remark how 'jolly glad' they are to see Madame Inventories leaving. The caption reads, quoting Byron, 'Farewell, and if for ever, then for ever fare thee well!' – and '"Hooray!" say the Theatrical and Music-hall Managers'.

These illustrations demonstrate one of the ways in which exhibitions were of central concern to London's musical life. Their musical influence was also

Figure 2. 'Madame Inventories. Her Last Appearance This Season', *Punch*, 14 Nov. 1885, p. 231. Periodicals Collection, SLV.

wide-reaching across the Empire, in terms of the sheer amount of music that they contained, and the large audiences that attended. Despite the influence of the exhibitions on musical life in late-nineteenth-century Britain and the colonies, however, these events have been generally overlooked in scholarly explorations of music so far. Similarly, there is little engagement with music in considerations of British and colonial exhibitions overall, despite exhibition studies being a wide and varied discipline.

By comparison, music at exhibitions in the French tradition is far better studied due to the pioneering work of Annegret Fauser, as well as contributions by Jann Pasler and a number of other scholars, with much research focusing on Claude Debussy (1862–1919) and his 1889 Exposition Universelle encounter with the Javanese gamelan.[9] There is also much scholarly discussion of music at late-nineteenth-century North American World's Fairs, particularly of the 1893 World's Columbian Exposition, and its engagement with non-Western musics.[10] Musicological considerations of music at British exhibitions have generally focused on the Great Exhibition, especially the representation of music through exhibits of instruments. As Flora Willson argues, these objects might be functionally understood as representing music through 'a putative, literal materialization of an epistemology of music' closely tied to 'the emergence of the work-concept'.[11] Yet discussion of 'works', or any conception of musical performance that occurred in this space is yet to be interrogated. Kerry Murphy, meanwhile, expands the discussion of these instruments to a geopolitical perspective in her exploration of Hector Berlioz (1803–69) as a Great Exhibition juror. Here, instruments represent more than just 'music', but rather national interests, used provocatively by the press to pit countries against one another.[12]

Music at Australian exhibitions has also been discussed in some detail, with pioneering studies including Mimi Colligan's exploration of music at the Melbourne exhibitions, Rosalyn Maguire's work on the Sydney Exhibition's musical director Paolo Giorza (1832–1914), Jennifer Royle's discussion of Frederic Cowen (1852–1935) and music at Melbourne 1888, and Julja Szuster's chapter on

---

[9] Annegret Fauser, *Musical Encounters at the 1889 Paris World's Fair* (Rochester, 2005); Jann Pasler, 'The Utility of Musical Instruments in the Racial and Colonial Agendas of Late Nineteenth-Century France', *Journal of the Royal Musical Association*, 129:1 (2004), 24–76, and 'Listening to Race and Nation: Music at the Exposition Universelle de 1889', in Florence Gétreau (ed.), 'La musique aux expositions universelles: Entre industries et cultures', *Musique, images, instruments: Revue française d'organologie et d'iconographie musicale*, 13 (2012), 52–74; see also the rest of this special issue. A number of other studies consider the musical representations of different countries at the Paris Expositions. For just one example of Spain in this context, see Manuelle Delannoy, 'La facture instrumentale espagnole aux expositions universelles parisiennes de 1855 a 1900', *Nassarre: Revista aragonesa de musicología*, 10:2 (1994), 9–17.

[10] For North American examples see, among others, David M. Guion, 'From Yankee Doodle thro' to Handel's Largo: Music at the World's Columbian Exposition', *College Music Symposium*, 24:1 (1984), 81–96; Mary Talusan, 'Music, Race, and Imperialism: The Philippine Constabulary Band at the 1904 St Louis World's Fair', *Philippine Studies*, 52:4 (2004), 499–526; and Krystyn R. Moon, 'The Quest for Music's Origin at the St Louis World's Fair: Frances Densmore and the Racialization of Music', *American Music*, 28:2 (2010), 191–210.

[11] Flora Willson, 'Hearing Things: Musical Objects at the 1851 Great Exhibition', in James Q. Davies and Ellen Lockhart (eds), *Sound Knowledge: Music and Science in London, 1789–1851* (Chicago, 2016), pp. 227–45, at p. 228.

[12] Kerry Murphy, 'Berlioz and the Piano at the Great Exhibition: The Challenge of Impartiality', in Barbara L. Kelly and Kerry Murphy (eds), *Berlioz and Debussy: Sources, Contexts and Legacies: Essays in Honour of François Lesure* (Aldershot, 2007), pp. 67–80.

music surrounding the 1887 Adelaide Exhibition.[13] Although much of this work is documentary, and these remain isolated studies, they provide foundations on which future scholarship on an interconnected tradition can build.[14]

Although few exhibition studies texts deal specifically with music, there are a number of important contributions that I draw on for methodological and historical foundation. The 1851 Great Exhibition has consistently attracted academic attention, inspiring some of the most significant studies on the British exhibition tradition. The earliest scholarly works examining this[15] – written in the 1950s around the Exhibition's centenary – are descriptive and moralistic products of their time, and have been challenged by every generation of scholars that followed.[16] Later Marxist, Gramscian, and Foucauldian analytical studies, however, particularly the work of Tony Bennett and Paul Greenhalgh, remain useful for understanding the exhibitions through frameworks of imperial propaganda and as part of the 'capitalist project'.[17] But it is the work of scholars such as John R. Davis, Jeffry A. Auerbach, Peter H. Hoffenberg, and

---

[13] Mimi Colligan and David Dunstan, 'A Musical Opening', in David Dunstan (ed.), *Victorian Icon: The Royal Exhibition Building, Melbourne* (Kew, 1996), pp. 107–14, and Colligan, 'More Musical Entertainments', in *Victorian Icon*, pp. 214–18; Roslyn Maguire, 'Paolo Giorza, Director of Music: The Most Accessible Art', in Peter Proudfoot, Roslyn Maguire, and Robert Freestone (eds), *Colonial City, Global City: Sydney's International Exhibition 1879* (Darlinghurst, 2000), pp. 129–147, and Maguire '"Pleasure of a High Order": Paolo Giorza and Music and Sydney's 1879 International Exhibition', *Context: Journal of Music Research*, 22 (2001): 41–50; Jennifer Royle, '"Preparing to Exhibit": Frederick Cowen in the Public Press Preceding Melbourne's Centennial International Exhibition, 1888–1889', *Context: Journal of Music Research*, 14 (1997): 53–62; Julja L. Szuster, 'Music of and at the Time of the Jubilee Exhibition', in Christine Garnaut, Julie Collins, and Bridget Jolly (eds), *Adelaide's Jubilee International Exhibition: The Event, the Building, the Legacy* (Darlinghurst, 2016), pp. 173–83.

[14] There are a few discussions that begin to connect aspects of these traditions together, such as the chapter 'Exhibitions and Festivals' in Jeffrey Richards, *Imperialism and Music: Britain 1876–1953* (Manchester, 2001), or Jennifer Royle's article, '"Turning the Wilderness into Flowers": Music as Triumph at Australia's International Exhibitions, 1879–1888', *Context: Journal of Music Research*, 22 (2001), 51–60. These works, however, focus on ceremonial music-making, rather than music in the day-to-day experience of exhibitions.

[15] Particularly Yvonne Ffrench, *The Great Exhibition: 1851* (London, 1950); Christopher Hobhouse, *1851 and the Crystal Palace: Being an Account of the Great Exhibition and its Contents, of Sir Joseph Paxton, and of the Erection, the Subsequent History and the Destruction of His Masterpiece* (London, 1950); Nikolaus Pevsner, *High Victorian Design: A Study of the Exhibits of 1851* (London, 1951).

[16] John R. Davis, *The Great Exhibition* (Stroud, 1999), p. xiii; Young, *Globalization and the Great Exhibition*, p. 12.

[17] Davis, *The Great Exhibition*, p. xv; Tony Bennett, 'The Exhibitionary Complex', in Reesa Greenberg, Bruce W. Ferguson, and Sandy Nairne (eds), *Thinking about Exhibitions* (London, 1996), pp. 58–80; Paul Greenhalgh, *Ephemeral Vistas: The Expositions Universelles, Great Exhibitions and World's Fairs, 1851–1939* (Manchester, 1988), p. 120.

Louise Purbrick that are most fruitful in breaking down the monumentalist, 'grand narrative' that surrounds previous discussions of the Great Exhibition.[18] Hoffenberg's other works, addressing the Great Exhibition's legacy and later British, Australian, and Indian events, have also been useful in framing my discussion here.[19] Although Hoffenberg refers little to music, he provides a convincing argument for the trope of 'progress' ubiquitous in all contemporary settler-colonial exhibitions; something that is also manifested clearly in the narratives projected around music. Several other important works on a similar theme, including those by David Dunstan, Graeme Davison, and Kate Darian-Smith and others, provide a valuable foundation for the study of colonial exhibitions, emphasising 'the contradictions and tensions' present in this imported tradition.[20]

The Key Players

This book consistently references two groups as participants in the discourse surrounding music at the exhibitions: the commissioners (or organisers), and the press.

THE COMMISSIONERS

The commissioners were the exhibitions' decision makers. While discussed in rather homogeneous terms, their influence and involvement varied significantly. These 'cultural bureaucrats' came from a variety of backgrounds: some had political or aristocratic links, while others were selected for their professional knowledge.[21] In addition to the executive commissioners who controlled the events overall, smaller committees were appointed by the governments of exhibiting countries. The job of these organisers was not only to solicit and arrange exhibits, but to be responsible for creating 'the ideas of "culture" and "society"' as they were presented through the displays.[22]

---

[18] James Buzard, Joseph W. Childers, and Eileen Gillooly (eds), 'Introduction', in *Victorian Prism: Refractions of the Crystal Palace* (Charlottesville, 2007), p. 2; Davis, *The Great Exhibition*; Jeffry A. Auerbach and Peter H. Hoffenberg (eds), *Britain, the Empire, and the World at the Great Exhibition of 1851* (Aldershot, 2008); Jeffry A. Auerbach, *The Great Exhibition of 1851: A Nation on Display* (New Haven, 1999); Louise Purbrick (ed), *The Great Exhibition of 1851: New Interdisciplinary Essays* (Manchester, 2001).

[19] Peter H. Hoffenberg, *An Empire on Display*; Peter H. Hoffenberg, 'Photography and Architecture at the Calcutta Exhibition', in Maria Antonella Pelizzari (ed.), *Traces of India: Photography, Architecture, and the Politics of Representation, 1850–1900* (Montréal, 2003), pp. 174–95; Peter H. Hoffenberg, *A Science of Our Own: Exhibitions and the Rise of Australian Public Science* (Pittsburgh, 2019).

[20] Graeme Davison, 'Exhibitions', *Australian Cultural History*, 2 (1982/3), 5–21; Kate Darian-Smith, Richard Gillespie, Caroline Jordan, and Elizabeth Willis (eds), *Seize the Day: Exhibitions, Australia and the World* (Clayton, 2008).

[21] Hoffenberg, *An Empire on Display*, pp. 34-5, 63.

[22] *Ibid*, p. 36.

The membership of the Executive Commission for the 1880s London exhibitions was relatively consistent, including the noted chemist Frederick Abel (1827–1902), director of the South Kensington Museum Philip Cunliffe-Owen, his nephew, the lawyer Edward Cunliffe-Owen (1857–1918), and the Marquis of Hamilton (1838–1913). This close-knit group – becoming known as the 'South Kensington Gang' – had such executive power over many years that they were sometimes accused of 'jobbery'. As a press report published as far away as South Australia stated, the 'Gang' had 'grouped themselves together … for the patriotic object of getting up exhibitions for the benefit of the public and of themselves'.[23] John Somers Vine, the official agent for the City of London to the Commission, was particularly influential; his connections with the printing firm given a large contract for the exhibitions courted controversy, as well as his 'weakness' for brass bands which apparently influenced the decision to spend over £100 a day employing bands (roughly £10,000 in 2020).[24]

In Australia, the executive commissioners tended to be among the 'most active and influential public figures' in the colonies, made up largely of European migrants, in government, judicial, and industry roles.[25] Others were involved in promoting colonial cultural endeavours, as trustees or board members of arts organisations. As such, the Executive Commission for both Melbourne exhibitions included politicians and businessmen such as John Benn (1821–95), William Mountford Kinsey Vale (1833–95), and John Pigdon (1832–1903), as well as the Victorian Premiers Graham Berry (1822–1904) and James Munro (1832–1908). Other important figures – all men – were also involved, such as engineer Alexander Kennedy Smith (1824–81) who had established the Institute for the Advancement of Science and the Philosophical Society of Victoria, William John Clarke (1831–97) who was a frequent donor to the Melbourne Church of England and the National Gallery of Victoria, and Robert Murray Smith (1831–1921), Council member of the University of Melbourne, and trustee of the Public Library, Museum, and National Gallery.

All these exhibitions also had extensive lists of patrons – usually headed by Queen Victoria – a president, and many honorary vice-presidents. In Australia, these usually included the Governors of the other colonies, whereas in Britain these were mainly aristocrats. In India, these positions were filled by imperial government officials, Maharajas, and Rajas of the different states. It is often unclear what influence, if any, those in titled roles had, other than to lend the events prestige. But this prestige did not always come from royal or aristocratic associations. Thomas Alva Edison (1847–1931) was a vice-president for Edinburgh 1890 – an exhibition dedicated to Electrical Engineering and Inventions – and, while there is no evidence he visited Scotland that year, his name on the list of vice-presidents gave the Exhibition an important sense of scientific legitimacy.

---

[23] 'Exhibition Exposures', *South Australian Register*, 27 Jun. 1887, p. 4.
[24] *Ibid*. Relative value calculated at *Measuring Worth* <https://www.measuringworth.com/calculators/ukcompare/> [accessed 24 Mar. 2021].
[25] Hoffenberg, *An Empire on Display*, p. 42.

THE PRESS

Analysis of press reports and stories is an important part of reception studies, especially in late-nineteenth-century contexts. The musical press expanded greatly over the nineteenth century, with nearly 200 music journals active in England, and content ranging from polemical tracts and opinion pieces, to works on education, and trade publications.[26] Many publications were designed to be read by both professionals and 'keen amateurs', reflecting an emerging forum in which, to quote David Kennerley, 'amateurs and professionals, performers and audiences, interacted as part of an increasingly cosmopolitan musical culture'.[27] Equally important, however, was the general interest periodical press and daily newspapers, which contained some of the most widely read discussions of music, given their volume of readership. This 'non-specialist' press was generally well-informed on musical matters, with many printing regular music columns and employing professional critics.[28] These various publication types had differing 'critical priorities', with the musical press determinedly advocating for the professional and artistic status of musicians and music.[29]

Among critics, there were also varying levels of investment in the music they discussed. Many late-nineteenth-century critics considered themselves as guardians of the art. This is seen notably in discussions by figures such as John Fuller-Maitland (1856–1936), who cast himself as a 'watchman' or 'doorkeeper' of music. These tropes, Merion Hughes argues, were 'drawn from a pre-modern, even biblical, context' where English music was a 'citadel, tower, [or] threatened city' that critics laboured to protect.[30] This sense of a need to 'defend' music from adulteration by commercial or 'lesser' forms translates into an ideological position seen in much of the criticism here. Critics took a defensive stance in relation to the use of music at the exhibitions, significantly influencing the way certain aspects of that music was received.

Another major issue arising through the use of the press relates to anonymity. The identity of the authors of the majority of articles I reference here remains unknown. For concision, except where the author has been identified (through signed notices, or later research), I refer to the responses I quote by their publication title.[31] This is complicated, however, by the fact that few

---

[26] Leanne Langley, 'The Musical Press in Nineteenth-Century England', *Notes*, 46:3 (1990), 583–92, at p. 585.

[27] David Kennerley, 'Debating Female Musical Professionalism and Artistry in the British Press, c.1820–1850', *The Historical Journal*, 58:4 (2015), 987–1008, at p. 992.

[28] Ibid, p. 993.

[29] Ibid.

[30] Meirion Hughes, *The English Musical Renaissance and the Press, 1850–1914: Watchmen of Music* (Aldershot, 2002), pp. 29–30.

[31] Merion Hughes suggests that contemporary sources and the 'internal stylistic evidence' of writings can help identify critics, where they held full-time employment at particular publications. The large number and geographic range of the publications used here, however, makes this research a task beyond the scope of this book. See Hughes, *English Musical Renaissance and the Press*, p. 8.

nineteenth-century periodicals can be seen as cohesive.[32] While there was certainly editorial discretion, these publications were often patched together from contributions by multiple authors. Consequently, an individual periodical may present many and conflicting viewpoints. Author anonymity was partly intended to promote objectivity, but it can also flatten out differences in opinion, implying one or two authors' views to be more universal than they may really be.[33] This becomes particularly problematic with regard to the aggressively racist reviews that I describe in the final chapters of this book. While there was clearly a sort of *Zeitgeist* of racist commentary, and despite any consensus that might be inferred from the multiple anonymous reviewers, care must be taken not to imply that opinions were necessarily unanimous, particularly given the number of named individuals who provide countering perspectives.[34]

The notion of consensus raises further questions about the representativeness of the press. Critics and their opinions must be viewed in the socio-historical context of their time.[35] Existing within the same society at the same time, critics and audiences shared a 'horizon of expectation', or a set of systems of reference that they brought to a work, formed through their shared social and historical experiences.[36] Because of this, in some circumstances, critics' views can be seen as representative of the wider public: by correlating the 'aesthetic assumptions' preserved in the press with their 'manifestations in behaviour' – to quote James Johnson – one can also make generalisations about the responses of 'those spectators whose behavior we see but whose thoughts are silent'.[37] While I have generally accepted this premise, there are clear instances where audience behaviour does *not* align with the critics' view. This is made evident by the press's own discomfort and explicit disapproval of the public response to certain musics. While critics cannot always be equated with audiences – in England, for example, the social and economic class of the critics might differ considerably from audience members at exhibitions attended by people from across the class spectrum – they may still provide helpful avenues to understanding the historical and social context of the events they describe.

---

[32] Laurel Brake and Julie F. Codell (eds), 'Introduction, Encountering the Press', in *Encounters in the Victorian Press: Editors, Authors, Readers* (Basingstoke, 2004), p. 1.
[33] *Ibid*, pp. 1–2.
[34] As is further demonstrated in Bennett Zon's *Representing Non-Western Music in Nineteenth-Century Britain* (Rochester, 2007).
[35] Jim Samson, 'Reception', *Grove Music Online* (2001) <http://www.oxfordmusiconline.com> [accessed 24 Mar. 2021].
[36] This is one of the major tenets of reception theory, which emerged through the work of literary scholar Hans Robert Jauss during the 1960s and '70s, advocating for a change in scholarly focus from the author or the work itself, to how it is interpreted by audiences. See Hans Robert Jauss, *Toward an Aesthetic of Reception*, trans. Timothy Bahti (Minneapolis, 1982).
[37] James H. Johnson, *Listening in Paris: A Cultural History* (Berkeley, 1995), p. 5.

❧ *The Exhibitions*

Thirteen exhibitions held in the British Empire between 1879 and 1890 are considered in this book: Sydney 1879, Adelaide 1887, and Melbourne 1880 and 1888 in the Australian colonies; the themed 1883 Fisheries, 1884 Health, 1885 Inventions, and 1886 Colonial and Indian Exhibitions in London, and Liverpool 1886 in England; Edinburgh 1886 and 1890, and Glasgow 1888 in Scotland; and Calcutta 1883 in India. For clarity, these are referred to by city and opening year (summer exhibitions in Australia and India generally fell over two calendar years) or, where relevant, by their theme. All these exhibitions were self-described as 'international' in scope and had significant musical elements.

My exploration of these exhibitions is informed by a wealth of archival material, in addition to reports from the press, although the depth and variety of these sources differs considerably between the exhibitions. Information about those held in London, for instance, can be found in the archive of the Royal Commission for the Exhibition of 1851, located at Imperial College in London, which holds detailed minute books concerning the organisation committee's activities, while the Victoria and Albert Museum archives hold manuscript letters between the various organisers. In contrast, documents associated with the administration of the Sydney 1879 Exhibition are lost, presumably destroyed in the fire that obliterated the Garden Palace in 1882. A similar situation exists in relation to Melbourne, where sections of the exhibition building were devastated by fire in the 1950s. The archive for Liverpool 1886 is similarly missing, in all likelihood destroyed in the 1941 Blitz.[38]

For most exhibitions, the most significant archival sources that survive are official publications, curated specifically by the organisers. These are deliberately self-conscious records, and though requiring caution, have been used to fill in major historical gaps. The 1,154-page Sydney 1879 *Official Record*, for example, details the debates of the Executive Committee during the Exhibition's planning, including several proposals for the musical arrangements, which can then be corroborated by press reports. Documents relating to exhibiting firms are also disparate in range and depth. A file in the British Library manuscripts collection, for example, contains extensive documentation of piano manufacturer James Stephen's exhibits at London 1885.[39] Yet other exhibitors at the same event have completely disappeared from the records.

This book is arranged thematically, rather than chronologically, exploring music in the context of race, class, public education, economics, and entertainment. Each chapter examines a different theme, moving gradually from object-based discussions to performance contexts. The opening two chapters give some historical background, using examples from earlier exhibitions in London between the Great Exhibition of 1851 and the 1870s, where traditions

---

[38] Murray Steele, *Liverpool on Display* (United Kingdom, 2012), preface [no page number].
[39] [A Collection of Miscellaneous Printed and MS. Material Relating to Pianofortes. Compiled by J.L. Stephen], BL, General Reference Collection, 07902.b.1/9.

were established that became a model for later events. These chapters explore methodological issues involved in 'exhibiting' music, and systems of representation of musical objects in Victorian commodity culture, before moving on to consider how musical instruments were displayed in the 1880s. Chapter Three then interrogates the use of these instruments in demonstration recitals. Chapter Four considers the different modes of interpretation of museum displays of historic musical objects, while Chapter Five examines music as 'high art' as a tool of the rational recreation movement and a marker of cultural 'progress'. Chapter Six contrasts this with music presented for entertainment in the exhibitions' pleasure gardens. Chapter Seven deals with issues of nationalism arising in the reception of music, before the last two chapters explore non-Western musics through the curation of musical objects, and the reception of music performance.

This book does not consider the many smaller-scale exhibitions, or those without an international scope, that were also held in the British Empire in the 1880s. These included intercolonial exhibitions in Australia, 'Juvenile' exhibitions – held to encourage people under the age of twenty-one to participate in 'works of industry and usefulness'[40] – or a number of local 'Jubilee' exhibitions, celebrating Victoria's 1887 Golden Jubilee. For this reason, no exhibitions held in New Zealand are covered. The 1882 Christchurch Exhibition was far smaller than the preceding Sydney and Melbourne exhibitions,[41] while the 1885 New Zealand Industrial Exhibition focused only on local trades and industries.[42] The 1889 New Zealand and South Seas Exhibition held in Dunedin was largely a private enterprise to extend New Zealand's trade with the Pacific islands, and the majority of international exhibits had already been displayed at Melbourne 1888.[43] In contrast, the 1886 Colonial and Indian Exhibition, while not titled an 'international' exhibition, has been included. The intentions of its organisers were categorically global, and the musical exhibits and performances greatly varied. Other themed international exhibitions – such as the London 1881 International Medical and Sanitary Exhibition, or the 1884 International Forestry Exhibition in Edinburgh – however, have been excluded, due to a lack of musical content.

Although I aim to cover all the major musical themes that emerged at the exhibitions, there are a few musical topics I exclude from discussion. First, apart from in Chapter One, I do not examine ceremonial music. This music

---

[40] 'Significance – Item NU 35421 Medal – Australian Juvenile Industrial Exhibition, Ballarat, Victoria, Australia, 1878', *Museums Victoria* <https://collections.museumvictoria.com.au/items/273850> [accessed 24 Mar. 2021].

[41] Philip Jane, 'Music in Christchurch during the 1882 International Exhibition', *Journal of New Zealand Studies*, 17 (2014), 21–38, at p. 22.

[42] 'The 1885 New Zealand Industrial Exhibition', *Museum of New Zealand* <https://collections.tepapa.govt.nz/topic/864> [accessed 24 Mar. 2021].

[43] Conal McCarthy, 'Dunedin 1889–1890', in John E. Findling and Kimberly D. Pelle (eds), *Encyclopedia of World's Fairs and Expositions* (Jefferson, 2008), pp. 108–10, at p. 108.

14   EXHIBITIONS, MUSIC AND THE BRITISH EMPIRE

functions similarly at exhibitions as at any state ceremony, and in many cases has been extensively covered in the literature elsewhere.[44] Equally, not being a history of economics or manufacturing, I am not concerned with the actual process of juries and awards. While this was a fraught topic in the music trades press, by the 1880s, most major firms had already received medals at previous exhibitions and were choosing to exhibit *hors concours*. Additionally, by this time the general public had little interest in this topic – at least, in comparison to the musical activities I do discuss. Finally, while many British exhibitions (and Adelaide 1887) held concurrent choral and band competitions, I do not consider these here. Such competitions were important traditions in British music-making, but were local events, with competitors rarely coming from outside of the host cities.

A Catalogue of Exhibitions

Recognising that a large number of exhibitions are explored in this volume, I provide here – before beginning Chapter One – a series of short descriptions of each exhibition under consideration, giving background information, important features, and details of the kinds of musical activity that can be expected to be discussed at each. While this section can be read from start to finish to reveal the gradual shifts in musical focus that occurred across the decade, it is not required reading to follow the narrative of the chapters that follow. It can instead be used as a point of reference to return to throughout the book for basic information concerning each exhibition, should any reminders be needed.

SYDNEY INTERNATIONAL EXHIBITION, 1879

17 September 1879 – 20 April 1880
As the first international exhibition in the Southern Hemisphere, Sydney 1879 broke new ground.[45] Housed in the Domain and designed by architect James Barnet (1827–1904), the spectacular Garden Palace's (Figure 3) interior hierarchy was modelled on the 1876 Philadelphia World's Fair. This placed New South Wales's exhibits at the centre, flanked by the other Australian colonies. British exhibits took up a quarter of the total space, while the 'longitudinal ceremonial axis' of the building 'divided the Old World from the New', with a large display by the United States placed opposite.[46] The opening of the Exhibition was a public holiday, and the ceremony contained a new cantata by Paolo Giorza,

---

[44] For Australian examples, see Maguire, 'Pleasure of a High Order', and Royle, 'Turning the Wilderness into Flowers'; Hamish MacCunn's setting of the 8th Psalm for the opening of Edinburgh 1890 has been discussed in Jennifer Oates, *Hamish MacCunn (1868–1916): A Musical Life* (New York, 2016) and Alasdair Jamieson, *The Music of Hamish MacCunn* (Bloomington, 2013).

[45] Kirsten Orr, 'Sydney 1879–1880', in John E. Findling and Kimberly D. Pelle (eds), *Encyclopedia of World's Fairs and Expositions* (Jefferson, 2008), pp. 65–7, at p. 65.

[46] Ibid.

Figure 3. Australian International Exhibition, Sydney, 1879–80 at the Garden Palace [no date]. SLV, Accession no: H24950.

the Milanese composer appointed the Exhibition's musical director. Through the seven months that it was open, there was much musical entertainment, including piano, organ, and instrumental recitals, and brass bands and light orchestras playing in the grounds. A regular series of orchestral concerts and six full-scale oratorios were produced over the course of the Exhibition. Over a million people visited – the largest attendance in proportion to population of any exhibition up to that point.[47] While the Exhibition made a financial loss of over £100,000, it was generally agreed that local spending by visitors more than compensated for this.[48]

MELBOURNE INTERNATIONAL EXHIBITION, 1880

1 October 1880 – 30 April 1881

Melbourne 1880 represented for many 'an Australian coming-of-age'.[49] This exhibition was politically volatile from its conception, with parliamentary debates between free-trade advocates and the protectionist government stifling its progress, until Victoria's success at the 1878 Paris Exposition Universelle convinced political leaders of its value.[50] London-trained Cornish architect Joseph Reed (1823–90) designed the now World Heritage Listed exhibition building on

---

[47] *Ibid*, p. 66.
[48] Aram A. Yengoyan, 'Sydney 1879–1880', in John E. Findling and Kimberly D. Pelle (eds), *Historical Dictionary of World's Fairs and Expositions, 1851–1988* (New York, 1990), pp. 72–3, at p. 72.
[49] Dunstan, *Victorian Icon*, p. 3.
[50] David Dunstan, 'Melbourne 1880–1881', in *Encyclopedia of World's Fairs*, pp. 67–70, at p. 67.

a largely ecclesiastical theme, with a dome – the second highest in the world at the time – replicating Florence cathedral.[51] The opening of the Exhibition was declared a public holiday, with a grand procession through the streets of Melbourne. At the ceremony, a choir performed the cantata, *Victoria*, composed by French-born Melbourne resident Leon Caron (1850–1905).[52] Significant musical events included performances by the Austrian Strauss Band (the first European professional orchestra to tour Australia),[53] other bands in the grounds, daily organ and instrumental recitals, and a collection of Indian instruments, sent by Bengali musicologist Sourindro Mohun Tagore (1840–1914), exhibited in the British India Court.[54]

CALCUTTA [KOLKATA] INTERNATIONAL EXHIBITION, 1883

4 December 1883 – 10 March 1884

Calcutta was the first exhibition in the British Empire held in 'a subject rather than settler community'.[55] It was organised by Jules Joubert (1824–1907), a French-Australian businessman and experienced exhibition manager, with a rather uncompromising nature that caused much conflict.[56] Though initially an Anglo-Indian undertaking, the regional committees were predominantly Indian and had significant input on the displays.[57] Yet the space was starkly divided, with the permanent Indian Museum housing goods from outside India while a temporary iron annex held 'native' manufactures.[58] The opening ceremony went very badly, with monsoonal rain, and a planned spectacular electric light show that failed at the ceremony's climax.[59] It included a cantata, composed by Herr Mack (a 'local musical celebrity') and performed by the Italian Opera Company.[60] (Some critics noted the strangeness of 'an English Exhibition in the capital of India' being 'celebrated by a Cantata sung in Italian!')[61]

---

[51] John Powell, 'Melbourne 1880–1881', in *Historical Dictionary of World's Fairs*, pp. 74–5, at p. 74.

[52] Dunstan, 'Melbourne', p. 68.

[53] Graeme Skinner, 'Austrian Strauss Band', *Australharmony*, <https://www.sydney.edu.au/paradisec/australharmony/register-organisations-from-1861-A-Z.php> [accessed 18 Mar. 2021].

[54] See Reis W. Flora, 'Raja Sir Sourindro Mohun Tagore (1840–1914): The Melbourne Connection', *South Asia: Journal of South Asian Studies*, 27:3 (2004), 289–313.

[55] Renate Dohmen, '"A Fraught Challenge to the Status Quo": The 1883–84 Calcutta International Exhibition, Conceptions of Art and Industry, and the Politics of World Fairs', in Kate Nichols, Rebecca Wade, and Gabriel Williams (eds), *Art versus Industry? New Perspectives on Visual and Industrial Cultures in Nineteenth-Century Britain* (Manchester, 2016), pp. 199–216, at p. 199.

[56] See Joubert's own account of the exhibition in his autobiography *Shavings and Scrapes from Many Parts* (Dunedin, 1890).

[57] Hoffenberg, 'Photography and Architecture at the Calcutta Exhibition', pp. 177, 181.

[58] Thomas Prasch, 'Calcutta 1883–1883', in *Encyclopedia of World's Fairs*, pp. 75–7, at p. 76.

[59] Ibid, p. 75.

[60] 'Opening Ceremony', *Friend of India & Statesman*, 4 Dec. 1883, p. 14.

[61] 'Account of the Opening of the Exhibition', *Indian Mirror*, 6 Dec. 1883, p. 3.

Continual rain, electrical blackouts, and a series of fires damaged the building and exhibits,[62] and British exhibitors mostly boycotted the event, rejecting its implication that India 'could fully, and increasingly equally, participate in the subcontinent's governance'.[63] Yet the Exhibition proved remarkably – and financially – successful, with over one million visitors, and 2,500 exhibitors.[64] The musical arrangements, however, were haphazard with occasional band performances and a small number of instrumental recitals.

INTERNATIONAL FISHERIES EXHIBITION, 1883

12 May 1883 – 31 October 1883

The first of four themed international exhibitions at South Kensington was dedicated to fisheries and 'maritime objects of all kinds',[65] apparently appealing to those with 'piscatorial tastes' as well as anyone interested in machinery, architecture, business, art, or design.[66] Displays included – beyond a live aquarium and fishing-related exhibits – natural history drawings, fossils, and preserved specimens from around the world, oceanographic and scientific equipment, and a collection of sea-related art. Lectures were held on the lives of fishing industry workers, amateur angling, 'saving life at sea', and environmental protections, as well as sea-related fables and mythology, leading to the publication of many volumes, including one entitled *Sea Monsters Unmasked*.[67] There were also exhibits of furniture and decorative objects with an aquatic theme. Fish as a food was prominent, with displays of techniques for cooking, preservation, and refrigeration of different varieties of fish, and restaurants serving fish. The Fisheries Exhibition was described as 'remarkably successful', visited by nearly two and a half million people and making a considerable profit, which was donated to a fund for orphans of sea fishermen.[68] Music was surprisingly prevalent here, although none of it was fish-related. Most was intended only as supplementary entertainment, with organ recitals and military bands heard every day.[69]

INTERNATIONAL HEALTH EXHIBITION, 1884

8 May 1884 – 30 October 1884

---

[62] 'The Exhibition and the Weather', *Englishman*, 6 Dec. 1883, p. 5.
[63] Dohmen, 'A Fraught Challenge to the Status Quo', p. 204.
[64] Prasch, 'Calcutta', p. 76; John Powell, 'Calcutta, 1883–1884', in *Historical Dictionary of World's Fairs*, pp. 82–3, at p. 82.
[65] 'The Fisheries Exhibition', *Saturday Review of Politics, Literature, Science and Art*, 56:1462 (3 Nov. 1883), p. 559.
[66] 'The Fisheries Exhibition at South Kensington', *British Architect*, 19:20 (18 May 1883), 243–5, at p. 243.
[67] Henry Lee, *Sea Monsters Unmasked* (London, 1883).
[68] 'Subsequent use of the Gardens/International Fisheries Exhibition, 1883', *Seventh Report of The Commissioners for the Exhibition of 1851 to the Right Hon. Henry Matthews, &c., &c., One of Her Majesty's Principal Secretaries of State* (London, 1889), RC/A/1851.
[69] 'The Society of Arts', *Musical Standard*, 25:992 (4 Aug. 1883), p. 70.

The second themed London exhibition explored health and education: concepts believed to be closely allied. Displays were intended to broadly illustrate how 'food, dress, the dwelling, the school, and the workshop' influenced health, with exhibits including building materials, techniques for heating and ventilation, model 'sanitary' and 'insanitary' houses,[70] and a life-size replica of Cheapside before the Great Fire in which visitors could gauge the 'progress' of construction.[71] Dress was illustrated by exhibits of techniques for making clothing, fabric, millinery, footwear, lace, and gloves, but the largest part of the Exhibition was dedicated to food. Displays detailed the production of meat, vegetables, cereals, dairy products, cold-storage, and ice-making, classes were given on 'cheap cooking', and the building contained numerous restaurants.[72] The Education section encompassed a variety of topics on teaching and gymnasia across the world, and included fourteen conferences, with one covering music education in schools. Over two thousand exhibitors displayed objects or information, and the event was attended by more than four million people, making over £15,000 profit.[73] Like the Fisheries Exhibition, music played an important role in the entertainment, with the popularity of organ recitals and bands far outstripping that of the educational displays on recent developments in sanitation. A notable musical aspect of this exhibition was a band from China, performing regularly in the building's Chinese restaurant.

INTERNATIONAL INVENTIONS EXHIBITION, 1885

4 May 1885 – 9 November 1885

Known as the 'Inventories', and hosting over four million visitors, the third London exhibition demonstrated modernity by displaying objects invented since the city's last major exhibition in 1862 (see floor plan, Figure 4). Its second division, dedicated to music, had one section showing instruments built after 1800 (the cut-off of 1862 appearing unreasonably recent in this field), and another illustrating music's history through 'ancient' musical objects.[74] The building was mostly unaltered from the previous exhibitions – maintaining the aquarium and Old London Street – with added murals 'representing the progress of the various industries'.[75] The subway that today connects South Kensington Underground station with the nearby museums was also built for

---

[70] 'International Health Exhibition', *British Architect*, 22:14 (3 Oct. 1884), p. 163.
[71] See Annmarie Adams, 'The Healthy Victorian City: The Old London Street at the International Health Exhibition of 1884', in Zeynep Çelik, Diane Favro, and Richard Ingersoll (eds), *Streets: Critical Perspectives on Public Space*, (Berkeley, 1994), pp. 203–21.
[72] Douglas Galton, 'The International Health Exhibition', *Art Journal*, 46 (May 1884), 153–6, at p. 156.
[73] 'International Health Exhibition, 1884', *Seventh Report of The Commissioners for the Exhibition*, RC/A/1851.
[74] Draft memorandum, Henry Truman Wood to Alfred Hipkins, 15 May 1884, Hipkins Papers Vol. 2, BL, Brit. Mus. Additional MS. 41,637.
[75] 'At the Inventions Exhibition', *British Architect*, 23:19 (8 May 1885). 224–6, at p. 225.

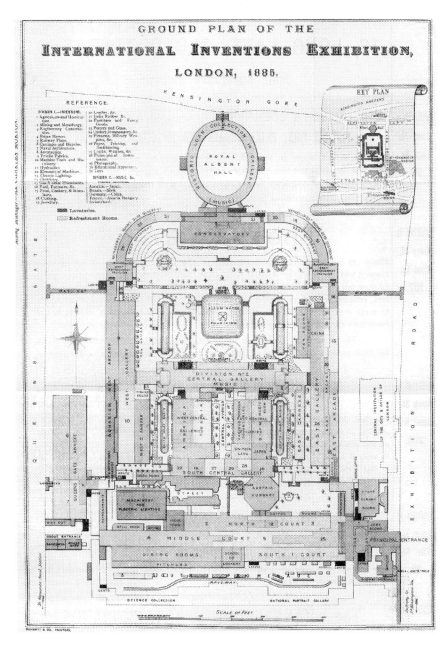

Figure 4. 'Ground Plan of the International Inventions Exhibition, London, 1885', *Metropolitan Railway and International Inventions Exhibition Guide, South Kensington, 1885* (London, 1885). Special Collections Research Center, Henry Madden Library, California State University, Fresno.

this exhibition. Collections of smaller 'fancy goods' complemented larger scale exhibits of mining, agriculture, engineering, and railway technologies.[76] Some displays placed electric and gas lighting in competition, while a collection of military equipment provided, according to the *British Architect*, 'a grim contrast' to the Health Exhibition's exploration of how to 'best prolong human life'.[77] In the machinery hall, visitors could observe textile and candle-making, and see the *Graphic* and *Illustrated London News* printed on site. Two associated conferences were also held: one on patent laws and another on musical pitch.[78] Instrumental and organ recitals, and bands in the grounds supplemented a series of concerts of 'ancient' music, Eduard Strauss's Orchestra, and weekly performances by the Court Band of the King of Siam.

COLONIAL AND INDIAN EXHIBITION, 1886

4 May 1886 – 10 November 1886

The Colonial and Indian Exhibition – or 'Colinderies' – was the last annual London exhibition. With Home Rule struggling in India and the Australasian colonies contemplating independence, this exhibition was a propaganda tool for the British Empire and 'a bonanza of national self-aggrandisement'.[79] Technically not an 'international' exhibition – displaying only products from within the Empire – it remained global in scope, advocating for the economic and cultural importance of the networks that the Empire comprised. Surrounded by more pomp and pageantry than previous exhibitions, it was opened by Queen Victoria, sitting on a throne looted during the capture of Lahore, being itself a piece of 'imperial war booty'.[80] The ceremony included Emma Albani (1847–1930) singing 'Home Sweet Home', and the National Anthem, sung partly in Sanskrit. The competitive elements and classificatory schemes of previous exhibitions were abandoned, and exhibiting governments arranged their own displays. India was the largest section, and while the Australian sections were significant, they showed no Indigenous objects, instead emphasising Western ideals. Where Indigenous peoples featured, it was through clay models, demonstrating Social Darwinist constructions of race, or, in one particularly exploitative manifestation, the India court included a 'living ethnological

---

[76] *Ibid.*

[77] *Ibid.*

[78] Anthony David Edwards, *The Role of International Exhibitions in Britain, 1850–1910: Perceptions of Economic Decline and the Technical Education Issue* (Amherst, 2008), p. 164.

[79] John MacKenzie, 'Empire and Metropolitan Cultures', in Andrew Porter (ed.), *The Oxford History of the British Empire: Volume III: The Nineteenth Century* (Oxford, 1998), pp. 270–93, at p. 283; Tim Barringer, 'The South Kensington Museum and the Colonial Project', in Tim Barringer and Tom Flynn (eds), *Colonialism and the Object: Empire, Material Culture, and the Museum* (London, 1998), pp. 11–27, at p. 23.

[80] Hoffenberg, *An Empire on Display*, p. 259.

display' of 'Indian artisans'.[81] Like previous exhibitions, there were dining halls, organ recitals, and pleasure gardens, as well as the left-over aquarium and Old London Street. Some colonies also established emigration bureau offices. This was the most successful exhibition of the era, drawing over five and a half million attendees and generating £35,000 profit.[82]

EDINBURGH INTERNATIONAL EXHIBITION OF INDUSTRY, SCIENCE, AND ART, 1886

6 May 1886 – 30 October 1886

Scotland's first international exhibition coincided with the Colonial and Indian Exhibition, opening only two days later. Organisers had hoped to attract the same international visitors, but many colonies lacked the resources to provide exhibits for both. Thus, while intended to be 'international' (and did see international participation), the main aim of this exhibition became showcasing 'the resources, manufactured objects, and art of Scotland'.[83] It included the first display of electric lighting in Scotland, with a 'Machinery in Motion' court where visitors could see the engines that lit the building. The walls of the building – designed by architects John Burnet and Son (1814–1901, and 1857–1938) – were adorned with a collection of paintings lent by major British and international institutions. There were also several novelties, including a section on 'women's industries',[84] and another on 'artisan' goods by working-class exhibitors.[85] This exhibition differed slightly from others in that selling prices of the exhibits were displayed (a practice usually banned), but objects were not permitted to be sold.[86] The Exhibition also featured an 'Old Edinburgh' street – an historical reconstruction of buildings from the Royal Mile – promoting the idea of 'living history', with exhibitors in this area dressing in period costume.[87] It also contained all the usual entertainment, with organ recitals, restaurants, a lake, fountains, and a bandstand. More than two million visitors attended, viewing 1,500 individual exhibits, making a reasonable profit of £5,555.[88]

---

[81] MacKenzie, 'Empire and Metropolitan Cultures', p. 284; Saloni Mathur, 'Living Ethnological Exhibits: The Case of 1886', *Cultural Anthropology* 15:4 (2001), 492–524, at p. 493.

[82] Thomas Prasch, 'London 1886', in *Encyclopedia of World's Fairs*, pp. 88–92, at p. 89.

[83] Laurie Dalton, 'Edinburgh 1886', in *Encyclopedia of World's Fairs*, pp. 87–8, at p. 87.

[84] *Women's Industries: Edinburgh 1886 International Exhibition of Industry, Science & Art* (Edinburgh, 1886), p. iv.

[85] Dalton, 'Edinburgh', p. 87.

[86] *International Exhibition of Industry, Science and Art, Edinburgh 1886: The Official Catalogue* (Edinburgh, 1886), p. 18.

[87] Dalton, 'Edinburgh', p. 87.

[88] *Ibid*, p. 88; Ken Carls, 'Edinburgh 1886', in *Historical Dictionary of World's Fairs*, pp. 93–4, at p. 93.

LIVERPOOL INTERNATIONAL EXHIBITION OF NAVIGATION, COMMERCE, AND INDUSTRY, 1886

11 May 1886 – 8 November 1886

The Liverpool Exhibition was intended to emphasise the city's position as '*the major Northern town*'.[89] Opening four days after Edinburgh, this was not the first British exhibition beyond London, but the Liverpool authorities were keen to promote themselves as the 'first' of something, so the Exhibition was lauded as the first in England (outside London) and the first devoted to 'travelling by sea and land'.[90] The building was constructed from materials reused from the Antwerp 1885 Exhibition,[91] but its construction was marred by disaster when parts of the structure collapsed, killing one worker and injuring others. The opening, attended by the Queen – who unexpectedly knighted Liverpool mayor David Radcliffe (1834–1907) during the ceremony – was musically controversial.[92] The poor acoustics of the main building meant the orchestra could not be heard, and a specially-composed overture by the orchestra's conductor Frederic Cowen was cut short on the order of the mayor, greatly offending Cowen.[93] Some critics blamed Liverpool itself for this, arguing that this was typical of 'the most unmusical city in the kingdom'.[94] But there was much other music throughout the Exhibition, with the usual bands in the grounds – including the Viennese Ladies' Orchestra – and instrumental recitals. The majority of the Exhibition's attractions were outdoors, with colourful electric lamps, promenades and bandstands accompanied by a working bakery and dairy, billiard room, tethered or 'captive' hot air balloon, toboggan rides (Figure 5), a supposedly exact replica of the Eddystone lighthouse, and several 'native village' pavilions.[95]

ADELAIDE JUBILEE INTERNATIONAL EXHIBITION, 1887

21 June 1887 – 7 January 1888

The first international exhibition in South Australia celebrated both the colony's fiftieth anniversary and Queen Victoria's Jubilee. The idea of an Adelaide exhibition had been approved in 1882, but the proposal faced strong opposition from regional areas, where it was seen as metropolitan extravagance.[96] South Australia was colonised on the condition that it not 'be a charge on the Mother

---

[89] Steele, *Liverpool on Display*, p. 3.
[90] *International Exhibition of Navigation, Travelling, Commerce, & Manufacture, Liverpool 1886: Official Guide* (Liverpool, 1886), p. 7.
[91] *Ibid.*
[92] Steele, *Liverpool on Display*, p. 24.
[93] 'Music in Liverpool', *Musical Times*, 27:520 (1 Jun. 1886), p. 339.
[94] 'Musical Notes', *Liverpool Mercury*, 3 Jun. 1886, p. 6.
[95] 'The Liverpool International Exhibition', *British Architect*, 25:20 (14 May 1886), 512–13, at p. 513.
[96] Wray Vamplew, 'Adelaide 1887–1888', in *Historical Dictionary of World's Fairs*, pp. 98–9, at p. 98.

Figure 5. 'Tobogganing at the Liverpool Exhibition 1886', *The Queen: The Lady's Newspaper*, 20 Nov. 1886, p. 596. © Illustrated London News Ltd/Mary Evans.

Country' and that settlers be 'capitalists able to profitably work the land'.[97] This ethos fit well with most exhibitions' aims, but by 1887, the colony was in the midst of a serious economic depression. Organisers hoped the Exhibition would help with economic recovery, show off Adelaide as equal to its 'inter-colonial rivals', and bring together the Australian colonies through newly established rail links between the capital cities.[98] The building – designed by Latham A. Withall (1853–1925) and Alfred Wells (1859–1935) – had a classical façade and impressive dome, and was surrounded by elaborate ornamental grounds with lighting, fountains, and rock gardens and grottoes showcasing native plants.[99] Also in the grounds were, for a short time, two camps of Ngarrindjeri and Narungga Indigenous Australians, who performed in the building's main hall on several occasions.[100] In terms of music, there were

---

[97] Lara Anderson, 'Adelaide 1887–1888', in *Encyclopedia of World's Fairs*, pp. 92–4, at p. 92.

[98] Garnaut, Collins, and Jolly, *Adelaide's Jubilee International Exhibition*, p. xii.

[99] Julie Collins, 'An Architectural Ornament: The Adelaide Jubilee International Exhibition Building', in *Adelaide's Jubilee International Exhibition*, pp. 67–81, at p. 73; Louise Bird, 'Making the Right Impression: The Jubilee Exhibition Ornamental Grounds', in *Adelaide's Jubilee International Exhibition*, pp. 101–14, at p. 108.

[100] See Tom Gara, 'Aboriginal Participation in the Adelaide Jubilee International Exhibition', in *Adelaide's Jubilee International Exhibition*, pp. 157–69.

organ recitals, brass bands, and occasional performances by singers and instrumentalists, the Adelaide Liedertafel, the Adelaide Orchestra, and St Peter's Cathedral choir.[101] Over 2,200 exhibitors came from twenty-six countries, and an attendance of over 789,000 far exceeded expectations in a city with a population of around 300,000.[102]

GLASGOW INTERNATIONAL EXHIBITION OF SCIENCE, ART, AND INDUSTRY, 1888

8 May 1888 – 10 November 1888

The second international exhibition in Scotland was organised in Glasgow to raise funds for a new art gallery and museum.[103] As such, in addition to the expected industrial displays, the visual arts were central to the arrangements, with seven picture galleries and one sculpture gallery holding works borrowed from major collections across Britain.[104] The building, designed by James Sellars (1843–88), used a striking combination of Moorish, Byzantine, and Indian influences with an expansive dome flanked with minarets.[105] Like the Edinburgh Exhibition, Glasgow had an 'artisan' section showing 'curiosities' made by members of the working class, and a women's section that surprised many by 'the most masculine productions' that it contained.[106] Musically, bands in the grounds and organ recitals were prominent, and the grounds themselves offered other extravagant entertainments. These included illuminated fountains, a Dutch cocoa house, Indian and Ceylonese tea rooms, dairy maids from across Europe giving live demonstrations, a reproduction of an 'ancient Episcopal palace', and a separate display of the Queen's Jubilee gifts. A shooting gallery and a switchback railway completed the carnival entertainment, while gondolas, steered by Venetian gondoliers, gave rides on the River Kelvin.[107] The Exhibition was attended by six million people.[108] The profits of nearly £42,000 were used to build the city's art gallery and museum, which were formally opened at the 1901 Exhibition and still stand today.[109]

MELBOURNE CENTENNIAL INTERNATIONAL EXHIBITION, 1888

1 August 1888 – 31 January 1889

The colony of New South Wales faced ongoing problems with debt through the 1880s. Therefore, when plans to hold an international exhibition

---

[101] Szuster, 'Music of and at the Time of the Jubilee Exhibition', p. 173.
[102] Lesley Abell, 'Travellers, Tourists, and Visitors to the Adelaide Jubilee International Exhibition', in *Adelaide's Jubilee International Exhibition*, pp. 129–39, at p. 139.
[103] Susan Bennett, 'Glasgow 1888', *Encyclopedia of World's Fairs*, pp. 95–7, at p. 95.
[104] J.M. Gray, 'The Glasgow International Exhibition', *The Academy*, 19 May 1888, p. 348.
[105] Ken Carls, 'Glasgow 1888', in *Historical Dictionary of World's Fairs*, pp. 103–4, at p. 103.
[106] 'The Glasgow Exhibition', *Saturday Review*, 65:1700 (26 May 1888), p. 629.
[107] Bennett, 'Glasgow', p. 96.
[108] Carls, 'Glasgow', p. 104.
[109] Bennett, 'Glasgow', p. 96.

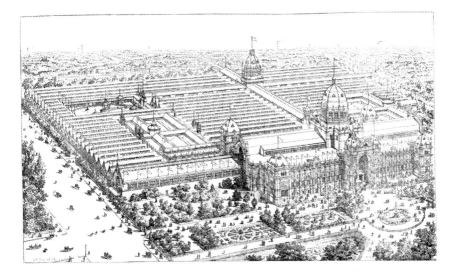

Figure 6. 'Melbourne Centennial Exhibition of 1888: Bird's-Eye View of the Buildings', *Australasian Sketcher with Pen and Pencil*, 9 Aug. 1888. SLV, Accession no: A/S09/08/88/120.

commemorating the centenary of Australia's European settlement were put forth, it was financially prosperous (but far younger) Victoria that was in a position to host the event. The old 1880 building was expanded (Figure 6), redecorated with brighter colours and lavish gilding,[110] and gained a nine-acre annex for displaying moving machinery.[111] This exhibition was the largest ever held in the antipodes, with more than ninety different countries exhibiting. There were vast picture galleries, displays of industrial products, 'fancy articles' such as jewellery and perfume, and most strikingly, a sixty-foot-tall gilt wood obelisk representing the total gold produced by Victoria since the 1851 gold rush.[112] There were numerous other attractions, including a fernery, aquarium, conservatory, and aviary, an ornamental lake, and opportunities to drink 'colonial wines in bars ... on a very extensive scale'.[113] Music was an important feature of this event, with the commissioners employing Frederic Cowen to conduct a full orchestra, performing many major European works for the first time in Australia.[114] As initial interest began to decline, more attractions were added, including a switchback railway, conjuring acts, and displays by Swiss yodellers.

---

[110] David Dunstan, 'Melbourne 1888–1889', in *Encyclopedia of World's Fairs*, pp. 97–9, at p. 97.
[111] 'A Walk Through the Exhibition', *Argus Exhibition Supplement*, 2 Aug. 1888, p. 5.
[112] Ibid.
[113] Ibid.
[114] Dunstan, 'Melbourne', p. 98.

More than two million people attended (double the population of Victoria), yet the overall financial loss was more than twice that anticipated.[115]

EDINBURGH INTERNATIONAL EXHIBITION OF ELECTRICAL ENGINEERING, GENERAL INVENTIONS, AND INDUSTRIES, 1890

1 May 1890 – 1 November 1890

The 1890 Edinburgh Exhibition was held to commemorate the completion of the Forth Bridge, in a celebration of inventions and engineering.[116] Held in parkland in Meggetland, the building – designed by W. Allan Carter and Frank Simon (1862–1933) – was considerably larger than the previous Edinburgh Exhibition. At its centre was a concert hall where orchestral music and oratorio was heard. In addition to bands in the grounds, organ recitals, and instrumental demonstrations, the National Telephone Company had a kiosk in which music was transmitted from distant towns by telephone,[117] and there were opportunities to hear examples of music recorded on Edison's phonograph. There was also an historical collection of 'ancient' musical instruments. Like the previous Scottish exhibitions, there were women's and artisan sections, and a separate fine arts gallery. The outdoor entertainment was extravagant, including a model Doge's Palace housing a Venetian glass factory, a reproduction Swiss chalet, a fruit kiosk, cocoa stands and tea rooms, 'fish dining rooms' staffed by waitresses in 'Newhaven fishwive [sic] costume',[118] a reproduction of the Hampton Court maze, fortune tellers, a shooting gallery, a swimming bath, a switchback railway, merry-go-round, and an 'Ocean Wave' ride. There were also sporting grounds for military tournaments and highland games.

Trends and comparisons across the decade of the 1880s and the Empire are explored in this book with reference to each of the thirteen exhibitions described above. Yet not all exhibitions are discussed in the same level of detail. While the 1885 Inventions Exhibition in London, for example, plays a significant role in many of the chapters – as the Exhibition with the widest variety of musical content and engagement – the Edinburgh 1886 Exhibition, in contrast, appears less frequently, as much of its music was similar to that offered by other exhibitions of the era. Discussions of all the exhibitions, however, help to make up a broader picture of the musical currents that spanned across the Empire.

---

[115] *Ibid.*

[116] 'International Exhibition, Edinburgh, 1890', *British Architect*, 32:19 (8 Nov. 1889), p. 338.

[117] See Sarah Kirby, '"Sweet Music Discoursed in Distant Concert Halls": The Telephone Kiosk at the 1890 Edinburgh International Exhibition', *Context: Journal of Music Research*, 44 (2019), 51–59.

[118] 'The Edinburgh International Exhibition', *Edinburgh Evening Dispatch*, 1 May 1890, p. 4.

Chapter 1

Exhibiting Music

> The painter's hues stand visible before us
> In power and beauty; we can trace the thoughts
> Which are the workings of the poet's mind:
> But music is a mystery, and viewless
> Even when present, and is less man's set,
> And less within his order; for the hand
> That can call forth the tones, yet cannot tell
> Whither they go, or if they live or die,
> When floated once beyond his feeble ear.
> —L.E.L. [Letitia Elizabeth Landon], Erinna (1827).[1]

'This', wrote the *Musical Times* in 1873, quoting Landon, 'is why music has hitherto had no place in artistic exhibitions'.[2] For as long as exhibitions had been held in Britain, there had been vigorous debate in the musical press about the position, representation, and use of music in such spaces. Yet it was exactly that fleeting quality – the intangibility of form that made it so attractive to poets – that made music's inclusion in the physical exhibition space elusive. This outcome, however, the *Musical Times* felt was 'not inevitable'.[3]

In purporting to display all branches of human achievement, over the decades, many exhibition organisers attempted to include music in their designs. But how to do it? Musical instruments – the physical products of a manufacturing industry – could be easily put on display. Yet many commentators argued that silent instruments could never adequately constitute an exhibit of 'music'; that these were merely representations of the mechanical means by which music *could* be produced. Performances of the 'great works' could be given, as if to exhibit their qualities, but these too were considered insufficient as they lacked the permanence of visual art displays. A physical art-object could be on show for six months at an exhibition: hardly comparable to a single performance of a musical work. Additionally, music was considered entertainment, and many visitors came with the intention of listening to music and enjoying themselves, without any particular concern for music's representation or status as 'art'. Debates surrounding these issues were considered with

---

[1] Letitia Elizabeth Landon, 'Erinna', in *The Works of L.E. Landon in Two Volumes*, vol. 1 (Philadelphia, 1838), pp. 183–7, at p. 185.
[2] 'Exhibition Music', *Musical Times and Singing Class Circular* 16:362 (1 Apr. 1873), pp. 40–1, at p. 41.
[3] Ibid.

some urgency, as music's presence – and the difficulty of putting it 'on display' – called into question the all-encompassing rhetoric that claimed exhibitions as universal showcases of human industry and culture.

The historical precedent for 'exhibiting' music at international exhibitions was first set in London with the Great Exhibition of 1851, and was continually re-established through the exhibitions of the 1860s and '70s that followed. Music appeared in a variety of forms at all these exhibitions: as an art to be revered and studied, as an entertainment to be listened to and enjoyed, as a means of advertising musical instruments, and as a spontaneously produced (and sometimes quite annoying) element of the overall exhibition soundscape. In terms of negotiating music within the official exhibitionary space, through these events, organisers were gradually driven towards the concept of a 'musical museum', based largely on the work-concept.[4] At the same time, however, music was a constant part of the day-to-day experience of the public, through spontaneous or informal performance, or through music presented purely for entertainment such as military bands and popular organ recitals. All of these forms – from the idea of 'exhibiting' music to what its public role and function should be – are examined in this chapter.

Codifying Expectations of Music and Display

The 1851 Great Exhibition of the Works of Industry of All Nations, as it was officially titled, was held in the monumental Crystal Palace, a temporary structure of glass and iron erected in London's Hyde Park. The internal structure, processes of organisation, and surrounding rhetoric of the Great Exhibition were central in shaping public expectations of future international exhibitions. Its legendary status held such an important place in the collective imagination that attendees of other exhibitions – whether they had experienced the original or not – were affected by 'the ghost of 1851' in how they perceived the events in 'material and imaginative terms'.[5] While the 1862 International Exhibition built on 1851's model quite directly, the 1870s exhibitions were more experimental, showing a limited selection of themed objects each year: wool, pottery, and horticulture in 1871; cotton, jewellery, paper, and musical instruments in 1872; a variety of other fabrics, steel products, carriages, and food in 1873; and lace, civil engineering and architecture, heating, leather, bookbinding, and wine in 1874.[6] These themed exhibitions were intended to be held annually for ten

---

[4] See Lydia Goehr, *The Imaginary Museum of Musical Works: An Essay in the Philosophy of Music* (Oxford, 1992).

[5] Peter H. Hoffenberg, *An Empire on Display: English, Indian, and Australian Exhibitions from the Crystal Palace to the Great War* (Berkeley, 2001), pp. 7, 5.

[6] Peter H. Hoffenberg, '1871–1874: The South Kensington International Exhibitions', in Dino Franco Felluga (ed.), *BRANCH: Britain, Representation and Nineteenth-Century History* (2017) <http://www.branchcollective.org/?ps_articles=peter-h-hoffenberg-1871-1874-the-south-kensington-international-exhibitions/> [accessed 2 Feb. 2021]; 'Official Notices and Documents', *The Key*, 13 May 1871, p. 3, RC/A/1851.

years, but were called off after 1874 due to a lack of interest. Although ultimately unsuccessful, they nonetheless formed a model for later themed exhibitions, helping to codify the expectations surrounding concepts of musical 'display'.

The early London exhibitions were also closely intertwined with the development of the public museum, influencing and being influenced by this process. While both private and public museums had existed in various forms through the previous centuries, it was a direct consequence of the Great Exhibition's success that the state began actively developing a public museum culture in Britain.[7] All of the 1870s and '80s London exhibitions were held in South Kensington on a site between Kensington Gore and Cromwell Road (see Figure 7), and the present-day institutions on this site form an important part of their legacy. The profits of the Great Exhibition allowed the purchase of this estate – nicknamed the 'Albertopolis' – and its first permanent museum, the South Kensington Museum (now the Victoria and Albert) was established to hold 'miscellaneous collections', some from the Great Exhibition itself.[8] The Natural History Museum, Royal Albert Hall, and other educational spaces followed.

Exhibitions and museums of the nineteenth-century British tradition were also central pillars of the rational recreation movement: an ideological, middle-class effort to promote public education and exert a 'civilising influence' over the working classes.[9] These rational recreation enterprises in many cases involved promoting the reform of popular amusements in a way that contributed to a widespread drive for 'social amelioration'.[10] With these aspirational and educational aims in mind, both exhibitions and museums introduced initiatives to encourage the working classes to attend for their own supposed intellectual benefit. These schemes were often practical, including days with reduced or free entry, and extended opening hours into the evenings and on weekends.[11] Exhibitions, however, placed much emphasis on spectacle as a 'vehicle for popular amusement', and this, alongside their significant commercial implications, left some feeling that they were inferior to the serious-minded permanent museum.[12] As George Wagstaffe Yapp wrote in 1852, the vast 'accumulation' of objects at the Great Exhibition 'however startling, is not of the most beneficial description', making it not 'a pleasant place of study'.[13]

In terms of music, exhibitions of the nineteenth century held more stake in attempting to display music than traditional museums. Many museums, during the later decades of the century, did establish collections of musical

[7] Christine Garwood, *Museums in Britain: A History* (Oxford, 2014), p. 26.
[8] *Ibid*.
[9] *Ibid*, p. 31.
[10] Peter Bailey, *Leisure and Class in Victorian England: Rational Recreation and the Contest for Control, 1830–1885* (London, 1978), p. 35.
[11] Garwood, *Museums in Britain*, p. 27.
[12] Christopher Whitehead, *The Public Art Museum in Nineteenth Century Britain: The Development of the National Gallery* (Aldershot, 2005), p. 70.
[13] George Wagstaffe Yapp, *Art Education at Home and Abroad* (London, 1852), pp. 36–8; quoted in *Ibid*.

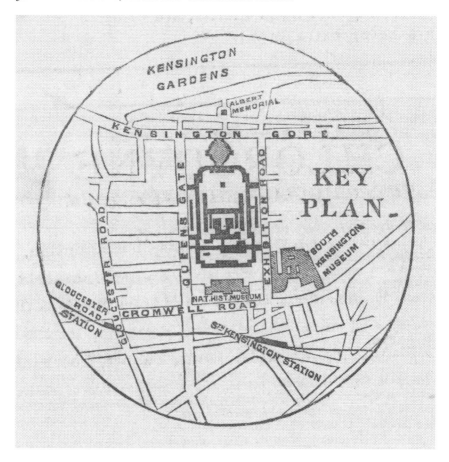

Figure 7. Location of the London exhibition buildings in the 1870s and '80s between the Albert Hall on Kensington Gore and the Natural History Museum on Cromwell Road. *International Health Exhibition: Official Guide* (London, 1884), [title page]. NLA, RB Ec 168 PV/2.

instruments, usually intended to retrospectively illustrate different periods and traditions of musical history. The exhibitions, on the other hand, were largely intended to promote advances in human industry, and the achievements of humanity in art and science, making it much more pressing that they incorporate 'music' as an art than any museum space had to that point. The questions that arose in the attempt to put music – a temporal art – in a space designed to house plastic works, are still asked by modern curators. Namely, 'how does one feature music in museums when its natural place would rather be the concert hall or the private home where one listens or plays music?'[14]

[14] Eric de Visscher, 'Sight and Sound: From a Museum of Instruments to a Museum of Music', *Music in Art: International Journal for Music Iconography*, 39:1–2 (2014),

❦ Locating 'Music'

In order to 'display' music at the exhibitions, it was first necessary to decide where it should be located within the rigidly compartmentalised taxonomic structures that governed the exhibitions' layouts. The Great Exhibition was uncharted territory in this respect, and the commissioners – with an executive made up mainly of engineers, military figures, and politicians, including chairman Colonel William Reid (1791–1858), Henry Cole (1808–82), and Charles Wentworth Dilke (1810–69) – did not include any musical experts. There was therefore much speculation and anxiety in the musical press before the Exhibition's opening as to what music really was and what would constitute an adequate representation of it within the exhibition space, particularly in comparison to the plastic arts. Other temporal arts such as dance and drama seem not to have elicited the same level of concern. In the case of dance, this may simply have been because the form as a distinct art lacked a comparable critical forum to the nineteenth-century British musical press. The theatrical and dramatic community, in contrast, appear largely concerned with the Exhibition as a rival for the public's attention, rather than by lofty questions about the representation of their art.[15] In one way, at least, the British theatre tradition was also prominently acknowledged within the Exhibition by a statue of Shakespeare by John Bell (1811–95), which was among the few exhibits labelled a 'principle landmark' on official maps.[16] The question of representing music, however, tapped into long-held critical anxieties and debates about the nature of the form. Contemporary publications frequently ran articles attempting to answer 'what is music?', with responses ranging from 'simply a succession of sounds regulated by the laws of melody and rhythm', to 'the first art of the feelings', 'the heart's own language', or quoting Martin Luther, 'the fairest and most glorious gifts of God'.[17] In responding to the Exhibition, however, critics found it simpler to define what it *wasn't*.

At the Great Exhibition, the only official display relating to music was a collection of instruments. While some recent scholarship has argued that no 'critical appraisals' of the Exhibition record any 'anxiety about the presence of musical instruments',[18] this in fact became an extremely fraught issue in the press. Critics argued that instruments could only demonstrate aspects of mechanical construction, or technologies of sound production. As the *Musical World* stated, it would be an 'absurd' mistake by the commissioners in 'confounding "music" with "instruments of music"', though the latter are to the

---

237–41, at p. 237.
[15] Marty Gould, 'Anticipation, Transformation, Accommodation: The Great Exhibition on the London Stage', *Victorian Review*, 29:2 (2003), 19–39, at p. 22.
[16] Clare Pettitt, 'Shakespeare at the Great Exhibition of 1851', in Gail Marshall and Adrian Poole (eds), *Victorian Shakespeare*, vol. 2 (London, 2003), pp. 61–83, at p. 61.
[17] 'What is Music?', *Musical World*, 22:18 (3 Sep. 1859), pp. 2–3.
[18] Flora Willson, 'Hearing Things: Musical Objects at the 1851 Great Exhibition', in James Q. Davies and Ellen Lockhart (eds), *Sound Knowledge: Music and Science in London, 1789–1851* (Chicago, 2016), pp. 227–46, at p. 237.

former no more than the bricks and mortar to a monument'.[19] No matter how well constructed or prominently placed, it was argued, this would reduce the art of music to matters of technical invention. As the same article continued,

> to confound the abstract science of sound, a matter of dry mathematical calculation, with the art of music itself, which appeals no less to the heart and the imagination, in its highest manifestations, than to the ear alone, in its lowest, is to confound the science of verbal derivation with the magnificent art of poetry.[20]

Not only were instruments the sole display relating to music at the Great Exhibition, but these were shown in a single combined class – superintended by two military men, Lieutenant-Colonel John Lloyd (1800–54) and Lieutenant William Trevor (1831–1907) – entitled 'Philosophical, Musical, Horological and Surgical Instruments'. These instruments (barring the grand, prominent pipe organs) were relegated to an upper gallery of the Crystal Palace between displays of anatomical models, cutlery, and glass chandeliers.[21] This approach, it was argued, came nowhere near adequately representing 'music'.

The narrative surrounding the inadequacy of instruments representing 'music' continued through the exhibitions that followed, and by 1873 the *Musical Times* was arguing about this in Biblical terms: 'Jubal's "chorded shell" was a wonderful instrument according to Dryden, but duly labelled and showed at a fine art exhibition ... it would scarcely have attracted much attention'.[22] Although performance began to take on a greater role at later exhibitions, displays of instruments remained the most constant music-related exhibit, and the musical press remained dissatisfied.

When the *Musical Times* argued that 'you cannot set up a gallery of this ethereal art as you can of painting and sculpture', they were tapping in to broader contemporary aesthetic arguments about music's ephemerality.[23] Descriptions of music as independent from the physical objects that facilitate its production – such as instruments or scores – appear throughout nineteenth-century musical literature, illustrating a dichotomous understanding of the plastic and temporal arts. As an essay reprinted in an 1857 *Musical Times* argued, the condition of music was 'a strange thing' that did not in itself exist: 'it is there – but gone again' in the moment of its performance, always putting on 'mortality afresh ... being born anew, but to die away and leave only dead notes and dumb instruments behind'.[24] Decades later, another author in the *Orchestra Musical Review* suggested that music could not exist in the material world, discounting both representations of music on 'the printed page' and in 'the vibrations' that

---

[19] 'The Great National Exhibition', *Musical World*, 16:2 (11 Jan. 1851), pp. 17–19, at p. 19.
[20] *Ibid*, pp. 18–19.
[21] 'Sect. II. Class 10', in *Official Descriptive and Illustrated Catalogue, by Authority of the Royal Commission* (London, 1851), pp. 404–5.
[22] 'Exhibition Music', *Musical Times*, p. 40.
[23] *Ibid*.
[24] 'Conditions of Music', *Musical Times*, 8:171 (1 May 1857), p. 42.

travel from 'instrument to ear'. Music, they concluded, was of 'another and a higher kind', whose substance was 'ethereal'.[25]

Couched in literary and sentimental Victorianisms as they are, these discussions display an approach to conceptualising music similar to those presented by many nineteenth-century European philosophers. E.T.A. Hoffmann, in his 1831 essay 'Beethoven's Instrumental Music', described music as existing outside of the physical world. Not bound like poetry to words that suggest 'definite emotions', and as 'the art diametrically opposed to plastic', Hoffmann considered music to exist instead in the 'realm of the infinite'.[26] Hoffmann was well-known in Britain, with English translations of his works appearing as early as the 1820s, so it might be assumed his thoughts on this were also known.[27] Similar sentiments appear in Heinrich Heine's work, particularly the ninth from *Letters on the French Stage*, widely reprinted in nineteenth-century English music periodicals. Originally written in 1837, Heine questions 'what is music?', reflecting on it as a 'marvel', existing 'between thought and manifestation'.[28] In the following decade, Søren Kierkegaard's 1843 *Either/Or* also describes music as obtainable 'only in the moment of its performance', existing only in 'an unreal sense' at other times.[29] Such discussions of music's material form continued throughout the century, appearing in many works of aesthetic philosophy beyond those specifically considering music (including, notably, Walter Pater's often-quoted statement that 'all art constantly aspires towards the condition of music').[30] While these disparate examples are not exhaustive, they show that the arguments brought forward by the necessity of placing music in the physical sphere tapped in to ongoing philosophical debates in the wider community.

Equivalents for these ideas can also be found in twentieth-century theoretical musicology. As Lydia Goehr argues, musical works are 'ontological mutants' that do not exist as 'concrete, physical objects'.[31] Roman Ingarden similarly argues that the musical work is both distinct from and does not exist as the 'conscious experiences' of the composer or listeners, cannot be 'identified with

---

[25] 'Music versus Materialism', *Orchestra Musical Review*, 186 (19 Dec. 1885), pp. 450–1, at p. 450.

[26] Ernst Theodor Amadeus Hoffmann, 'Beethoven's Instrumental Music (1813)', in Ruth Solie (ed.), *Source Readings in Music History*, rev. ed. Leo Treitler, vol. 6 (New York, 1998), pp. 151–6, at pp. 151–2.

[27] Karl Leydecker, 'Hoffmann, E.T.A.', in Peter France (ed.), *The Oxford Guide to Literature in English Translation* (Oxford, 2000), p. 331.

[28] Heinrich Heine, *Letters on the French Stage*, trans. Charles Godfrey Leland, The Works of Heinrich Heine, vol. 8 (New York, 1892–1905); repr., for example: 'Rossini and Meyerbeer', *Musical World*, 37:27 (2 Jul. 1859), pp. 428–9, and 'Letters by Heinrich Heine', *Monthly Musical Record*, 17:203 (1 Nov. 1887), pp. 247–9.

[29] Søren Kierkegaard, *Either/Or*, trans. David F. Swenson and Lillian Marvin Swenson (Princeton, 1972), p. 55.

[30] Walter Pater, *The Renaissance: Studies in Art and Literature* (London, 1888), p. 135.

[31] Goehr, *The Imaginary Museum*, pp. 2–3.

its various performances', and is entirely distinct from the score.[32] Just as similar ideas had been explored through the nineteenth century, the exhibitions, with their expectation that music be represented in physical space, forced an examination of these theoretical problems in real terms, becoming sites of physical attempts to reconcile such ideas.

THE MUSICAL WORK AS OBJECT

The consensus that musical instruments – while perhaps interesting displays of manufacturing – were not exhibits of 'music' itself, meant that the press demanded and organisers searched for solutions elsewhere. From the philosophical debates regarding the nature of music over the nineteenth century, there was a general agreement in discussions of exhibitions that the best way of representing music was through the performance of musical works. This was fitting, as the concept of the 'work' itself emerged in the late eighteenth century through a movement towards understanding music as a fine art, in need of 'enduring products – artefacts comparable to other works of fine art'.[33]

The opening ceremonies of the exhibitions were the most obvious place to perform musical works, yet the Great Exhibition was notoriously lacking in this respect. The ceremony included massed choirs singing only the National Anthem and the 'Hallelujah' chorus from *Messiah*. The National Anthem was then heard again, passed from organ to organ, following the royal family's procession around the building. With William Sterndale Bennett (1816–75) as the superintendent of music and George Smart (1776–1867) directing, it was perhaps unfair of *Musical Times* editor Henry C. Lunn (1817–94) to reflect two decades later that the Exhibition was marred by its officials' lack of 'knowledge' and 'sympathy with music'.[34] The choice of *Messiah* was, in fact, entirely fitting to the vast, cathedral-like space of the Crystal Palace, as 'a religious piece which could be played in secular surroundings'.[35] In any case, this ceremony did not constitute an active attempt to 'exhibit' music, and music merely fulfilled its usual ceremonial function.

Organisers of the next exhibition in 1862, in response to the criticism of 1851, made a conscious attempt to centre music in the opening ceremony. The executive commission – headed by the Earl Granville (1815–91) and taking musical advice from Henry Chorley (1808–72) – commissioned several composers to write new works representing different countries. This was one of the first attempts at an exhibition to use musical works as representative, sonic objects. While not 'anticipat[ing] any satisfactory result' as to the adequate representation of music, the *Musical World* argued that, unlike at the Great Exhibition, music had 'this time been allowed to assert its right to a fitting place in the

---

[32] Roman Ingarden, *The Work of Music and the Problem of Its Identity*, trans. Adam Czerniawski, ed. Jean G. Harrel (Basingstoke, 1986), p. 2.

[33] Goehr, *The Imaginary Museum*, p. 152.

[34] Henry C. Lunn, 'Music at the Opening of the International Exhibition', *Musical Times*, 15:340 (1 Jun. 1871), pp. 103–5, at p. 103.

[35] John Davis, *The Great Exhibition* (Stroud, 1999), p. 127.

temple of the world's genius'.[36] The Exhibition's definition of 'internationalism' was rather Eurocentric, limited only to Britain, Germany, and France through, respectively, an ode by Sterndale Bennett, a *Fest-Ouvertüre im Marschstyl* by Giacomo Meyerbeer (1791–1864), and a *Grand Triumphal March* by Daniel Auber (1782–1871). Giuseppe Verdi (1813–1901) had also provided a cantata, *Inno delle nazioni*, but this was rejected by the organisers. The press reported that this was because it contained a quotation from the overtly political 'La Marseillaise' – potentially controversial in a British ceremony – but the organisers themselves (now supported by recent scholarship) argued that the work was simply submitted too late.[37] The Bennett, Meyerbeer, and Auber works were reviewed as 'a decided success'.[38] Despite this, little was made of the idea of these works as representative of individual nations, or of 'music' itself.

The next Exhibition in 1871 explicitly presented musical works as exhibition objects, in an opening ceremony entitled an 'Exhibition of Musical Art'.[39] Opening with the overture to *Der Freischütz* by Carl Maria von Weber (1786–1826) and closing with *Semiramide* by Gioachino Rossini (1792–1868), the highlight of this sonic 'Exhibition' was four works commissioned by different composers to represent 'the varied styles of national music'.[40] Ciro Pinsuti (1829–88) represented Italy with a chorale on words by Lord Houghton (1809–55), Charles Gounod (1818–93) presented the motet *Gallia* for France, Ferdinand Hiller (1811–85) provided a *Triumphal March* for Germany, and for Britain was the cantata *On Shore and Sea* by Arthur Sullivan (1842–1900). The general consensus in the press was that these works were unconvincing as musical representations of different nations, with a contributor to *The Sunday Times* writing that, owing to 'a singularly unanimous misconception', the composers had merely composed in their own styles.[41]

From the Great Exhibition onwards, exhibitions' floorplans and distribution of goods encouraged the 'study and comparison of individual nations' through and alongside that of individual products.[42] Audiences clearly expected this 'Exhibition of Musical Art' to provide a similar forum, bringing each nation's musical qualities 'into the small compass of one programme; just as in the Exhibition galleries the productions of various nations are grouped within one field of vision'.[43] 'National' musics, however, rarely contain any intrinsic markers of a nation, with their apparent national qualities instead emerging through

---

[36] 'The Musical World', *Musical World*, 39:29 (20 Jul. 1862), p. 456.
[37] 'Her Majesty's Theatre', *Musical World*, 40:22 (31 May 1862), p. 339; Roberta Montemorra Marvin, *The Politics of Verdi's Cantica* (Farnham, 2014), p. 46.
[38] 'The Music at the International Exhibition', *Musical World*, 40:18 (3 May 1862), pp. 282–4, at p. 282.
[39] 'Music at the International Exhibition', *Musical World*, 49:18 (6 May 1871), p. 276.
[40] Lunn, 'Music at the Opening', p. 103.
[41] 'Music at the International Exhibition', *The Sunday Times*, 7 May 1871, p. 3.
[42] Paul Young, *Globalization and the Great Exhibition: The Victorian New World Order* (Basingstoke, 2009), p. 70.
[43] 'Music at the International Exhibition', *The Sunday Times*, p. 3.

historical processes or extrinsic signifiers.[44] The way the 1871 opening was promoted, however, suggested that such markers would be not only present, but aurally perceptible and easily comparable, leading to much frustration in the press.

Despite broad agreement that the works were poor musical representations, there was little consensus on what should constitute each national style. Pinsuti – accused of providing only 'one of those part-songs' that were his 'speciality' – gave a work that reminded one reviewer of a 'cross between the Teutonic part-song and the Anglican glee'.[45] His composition lacked the 'colour', and 'warmth and emotionalism' apparently distinctive to Italian music.[46] For Gounod, 'nobody', the *Musical World* argued, would associate *Gallia* 'with the lightsome genius of "La Belle France"'.[47] However, with the ceremony occurring alongside the end of the Franco-Prussian War and Paris Commune, other critics argued that its tone could indeed represent present-day France, in an 'earnest outpouring of deep and heartfelt grief'.[48] Gounod, conducting the work himself, apparently in tears, received a standing ovation. Hiller's *Triumphal March*, in contrast, was described by Lunn as appropriate to 'glorify the victorious deeds of his countrymen', but by others as 'a bitter failure' in representing Germany, lacking Wagner's particular understanding of 'the head, hands, and feet of the Teuton'.[49] Following the Gounod, this work was not warmly received, and Hiller left the hall immediately after its conclusion.[50] Criticism of Sullivan's representation of England seems largely confined to the cantata's subject matter, set in sixteenth-century Genoa and depicting conflict between Italian Christians and North African Muslims. Such a text left Sullivan little room to 'get in even a little bit of English music edgeways'.[51] It was suggested that he should have provided something more 'intensely national', with pastoral works like Bennett's *May Queen* or *May Day* by George Macfarren (1813–87) given as potential models.[52]

Although critics found no explicitly national sonic markers in these works, the programme itself was considered important as an indication that organisers were progressing from static displays of instruments in representing music; that music was finally admitted into 'a scheme especially intended to exhibit the result of human genius and skill'.[53] Yet a single concert still felt inadequate in comparison to the displays of plastic arts. *The Times* argued in 1873 that

[44] Carl Dahlhaus, *Nineteenth-Century Music*, trans. J. Bradford Robinson (Berkeley, 1989), p. 39.
[45] 'Music at the International Exhibition', *The Sunday Times*, p. 3; 'Music', *Graphic*, 3:75 (6 May 1871), pp. 410–11, at p. 410.
[46] 'The International Exhibition', *Orchestra*, 16:397 (5 May 1871), p. 68–9, at p. 69.
[47] 'Music at the International Exhibition', *Musical World*, p. 276.
[48] Lunn, 'Music at the Opening', p. 104.
[49] 'The Exhibition Music', *Orchestra*, 16:397 (5 May 1871), p. 74–5, at p. 74.
[50] Jeffrey Richards, *Imperialism and Music: Britain, 1876–1953* (Manchester, 2001), p. 25.
[51] 'The International Exhibition', *Orchestra*, p. 69.
[52] 'Music', *Graphic*, p. 411.
[53] Lunn, 'Music at the Opening', p. 103.

paintings and sculptures 'may be seen and judged, day after day, without the intervention of a medium', unlike music, which required 'a medium, in the shape of a performer ... to give audible utterance to the thoughts of the composer'.[54] While the concept of the musical 'work' was an 'equivalent commodity, a valuable and permanently existing product that could be treated in the same way as the objects of the already respectable fine arts', exhibitions faced great difficulty in giving music equivalent space.[55] As Edmund Gurney explained in his 1880 *The Power of Sound*, musical works – with no equivalent in the physical world – were 'not, like pictures, contained in a national gallery which can be walked round once a week'.[56] It was therefore important for exhibition organisers to find ways of presenting music with more permanence than single performances, in a manner more comparable to a museum of plastic art-objects.

A REAL EXHIBITION OF MUSICAL WORKS

The solution proposed at the 1873 Exhibition, in a joint venture between the commissioners and Novello, attempted to put music 'on view' like the plastic arts, through six months of daily orchestral concerts.[57] These were held in the Albert Hall, conducted by Joseph Barnby (1838–96) or Carl Deichmann (1827–1908), had an orchestra 'chosen with special care' from 'the most esteemed London professors', and played music exclusively 'of a high class'.[58] With programmes supposedly covering 'all schools of orchestral music which may fairly claim to be considered classical', from Bach to still-living composers, the *Graphic* described this series as an 'absolute novelty' and the first time that music had been presented in a way that truly 'constitute[d] an exhibition'.[59] While the programmes were not exactly the same every day, a sense of permanence was achieved through the regularity of these concerts, each consistently structured containing a symphony or concerto, two overtures, and selections of vocal music.[60] Works, and sometimes entire programmes were repeated in close succession (see Table 1 for the programmes of the first week), providing a physical space where listeners could contemplate pieces as if in a 'collection of works of art' and 'divorced from everyday contexts'.[61] Although the programmes changed, individual works remained present over weeks, and in some cases, across the whole season, and 'music' as a whole was a constant in a way that attempted to counter the impermanence and ephemerality of the form.

Goehr argues that, over the nineteenth century, the problem of preserving musical works in comparison to the fine arts was collectively resolved through the formation of a 'metaphorical' museum, appropriate to music's 'temporal

---

[54] 'Music at the International Exhibition', *The Times*, p. 6.
[55] Goehr, *The Imaginary Museum*, pp. 173–4.
[56] Edmund Gurney, *The Power of Sound* (London, 1880), p. 302.
[57] 'Exhibition Music', *Musical Times*, p. 41.
[58] 'Exhibition Music', *Musical World*, 51:14 (5 Apr. 1873), p. 220.
[59] 'Music', *Graphic*, 7:178 (26 Apr. 1873), p. 399.
[60] 'Exhibition Music', *Musical World*, p. 220.
[61] Goehr, *The Imaginary Museum*, p. 173–4.

Table 1. Daily Orchestral Concerts, Royal Albert Hall, Opening Week 14–18 April 1873

Work	Composer
14 & 15 April, 12 noon	
Overture *Exhibition*	Daniel Auber
Recit. And Air 'With Verdure Clad' (sung, Helen Walton [dates not known])	Joseph Haydn (1732–1809)
Symphony 'Scotch,' in A minor	Felix Mendelssohn (1809–47)
Recit. And Air 'O, Ruddier than the Cherry' (sung, James Thurley Beale [1847–97])	George Frideric Handel (1685–1759)
Selection *Lohengrin*	Richard Wagner (1813–83)
14 & 15 April, 4:00pm	
Overture *William Tell*	Gioachino Rossini
Aria 'Vedrai carino' (sung, Helen Walton)	Wolfgang Amadeus Mozart (1756–91)
Symphony 'Surprise'	Haydn
Song 'I'm a Roamer' (sung, James Thurley Beale)	Mendelssohn
Organ Concerto No. 1 (perf. William Thomas Best [1826–97])	Handel
March *Reine de Saba*	Charles Gounod
16 April, 4:00pm	
Overture *Exhibition*	Auber
Song 'There is a Green Hill' (sung, Emily Dones [1848–1922])	Gounod
Symphony No. 8	Ludwig van Beethoven (1770–1827)
Air 'It is Finished' from *St John Passion* (sung, Emily Dones)	Johann Sebastian Bach (1685–1750)
Selection *Lohengrin*	Wagner
17 April, 4:00pm	
Overture *Die Zauberflöte*	Mozart
Aria 'Batti, batti' (sung, Edith Dalmaine [*fl.* 1868–75])	Mozart
Symphony No. 8	Beethoven
Canzonet 'Fidelity' (sung, Edith Dalmaine)	Haydn
Overture *Mock Doctor*	Gounod
18 April, 4:00pm	
Overture *Die Zauberflöte*	Mozart
Recit. and Air 'Angels Ever Bright and Fair' (sung, Katherine Poyntz [*c.*1841–?])	Handel
Symphony, 'Reformation'	Mendelssohn
Air 'In questo semplice' (sung, Katherine Poyntz)	Gaetano Donizetti (1797–1848)
Saltarello	Gounod

Source: Programmes as reported in *The Key*, 14–18 Apr. 1873, RC/A/1851.

and ephemeral character'.[62] When tangibly confronted with this problem, the organisers of the 1873 Exhibition also moved towards a concept of a 'musical museum'. Of course, the idea of such a project was not new: examples range from Franz Liszt (1811–86) suggesting daily ceremonial performances of 'all the best' works in 1835 as a sort of 'musical museum',[63] to less systematic processes whereby opera houses and symphony halls gradually became 'virtual, repertorial museum[s]' through 'the repetition ad infinitum of canonic works'.[64] What these institutions did inadvertently, through the organic process of canon-formation or in direct attempts to preserve older music, the exhibitions did in a deliberate, practical way.

While the 1873 concerts were praised across the press, these performances were unable to sustain public attention, and attendance steadily decreased. Yet the *Musical Times* argued that the importance of the series in representing music meant that this should not be considered a failing:

> The public came or stayed away – more often they stayed away than came – but every afternoon ... the prescribed work was done as carefully as though the Hall had been full ... It brought a new element into the public demonstration of art – an element above and beyond the question of pecuniary gain, and taking music into account before aught else.[65]

It is perhaps through this lack of attendance that the idea of an equivalent permanence between this music and the plastic art-object can be most strikingly perceived. The physical art work in a physical gallery remains, regardless of whether it is viewed. At 1873, musical works also remained present, whether anyone was listening or not.

ࣃ Experiencing Music

The musical press was deeply invested in promoting the importance of music at the exhibitions in grand terms, debating its presence and theoretical, philosophical, and aesthetic function. With a goal to champion music as a serious and vital art – particularly in relation to other arts – their comments come largely from this ideological standpoint and may not have been in line with the experiences of the general public. Equally, the focus on 'music' from a work-based, conceptual viewpoint meant that reporting in music periodicals tended to ignore the music-making that appeared throughout the exhibitions almost incidentally. Exploring the general or daily press, on the other hand, gives a different perspective. Through reports of the everyday activity of the exhibitions – sometimes only passing comments – it becomes clear just how ubiquitous

---

[62] Goehr, *The Imaginary Museum*, p. 174.
[63] Franz Liszt, quoted in Alan Walker (ed.), *Franz Liszt: The Virtuoso Years 1811–1947* (Ithaca, 1987), pp. 159–60.
[64] Katharine Ellis, 'Olivier Halanzier and the Operatic Museum in Late Nineteenth-Century France', *Music & Letters*, 96:3 (2015), 390–417, at p. 391.
[65] 'Daily Exhibition Concerts', *Musical Times*, 16:370 (1 Dec. 1873), pp. 319–20.

music was to the experience of attending an exhibition, often through the actions of members of the public themselves.

SPONTANEOUS MUSIC-MAKING

The first clues to the existence of music – beyond official programmes – lie in the press's acknowledgement of its absence. Due to the monumental size and scope of exhibitions, in almost every case, they were never completely ready by opening day. In addition, music was usually one of the last things arranged, meaning that the opening weeks and months were often devoid of formally organised performance. In the first week of the Great Exhibition *The Times* mused on this absence:

> the overtaxed sight wishes and longs for relief in the great palace of wonders. The longer one stays and the oftener one visits the building the more irresistible does the craving for music become. Everybody feels and expresses this want, and the occasional half-notes of an organ, or the faint tinkling sounds of a piano, as they fall upon the ear, only aggravate the general desire.[66]

These sentiments were echoed across the press over the first month, including calls in the *Morning Post* for the 'hitherto silent' collection of instruments to be put to use.[67]

As the weeks went on, however, despite a lack of officially organised performance, there quickly became no shortage of music provided by the public. In what appears to have been the nineteenth-century equivalent of a 'flash mob', visiting groups from local and provincial schools and factories travelled to the Exhibition, marching through the surrounding parks and gardens accompanied by their school or company bands, before giving unannounced performances within the building. Notably, at the end of July the Engineers of the Katesgrove Ironworks processed from a steamboat at Westminster Bridge to the Exhibition with their band, 'singing in chorus some spirited and appropriate verses', including a song called 'The Working Man' written by one of their members.[68] In the same week, a group of 'West of England firemen' arrived, 'mounted on their engines and accompanied by a brass band'.[69] It was reported that other visitors greatly enjoyed these events, but such spontaneous music-making did not always go well. The following month an impromptu Temperance demonstration held inside the Crystal Palace erupted into violence when their singers – described as 'well-disciplined in provincial music' – performed one song in Welsh.[70] This song supposedly had the 'effect of exciting one of the auditors to such a degree that he made a violent attack on three women'. The organisers dealt with this situation by issuing an order 'requesting all persons to abstain from singing, or, at all events, if they do sing, not to choose the Welsh

---

[66] 'The Great Exhibition', *The Times*, 7 May 1851, p. 7.
[67] 'The Great Exhibition', *Morning Post*, 29 May 1851, p. 6.
[68] 'The Great Exhibition', *Morning Chronicle*, 29 Jul. 1851, p. 5.
[69] 'The Great Exhibition', *Lloyd's Weekly Newspaper*, 3 Aug. 1851, p. 11.
[70] 'The Great Exhibition', *Examiner*, 9 Aug. 1851, pp. 504–5, at p. 504.

language'.[71] This came at a time of ongoing tensions and negative sentiments toward the Nonconformist Welsh-speaking community in England, and this incident caused the commissioners to attempt greater control over the music allowed in the space.[72]

Of all the spontaneous public performances, school groups were by far the best received. In mid-July, 332 students and teachers of the Duke of York's School 'obtained permission' from the commissioners for their band to perform inside the building. They 'treated the assembled company to some well-executed pieces of music' before 'the little heroes marched out with all the honours of peace, keeping time to an exhilarating quick step'.[73] The public response to this performance – who were 'profuse in their commendations' – suggested, according to the *Daily News*, that regular music would add greatly to the Exhibition's attractions. They felt that the boys had proved that the building's infamously poor acoustics could be overcome, being heard with 'distinctness' within the 'wilderness of glass'.[74] Other school groups followed this example with fervour, and performances from a variety of visiting bands became an almost daily occurrence, to an enthusiastic reception. It is not clear whether these performances were given with advance permission from the organisers, but they continued until a Caledonian public school arrived with their band in full Highland dress and were refused permission to perform. This, the commissioners stated, was because they believed 'that this practice of volunteer music is gradually growing into a nuisance'.[75] Despite this apparent ban, press reports suggest school groups – including 1,555 children from Woolwich – were still attending, 'with a band of music and flags flying' well over a month later.[76]

Although music was better organised at the 1862 Exhibition, impromptu performances by the public continued to have a place. Visiting school groups still arrived, accompanied by their bands, to give unannounced performances.[77] In addition, talented amateurs occasionally also played the exhibited instruments. The *Daily News*, for example, reported that 'visitors who linger late in

---

[71] *Ibid*, p. 505.
[72] For example, only a few years before the Exhibition, English Anglican government commissioners led an inquiry into the Welsh education system, publishing their conclusion that the Welsh 'were liars, cheats, thieves and sexually promiscuous', and this related to their being 'Welshspeaking Nonconformists'. See Gwyneth Tyson Roberts, '"At Once Illogical and Unfair": Jane Williams (Ysgafell) and the Government Report on Education in Mid Nineteenth-Century Wales', *Women's Writing*, 24:4 (2017), 451–65. There are several studies of Anglo-Welsh relations and the use of the Welsh language in mid-nineteenth century England. See, for example, Emrys Jones, 'The Welsh Language in England c. 1800–1914', in Geraint H. Jenkins (ed.) *A Social History of the Welsh Language: Language and Community in the Nineteenth Century* (Cardiff, 1998), pp. 231–60.
[73] 'The Great Exhibition', *Daily News*, 15 Jul. 1851, p. 5.
[74] *Ibid*.
[75] 'The Great Exhibition', *Daily News*, 19 Jul. 1851, p. 5.
[76] 'The Great Exhibition', *Illustrated London News*, 23 Aug. 1851, p. 235.
[77] 'The International Exhibition', *Daily News*, 3 Jul. 1862, p. 5.

the evening' were frequently attracted to the Austrian Court by 'the sound of music'. There, Franz Holzhuber (1826–98) – an assistant in the Austrian ironwork department – on finishing work, would find any available Austrian piano and spend his evening singing and playing German songs of a 'soft and pleasing character'.[78] These unofficial performances, 'not to be found in any of the bills', became very popular with visitors.[79] Such public, spontaneous performance, either by individuals or groups, continue to feature regularly in incidental press reports until the 1870s, and this practice seems to have formed an expected musical element of the exhibitions.

MUSIC 'IN ABUNDANCE' AND 'FREQUENTLY IN COLLISION'

On one hand the spontaneous or unorganised performance of music within these exhibitions displayed a remarkable public determination to have music, whether officially provided or not. On the other, this determination created many logistical problems. From not enough music in the early stages of opening, it was quickly found that many exhibitions began to have altogether too much. Sensing an opportunity to demonstrate their instruments, and the public desire for music, exhibitors of instruments in 1851 began to invite performers to play their wares. Although there is rarely mention in the press of the players or programme, the names of the makers involved in these concerts are common, and some iconographic evidence for such recitals remains (see, for example, Figure 8). For instance, in May, a piano by Broadwood was 'placed in the English nave' where 'the performances of a clever amateur or professor attracted a crowd of admiring auditors'.[80] Similarly, on one of her many visits to the Crystal Palace, Queen Victoria listened to a performance on one of the Érard grand pianos, which demonstrated 'the wonderful power and brilliancy of the instrument'.[81]

Such performances, however, were often given with little consideration for their surroundings, and many instruments were played at the same time in close proximity. The results of this were predictably cacophonous. One report in the *Daily News* described a 'sort of cats'-concert' given in the American court. Here, 'the detestable piano-violono' (a combined instrument with a violin 'literally attached' to a piano, with four bows that 'sawed' the strings connected to separate piano keys),[82] Spiegelhalter's Euterpion (a form of automatic barrel organ), and several other instruments were heard at once, creating a 'din' described as 'worse than a universal tuning of stringed instruments in exceedingly damp weather'.[83] The amount of music in constant performance within the Great Exhibition grew so intense that by September the building was

---

[78] 'The International Exhibition', *Daily News*, 21 Jul. 1862, p. 2.
[79] *Ibid.*
[80] 'The Great Exhibition', *Standard*, 19 May 1851, p. 1.
[81] 'The Great Exhibition', *Daily News*, 19 Jul. 1851, p. 5.
[82] *The Crystal Palace and its Contents, being an Illustrated Cyclopaedia of the Great Exhibition of the Industry of All Nations, 1851* (London, 1852), p. 91.
[83] 'The Great Exhibition', *Daily News*, 15 Jul. 1851, p. 5.

Figure 8. 'Érard's Pianoforte and Harps', *The Crystal Palace and its Contents, being an Illustrated Cyclopaedia of the Great Exhibition of 1851* (London, 1852), p. 200. Universitätsbibliothek Heidelberg, CC-BY-SA 4.0.

described as housing as 'a perfect *émeute*' [riot], where several grand organs and other instruments 'bellowed forth', while 'the largest of the Sax-horns marched up and down the foreign nave'.[84] The organs came to be 'looked upon as a common enemy' by nearby exhibitors, and in one case, supposedly the 'gamut of thunder … twice invalided' an exhibitor 'whose duties place[d] him in the hottest of the fire'.[85] In light of such a cacophonous soundscape, Berlioz's well-known description in *Les Soirées de l'orchestre* of the empty Crystal Palace early one morning becomes even more poignant, as he savours the quiet and seclusion:

> The deserted inside of the Exhibition palace at seven in the morning was a spectacle of original grandeur: the vast solitude, the silence, the gentle light coming from the transparent roof, the dried-up fountains, the silent organs, the motionless trees, this harmonious display of opulent goods brought from the four corners of the world by rival peoples. These ingenious creations … all the causes of movement and noise – while human beings were absent, everything seemed to be holding a mysterious conversation together in the strange language that can be heard with the ear of the mind.[86]

---

[84] 'The Great Exhibition', *Daily News*, 13 Sep. 1851, p. 6.
[85] 'The Great Exhibition', *Daily News*, 24 Sep. 1851, p. 5.
[86] Hector Berlioz, *Les Soirées de l'orchestre* (Paris, 1854); trans. and repr. as 'Berlioz in London: Crystal Palace – 1851 Exhibition', *The Hector Berlioz Website* <http://www.hberlioz.com/London/BL1851Exhibition.html/> [accessed 2 Feb. 2021].

To rectify the factors that caused such aural chaos at 1851, in 1862 piano manufacturers Collard & Collard and Broadwood & Sons donated two grand pianos to be used for organised professional performance.[87] These instruments were placed at a distance under the building's east and west domes, but this did not resolve the larger problems with noise. Uncoordinated recitals at different manufacturers' stands were unmitigated by the presence of the 'professional' pianos, and the *Daily News* reported that they were 'sorry to find … pianos, horns, organs … all going together' with music both 'in abundance' and 'frequently in collision'.[88] In the first month, with construction work on the building still ongoing, the soundscape was described as 'the reverse of agreeable', while *The Times* stated that their earlier suggestion 'that occasional performances of music would add considerably' to the Exhibition's attractions was not intended to aid 'in the creation of the terrible jangle which prevails'.[89] The noise also had an effect on the professional performers engaged by Broadwood and Collard & Collard. Austrian pianist Ernst Pauer (1826–1905) had to play with 'a vigorous hammering' immediately above him, turnstiles keeping up 'an unceasing "click, click"' nearby, and, 'in the middle of one of his most delicate pianissimos' the cork of a bottle of ginger-beer was apparently released near his head.[90] It was not until late in the 1862 season that a timetable of performances was created to avoid instruments clashing. The *Illustrated London News* regarded this arrangement to work well, with 'the annoyance' of having multiple instruments playing at once 'thus averted'.[91] By the exhibitions of the 1880s, such a system was rigorously enforced, to the extent that – at London 1885, for example – the public were banned from touching the displayed instruments.

Problems relating to noise and space also raised issues with judging the instruments. In 1862, some in the continental European press were annoyed by the British organisers' decision to trial the instruments where they were exhibited. As a report from Vienna – reprinted in the *Musical World* – stated, 'what piano player – and that is almost as much to ask as what European – does not know the immense influence of the locale on a Piano?'[92] They suggested a more methodical approach, like that used by the jury at the 1855 Paris Exhibition, who tested each instrument in exactly the same space, with the same piece of music.[93] In an attempt to counter such criticism, in 1872

---

[87] 'Pianoforte Playing at the Great Exhibition', *Musical World*, 40:20 (17 May 1862), pp. 308–9, at p. 308.
[88] 'The International Exhibition', *Daily News*, 23 Jun. 1862, p. 2.
[89] 'The International Exhibition', *Daily News*, 21 May 1862, p. 5; 'The International Exhibition', *The Times*, 19 Jun. 1862, p. 14.
[90] 'The International Exhibition', *Daily News*, 26 May 1862, p. 2.
[91] 'The International Exhibition', *Illustrated London News*, 12 Jul. 1862, p. 42.
[92] 'Pianofortes at the International Exhibition (from the "*Presse*" of Vienna)', *Musical World*, 40:35 (30 Aug. 1862), pp. 554–5, at p. 554.
[93] *Ibid*. This process was humorously described by Berlioz in 'Exposition Universelle: Les Instrumens de musique à l'Exposition universelle', *Journal des Débats*, 9 Jan. 1856, 3. Also available at *The Hector Berlioz Website* <http://www.hberlioz.com/feuilletons/debats560109.htm/> [accessed 2 Feb. 2021].

the commissioners organised public recitals on the competing instruments. Unlike the recitals at 1862, given by performers selected by the exhibitors, in 1872 Pauer was appointed to run these concerts.[94] But the vague terms released by the commissioners give little evidence that the jury practices had actually changed, stating the instruments would be either heard in the Albert Hall, or 'tried without removal from their exhibition allotments'.[95]

MUSIC AS LEISURE AND ENTERTAINMENT

When the *Musical Times* asserted in 1873 that music had had 'no place in artistic exhibitions', they conceded that they were not including music employed 'as an amusement and a relaxation'.[96] In doing so, they foregrounded another debate circulating about music's place at exhibitions: the relative importance between music as an elevated art, and music as entertainment. For all the official rhetoric about 'progress' and education, exhibitions were also commercial, mass-entertainment sites.[97] They were expensive to run and entry was ticketed, so it was important – however much the organisers tried to avoid mentioning it – to attract consistent attendance. Catering to a wide spectrum of social and cultural groups and tastes, organisers had to balance their rational-recreationalist ideals of public education and 'high art' against drawing a paying audience looking for entertainment. Knowing that popular music – in particular brass and military bands – would encourage ticket sales, the organisers worked to supply entertainment that was attractive to the widest audience.

The idea of music as pure entertainment angered some in the musical press, with the *Musical Times* in 1871 arguing that the commissioners had proved that they had no interest in 'artistic progress'.[98] The *Musical Standard* cynically compared the employment of bands at the exhibitions with their success at Wombwell's menagerie and other travelling circuses.[99] The utilitarian view of music as a tool to draw the public was considered degrading to the profundity of the art by those who staunchly championed performed music as an exhibition-object. Much to the musical press's chagrin, band and secular organ recitals containing medleys, pot-pourris, and selections of popular tunes, came to be regarded as one of the main highlights of the exhibitions. This music was not intended to be listened to with great focus, but rather to accompany viewing objects, or while promenading in the gardens. While unappreciated in the musical press, it was this music – considered of the lowest cultural status of any heard at the exhibitions – that was the most well-liked by the public.

Organ recitals were prominent at all exhibitions in the British Empire, yet at the Great Exhibition – as in most of its musical aspects – these were

---

[94] 'International Exhibition', *Era*, 16 Jun. 1872, p. 12.
[95] [no title], *Musical World*, 50:4 (27 Jan. 1872), p. 61.
[96] 'Exhibition Music', *Musical Times*, p. 40.
[97] Maurice Roche, 'Mega-Events, Culture and Modernity: Expos and the Origins of Public Culture', *International Journal of Cultural Policy*, 5:1 (1998), 1–31 p. 17.
[98] Lunn, 'Music at the Opening', p. 103.
[99] 'The Coming Exhibition', *Musical Standard*, 14:342 (18 Feb. 1871), p. 69.

poorly organised.[100] As the *Standard* noted in May 1851, although the organs were 'labelled with promises' of concerts, at the stated hours 'we hear[d] little music'.[101] Despite this, when performances were given, they were positively received. John Thomas Cooper (1819–79), the organist at both St Sepulchre and St Paul's, was one of the most frequent performers, but appearances were also made by W.T. Best, George Washbourne Morgan (1821–92), and the visiting Adolf Hesse (1809–63), a 'professor of some eminence', composer, and principal organist at the Bernhardinerkirche in Breslau (now Wrocław).[102] Programmes, containing a few works specifically written for organ by Bach or Handel, generally consisted of arrangements, overtures, and selections of popular works, and included, at one point the novelty of a song composed by Prince Albert.[103]

Along similar lines, band music became an increasingly important part of the musical entertainment at the exhibitions, heard regularly in the grounds.[104] In 1862, a significant proportion of this music was provided by the Kensington Volunteers, but other bands, including the Grenadier and Coldstream Guards, the Royal Artillery, and – according to one report – a band lent by the Pasha of Egypt from his yacht, were heard by the Exhibition's close.[105] In 1871, following the success of the opening ceremony's 'Exhibition of Musical Art', the commissioners described the organ recitals and bands as further 'daily exhibitions' of music.[106] With the intention of making the entertainment 'thoroughly international', musicians from across Europe were invited, in return for payment and accommodation, to perform twice per day for a fortnight.[107] Through this scheme, several European bands – including the King of Sweden's First Regiment of Guards, the Belgian Regiment of Guides, and the French Garde républicaine – became extremely popular with the British public, with the press reporting rapturous applause and large attendances throughout.[108] In such

---

[100] For more on the organs at the Great Exhibitions see Makiko Hayasaka, 'Organ Recitals as Popular Culture: The Secularisation of the Instrument and Its Repertoire in Britain, 1834–1950', (unpublished Ph.D. thesis, University of Bristol, 2016).
[101] 'The Great Exhibition', *Standard*, 19 May 1851, p. 1.
[102] 'The Great Exhibition', *Morning Chronicle*, 9 Jun. 1851, p. 2; 'The Great Exhibition', *Standard*, 30 Jun. 1851, p. 3; 'The Great Exhibition', *Morning Chronicle*, 8 Sep. 1851, p. 3; 'The Great Exhibition', *Standard*, 21 Jul. 1851, p. 1.
[103] 'The Great Exhibition', *Standard*, 21 Jul. 1851, p. 1; 'The Great Exhibition', *Morning Chronicle*, 9 Jun. 1851, p. 2; 'The Great Exhibition', *Morning Chronicle*, 12 Jun. 1851, p. 2.
[104] 'The International Exhibition', *Daily News*, 9 May 1862, p. 6; 'The International Exhibition', *Daily News*, 6 Sep. 1862, p. 2.
[105] 'The International Exhibition', *The Times*, 27 May 1862, p. 7; 'The International Exhibition', *Morning Post*, 5 Jul. 1862, p. 5.
[106] 'The Organ of the Royal Albert Hall – International Exhibitions in Music', *Dwight's Journal of Music*, 31:3 (6 May 1871), pp. 20–1, at p. 20.
[107] *Ibid.*
[108] *Ibid.*

performances, the usual programmes of popular opera fantasias and overtures were supplemented with examples of their own national musics.[109]

The environment in which secular organ recitals and bands were heard encouraged significant debate about their appropriateness. Because the organs were heard inside the buildings, surrounded by the bustle of visitors, competing stalls, and other entertainment, *The Times* suggested that such music 'should not be of too engrossing a character' so as to not distract from the other exhibits.[110] This highlights exactly the perception lamented by the musical press: that music should be seen only 'as an amusement and a relaxation', and not be the focus of one's attention.[111] The bands in the gardens were similarly just one element of the outdoor entertainment, being surrounded by colourful lighting, large fountain displays, vast spaces for promenading, and – at later exhibitions – carnival amusements.

While much of the criticism of the bands reflected their 'uneasy cultural position' in Britain due to their working-class associations, discussions about music – and audiences – as 'mindless', were not only confined to working-class audiences.[112] During the 1862 Exhibition, *The Times* was surprised to note that recitals on exhibited instruments drew their largest crowds on 'shilling days', where the entry price was reduced. At these times, 'each and every instrument drew around it such a quiet and attentive audience as they can never command on fashionable days'.[113] This suggests to their readers, albeit rather patronisingly, that the working classes were more discerning than expected, taking an interest in a wide variety of musical activities. *The Times* also argued that in audiences made up of wealthier people, the main attraction was to promenade and be seen, with music 'only an accident of the situation'.[114] This was, interestingly, almost exactly the criticism levelled at bands by the musical press, who lamented music being seen as only incidental to being entertained overall.

The popularity of organ recitals and bands was one of the main successes of the exhibitions between 1851 and the 1870s, drawing crowds where even the exhibits themselves failed. While the exhibitions had been relatively financially and popularly successful up to 1871, by 1872 public enthusiasm was beginning to wane. The 1872 Exhibition closed 'without any kind of ceremony' and the final weeks were regarded by the press as thoroughly depressing; yet music, provided by bands, remained steadily attractive. As the *Morning Post* explained, the only 'bright feature' of the final day was the Royal Horse Guards band,

---

[109] 'The Swedish Military Band', *Musical World*, 49:31 (5 Aug. 1871), p. 488; 'The International Exhibition', *The Times*, 2 Oct. 1871, p. 9.

[110] 'The Great Exhibition', *The Times*, p. 7.

[111] 'Exhibition Music', *Musical Times*, pp. 40–1.

[112] Trevor Herbert, 'Victorian Brass Bands: Class, Taste and Space', in Andrew Leyshon, David Matless, and George Revill (eds), *The Place of Music* (New York, 1998), pp. 104–28, at p. 106.

[113] 'The International Exhibition', *The Times*, 8 Jul. 1862, p. 10.

[114] *Ibid.*

whose music helped in 'chasing away melancholy'.[115] The programmes of both the popular organ recitals and bands across all these exhibitions are remarkably similar to those given at the exhibitions of the 1880s, and – perhaps inadvertently – demonstrate the most successful 'exhibition' of music. The conditions considered necessary for showing music comparably to the plastic arts – that is, frequent repetition of the same work, as argued by the commentators discussed above – occurred, not through the best attempts of the organisers to display 'high art', but instead through the popular entertainments where works were repeated precisely because they were well-received.

If attendees were beginning to tire of exhibitions by 1872, they had completely lost interest by 1874 and 'exhibition fatigue' had well and truly set in.[116] The musical press does not appear to mention the Exhibition of 1874, despite regular military bands remaining in the gardens and Albert Hall. Yet not even these managed to draw a crowd. As the *Illustrated London News* put it:

> Long corridors with hardly anyone in them ... such was the International Exhibition ... so few and uninterested its visitors. The admission was only a shilling, and yet neither rich nor poor were attracted. Every class pronounced it a failure; and it was, indeed, the most depressing of places ... if there is one thing drearier than all others it is a very big place with very few people in it.[117]

It was not until nearly a decade later that London held another international exhibition, once the tradition had been reinvigorated by a series of exhibitions in a new context: the colonies. The precedents set by the exhibitions of the 1850s to '70s, however, and the themes arising through this discourse – discussions about music as an art and its representation through objects, music as a means of popular entertainment and public engagement, or of its educational value – all developed further through the exhibitions of the 1880s. It is this set of ideas that frame the chapters that follow.

---

[115] 'The International Exhibition', *Morning Post*, 21 Oct. 1872, p. 6.
[116] Alexander C.T. Geppert, *Fleeting Cities: Imperial Expositions in Fin-de-Siècle Europe* (New York, 2010), p. 201.
[117] 'The End of the Exhibition', *Illustrated London News*, 31 Oct. 1874, p. 427.

CHAPTER 2

The Musical Object

In the opening chapter of his seminal work *The Commodity Culture of Victorian England*, Thomas Richards sums up the single idea at the centre of the 1851 Great Exhibition's conception: 'that all human life and cultural endeavour could be fully represented by exhibiting manufactured articles'.[1] This exhibition – this 'first outburst of the phantasmagoria of commodity culture' – would significantly change how the Victorian public understood material culture in ways that still resonate today.[2] The Great Exhibition, while not the first exhibition of manufactured objects in Europe, was by far the most influential, and the systems of representation it established were perpetuated in the events of later decades. The idea of spectacle and phantasmagoria was central to the display of objects at 1851 and later, as the vast spaces and overwhelming number of products dazzled consumers into losing sight of the commercial nature of the goods they were invited to inspect. The presence of the arts at these exhibitions helped establish this grander narrative and, it was hoped, averted the descent of such events into 'mere' trade fairs.[3] In combining the arts, manufacturing, and entertainment, exhibitions left attendees with a sense of 'kaleidoscopic synthesis', that the universe had been systematically ordered in such a way that arbitrary commercial decisions might be reconciled with grander ideas of art and learning.[4]

As large-scale displays of material culture, international exhibitions could easily accommodate most raw materials, commercially manufactured commodities, and visual art-objects into their grand structures of display. In most cases, the buildings' layouts transitioned seamlessly from machinery halls, to courts of commercial goods, to picture and sculpture galleries. Yet as we have seen, representing 'music' in this context was not so simple. Despite critics' protestations, displays of physical, musical instruments were the most consistent representation of 'music' that the exhibitions held. These objects, like all those around them, were both 'spectacularised' as commodities and subsumed into the phantasmagoria of the exhibition spaces, but that did not mean that

[1] Thomas Richards, *The Commodity Culture of Victorian England: Advertising and Spectacle, 1851–1914* (Stanford, 1990), p. 17.
[2] Ibid, p. 18.
[3] Paul Greenhalgh, *Ephemeral Vistas: The Expositions Universelles, Great Exhibitions and World's Fairs, 1851–1939* (Manchester, 1988), p. 198.
[4] Andrzej Piotrowski, 'The Spectacle of Architectural Discourses', *Architectural Theory Review*, 13:2 (2008), 130–44, at p. 134.

they were not also encountered as individual objects, loaded with their own cultural meaning.[5] The idea of a 'musical commodity' – as one might classify an instrument – was something that bridged a gap between manufactured object and work of art. It was itself manufactured, but also facilitated the production of music. This position raised philosophical problems for the systems of taxonomy on which exhibitions relied to classify their contents.

Regardless of how musical instruments were catalogued, or where they were placed in the buildings, the public's first experience of these objects would generally not involve hearing them making music. Instead they were initially encountered as silent, static objects. Without a sonic reference point, critics in the press and members of the public still interpreted these objects through frameworks informed by their cultural position as related to music. Sometimes, this was through an assessment of the instruments' external, aesthetic features. At other times, they were perceived as significant for their associations with important historical figures. For other instruments, the way various countries' commissioners invested in their display built up national mythologies around them.

In exploring these ideas, in this chapter and the next, I use the piano as a case study. The piano was one of the most abundant instruments displayed at all the exhibitions. While there were certainly many other groups represented – brass, for example, was commonly displayed in Britain due to the marketing efforts of firms such as Besson and Boosey – at London 1885, over ninety different manufacturers displayed pianos, as well as other keyboard instruments such as harmoniums and organs, or component parts like keys, actions, soundboards, and wires. In Melbourne 1888, too, nearly one hundred manufacturers exhibited pianos.[6] At both of these exhibitions, many of these makers sent multiple instruments. Aside from being the most numerous instrument, pianos were also among the most conspicuous through their size and capacity for external decoration. Their multiple moving parts and complex construction also made them interesting as mechanical exhibits, independent of their cultural associations. To quote Arthur Loesser, during the Industrial Revolution:

> any zealot for factory production would have cast a lecherous eye upon the pianoforte's tens of identical wooden keys, its dozens of identical jacks and hammer-shanks, its greater dozens of identical turning pins and hitch pins, and its yards of identically drawn wire. The pianoforte was the factory's natural prey; purely on the basis of its structure, it was the instrument of the time.[7]

The most important reason for focusing on pianos here, however, is their social significance. Pianos were central to musical daily life, with the proliferation of amateur music-making in nineteenth-century Britain and the colonies largely facilitated by their increasing affordability and improved construction.

---

[5] Steve Edwards, 'Photography; Allegory; and Labor', *Art Journal*, 55:2 (1996), 38–44, at p. 38.

[6] Cyril Ehrlich, *The Piano: A History*, rev. ed. (Oxford, 1990), p. 86; See also *Official Catalogue of Exhibits: Centennial International Exhibition, Melbourne, 1888–9* (Melbourne, 1888), pp. 125–6.

[7] Arthur Loesser, *Men, Women and Pianos: A Social History* (New York, 1990), p. 233.

This was well recognised during the exhibitions and was repeatedly highlighted in contemporary literature. Edward Rimbault's *The Pianoforte, its Origin, Progress, and Construction* of 1860 opens describing the piano as 'the "household orchestra" of the people'.[8] Equally, the *Report of the Jury* on the pianos exhibited at the Great Exhibition contains passages by Sigismund Thalberg (1812–71), describing 'the social importance of the piano' as being 'far greater than that of any other instrument of music'.[9] This was equally true in the colonies. As Oscar Comettant (1819–98) – visiting the Melbourne Exhibition as a member of the international jury – joked of Australia in 1880, the piano was considered so necessary that people, 'rather than not have one of these sonorous instruments in the drawing-room ... would go without a bed; they would sleep on the piano while waiting to complete their furnishings'.[10]

By the late nineteenth century, the prevalence of pianos in domestic life meant that most exhibition visitors would have had some visual familiarity with them, and therefore some competence in evaluating them on aesthetic terms. Similarly, many would have experience either playing an instrument, or hearing one played. As the *Musical World* stated at London 1885, 'everybody appreciates them more or less', and 'almost everybody believes that he is, or might be with very little trouble, able to play them'.[11] This was not, however, the case for all instruments at the exhibitions, where, alongside the pianos and other common instruments were also a number of new (and at times, quite bizarre) Victorian-invented instruments. This chapter closes with an analysis of the reception of such instruments. For the public, the capacity to appreciate the cultural significance of an instrument broke down when the instrument was unfamiliar. Such musical curiosities became, instead, objects of enquiry, rather than elevated cultural products. This made them less successful in navigating the divide between the commercial and art worlds, but also less implicated in the debates about music as 'art' as discussed in Chapter One. Such instruments, too, could more easily fit within the general taxonomic categorisations than the standard instruments.

---

[8] Edward Francis Rimbault, *The Pianoforte, its Origin, Progress, and Construction* (London, 1860), p. v.

[9] Sigismund Thalberg, quoted in Peter and Ann Mactaggart, *Musical Instruments in the 1851 Exhibition: A Transcription of the Entries of Musical Interest from the Official Illustrated Catalogue of the Great Exhibition of the Art and Industry of All Nations, with Additional Material from Contemporary Sources* (Welwyn, 1986), pp. 96–7.

[10] Oscar Comettant, *In the Land of Kangaroos and Gold Mines* [Au pays des kangourous et des mines d'or], trans. Judith Armstrong (Adelaide, 1980), p. 137.

[11] D.T., 'Music at the Inventions Exhibition', *Musical World*, 63:23 (6 Jun. 1885), 349–50, at p. 349.

❦ *Phantasmagoria and the Spectacularised Commodity*

In his 1930s *Arcades Project*, Walter Benjamin describes exhibitions as 'places of pilgrimage to the fetish Commodity' and 'a phantasmagoria into which people entered in order to be distracted', setting the tone for much of the current theoretical discourse on the phenomenon of international exhibitions.[12] The term 'phantasmagoria' – originally the name given to early nineteenth-century 'magic lantern' optical illusions – by the mid-nineteenth century had taken on the additional meaning of a 'startling or extraordinary' dreamlike scene, made up of multiple changing elements.[13] In Benjamin's use of the term to describe exhibitions, one can read elements of both of these definitions, from the illusory qualities of the magic lanterns, to the overwhelming, extraordinary, or dreamlike multi-element vista, where commodities are experienced as both deceptive and spectacular. Incorporating elements of Karl Marx's theories of commodity fetishism[14] and the 'magical quality of commodities and their power over the consumer', phantasmagoria is a way of theorising the effects of capitalism in the visual and psychological realms with particular relevance to exhibitions.[15]

The phantasmagorical qualities of exhibitions related to both their enormous and spectacular internal spaces, and the vastness and 'unparalleled opulence' of the concepts they encompassed.[16] On a purely logistical level, exhibitions involved the disruption and remodelling of entire cities, and the expenditure of vast amounts of money.[17] In ideological terms, they were the physical embodiment of the 'classificatory gaze' prevalent in nineteenth-century British thought, representing 'a panoramic view' where all human knowledge was supposedly

---

[12] Walter Benjamin, *The Arcades Project*, trans. Howard Eiland and Kevin McLaughlin (Cambridge, 1999), p. 7.

[13] 'phantasmagoria, n.', *OED Online* <http://www.oed.com/view/Entry/142184/> [accessed 5 Feb. 2021].

[14] Discussions of commodities and exhibitions invariably invoke Marx's concept of commodity fetishism; yet the term 'fetishism' has a highly specific, technical meaning, which is often misunderstood in such discussions. See, Timothy D. Taylor, 'The Commodification of Music at the Dawn of the Era of "Mechanical Music"', *Ethnomusicology*, 51:2 (2007), 281–305, particularly pp. 297–301. In Marx's view, commodity fetishism occurs in the way the apparent 'value relation between the products of labour which stamps them as commodities' conceals the social relations between the people whose labour produced them. See Karl Marx, *Capital: A Critique of Political Economy*, first published in German in 1867, first English edition in 1887, <https://www.marxists.org/archive/marx/works/download/pdf/Capital-Volume-I.pdf> [accessed 5 Feb. 2021], p. 48.

[15] Amy F. Ogata, 'Viewing Souvenirs: Peepshows and the International Expositions', *Journal of Design History*, 15:2 (2002), 69–82, at p. 69.

[16] Susan Pearce, *On Collecting: An Investigation into Collecting in the European Tradition* (Florence, 2007), p. 134.

[17] Greenhalgh, *Ephemeral Vistas*, p. 1.

available to inspect.[18] Yet, for the actual objects – ostensibly the reason for these events – the vastness of the spaces could overwhelm them. Despite an official rhetoric suggesting that exhibitions provided a survey of the human world's products and achievements, their collections appeared less like an 'exact census' of goods, and more like an immense mass of commodities 'expanding profligately in every direction'.[19]

The presence of such quantities of diverse items, displayed within the same colossal space, also overwhelmed audiences through the newly conceived practice of 'commercial enchantment'.[20] Dazzled visitors – 'no longer bound by any preconceived logic of understanding or judgment' – were left bewildered, in a state of 'irrational reverence' that erased the separation between academic knowledge and commercial interests.[21] But the spectacle and phantasmagoria went beyond the displayed commodities too. Exhibition buildings were structured so that, while everyone could see the objects on display, there were also places from which one could be seen oneself: look-outs from which the mass of visitors could be surveyed, in a manner often described as paralleling Bentham's panopticon.[22]

Such spectacle and 'irrational reverence' was compounded by the religious overtones that exhibition buildings and their official rhetoric commanded. Cathedrals were some of the few contemporary buildings remotely comparable in size and scale, and exhibition spaces were commonly referred to as cathedrals or temples of commerce. Exhibition buildings were also frequently laid out in the church's traditional cruciform shape, and the various galleries and branches of the buildings were officially referred to as 'transepts' and 'naves'. Despite being secular festivals, biblical quotes were also sometimes incorporated into the decorations (Figure 9), or on associated publications. The Great Exhibition, for example, was given 'religious legitimation' by incorporating Psalm 24 from the 1662 Book of Common Prayer translation into the *Official Catalogue* ('the earth is the Lord's and all that therein is; the compass of the world and they that dwell therein').[23] This meant that, despite the overt commercialism of the event, it could be interpreted as exhibiting 'the riches of God's creation'.[24] While the psalm was not printed in the catalogues of the 1880s, other semi-religious aspects remained, including the nearly ubiquitous performance of the 'Hallelujah' chorus at exhibitions' opening and closing ceremonies. The

---

[18] Pearce, *On Collecting*, p. 132.
[19] Richards, *Commodity Culture of Victorian England*, p. 27.
[20] Andrzej Piotrowski, 'Architecture and the Evolution of Commercial Culture', *International Journal of the Constructed Environment*, 1:1 (2011), 51–64, at p. 53.
[21] Ibid.
[22] Tony Bennett, 'The Exhibitionary Complex', in Reesa Greenberg, Bruce W. Ferguson, and Sandy Nairne (eds), *Thinking About Exhibitions* (London, 1996), pp. 58–80, at p. 62.
[23] Geoffrey Cantor, 'Science, Providence, and Progress at the Great Exhibition', *Isis*, 103:3 (2012), 439–59, at p. 445.
[24] Ibid.

Figure 9. Interior of the Glasgow exhibition building, 1888, with the text 'By knowledge shall thy chambers be filled with all pleasant riches' from Proverbs 24:4. 'The Glasgow Exhibition: The Main Avenue', *Illustrated London News*, 25 Aug. 1888, p. 221. © Illustrated London News Ltd/Mary Evans.

overall experience of attending was also likened to a 'religious ritual', with contemporary sources from even scientifically minded figures making religious allusions.[25] As biologist Thomas Henry Huxley (1825–95) described the Great Exhibition, it was a place to be approached 'with awe and reverence, as if … on a sacred pilgrimage to a holy shrine'.[26] These religious connotations would certainly have reinforced the spectacular impression made by the events, and facilitated a further reverence for the objects held within.

Many of the objects on display were themselves either elaborate or extravagant too. As the *Illustrated London News* put it, at the Great Exhibition visitors could look at 'a tissue nobody could wear; at a carriage in which nobody could ride; at a fireplace which no servant could clean if it were ever guilty of a fire … at a musical instrument not fit for one in fifty thousand to play', such was the

[25] Pearce, *On Collecting*, p. 139.
[26] Bernard Lightman, 'Science and Culture', in Francis O'Gorman (ed.), *The Cambridge Companion to Victorian Culture* (Cambridge, 2010), pp. 12–42, at p. 15.

ostentation of the design.[27] These kinds of objects, displayed alongside more commonly available products, helped transform the commodities as a whole: they became not everyday items, but objects of 'high spectacle', participants in a 'fundamental shift in viewing that favoured the phantasmagorical'.[28] Within this spectacular, phantasmagorical space, objects and commodities became 'no longer the trivial things' as they appeared at first sight to Marx in *Capital*, but instead, were an all-encompassing, 'sensual feast for the eye'.[29]

MUSICAL COMMODITIES

While it is tempting to analyse exhibitions entirely from the perspective of large-scale spectacle, exploring them only in terms of the 'fantastic and mesmerizing' can risk overwhelming discussions at an object-specific level.[30] People did attend exhibitions to 'gaze in wonder, to stand spellbound … to wander awestruck before the fantastic multiplicity of things', but within that psychological and physical space they also encountered and interacted with individual commodities.[31] A commodity, as Marx defines it, is broadly 'an object outside us … that by its properties satisfies human wants of some sort or another'.[32] These material objects are not culturally static or devoid of external meaning, abounding – according to Marx – in 'metaphysical subtleties and theological niceties'.[33] This was as much the case for musical instruments as any other commodity, and throughout the Victorian period, these objects were attributed with multiple social and cultural meanings.

The variety of meanings that musical instruments held made them difficult to taxonomically categorise, yet the display-structure of the exhibitions compelled organisers to do just that. This problem was fundamentally related to one of the most fraught aspects of the exhibitions' relationship with material culture: the sometimes arbitrary distinction between industrial products and art-objects. Even today, commercialism and capitalism as broad categories have 'problematic relationships' with the arts, particularly when the creative process is believed to be separate from the 'profit motive'.[34] This was also true in the nineteenth century, where many writers made clear their discomfort with the conflation of 'commerce and culture'.[35] Musical instruments, in particular, sit awkwardly within this field. They are demonstrably manufactured objects,

---

[27] 'Exhibition Notes No. 1', *Illustrated London News*, 14 Jun. 1851, pp. 493–4. Quoted in Richards, *Commodity Culture of Victorian England*, p. 33.
[28] Ogata, 'Viewing Souvenirs', p. 73.
[29] Richards, *Commodity Culture of Victorian England*, p. 21.
[30] Edwards, 'Photography; Allegory; and Labor', p. 38.
[31] Ibid.
[32] Marx, *Capital*, p. 27.
[33] Ibid, p. 47.
[34] Kate Nichols and Rebecca Wade, 'Art versus Industry? An Introduction', in Kate Nichols, Rebecca Wade, and Gabriel Williams (eds), *Art versus Industry?: New Perspectives on Visual and Industrial Cultures in Nineteenth-Century Britain* (Manchester, 2016), pp. 1–18, at p. 3.
[35] Ibid.

made up of mechanical parts and capable of being bought and sold as commodities. Yet they are also vehicles for the creation of music and the realisation of musical works.

In the twentieth century, such objects have been labelled 'cultural commodities', existing somewhere between the extremities of total art-object and prototypical industrial product. Bernard Miège offers several categories into which 'cultural commodities' can be divided, considering musical instruments to fit within a class of objects that are 'reproducible products not requiring the involvement of cultural workers in their production'.[36] While not necessarily art-objects themselves, instruments – like other, perhaps more obvious twentieth-century technologies such as the radio and recording devices – are objects capable of either producing or reproducing music. What gives these a distinct presence as 'cultural commodities' is the way in which their association with 'cultural' forms attribute them with a greater social value. As Pierre Bourdieu argues, material objects owned by an individual can represent possession of both symbolic and cultural capital. In this way, musical instruments are able to represent not only economic capital or monetary value, but cultural capital in its objectified state as 'cultural goods'.[37] Although they are not owned by the members of the public attending exhibitions (and, in most exhibition contexts, cannot even be bought) these objects were presented in a manner that gave the impression that they 'would one day be democratically available to anyone and everyone'.[38]

The musical instrument as cultural commodity is distinct from, but not unrelated to the *musical work* as a commodity. In the era before recorded sound, musical instruments were required to produce instrumental music. This may seem like stating the obvious, but it is important to underline that while these instruments themselves exist in commodity form, they are also 'inextricably intertwined with the musical commodities they contribute to producing'.[39] Ultimately the status of both commodities – instrument and work – are mutually dependent: commodified musical works could not exist without the objects that facilitate their production. By the same token, instruments would be rather pointless without music to play on them.[40] It was this inextricable link between musical-work-as-art-object and the instrument necessary for producing it that caused the difficulty in categorising musical instruments at these exhibitions.

In addition to this complex relationship, many instruments were also regarded as aesthetic objects in their own right. This aspect of their physical existence was also one of the elements that allowed them to acquire embodied cultural capital. Highly crafted or decorated instruments provided evidence of a skilled artisan's labour 'congealed' on their surfaces, and the aesthetically

---

[36] Bernard Miège, 'The Cultural Commodity', trans. Nicholas Garnham, *Media, Culture and Society*, 1:3 (1979), 297–311, at p. 302.
[37] Pierre Bourdieu, 'The Forms of Capital', in John Richardson (ed.), *Handbook of Theory and Research for the Sociology of Education* (New York, 1986), pp. 241–58, at pp. 246–7.
[38] Richards, *Commodity Culture of Victorian England*, p. 19.
[39] Taylor, 'Commodification of Music', p. 283.
[40] *Ibid.*

elaborate instruments displayed at the exhibitions assert 'a wholeheartedly materialist world order'.[41] Whatever the 'crass materialism and social rapaciousness' represented by the overwrought aesthetic qualities of these instruments might have been, 'the arts' and 'music especially' were theoretically 'employed ... to mitigate, if not to subvert' these excesses.[42]

TAXONOMIES AND SYSTEMS OF REPRESENTING MUSIC

The nineteenth-century's burgeoning commodity culture created a number of problems, one of which was creating a 'stable system of representation' for the vastly increasing number of new products.[43] Exhibitions articulated this problem starkly by their organisational processes, explicitly attempting to create 'a dominant form of representation' for the new commodity culture.[44] This framework of representation came in the form of a highly-curated taxonomy, into which every displayed product was supposed to fit. While these systems were established to organise the enormous collections of objects into smaller, more comprehensible departments, they also represent a clear attempt to order and make sense of capitalist society itself.[45] The phantasmagorical nature of exhibitions may have created the impression of an overwhelming and perhaps chaotic mass of objects, but this belied the fact that they were actually highly ordered through these strict systems of classification.

Exhibition taxonomies and classificatory systems by their very nature created additional problems for the organisers, particularly in their categorising products or commodities related to art. Despite the official rhetoric that espoused a grand union between the art and manufacturing worlds, exhibition taxonomic schemes almost universally separated the products of industry from the fine arts.[46] This caused particular difficulties in categorising art objects created through industrial means. Stained glass and photography are two such examples, which were classed respectively as manufacturing and machinery in several early exhibitions, causing much debate about their status as fine arts.[47] Musical instruments, through their status as cultural commodities, inextricably linked to the art of music, faced similar issues of classification.

---

[41] Richard Leppert, 'Material Culture and Decentred Selfhood (Socio-Visual Typologies of Musical Excess)', in Stan Hawkins (ed.), *Critical Musicological Reflections: Essays in Honour of Derek B. Scott* (Farnham, 2012), pp. 101–24, at p. 103 and p. 105.

[42] Ibid, p. 106.

[43] Richards, *Commodity Culture of Victorian England*, p. 3.

[44] Ibid.

[45] Jasmine Allen, '"Why Are the Painted Windows in the Industrial Department?" The Classification of Stained Glass at the London and Paris International Exhibitions, 1851–1900', in Nichols, Wade, and Williams (eds), *Art versus Industry?*, pp. 61–80, at p. 61; Edwards, 'Photography; Allegory; and Labor', p. 38.

[46] Allen, 'Why Are the Painted Windows in the Industrial Department?', p. 63.

[47] See for example Jasmine Allen's discussion of stained glass, which could be seen simultaneously as 'an applied art, art-manufacture, craft, decorative art, industrial art, manufactured product and commodity' in *Ibid*, p. 61. For a discussion of photography, see Edwards, 'Photography; Allegory; and Labor', p. 39.

The system of classification used throughout the British, Australian, and Indian exhibitions considered here was developed for the Great Exhibition by Lyon Playfair (1818–98) not, as commonly thought, by Prince Albert. Playfair – a politician and trained organic chemist – established his system in discussion with committees from the manufacturing industry, and as such, the final scheme largely reflected these manufacturers' interests and concerns.[48] Thus, the Great Exhibition was divided into four main categories: raw materials, machinery, manufactures, and fine arts, which were themselves divided into thirty smaller classes. While the labelling of classes changed, new classes were added, and objects were sometimes reclassified across the later exhibitions; the grand scheme of every exhibition that followed was based on this model.

A dialectical analysis of 'the problem of taxonomy' is a useful way to explain where taxonomic categories fail and are rebuilt.[49] Such an analysis is presented in Table 2, which shows the different ways musical instruments were classified within the British exhibitionary tradition from the Great Exhibition to 1890. It can be seen here that the classification of musical instruments in 1851 as 'machinery' and the strikingly broad class of 'Philosophical, Musical, Horological, and Surgical Instruments' broke down. By the end of the 1880s, the classificatory category for instruments had been reconceptualised as 'Education', while sometimes still within a broad class of 'Scientific or Philosophical' objects.

The taxonomic categorisation of musical instruments as 'machinery' in the early British exhibitions was considered wholly inadequate and unrepresentative. As this classificatory category broke down, it was revised, and instruments were gradually reclassified as 'educational' objects, and categorised as representative of applied liberal arts. It is possible, in London at least, that this change developed in response to the criticism of the classification of musical instruments outlined previously. But this shift also demonstrates the increasing importance of music within the exhibitions, and the social status of the objects used to create it. This occurred as the exhibitions moved to the colonies, where such objects grew in significance as markers of sophistication and cultural status.

ཉ་ Silent Encounters with Musical Objects

Most visitors' initial encounters with musical instruments were through physical displays in which the instruments sat silent. These were usually presented at independent stands curated by manufacturers within the larger national courts (see Figure 10 of the French piano court at Melbourne 1880). Such displays presented instruments primarily as either aesthetic or mechanical objects; yet despite their silence, the overwhelming associations of these instruments was with the music they *could* produce. Unlike the exhibitions of the 1850s, '60s, and '70s discussed in Chapter One, by the 1880s, visitors were precluded from

---

[48] Edwards, 'Accumulation of Knowledge', p. 36.
[49] Edwards, 'Photography; Allegory; and Labor', p. 40.

Table 2. Classification of Musical Instruments at International Exhibitions in the British Empire, 1851–1890

Year & Exhibition	Location	Category	Class
1851 Great Exhibition	London	Machinery	Class 10: Philosophical, Musical, Horological, and Surgical Instruments
1862 International Exhibition	London	Musical Instruments	
1865 International Exhibition	Dublin	Machinery	Section 10: Philosophical Instruments and Processes depending upon their use; Photographic Apparatus, Musical, Horological, and Surgical Instruments
1871 International Exhibition	London	No instruments displayed	
1872 International Exhibition	London	Industrial Department	Class 10: Musical Instruments
1873 International Exhibition	London	No instruments displayed	
1874 International Exhibition	London	No instruments displayed	
1879 International Exhibition	Sydney	Education and Science	Scientific and Philosophical Instruments and Methods Class 313: Musical Instruments and Acoustic Apparatus
1880 International Exhibition	Melbourne	Education and Instruction, Apparatus and Processes of the Liberal Arts	Class 13: Musical Instruments
1883 International Exhibition	Calcutta	Education and Application of Liberal Arts	Class 14: Musical Instruments
1884 Health Exhibition	London	No division for music	
1885 Inventions Exhibition	London	Music (own Division)	Group 32: Instruments and Appliances Constructed or in Use Since 1800
1886 Indian & Colonial Exhibition	London	Classification decided by exhibiting commissions	
1886 Shipping & Navigation Exhibition	Liverpool	Group 23: Musical Instruments	

—(continued)

Table 2—*concluded*

Year & Exhibition	Location	Category	Class
1886 International Exhibition of Industry Science and Art	Edinburgh	Educational Appliances	Court 7: Music
1887 International Jubilee Exhibition	Adelaide	Education and Science	Scientific and Philosophical Instruments and Methods Class 364: Musical Instruments and Acoustic Apparatus
1888 International Exhibition	Glasgow	Class 21: Music and Musical Instruments	
1888 Centennial Exhibition	Melbourne	Education and Instruction, Apparatus and Processes of the Liberal Arts	Class 13: Musical Instruments
1890 International Exhibition of Electrical Engineering, General Inventions and Industries	Edinburgh	Arranged by nation, without further classification	

making physical contact with the exhibited objects. This meant, in the case of musical instruments, audiences had no experience of their actual function, apart from when they were used in organised demonstrations. This created an 'illusionistic tease' for visitors where, like the poetic ode – a form that invites readers into 'metaphysical communion through an object' without physical contact – exhibitions compelled viewers to suppress the desire to touch, relying instead on imagination in an 'almost synaesthetic process of evocation'.[50]

Yet the presentation of musical instruments as silent museum-objects detached from the context of their function elicited mixed critical and public responses. The musical trade press often presented large supplementary exhibition volumes of their publications, offering extensive descriptions of the technical specifications of each instrument. These would presumably have been of little interest to any but a specialist audience; it is doubtful how many general visitors would know (or be particularly interested in) the difference between a piano with a 'patent lever butt repetition check action' or an 'imperial check repeating action', as were displayed at London 1885. So in addition to

---

[50] Marius Kwint, 'Introduction: The Physical Past', in Marius Kwint, Christopher Breward, and Jeremy Aynsley (eds), *Material Memories: Design and Evocation* (Oxford, 1999), pp. 1–16, at p. 6.

Figure 10. French Court, Great Hall, Melbourne Exhibition Building, 1880–1, Museums Victoria, MV 107908. https://collections.museumsvictoria.com.au/items/1563175.

these descriptive articles, responses were published that sought meaning for these instruments beyond their mechanical parts, placing them squarely in the cultural or artistic realm.

Many in the press went to great lengths to depict the instruments as explicitly linked to music as an art. The *Lady's Pictorial* stated in 1885 that the prominence given to musical instruments at the Inventions Exhibition was evidence for the 'spreading cultivation of the art of music'.[51] Similarly, the *Piano, Organ and Music Trades Journal* described the division relating to music at the same exhibition as recognition of music's 'high significance', stating that 'its claims as an art are unique', being 'not confined to a cultured few', but rather having 'a universal prevalence throughout the world'.[52] This article is brimming with biblical and classical references: from the creation of the earth where 'the morning stars sang together' to the way 'music appeared in intimate relation with life and religion' to St Paul, and on to quotes from Shakespeare and Greek philosophy.[53] The author concludes that 'music educates and elevates, soothes and delights us' in a way 'that no other art ever did or ever can', with the implication that

[51] 'Musical Exhibits at South Kensington', *Lady's Pictorial*, 25 Jul. 1885, p. 16.
[52] 'The International Inventions Exhibition 1885: Special Description of the Exhibits in the Music Division', *Piano, Organ and Music Trades Journal,* May 1885, p. 55.
[53] *Ibid.*

the Exhibition's displays of instruments are a vehicle for this.[54] It is interesting that a trade journal – rather than a publication dedicated to the 'art' of music exclusively – should write in such an emotive way, particularly given that this section precedes a massive article detailing the technical specifications of many of the instruments on show. While the writer may have genuinely felt strongly about the importance of music, in such a publication this perhaps demonstrates an attempt to legitimise the commercial aspects of industry by invoking its connection to the apparent higher purposes of art. This was a common technique in exhibition-related literature: as Graeme Davison has argued, 'the idea that high culture must grow from the seed of more practical endeavours was a consoling notion to men immersed in money-making'.[55]

INSTRUMENTS AS AESTHETIC OBJECTS

The most obvious way to associate silent instruments with the artistic world was through their physical aesthetic qualities. Thus, in addition to descriptions of iron frames, repetition actions, and soundboards of pianos, many publications printed long explanations of the visual qualities of the woods used in their cases, their ornamental inlays, and additional decorative features. One of the Blüthner pianos shown at Melbourne 1888 was described as a 'beautiful piece of piano architecture', with 'a beautifully panelled front relieved by carved pilasters and panels of dark walnut with diagonal borders and antique candelabra and handles'.[56] The *Horsham Times* explained that this piano, 'independently of its qualities as a musical instrument', could be considered a 'wonderfully handsome piece of furniture'.[57] A drawing-room grand piano by Collard & Collard shown at Glasgow 1888 was described almost entirely by its outward appearance, its mechanism summed up as simply having 'all the most recent improvements'.[58] A Pleyel exhibited at London 1885 was similarly described by its physical qualities: the 'upright black and gold' piano in the style of Louis XV, was 'one of the most handsome instruments ever exhibited', with three-branch candelabras at the corners, 'richly gilt' mouldings, and 'exquisite' front panels that depicted 'a group of shimmering Cupids performing on diverse musical instruments'.[59] Perhaps as a way of legitimising what may have been seen as a rather trivial aspect of these instruments – their exteriors – the *London and Provincial Music Trades Review* attempted to give some historical context, explaining that the

---

[54] *Ibid.*
[55] Graeme Davison, 'Exhibitions', *Australian Cultural History*, 2 (1982/1983), 5–21, at p. 14.
[56] 'In the Piano Saloon', *Horsham Times*, 14 Sep. 1888, p. 1.
[57] *Ibid.*
[58] 'The Glasgow International Exhibition', *Magazine of Music*, 5:6 (Jun. 1888), 138–9, at p. 138.
[59] 'Exhibition Notes', *Piano, Organ and Music Trades Journal*, Jul. 1885, p. 95.

'genuine art work on piano cases' was simply 'a reversion to older times' and the painting of harpsichord lids by 'more or less eminent masters'.[60]

The assessment of instruments based on their outward appearance was clearly due to the fact that they generally could not be heard, yet still had to be evaluated by the press in some way. The *Magazine of Music* pointed this out plainly in 1885, stating that their reporting would be 'inevitably related to exteriors rather than to interiors and sonic qualities'.[61] This slightly tongue-in-cheek article considered that few people viewing the displays of musical instruments would have:

> realised fully the capacities of the piano as an article of furniture. It appears in an endless variety of guises – in all sorts of material from ebony to satin wood, and with all sorts of decoration, from plain carving to splendours of gilt and paint, and ingenuities in enamel and mosaic. One wonders if it would ever be possible to live on terms of intimacy with such royal instruments; profanation by any vulgar tunes is altogether out of the question.[62]

While this article may be read as facetious, in certain circumstances, it was considered perfectly reasonable for some social classes to view musical instruments as 'non-functional symbolic goods'.[63] Beautifully crafted instruments were evidently not only 'objects to be played' but were 'objects to be seen'.[64] This was largely the practice of the middle and upper classes, where an instrument with an elaborate exterior that served no functional purpose could symbolically suggest that its owners had enough social and economic capital to 'ignore the gross functionality of the instrument in favour of its purely visual qualities'.[65] Even tacit acknowledgement of this would have lent the similarly elaborate instruments on display at the exhibitions some public interest.

There were also attempts, however, to place these still, silent instruments in a more domestic context. In contrast to instruments that drew attention for their exceptional aesthetic qualities, others made a virtue out of their normality. Brinsmead, for example, exhibited pianos at Melbourne 1880 that were expressly advertised as being 'not specially manufactured for the occasion', but rather exactly what the general public could buy.[66] Other reports highlighted the practical uses of the instruments, placing them in a recognisable context. The *South Australian Register* described a Thürmer piano with a 'damp stop' shown at Adelaide 1887 as 'a perfect boon to people living in the neighbourhood

---

[60] 'Inventions at the Exhibition', *London and Provincial Music Trades Review*, 15 Jun. 1885, p. 27.
[61] 'Staccato', *Magazine of Music*, 2:15 (Jun. 1885), 63–5, at p. 63.
[62] Ibid.
[63] Karen Yuen, 'Fashioning Elite Identities: Dante Gabriel Rossetti, Edward Burne-Jones, and Musical Instruments as Symbolic Goods', *Music in Art*, 39:1–2 (2014), 145–58, at p. 147.
[64] Ibid.
[65] Ibid.
[66] 'Melbourne Exhibition', *Musical Opinion and Music Trade Review*, 3:37 (1 Oct. 1880), 28–9, at p. 28.

of a family with several girls learning the piano'.[67] The *Art Journal* also placed the pianos shown at London 1885 in the domestic sphere, describing how the instruments 'seen stretching away down the centre of the gallery' at the Exhibition could also be seen 'facing us as we sit by our hearths, from the splendid grands in the most highly finished cases to the cottage, modestly unobtrusive, but certainly, as regards the great English makers, not the less of solid and excellent workmanship'.[68]

IMPORTANCE BY ASSOCIATION

Another way these silent instruments could be reanimated with a sense of the world of high art was through associations with important musical figures. This was nowhere more obvious than in the reception of two pianos exhibited independently by Broadwood and Pleyel at London 1885, both having apparently been played by Fryderyk Chopin (1810–49). While these instruments could have been easily displayed in the historic section of this exhibition (see Chapter Four), they were instead shown among the other modern pianos by their manufacturers. Pleyel's piano – their 'centre of attraction' – was built in 1839, and had been owned by Chopin in Paris. The Broadwood piano, on the other hand, was supposedly used by Chopin while he was visiting England in 1848. In a pamphlet issued by Broadwood describing their displays, Alfred Hipkins (1826–1903) explained how Chopin had played several of their instruments during his trip, and that the Grand Piano No. 17,047 – the one on display – had been used in a number of recitals.[69] The press reception of both these instruments made very clear the philosophical contrast between the other newly manufactured instruments on show, and those ascribed cultural value by their association with artists.[70] The *Magazine of Music* described seeing one of Chopin's pianos at the Exhibition as being 'like stumbling across a poem in a sale catalogue'.[71] The *Musical World* also felt that the presence of these slightly older instruments created more 'provocation to contrast rather than comparison', having become relics of a past era. Few other 'branches of manufacture' as that of pianos, they wrote, displayed such a 'feverish race towards perfection'.[72]

Despite not being played during the Exhibition, descriptions of these instruments invoked a great deal of romantic imagery. The *Lady's Pictorial* described how the Pleyel piano had become a place of 'pilgrimage' to devotees of Chopin's music. The writer described how a woman – apparently a former student of Chopin – had approached the piano at Pleyel's stand, 'reverentially kissed it, and then silently withdrew'.[73] Equally, the *Piano, Organ and Music Trades Jour-*

---

[67] 'British and Foreign', *South Australian Register*, 30 Jun. 1887, p. 4.
[68] 'Music at the Inventions Exhibition, 1885', *Art Journal*, 50 (May 1885), 153–6, at p. 154.
[69] Alfred J. Hipkins, *List of John Broadwood & Sons' Exhibits, International Inventions Exhibition, Division – Music* (London, 1885), p. 12.
[70] 'Staccato', *Magazine of Music*, p. 63.
[71] Ibid.
[72] D.T., 'Music at the Inventions Exhibition', p. 349.
[73] 'Musical Exhibits at South Kensington', *Lady's Pictorial*, 25 Jul. 1885, p. 16.

nal published several quotations from sources contemporary to Chopin about the Pleyel, amplifying the sense of the cultural significance surrounding the instrument. One contemporary writer had stated, they explained, that the piano had been housed in Chopin's apartment, which was often lit only by candles, and that he particularly liked Pleyel instruments for their 'slightly veiled yet silvery sonorousness and easy touch'.[74] It was suggested that, when played by Chopin, the piano produced sounds 'which one might think proceeded from one of those harmonicas ... so ingeniously constructed by its ancient masters from the union of crystal and water'.[75] This reference to the glass harmonica – an instrument invented by Benjamin Franklin (1706-90) in the late eighteenth century – further mythologised the Pleyel piano by associating Chopin's interest in it with the popular conception of the glass harmonica as capable of bringing about 'nervous' illness, madness, and even summoning ghosts.[76] Such imagery deliberately attempted to heighten the romantic associations evoked by the connection between Chopin and the physical instrument. Highlighting the trope of the 'tragic artist', the *Music Trades Journal* explained that 'while Chopin was strong and healthy' he preferred to play on an Érard, but had found the 'remarkable ... metallic ring and very light touch' of the Pleyel more intimate toward the end of his life'.[77] This article also related a list of works supposedly composed by Chopin on the instrument, including a number of Preludes, Études, Nocturnes, and Mazurkas, as well as the Funeral March, the F minor *Fantaisie*, and rather confusingly, a Scherzo in D minor (they perhaps meant the Scherzo no. 3 in C sharp minor, written about the same time as the others).

INSTRUMENTS AS NATIONAL OBJECTS

A further way that instruments could embody cultural meaning beyond their physical attributes was by association with their country of construction. A notable example of this is the piano manufactured by William Ezold (?–1907) shown at Sydney 1879 (Figure 11). Reportedly the first piano ever built entirely in Sydney, it received an enormous amount of press interest, far surpassing that afforded to any other instrument. A substantial article in the *Sydney Mail* described the Ezold piano as marking 'a new stage in the industry of New South Wales', where 'all honour' should be given 'to the courageous worker who has shown of what Sydney is capable in this art'.[78] The *Sydney Morning Herald* argued that this piano should be seen as 'evidence of progress in one of the fine

---

[74] 'Exhibition Notes', *Piano, Organ and Music Trades Journal*, Jul. 1885, p. 95.
[75] *Ibid.*
[76] See Gerhard Finkenbeiner and Vera Meyer, 'The Glass Harmonica: A Return from Obscurity', *Leonardo*, 20:2 (1987), 139–42, and Stanley Finger, *Doctor Franklin's Medicine* (Philadelphia, 2006), particularly chapter 14 'From Music Therapy to the Music of Madness', pp. 235–50.
[77] 'Exhibition Notes', *Piano, Organ and Music Trades Journal*, Jul. 1885, p. 95.
[78] 'Pianofortes in the Exhibition', *Sydney Mail and New South Wales Advertiser*, 22 Nov. 1879, p. 893.

Figure 11. 'A Colonial-Made Pianoforte – Mr. Ezold's Exhibit in the New South Wales Gallery', *Illustrated Sydney News*, 20 Dec. 1879, p. 5. NLA http://nla.gov.au/nla.news-article63335847.

arts' within the colony.[79] Such comments exemplify the status of the piano in late nineteenth-century Australia where it was seen as a symbol of European cultural and social values.[80] The piano's symbolic value had a long legacy in Australia. Early settlers had frequently brought pianos with them, even when they had little other furniture, as a way of reinforcing 'their sense of superiority to the natives' by demonstrating their 'certainty that civilised (in other words, European) values would prevail' in the new colonies.[81]

The cultural tenets associated with the piano in Europe – namely gentility and economic prosperity – were especially important in the context of Australian exhibitions, and at Sydney 1879 in particular, as the first appearance of the colonies on the grand exhibition-hosting stage. For this reason, the *Sydney Mail*'s article went to great efforts to remind readers of Ezold's associations with European manufacturing, having been previously employed by Kaps in Dresden, and being 'known to more than one of the large German houses as

[79] 'Sydney International Exhibition', *Sydney Morning Herald*, 15 Oct. 1879, p. 3.
[80] Deborah Crisp, 'The Piano in Australia, 1770 to 1900: Some Literary Sources', *Musicology Australia*, 18:1 (1995), 25–38, at p. 26.
[81] *Ibid*, p. 25.

a skilled and thorough worker'.[82] In an attempt to legitimise the instrument on European terms and as part of a larger, respected tradition, the *Mail* continued by arguing that through working in the colonies Ezold was able to apply a variety of techniques 'gained in his experience of the productions of different makers'.[83] The Ezold piano represented, then, a locally produced culmination of European high culture.

Pianos at the exhibitions could also symbolise social and trade relations between countries. The Australian exhibitions saw a great deal of tension in the British press about colonial assessments of English instruments, laced with what Cyril Ehrlich describes as an 'undercurrent of thinly veiled contempt for antipodean philistinism'.[84] Few English makers received awards at Sydney 1879, and many in the British press then threatened that such 'unsatisfactory results' would be 'a heavy blow' to the success of the upcoming Melbourne Exhibition.[85] At Melbourne the following year, the *Monthly Musical Record* was again disappointed that 'truly admirable' instruments by Brinsmead and Broadwood had attracted only 'somewhat vitiated' local interest. They argued that because Australians had become accustomed to 'the thin wiry sound' of 'cheaper' French and German pianos, they were unable to recognise the superior tone of the British instruments.[86] These condescending articles were part of an ongoing debate in the British trade press about protectionism, and anxiety about competition for sales in the colonies.

Such discussions continued at Melbourne 1888, with the *Musical Opinion and Music Trade Review* lamenting the 'energy' with which German pianos were presented, while arguing that British manufacturers had restricted their own sales by treating the Australian market with complacency. This almost self-flagellatory report describes the 'inherent conservatism of the British mind' as causing English makers – once 'command[ing] the bulk of the trade' – to lose out to the growing German industry.[87] It seems that there was indeed complacency among British piano exhibitors, with reports noting that some instruments in their court were never cleaned – leading passers-by to write 'shame' in the dust with their fingers – and many were left untuned.[88] This was in striking contrast to the German piano court, where 'men in uniform, paid by the German commissioners' were 'continually cleaning and dusting' between the daily recitals.[89] The German efforts were appreciated by the Australian

---

[82] 'Pianofortes in the Exhibition', *Sydney Mail and New South Wales Advertiser*, 22 Nov. 1879, p. 893.
[83] *Ibid*.
[84] Ehrlich, *The Piano*, p. 86.
[85] *Ibid*, p. 83.
[86] 'Music in Melbourne, Australia', *Monthly Musical Record*, 11 (May 1881), p. 94.
[87] 'Pianos at the Melbourne Exhibition', *Musical Opinion and Music Trade Review*, 12:138 (1 Mar. 1889), 293–5, at p. 293.
[88] 'News from the Melbourne Exhibition', *Musical Opinion and Music Trade Review*, 12:136 (1 Jan. 1889), p. 190; Ehrlich, *The Piano*, p. 86.
[89] 'News from the Melbourne Exhibition', *Musical Opinion*, p. 190.

public; as the *Horsham Times* explained, 'a stroll past' the German pianos showed that 'the wants of Victorian buyers are very carefully catered to'.[90]

Musical Curiosities

One of the reasons that the above critical framing of pianos was possible was because audiences were already familiar with the instruments through encountering them in their everyday lives. Most people would have had some confidence in assessing a piano as a decorative object based on personal taste, understood the significance of an instrument owned by a great composer, or been intrigued by differences that could be described by national variation. But what happens when an unfamiliar musical object, without the cultural significance of a piano, is displayed under the same circumstances?

International exhibitions, as ventures intended to demonstrate 'progress' in industry, frequently became forums for presenting what now appear as some quite bizarre Victorian inventions. The music department of London 1885 – the Inventions Exhibition – was particularly fruitful in this respect. The miscellaneous musical exhibits included, 'musical dominoes', a variety of music stands that either self-turned pages or folded up into other objects such as walking sticks, and amusingly, a violin case that could be 'converted into a life-preserver' that 'might be useful in case of shipwreck'.[91] There were also several machines intended for transcribing music, such as Fohr's Music Electrograph, which attached to a piano and transcribed music onto a stave as it was played.[92] Many such inventions were discussed in the 'scientific' sections of the general press, rather than by music critics, highlighting the importance of the cultural associations afforded to already well-known music-related objects. Without a tradition linking the physical objects to the actual 'art' of music, it was far more difficult to place these mechanical objects in a discussion of music itself.

For similar reasons, the majority of the 'new' instruments at the exhibitions discussed in the musical press were variations on or adjustments to the piano. Many 1880s inventors seem preoccupied with facilitating crescendo and diminuendo effects over a single note on a piano, and this is reflected in many new instruments also exhibited at London 1885. Burling & Burling's 'triplex euphonoid' pianoforte emitted sound from 'a powerful tubular pillar' through 'a valve at the top by means of a knee-pedal' creating a swell.[93] Richard Howson (1821–1911) showed a comparable instrument with an 'expression pedal', although its mechanism was not described in any detail, being simply labelled by the *Telegraph* as a 'contrivance' which 'is sufficiently ingenious'.[94] Other variations on piano tone-quality were created by changing the resonant

---

[90] 'In the Piano Saloon', *Horsham Times*, p. 1.
[91] 'Music', *Graphic*, 32:820 (15 Aug. 1885), p. 178.
[92] 'Scientific Notes', *Graphic*, 33:815 (11 Jul. 1885) p. 34.
[93] 'Music at the Inventions Exhibition', *Daily Telegraph*, 2 Jun. 1885, p. 3.
[94] *Ibid*.

material of the strings or altering the way the resonance was conveyed. Thomas Machell (1841/2–1915) exhibited a 'Dulcitone' piano with tuning-fork shaped steel bars instead of strings, which the *Telegraph* described as bringing 'forth sounds not untruthfully described as "pure, sustained, and sympathetic"' (quoting the inventor's description of the instrument, given to the Royal Philosophical Society of Glasgow).[95] Blüthner's 'aliquot' piano drew attention for its addition of a sympathetic fourth string tuned an octave higher on each note.[96] Metzler and Co. exhibited an 'organo-piano' which included an additional set of hammers 'put in rapid motion by a vibrating cylinder' sustaining notes for 'as long as the key is held down'.[97] This was not to be confused with the 'organ-piano' exhibited by Böhmer, which combined a piano with organ bellows (much like the late-fifteenth and sixteenth-century claviorgan).[98] Similar novelties were exhibited in Scotland, drawing press attention across Britain. At Glasgow 1888, Arthur Allison & Co. exhibited a piano with 'a patent mello attachment' which supposedly gave the effect of 'an organ or Spanish mandoline'.[99] Like many of the instruments described above, this could be used as an ordinary piano, but 'on turning a lever, a current of electricity is thrown on the wires, which produces the sweetest music imaginable'.[100]

One of the newly invented instruments that drew the most public interest at London 1885 was the vocalion: a combined free reed organ and Aeolian harp invented by James Baillie-Hamilton (1850–1921), a Scottish inventor of 'considerable financial means'.[101] Regular recitals were given on this instrument from its rather incongruous position in the Exhibition's Siamese Court. These concerts contained much standard organ repertoire including Handel, Bach, Louis Lefébure-Wely (1817–69), and Mendelssohn in what can be seen as an attempt to ingratiate the new and rather confusing instrument – as George Bernard Shaw (1856–1950) described it, 'a standing puzzle to the Inventions visitors' – with a familiar musical tradition. Large audiences were drawn to these recitals; however, it seems most people were more interested in understanding how the instrument worked than in listening to the music it produced. Shaw wrote, rather sardonically, that few fully understood it, yet 'the average sightseer is always ready to explain what he does not understand' and were happy to speculate. 'Statements that the vocalion is "a specious of horgan and 'armonium

---

[95] *Ibid*; Thomas Machell, 'On a New Musical Instrument', *Proceedings of the Royal Philosophical Society of Glasgow*, 15 (1884–5), 185–8, at p. 185.

[96] 'The Musical Exhibition', *Globe*, 1 Jun. 1885, p. 3

[97] 'Music at the Inventions Exhibition', *Daily Telegraph*, p. 3.

[98] 'Exhibition Notes', *Piano, Organ and Music Trades Journal*, p. 95; Donald Howard Boalch and Peter Williams, 'Claviorgan', *Grove Music Online* <http://www.oxfordmusiconline.com> [accessed 5 Feb. 2021].

[99] 'Glasgow International Exhibition', *Magazine of Music*, p. 138.

[100] *Ibid*.

[101] James Howard Richards, 'Baillie-Hamilton, James (John Buchanan) (1837–After 1926)', in Douglas Earl Bush and Richard Kassel (eds), *The Organ: An Encyclopedia* (New York, 2005), pp. 46–7, at p. 46.

combined" are freely forthcoming', he wrote, from bystanders observing these recitals.[102] The actual sound of the vocalion drew mixed responses. Overall, Shaw summed it up as 'better than the harmonium', although he stated that this was 'faint praise' given that 'it could hardly be worse than that detestable instrument'.[103]

The most dramatic new inventions at 1885 were the Orchestral Fire Organ, or Pyrophone, and the related electric Singing Candelabras and Lustres, which could not be demonstrated for reasons of safety, yet still drew considerable attention.[104] Invented by Frederic Kastner (1852–82), these instruments used burning gas to produce sound. The Pyrophone, appearing like an organ, was made up of nearly forty glass tubes, some ten feet high, in which gas jets burned. The Electric Singing Candelabra and Lustre functioned similarly, but were 'moved by electric magnets' so could be played from a distance.[105] A highly scientific description of these instruments appeared in the *Musical World*, although there was little discussion of their sound qualities. They noted, however, that while instruments of stone, wood, and metal were common, 'only a scientific German' could have conceived of using burning gas.[106] This created, amusingly, a small degree of national tension. While Kastner was German, some publications were keen to remind readers that it was in fact the English William Mullinger Higgins who 'discovered that a flame burning in a vertical glass tube could, under favourable circumstances, produce a sustained tone' more than a century prior.[107]

All these instruments – pianos and musical curiosities alike – were loaded with differing levels of cultural meaning by their association with the creation of music. Pianos had an explicit and firmly established place in the cultural consciousness of their audiences. While many in the press may not have considered the instruments alone as necessarily representative of 'music', they were still viewed as *musical* objects and were therefore an important cultural aspect of the exhibitions. This is made even clearer by the reception of new musical inventions, which were less successful in navigating the divide between the commercial and art worlds. As the public lacked familiarity with their sounds and construction, they became simply objects of curiosity, fitting less problematically into the taxonomic categorisations described above (such as 'machinery', 'scientific and philosophical', or 'educational' objects). This contrasts strikingly with the categorisation of traditional instruments that many had found so difficult to reconcile with their ideas of music as, primarily, art. Ultimately, however, only so much could be said about musical instruments as

---

[102] [George Bernard Shaw, unsigned], 'Pianoforte and Organ', *Dramatic Review*, 25 Jul. 1885, repr. in Dan H. Laurence (ed.) *Shaw's Music: The Complete Musical Criticism in Three Volumes*, vol. 2 (London, 1981), p. 318.
[103] [Shaw, unsigned], 'Pianoforte and Organ', p. 319.
[104] 'Kastner's "Pyrophone" at the Inventions', *Musical World*, 63:39 (26 Sep. 1885), p. 610.
[105] 'The Pyrophone', *Piano, Organ and Music Trade Journal*, Oct. 1885, p. 145.
[106] 'Kastner's "Pyrophone"', *Musical World*, 63:41 (10 Oct. 1885), p. 637.
[107] 'Exhibition Notes', *Piano, Organ and Music Trade Journal*, p. 95.

cultural products, or even as mechanical ones, without actual demonstration of their primary function – making music – so, as the next chapter explores, recitals on these instruments were given regularly.

CHAPTER 3

Sounding Instruments

In an 1885 *Magazine of Music* article, George Bernard Shaw described his frustration at the way musical instruments were exhibited at the London International Inventions Exhibition:

> No less satisfactory exhibition can be conceived than a collection of musical instruments surmounted by notices that visitors are requested not to touch. Even a Stradivarius violin is not pleasant to look at when it is standing on end in a glass case. You may not hold it to the light to make the lucid depths of the varnish visible … you cannot hear the sound, apart from which it is the most senseless object extant; and your personal independence is irritated by the feeling that what prevents you from satisfying your curiosity by force of arms is not your conscience, but the proximity of a suspicious policeman, who is so tired of seeing apparently sane men wasting their time over secondhand fiddles and pianofortes, that he would probably rather arrest you than not, if only you would give him a pretext for the capture.[1]

As understandable as the restrictions placed on touching or playing musical instruments were – particularly given the sonic chaos of the early exhibitions before such rules were introduced – Shaw was not the only one who was unsatisfied with these arrangements. The primary mode of engagement with objects displayed at exhibitions was visual, and as we have seen, as far as musical instruments were concerned, the press and public went to great lengths to give these 'senseless objects' meaning, without them needing to be heard. But for manufacturers and exhibitors, this ignored the primary function of the instruments. While some makers clearly took pride in the physical aesthetic qualities of their products, all wanted their instruments to be able to demonstrate their reason for existing: making music. Thus, at all the exhibitions in this study where instruments were displayed, the manufacturers themselves arranged public recitals to fully exhibit their wares.

Demonstration recitals were given on a variety of different instruments across the exhibitions. At London 1885, for example, there were concerts of wind instruments arranged by firms such as Boosey, Besson, and Metzler, violin recitals on instruments by Jeffrey James Gilbert (1850–1942) or George Gemünder (1816–99), and a few on the banjo by Arthur Tilley (1847–1921) playing his own instruments. Concertina recitals were also common, reflecting

---

[1] George Bernard Shaw, 'Musical Instruments at the Inventions Exhibition', *Magazine of Music*, 2:17 (Aug. 1885), pp. 111–12, at p. 111.

the tail-end of the English instrument's 'Victorian heyday',[2] with virtuoso performers such as Richard Blagrove (1826/7–95), and Edward Chidley (1830–99) and his daughter Amy (1866–1946) performing on Wheatstone & Co. instruments. Lachenal & Co.'s concertinas were also demonstrated by, among others, John Hill Maccann (c.1860–?, patentee of a new duet concertina),[3] and on one occasion by Madame Marie Debenham (1848–1937, née Lachenal), daughter of the instruments' creator. Accompanied by one of her daughters – styled Mademoiselle Debenham – on piano, this concert featured this 'most accomplished and charming concertina-player' performing 'Fantasias of English and Scotch airs', as well as arrangements of works by Gounod, Rossini, and Meyerbeer.[4] One of the more unusual demonstrations saw an ocarina orchestra performing works by Joseph Gung'l (1809–89), Sullivan, Verdi, Franz Schubert (1797–1828), and Emile Waldteufel (1837–1915) on a range of Mezetti's ocarinas. The largest number of demonstration recitals, however, at any exhibition, were on the piano. The focus of this chapter, therefore, as in the last, is on this instrument as a case study.

Piano recitals were sometimes given on the main floor of the exhibition buildings, as in the Australian exhibitions in Sydney 1879, Adelaide 1887, and Melbourne 1880 and 1888, where these recitals were held at the various exhibitors' stands. At the English and Scottish exhibitions, instead, they were given in separate, specially built music rooms. At Calcutta 1883 they were held in the building's quadrangle. While there was a clear central and strictly maintained timetable for these performances to avoid the clashing recitals seen at earlier exhibitions, the details of the concerts and employment of musicians was left up to the exhibiting firms. The only centrally enforced rule was that the public was not allowed to play the instruments. This rule, however, at London 1885 at least, also prompted public outrage. In response, for a time, the organisers allowed one day per week where exhibitors could open their displays to anyone, who were 'permitted to make as much noise as they like'.[5] This day was dubbed, perhaps aptly, 'pandemonium day'.[6] In any case, professional recitals remained the best way of hearing the musical qualities of the exhibited instruments.

The public demonstration of instruments in the context of a large-scale display of commercial objects strongly emphasised the fact that these performances were advertisements, and were intended to exhibit the sonic qualities

---

[2] Allan W. Atlas, 'The "Respectable" Concertina', *Music & Letters*, 80:2 (1999), 241–53, at p. 241.

[3] And, according to one of his publications, the Concertinist by command to the Prince of Wales. See John Hill Maccann, *The Concertinist's Guide* (London, 1888), front cover.

[4] 'The Courier', *Penny Illustrated Paper*, 1 Aug. 1885, p. 71. For more on Marie Lachenal see Faye Debenham and Randall C. Merris, 'Marie Lachenal: Concertinist', *Concertina Library* (2005) <http://www.concertina.com/merris/marie-lachenal/index.htm> [accessed 17 Feb. 2021].

[5] E.C. Locke, 'Playing Instruments at the Inventions Exhibition' [letter to the editor], *Musical Opinion and Music Trade Review*, 8:91 (1 Apr. 1885), p. 356.

[6] 'Musical Instruments Exhibition', *London and Provincial Music Trades Review*, 15 Apr. 1885, p. 13.

of instruments that the public had already inspected from a material and visual-aesthetic perspective. Such commercial demonstrations were not new; in France the Salles Érard and Pleyel – within which 'both player and piano could be applauded' – or in London, the Bechstein Hall, or the early nineteenth-century demonstrations of Flight & Robson's Apollonicon, provided a long legacy of performances being used to sell instruments.[7] However, at the exhibitions – institutions perceived to be largely educational – awareness that these recitals were so distinctly a commercial endeavour had a significant impact on the critical reception of the performances.

Despite some makers employing well-known and highly regarded performers to give these recitals, the overtly commercial context of these demonstrations influenced the way the press and public engaged with and assessed the performances. Critics felt compelled to evaluate the instruments as commodities first, before they could consider the music being played, the skills of the performer, or quality of the performance. Through the almost constant use of the same instruments, often by the same performers, playing necessarily limited repertoire, 'music' as a broad concept and the instruments themselves became the press's focus, rather than the performers, composers, or musical works heard on the programmes.

❧ *Performers and Manufacturers*

The two exhibitions in this study that saw the largest number of demonstration recitals were Sydney 1879 and London 1885. In Sydney, only twenty manufacturers – either themselves or through a Sydney agent – employed pianists. No official programme of these concerts has survived; however, press reports indicate that many performances were given in quick succession each day with, at its peak, five or six different demonstrations given in a single afternoon. This means that many hundreds of piano recitals were heard across the six-month exhibition season. Among the performers were the Exhibition's musical director, Paolo Giorza, playing on Ascherberg and Chickering instruments, Charles Huenerbein (c.1859–1908) on Blüthner, and Reginald Toms (1849–1922) on both Érard and Pleyel. Léontine Lamal (1837–?), the Belgian pianist and wife of Prosper Lamal (1836–95) – one of Belgium's representatives for the Exhibition – was a regular performer on the Belgian instruments by Goebel and Gunther and in the French court on a Bord. Jules Meilhan (?–1882) was frequently heard on the famous Australian-made Ezold upright, or on the Steinways in the American court, in concert with visiting Russian pianist Olga Duboin (*fl.*1874–1909). Cecilia Summerhayes (1840–1929) – among the most prolific performers – was heard three times a week on Bechstein, semi-regularly

---

[7] Leon Plantinga, 'The Piano and the Nineteenth Century', in R. Larry Todd (ed.), *Nineteenth-Century Piano Music*, 2nd ed. (New York, 2004), pp. 1–15, at p. 7. See also Rachel Cowgill, 'The London Apollonicon Recitals, 1817–32: A Case-Study in Bach, Mozart and Haydn Reception', *Journal of the Royal Musical Association*, 123:2 (1998), 190–228.

on Campo and Kaps's pianos, and daily on the Brindsmeads in either solo recitals or chamber concerts, accompanied by Huenerbein, violinist Ercole Ortori (1853–1930), a cellist known as Mr Massey, and the tenor Vernon Reid (c.1850–99). Several young women, including Maud Fitz-Stubbs (1861–1940), Lottie Hyam (1860–1946), and Emilie North (1858–85), also played regular recitals. In addition, a number of 'lady amateurs' – often Giorza's students – who were never named in any reviews, also performed throughout the season. This was a common practice in the late nineteenth-century Australian press, largely for propriety's sake, 'left over from when nice women did not go on the stage'.[8]

London 1885 also involved a large number of piano recitals. These were held in a 400-seat music room, with a stage large enough to hold two grand pianos, and two pipe organs at opposite ends of the space.[9] In London, as in other cities where a separate music room was used, the instruments had to be 'wheeled into' the space, retuned, then removed again before any more recitals could take place.[10] This meant that the turnaround time between demonstrations was far greater than in Sydney. Thus, while a larger number of makers, instruments, and performers were heard at London than elsewhere, the actual number of recitals was far smaller: only 175 in total, performed by eighty-nine different pianists, almost daily over the six months of the Exhibition.[11] The most famous pianists were drawn by Broadwood & Sons, with their programmes featuring Charles Hallé (1819–95), Ernst Pauer and his son Max von Pauer (1866–1945), and Agnes Zimmermann (1847–1925), among others. Zimmermann, alongside a number of other pianists including Johann Heinrich Bonawitz (1839–1917) also played on Blüthner & Co.'s instruments. Pleyel too had a striking number of well-known pianists, including Marie-Aimée Roger-Miclos (1860–1950), Luisa Cognetti (1857–1952), and Tito Mattei (1841–1914), while Steinway & Sons employed only German pianist Franz Rummel (1853–1901).

At many other exhibitions, such recitals were less consistent. At Melbourne 1880, these concerts were confined to a small group of performers: primarily, Carlotta Tasca (c.1849–1902) who played on Brinsmead, Henri Kowalski (1841–1916) on Phillipe Herz & Co., Alice Charbonnet (1858–1914) and Alberto Zelman (1832–1907) on Érard, and a pianist called Miss Matthias who gave recitals for Campo in the Belgian Court. These pianists were not always restricted to playing on a single company's instruments. Tasca often performed

---

[8] Jennifer Hill, 'Crossing a Divide? Maud Fitz-Stubbs as Amateur then Professional Musician in Late Nineteenth-Century Sydney', *Context: Journal of Music Research*, 19 (2000), 35–42, at p. 40.

[9] 'Music at the Inventions Exhibition, 1885', *Art Journal*, 50 (May 1885), 153–6, at pp. 154–5.

[10] 'Music at South Kensington', *Musical Times*, 26:508 (1 Jun. 1885), 317–19, at p. 317.

[11] A statistic that can be gleaned from the complete set of concert programmes that survives. See *The International Inventions Exhibition: Daily Programme, Musical and Other Arrangements (May 4th–November 9th 1885)* (London, 1885), held in the Senate House Library Special Collections, University of London.

in the German and French courts, and Charbonnet played for Pleyel-Wolff occasionally. While there were no Australian-made pianos shown in Melbourne, the *Argus* reported that 'a local exhibitor of bagpipes' had planned a 'practical demonstration of the excellence of the colonial instruments shown by him', although they wryly concluded that these could be employed at the end of the day 'for clearing the building of visitors'.[12] There were even fewer recitals drawing press attention at Melbourne 1888, presumably due to the vast amount of orchestral music on offer at this exhibition. A few recitals are documented, however, including Lalla Miranda (1874–1944) on Bechstein, Alice Sydney Burvett (1857–1919) on Pleyel, and recitals in the German court given three to four times per week by, among others, Benno Scherek (1854–1928), Blanche King (1860–1933), and Lizzie Martin (dates not known).[13]

The individual exhibitors played a fundamental role in organising these concerts, as can be seen clearly in the example of Calcutta 1883. Here, little music in any form was heard until Horace Brinsmead (1854–1908) – the company representative of Brinsmead & Sons, who had also been involved with Sydney 1879 and Melbourne 1880 – arrived in India several months into the Exhibition. Brinsmead immediately organised a concert in the building's quadrangle on one of his company's pianos, employing members of the touring Italian Opera Company to assist. As the *Englishman* (one of the few Anglo-Indian publications to cover the Exhibition in any detail) reported, these recitals were intended to 'display the power and tone of the beautiful instruments'.[14] These performances continued after Brinsmead left Calcutta, and were described as 'eminently successful', with large attendances and 'extremely good' music.[15] Pianist Signor Michele Angelo Valenza (1858–c.1915) was described as bringing out 'the tone of the grand Piano in the *Fantasia Sonnambula* in such a style as few people could have believed possible'. Audiences were describing as going away pleased, and 'wondering why someone had not done the same thing six weeks ago'.[16] No other manufacturers staged anything similar, and without Brinsmead, there would have been no instrumental demonstrations at Calcutta at all.

✥ *Commercialism and Critical Reception*

All of these recitals, regardless of who performed or what they played, were explicitly demonstrations of and advertisements for the instruments, and awareness of this fact impacted significantly on the critical reception of the music. In some cases, particularly in the London musical press, there was an outright rejection of the recitals as displays of musical 'art', as this could not be separated from their commercial, and therefore, unforgivably mercenary

---

[12] 'Exhibition Notes', *Argus*, 25 Oct. 1880, p. 7.
[13] 'Music at the Exhibition', *Argus*, 27 Oct. 1888, p. 18; 'News of the Day', *Age*, 6 Dec. 1888, p. 5.
[14] 'Calcutta Exhibition', *Englishman*, 22 Jan. 1884, p. 5.
[15] 'The International Exhibition', *Englishman*, 24 Jan. 1884, p. 5.
[16] *Ibid.*

aims. The *Musical Times*, in discussing London 1885, maintained that their concern was only with other exhibits that would interest 'high-class amateurs', barely acknowledging any recitals organised by manufacturers, even those by eminent musicians such as Hallé. They noted in an issue at the beginning of the Exhibition that demonstration recitals would 'not be included in any criticism' that they published because, they argued, such recitals would likely be 'generally indifferent in quality', given that the programmes were arranged in consultation 'between the artists and the manufacturers'.[17]

The daily press, while less scandalised by the overt commercialism of the recitals, still acknowledged that they were for advertising purposes. The *Evening Standard* even considered the competition between 'the finest instruments by modern makers' as one of the recitals' most interesting features.[18] The *Art Journal*, too, suggested that the competitive element would be good for audiences, as the manufacturers, 'for their own credit ... will, no doubt, engage the best available talent'.[19] In stark contrast to the rest of the musical press, those in the music trade press were keen to emphasise the commerciality of the demonstrations, expecting that the instruments shown would be appropriate to the needs and budgets of a middle-class audience. As *London and Provincial Music Trades Review* warned early in the London 1885 season, it would be 'unfair' of makers to demonstrate only their 'grands and the more expensive class of uprights' when most people had 'no room in their houses' for such instruments.[20] By only demonstrating instruments that would not be realistically within reach of their audiences, they suggested, 'these recitals bid fair to degenerate to a mere series of gratuitous concerts'.[21]

Acknowledgement of the commercialism of these concerts was consistent across all exhibitions, as was made manifestly clear in the reception of those given at Sydney 1879. Yet, this did not preclude audiences from also enjoying the music. Although these recitals were clearly 'given for trade purposes', as the *Evening News* reported, the music remained 'a most attractive feature of the Exhibition'.[22] The Brisbane *Telegraph* further explained that while at Sydney the recitals were arranged so that anyone wanting to 'form an estimate of the merits of any particular maker of instruments can do so with certainty', a pleasing side-effect was that the 'casual visitor is always able to hear some excellent performer'.[23] The critical reception at Melbourne 1880 also acknowledged this dual response. While the advertising intent of the recitals was highlighted in the press by consistent reference to the size of the audiences attracted to each manufacturer's stand, they also described them as an important and worthwhile

---

[17] 'Music at South Kensington', *Musical Times*, p. 318.
[18] 'The Inventions Exhibition', *Evening Standard*, 1 May 1885, p. 3.
[19] 'Music at the Inventions Exhibition, 1885', *Art Journal*, pp. 154–5.
[20] 'The Exhibition Recitals', *London and Provincial Music Trades Review*, 15 Jun. 1885, p. 11.
[21] *Ibid.*
[22] 'International Exhibition', *Evening News*, 28 Oct. 1879, p. 3.
[23] 'Sydney Exhibition', *Telegraph*, 30 Oct. 1879, p. 2.

'means of entertainment for the public'.[24] As the *London and Provincial Music Trades Review* described, also of Melbourne, 'the chief point' of these recitals was 'to attract people to the stands for purposes of advertisement' so that visitors could 'compare the various pianos by the evidence of their ears as well as of their eyes'.[25]

Exhibitors and manufacturers were deeply aware of the importance of these demonstrations as a means of advertising their wares, and this occasionally led to controversy or even acts of sabotage. At Sydney 1879, in an attempt to gain a commercial advantage, piano manufacturer Emil Ascherberg (1839–1904) had built 'at his own expense for the purpose of exhibiting his pianos' a much larger platform than the regular makers' stands which was placed in front of the grand organ (depicted in Figure 12). Ascherberg and his Sydney agent James Nicholson (1837–1907) did not allow other exhibitors to use this makeshift stage, as they did not want it being used for 'purposes hostile' to their own interests.[26] While a deal appears to have been struck with Brinsmead, as their instruments were also demonstrated on Ascherberg's platform, its presence caused much consternation among other exhibitors. The agents for Steinway in particular, after being denied a request to use the platform, moved one of their instruments to the floor directly in front of it. They then set to work nosily 'cleaning ... the keys and dusting' their piano while performances were being held on the competing instruments above it.[27]

❧ Musical Works or Commercial Products?

Throughout the critical reception of these recitals at all exhibitions – but particularly at Sydney and London – their explicitly commercial nature contributed to a sense that the music played was almost incidental to the demonstration of the instruments themselves. Compounded by the vast catalogue of instruments, enormous number of concerts, and variety of different performers and works heard, there was little room in the press for individual reviews of any specific performance. Particularly in London, the recitals were often described en masse, and reviews, where they do occur, are vague or very general. The *London and Provincial Music Trades Review* described the concerts at 1885 in no more detail than to acknowledge that 'a tolerably lengthy list of piano and other recitals' had been carried out at the Exhibition, and 'most of the principal makers have had their innings'.[28]

While Australian exhibition recitals received more press attention, the overall critical focus was on the instruments. Discussion of repertoire was

[24] 'Exhibition Notes', *Argus*, 25 Oct. 1880, p. 7.
[25] 'The Melbourne Exhibition', *London and Provincial Music Trades Review*, 15 Jan. 1881, p. 11.
[26] 'International Exhibition', *Evening News*, 24 Nov. 1879, p. 3.
[27] 'Music at the Garden Palace', *Sydney Morning Herald*, 24 Nov. 1879, p. 3.
[28] 'The Exhibition Recitals', *London and Provincial Music Trades Review*, 15 Jun. 1885, p. 11.

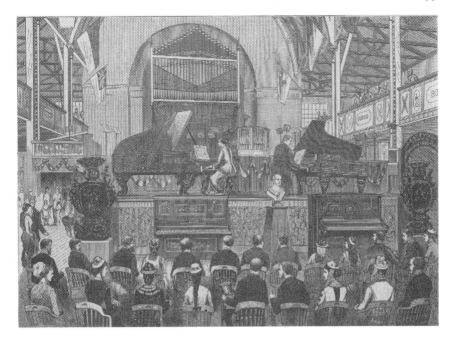

Figure 12. 'A Recital on Messrs Nicholson & Ascherberg's Pianofortes', *Illustrated Sydney News and New South Wales Agriculturalist and Grazier*, 29 Nov. 1879, p. 12. NLA http://nla.gov.au/nla.news-article63335817.

limited to the way certain works illuminated aspects of the instruments' tone or touch, and reviews of performers to the ways that they managed the specific qualities of the instruments. At Sydney 1879, Huenerbein's recitals on the Blüthner pianos in the German Court consisted primarily of selections from Mendelssohn's *Lieder ohne Worte*. The *Sydney Morning Herald*'s assessment of these performances focused mainly on the way 'the melodious tone' of the Blüthner instruments was 'peculiarly suited' to Mendelssohn.[29] Similarly, while Giorza often performed his own compositions on Ascherberg's pianos, the press concentrated on the 'splendid instrument' itself which, through Giorza's playing, showed a 'large capacity for distributing sound'.[30] His performance of arrangements by Thalberg – particularly a selection from *La Sonnambula* by Vincenzo Bellini (1801–35) – was described as fitting 'admirably' to the 'power of the grand piano'.[31] Meilhan's performances on Steinway's pianos, too, were reviewed to show how the pianist's skill was reflected in the qualities of the instrument. His interpretation of a number of Chopin works showed a 'delicate

---

[29] 'The Music at the Garden Palace', *Sydney Morning Herald*, 29 Nov. 1879, p. 5.
[30] 'Sydney International Exhibition', *Sydney Morning Herald*, 13 Oct. 1879, p. 5.
[31] 'Sydney International Exhibition', *Sydney Morning Herald*, 16 Oct. 1879, p. 6.

brilliancy' when 'given on the Steinway'.[32] In another recital, Meilhan exhibited a Steinway 'at its best' in the rapid passages of Beethoven's first sonata, where 'the full rich tone was much commented upon'.[33]

Cecilia Summerhayes – one of the most prolific performers at Sydney, giving over 125 individual performances – was considered an impressive pianist, having studied with Hallé, Thalberg, and Julius Benedict (1804–85). Her many recitals on Brinsmead's pianos often saw the instruments described in terms of her qualities as a performer.[34] Her 'perfect technique', 'elastic and tolerably vigorous' touch, and capability to perform 'as soft as the sigh of an evening zephyr' were apparently matched by the Brinsmead piano, which responded 'as if it were a thing of life, eager to be made instrumental in developing conceptions of the products of musical genius'.[35] While Summerhayes's playing was 'enjoyable ... [to] lovers of music', the piano's 'exquisitely soft and beautiful tone' and improved third pedal was 'strikingly apparent' when she played Brahms's 'Hungarian dance'.[36]

Such critical conflation of instrument, work, and performer was not always positive, and Giorza, giving performances for the American firm Chickering, was harshly criticised. These recitals were given on pianos whose lids had been removed so that audiences could examine and admire 'the exquisite workmanship and finish' of the inside of the instruments.[37] Yet 'the immense power' of the piano when played by Giorza, particularly in his variations on the 'Coronation March' from Meyerbeer's *Le Prophète,* was 'more astonishing than pleasing', and 'when taxed to its full power the melody of the tone' produced a 'strong metallic sound'.[38] The only point at which the repertoire choices of a performer were critiqued was in Madame Lamal's daily recitals in the Belgian Court. Her consistent presentation of works by Charles De Wulf – a composer of 'showy, yet not difficult works' – began to bore the press.[39] As the *Evening News* stated, 'we confess a desire to hear an occasional variety in style; *toujours Wulf* is as objectionable as *toujours perdrix*'.[40]

In the reception of the Sydney recitals, comment on the musical works quickly disappeared entirely, and by December 1879 the press no longer listed any individual works in their reviews. Part of the reason for the lack of interest in the works performed at both London and Sydney was due to the vast amount of music given overall. Both exhibitions had orchestral, choral, band, and other musical events throughout their season, which – without such overt commercialism – were perhaps more interesting to the musical press. In contrast,

---

[32] 'Sydney International Exhibition', *Sydney Morning Herald*, 24 Oct. 1879, p. 3.
[33] 'Sydney International Exhibition', *Sydney Morning Herald*, 30 Oct. 1879, p. 7.
[34] 'Sydney International Exhibition', *Sydney Morning Herald*, 9 Oct. 1879, p. 5.
[35] 'International Exhibition', *Evening News*, 9 Oct. 1879, p. 3.
[36] 'International Exhibition', *Evening News*, 13 Oct. 1879, p. 3.
[37] 'Music at the Garden Palace', *Sydney Morning Herald*, 6 Dec. 1879, p. 7.
[38] 'Music at the Garden Palace', *Sydney Morning Herald*, 17 Dec. 1879, p. 7.
[39] 'Sydney International Exhibition', *Sydney Morning Herald*, 16 Oct. 1879, p. 6.
[40] 'Sydney International Exhibition', *Sydney Morning Herald*, 17 Oct. 1879, p. 3.

at Melbourne 1880, where there were far fewer musical features overall, the reception of the demonstration recitals was consistent and attentive. Although many reports still described these recitals as commercial, noting the size of the audiences attracted by particular exhibitors, they frequently concluded by pointing out how appreciative these audiences were, and by commenting on the works and performers in relation to ideas such as 'artistic merit'. Kowalski was particularly admired for both his 'virtuosity and energy' in playing, and his own works as a composer. Many of his programmes included works written specifically for piano, but also paraphrases and variations on popular operatic and orchestral music.[41] Throughout his Melbourne recitals, only incidental reference is made to the Herz & Co. pianos on which he performed, but his paraphrase on Mozart's 'Don Juan', and his own works, *Danse Tzigane* and *Marche Hongroise*, were widely applauded. Kowalski often 'commemorated his travels with pianistic mementos that celebrated the places he had visited', and his *Belles de Melbourne* – apparently inspired by the women he had seen on the lawn at the Melbourne Cup – was described as 'quite a happy musical thought' and was frequently encored.[42]

❧ Performers as Objects and Commodities

The manner in which the demonstration recitals were presented at many exhibitions emphasised the way that the performers themselves could become viewed as objects or commodities. It was clear that the instrumentalists at the exhibitions were offering a service to the manufacturers to demonstrate their instruments, regardless of whether the audiences enjoyed or appreciated the 'artistic' side of the playing. This focus on the instruments above all else in the reception of recitals, however, saw the performers become basically interchangeable. During a Brinsmead concert at Sydney in December, for example, Summerhayes – perhaps understandably, given her intense performance schedule – was 'so severely' affected by a 'neuralgic headache that she was most unwillingly compelled to abandon' her performance halfway through.[43] Lottie Hyam, one of Giorza's students who had also been giving recitals on the Érard pianos, was in the audience and stepped in 'most good-naturedly' to complete the recital in a manner deserving of 'high commendation'.[44] Hyam went on to give two further recitals for Brinsmead the following week while Summerhayes recovered.[45]

At other points, it appears that Hyam herself was regarded as an object on display. As Figure 13 shows, the demonstration recitals placed performers and audiences in very close proximity to one another. This arrangement

---

[41] Kerry Murphy, 'Henri Kowalski (1841–1916): A French Musician in Colonial Australia', *Australian Historical Studies*, 48:3 (2017), 346–62, at p. 351.

[42] Ibid, p. 352; 'Exhibition Notes', *Argus*, 5 Nov. 1880, p. 6.

[43] 'Music at the Garden Palace', *Sydney Morning Herald*, 17 Dec. 1879, p. 7.

[44] Ibid.

[45] 'Music at the Garden Palace', *Sydney Morning Herald*, 30 Dec. 1879, p. 3.

Figure 13. 'Pianoforte Recitals – Messrs. John Brinsmead and Sons' Stand, in the Nave', *Illustrated Sydney News and New South Wales Agriculturalist and Grazier*, 1 Nov. 1879, p. 5. One of the pianists depicted here is presumably Cecilia Summerhayes, given her constant presence at the Brinsmead stand. NLA https://trove.nla.gov.au/newspaper/article/63335774.

occasionally led to unpleasant encounters between players and public. Hyam's debut recital, on an Érard grand in the French Gallery, was well-reviewed for her playing on an instrument that 'gave full scope to her powers'.[46] It was reported, however, that while she was performing, she was 'rendered uneasy by the fussiness of some individual who would get unpleasantly near her', proceeding to 'bore her' with his 'ceaseless and annoying importunity'.[47] Whatever that 'importunity' entailed, Hyam was clearly disturbed enough that she made cuts to the works she was performing, to finish the recital as quickly as possible.

One of the most fascinating aspects of these demonstration recitals overall lies in the tension between the commercial and 'art' worlds. These recitals made explicit the distinction between product and process, which in the usual circumstances of live musical performance is difficult to separate.[48] In general concert life, as Regula Burckhardt Qureshi argues, 'the piano is subject to economic relations of production as an item of manufacture, but it is exempt

---

[46] 'Music at the Garden Palace', *Evening News*, 27 Oct. 1879, p. 2.
[47] Enoemos, 'The Critic', *Australian Town and Country Journal*, 1 Nov. 1879, p. 41.
[48] Regula Burckhardt Qureshi, 'Mode of Production and Musical Production: Is Hindustani Music Feudal?', in Regula Burckhardt Qureshi (ed.), *Music and Marx: Ideas, Practice, Politics*, (New York, 2002), pp. 81–105, at p. 89.

from them as a tool of performance'.[49] To return to a Marxist interpretation of labour and value, the instrument maker's labour has 'exchange value' but the performer's has only 'use value'.[50] The fact that these demonstration recitals were organised specifically to advertise the instruments, however, demonstrates the intrinsic link between the musical work as cultural commodity and the physical commodities of musical instruments.[51] In terms of their 'cultural commodity' status, these recitals make explicit one of the different 'modes of insertion of cultural labour into the process of production'.[52] Unlike the singer who is described as an unproductive labourer in Marx's often quoted example, cultural products (in this case, musical works, played by performers) can be integrated 'into the process of circulation within the framework of the realization of value'.[53] As overtly commercial presentations of cultural products, with the aim of eventually selling more instruments, the cultural labour of the performers becomes 'indirectly productive'.[54] Exhibitions, therefore, contained the seeds of a rather larger twentieth-century phenomenon of 'on the one hand the promotion of culture by commerce and on the other the promotion of commerce by culture'.[55]

---

[49] Ibid.
[50] Ibid.
[51] Timothy D. Taylor, 'The Commodification of Music at the Dawn of the Era of "Mechanical Music"', Ethnomusicology, 51:2 (2007), 281–305, at p. 283.
[52] Bernard Miège, 'The Cultural Commodity', trans. Nicholas Garnham, Media, Culture and Society, 1:3 (1979), 298–311, at p. 301.
[53] Ibid. See also Karl Marx/Friedrich Engels, Werke, vol. 26, part 1 (Berlin, 1959), p. 377.
[54] Miège, 'Cultural Commodity', p. 301.
[55] Ibid, p. 310.

CHAPTER 4

Museums and the History of Music

Exhibitions were, undoubtedly, paeans to modernity. They were unapologetically forward-looking, and intended to demonstrate a model of industrial and artistic 'progress' that would – their official rhetoric argued – lead the world towards peace and prosperity. All the exhibitions in this study followed this narrative to some extent, but London 1885 and Edinburgh 1890 were the most unequivocally intended to 'exhibit' modernity. London was entitled an Exhibition of 'Inventions', while Edinburgh was one of 'Electrical Engineering, General Inventions, and Industries'. Yet both these exhibitions – in their music sections at least – were also the two events that engaged most vividly with the past. In contrast to exhibits of the newest musical instruments and technologies, both included striking museum displays of 'ancient' musical objects. These collections of instruments, manuscripts, scores, and miscellanea were intended to show music across time and around the world. In London, this contrast was extended into performed music too, with a series of concerts of 'ancient' music, given in the Music Room and the Royal Albert Hall.

Such a blatant juxtaposition of 'ancient' and modern musical objects at these exhibitions reveals a conceptual breach between past and present, demonstrating the late-nineteenth-century's ambivalent relationship with the past. Presented at a time where the social consequences of the Industrial Revolution were becoming increasingly apparent, 'ancient' musical objects were the subject of conflicting interpretations. One reading saw these displays through a developmentalist paradigm, believing them to demonstrate progress over time to the increasingly 'perfect' instruments of the present. In contrast, a Romantic interpretation considered historical instruments to represent an idealised past, imbuing them with a heightened sense of cultural significance that was considered lacking in the displays of new instruments. The temporal disconnect articulated in the displays of instruments illuminates 'a powerful act of dissociation' that scholars including Frederic Jameson and Anthony Giddens have described as essentially symptomatic of modernity.[1] The contrast created by these exhibits, then, regardless of the opposing interpretative poles appearing in their reception, powerfully emphasised the modernity of the exhibitions, and thus the present itself.

---

[1] Frederic Jameson, *A Singular Modernity: Essay on the Ontology of the Present* (New York, 2002), p. 25; Anthony Giddens, *The Consequences of Modernity* (Cambridge, 1991), pp. 38–41.

Both of these exhibitions used the term 'ancient' in addition to 'historic' to describe their displays. This first term, however, was loosely defined, and stretched common understandings of the term. 'Ancientness' as a concept and the notion of the present existing in dialogue with the past, developed over the nineteenth century, becoming 'integral features of intellectual and cultural life'.[2] Yet antiquity was generally regarded to cover classical Greece, Rome, and Egypt, as well as pre-Roman Britain through to the medieval and Gothic.[3] At London, however, any instrument built before 1800 was considered for inclusion, while in Edinburgh even early nineteenth-century instruments were shown. Although the term 'ancient' had been used in musical contexts for some time – significantly by the Academy of Ancient Music in the early eighteenth century, and in the 1776 Concerts of Ancient Music[4] – a 'mystique' developed around the word through the Romantic era as the fashion of 'digging up the past' grew.[5] This character was highlighted by the term 'ancient' at the exhibitions, and its use illuminated the temporal distance between the historical musical objects and the modern inventions of the other displays.

International Exhibitions and Representing the Past

From the Great Exhibition onwards, it was not unusual for international exhibitions to engage with the past, particularly in the context of illustrations of 'progress' through contrasting displays of historical objects. The Great Exhibition included a 'Gothic' court curated by A.W.N. Pugin (1812–52) containing, not historical artefacts, but replicas of medieval sculptures and ecclesiastical objects, and Gothic designs applied to newly-manufactured industrial goods.[6] While this display was popular for its spectacle, some felt that design referencing the past did not fit within the Exhibition's narrative of modernity and was dismissed as 'backward and outdated' and 'antithetical to progress'.[7] As one illustrated catalogue argued, the decorative revivalism was 'a mistake' as the 'pious but often mistaken act of laborious decorations' in the medieval period was 'lifeless, tame – not to say absurd – when copied in a more enlightened age'.[8]

---

[2] Nick Groom, 'Romantic Poetry and Antiquity', in James Chandler and Maureen McLane (eds), *The Cambridge Companion to British Romantic Poetry* (Cambridge, 2008), pp. 35–52, at p. 37.

[3] *Ibid*, p. 37.

[4] Peter Holman, *Life after Death: The Viola da Gamba in Britain from Purcell to Dolmetsch* (Woodbridge, 2010), pp. 303–4.

[5] Percy Lovell, '"Ancient" Music in Eighteenth-Century England', *Music & Letters*, 60:4 (1979), 401–15, at p. 402.

[6] John Davis, *The Great Exhibition* (Stroud, 1999), pp. 139–40.

[7] Jeffry A. Auerbach, *The Great Exhibition of 1851: A Nation on Display* (New Haven, 1999), p. 117.

[8] *The Crystal Palace, and its Contents: Being an Illustrated Cyclopaedia of the Great Exhibition of the Industry of All Nations, 1851* (London, 1852), p. 215.

The themed exhibitions in London in the 1880s also had occasional historic displays. The 1883 Fisheries Exhibition showed the Queen's renaissance-style 'state barge' supposedly 'built in the time of James I, and *re-venerated* by George II'.[9] At the 1884 Health Exhibition, visitors could view examples of the typical dress of 'the upper and lower classes at every change of fashion from the time of William the Conqueror to the present day'.[10] Most of the London themed exhibitions also contained a rather incongruous 'Old London' street: a life-size replica of Cheapside prior to the Great Fire. A similar installation of 'Old Edinburgh' was erected at the Edinburgh Exhibition of 1886. These reconstructed cities – intended more for entertainment than education – provided a prominent contrast to the encompassing exhibits of modernity and industrial progress.[11] In each instance, these displays were both intended and received – in contrasting the old with the new – to emphasise the newness of the new.

This was also true at exhibitions outside of Britain, particularly the 1889 Paris Exposition Universelle. Intended to commemorate the centenary of the French Revolution, the Exposition contained many retrospective elements including an exhibition of historic French paintings, a display depicting the 'History of Human Habitation', and a collection of historic musical instruments.[12] These instruments were shown in a room dedicated to 'the Histoire du Travail', with 'reconstructions and reproductions' filling chronological gaps in the represented objects. Newly made instruments of older models were included, such as an Érard harpsichord built in response to the 'current enthusiasm for all that touches on things from times past'.[13] The concept of 'historical retrospection' was here used to both celebrate the past and validate new achievements.[14]

Although no international exhibition in Britain had displayed historic musical instruments prior to 1885, in 1872 the South Kensington Museum held a Special Exhibition of Ancient Musical Instruments containing over 500 objects.[15] Curated by musicologist and collector Carl Engel (1818–82), this exhibition coincided with the 1872 London International Exhibition but was not part of it. However, as the *Monthly Musical Record* explained, a visitor to the International Exhibition, 'after having acquainted himself ... with the most

[9] 'The Fisheries Exhibition at South Kensington', *British Architect*, 19:20 (18 May 1883), 243–5, at p. 243.
[10] Douglas Galton, 'The International Health Exhibition', *Art Journal*, 46 (May 1884), 153–6, at p. 156.
[11] Wilson Smith, 'Old London, Old Edinburgh: Constructing Historic Cities', in Marta Filipová (ed.), *Cultures of International Exhibitions 1840–1940: Great Exhibitions on the Margins* (Burlington, 2015), pp. 203–30, at p. 203.
[12] Annegret Fauser, *Musical Encounters at the 1889 Paris World's Fair* (Rochester, 2005), p. 103.
[13] Ibid, p. 29, quoting Julien Tiersot, 'Promenades musicales à l'Exposition', *Le Ménestrel*, 55 (1889), p. 180.
[14] Fauser, *Musical Encounters*, p. 40.
[15] Carl Engel, *Musical Myths and Facts* (London, 1876), p. 73; *Science and Art Department: South Kensington Museum. Catalogue of the Special Exhibition of Ancient Musical Instruments MDCCCLXXII* (London, [1872?]), p. v.

recent improvements in the manufacture of musical instruments ... [could] cross the road to find himself face to face with the past'.[16] Press reports describe the appeal of the Special Exhibition as residing in the status of the instruments as relics of another era. The *Daily News* romantically described the 'well-worn and antiquated objects which in their day afforded delight and solace to many a heart; whose keys or strings were touched by fingers that long ago "for ever grew still"' (quoting Byron's *The Destruction of Sennacherib*).[17] While the concurrent running of the 1872 International Exhibition and the Special Exhibition inadvertently contrasted new musical instruments with old, at London 1885 and Edinburgh 1890, such a display choice was entirely deliberate.

❧ London 1885 and Edinburgh 1890: Modern Exhibitions and Ancient Instruments

Both London 1885 and Edinburgh 1890, in contrast to their striking displays of 'inventions', had distinct historical departments exclusively related to music. At London, a 'Loan Collection' lent by various institutions and individuals displayed 'ancient' musical instruments, manuscripts, and related objects, filling the circular gallery at the top of the Albert Hall (Figure 14). This display included three 'period rooms' – demonstrating Tudor England, eighteenth-century England, and another in the style of Louis XVI – where instruments were presented among contemporary furniture and decorations, and a fourth 'Oriental Room' showing non-Western instruments. At Edinburgh, following the successful examples of 'ancient' instrument exhibitions in London in 1872 and 1885, and Paris in 1889, the Exhibition's own collection was held in a 'moderate-sized but lofty and well-lighted room', prominently positioned near the building's entrance.[18] Curated by Robert A. Marr, (1850–1905, secretary for the Scottish Music Society and a respected local authority) and gathered from private and institutional collections, this display was divided into three sections: instruments, scores and manuscripts, and pictures. Whereas in London non-Western instruments had been shown in a separate room, at Edinburgh these were scattered throughout. At both London and Edinburgh, this physical separation of 'ancient' and 'modern' emphasised the contrast between past and present, demonstrating an aesthetic and ideological distinction between technical innovation, and the culturally and artistically loaded history of music.

Most instruments at both exhibitions came from private collections. At London these included string, keyboard, brass, and wind instruments, grouped by type and maker, rather than historical period, with examples from Stradivarius and Amati (including the famous 'Hellier Strad'), and the English, Venetian,

---

[16] 'The Collection of Ancient Musical Instruments at South Kensington', *Monthly Musical Record*, 2 (Aug. 1872), 114–15, at p. 114.

[17] 'Exhibition of Ancient Musical Instruments', *Daily News*, 1 Jun. 1872, p. 5.

[18] 'The Historic Musical Collection at the Edinburgh Exhibition', *Musical World*, 70:37 (13 Sep. 1890), 734–5, at p. 734.

Figure 14. John Dinsdale, 'Old Musical Instruments in Gallery of Albert Hall', *Sketches at the Inventories* (London, 1885), [pages not numbered].

Dutch, and German Schools of makers.[19] The date-range of the exhibits here was vast, with manuscripts and autographs of nineteenth-century composers displayed alongside supposedly prehistoric instruments. Of the latter, an instrument described as a 'Rock Harmonicon' was shown by relatives of Peter Crosthwaite (1735–1808) of the Keswick Crosthwaite Museum, which was supposedly found in the Greta river in Cumbria in the 1780s, and declared by 'more than 200 gentry … to be the first set of music stones that ever was in the World'.[20] Several important collections also came from European musical institutions. A notable display from the Brussels Conservatoire and its curator Victor Mahillon (1841–1924) was so vast that *The Times* suggested that any account 'would alone require more space than we can devote to the entire exhibition'.[21] Yet instruments from British institutions were limited, apart from a collection of non-Western instruments from the Royal College of Music, and a 1726 clavichord sent by the Maidstone Museum and Public Library, allegedly used by Handel while 'composing on journeys'.[22] This was due to resistance from

[19] 'Historical Music at the Inventions Exhibition', *Daily News*, 1 Jun. 1885, p. 3.
[20] Alfred J. Hipkins, *Guide to the Loan Collection and List of Music Instruments, Manuscripts, Books, Paintings, and Engravings: Exhibited in the Gallery and Lower Rooms of the Albert Hall* (London, 1885), pp. 45, 53.
[21] 'The Musical Loan Collection at South Kensington', *The Times*, 1 Jun. 1885, p. 12.
[22] Hipkins, *Guide to the Loan Collection*, p. 42. The *Musical Times* thought the assertion that Handel might have written oratorios while travelling to be 'ludicrous'. See 'The

many public institutions regarding lending objects to an exhibition with a commercial imperative. When the Marquis of Hamilton wrote from the Exhibition's Executive Council to the South Kensington Museum in 1885, asking to borrow instruments, Phillip Cunliffe-Owen, both the museum's director and an Exhibition commissioner, responded by stating his 'grave objections to lending objects' to an 'Exhibition where a charge is made to inspect them'.[23]

Edinburgh's collection – largely strings, keyboard, and wind instruments – was smaller by contrast, with the majority of objects coming either from private collections or the University of Edinburgh. Instruments included a 1780 spinet by Christian Shean (c.1711–94), a 'theorbo lute' by Home and Sons, and a cello by Barak Norman (1651–1724), 'the oldest maker of violoncellos in Great Britain'.[24] Yet there were few 'big names' beyond a 1736 violin by Gennaro [Januarius] Gagliano (fl. c.1740–c.1780) 'alumnus Antonii Stradivarii', a 1759 Neapolitan mandoline by Antonius Vinaccia (fl. c.1756–84), a 1684 viola da gamba by London maker John Betts (1755–1823) and another of 1696 by Joachim Tielke (1641–1719) of Hamburg.[25] Scottish exhibits drew particular attention with spinets by Edinburgh makers and a variety of 'highland' and 'union' bagpipes, including a 1781 set supposedly played at Waterloo. Historical models were displayed, including two reproduction piano actions created from surviving diagrams by Bartolomeo Cristofori.[26] Experimental and 'curious' early instruments were also prominent, including 'singular' examples of 'cithers with keyboards', and an 'extinct species' of lute of which the *Musical World* noted 'the banjo is a fashionable but degenerate modern representative'.[27]

Both exhibitions contained extensive collections of manuscripts and printed scores. These were lent, in London, by many university libraries and colleges including the Bodleian Library in Oxford and St John's College, Cambridge, and ecclesiastics including the Archbishop of Canterbury. In Edinburgh, again, most came from the University. At London many copies of masses and hymns were displayed, including a 'curiosity' in 'the hymn to the Virgin signed "Quoth Dominus Proweth," every word of which begins with a P',[28] works by John Taverner (1490–1545) and Thomas Ashwell (c.1478–after 1513), a 1457 Mainz Psalter lent by Lord Spencer, and several Handel scores from royal collections.[29] The library of the monastery of St Gall sent what was believed to be the earliest

---

Historic Loan Collection', *Musical Times*, 26:510 (1 Aug. 1885), pp. 453–5.

[23] Minutes, 12 Mar. 1885, United Kingdom, London: International Inventions Exhibition, 1885, V&A Archives, MA/35/96.

[24] 'The Historic Musical Collection at the Edinburgh Exhibition', *Magazine of Music*, 7:11 (Nov. 1890), p. 219.

[25] Samuel Lee Bapty (ed.), *International Exhibition of Electrical Engineering, General Inventions and Industries, Edinburgh 1890: Official Catalogue*, 2nd ed. (Edinburgh, 1890), p. 161.

[26] Bapty, *Official Catalogue*, p. 162.

[27] 'The Historic Musical Collection at the Edinburgh Exhibition', *Musical World*, pp. 734–5.

[28] 'The Musical Loan Collection at South Kensington', *The Times*, 25 Jul. 1885, p. 3.

[29] 'Historical Music at the Inventions Exhibition', *Daily News*, p. 3.

musical manuscript in existence, the 'Antiphonarium S. Gregorii' (although *The Times* noted it was 'in reality a *graduale*'), while elsewhere the 1473 folio 'Collectorium super Magnificat', thought to be the earliest printed music, was displayed.[30] English music was represented, including the unique manuscript of the thirteenth-century secular song 'Sumer is icumen in', and the *Polychronicon* of Ranulf Higden (*c*.1280–1364) 'Englyshed by Syr John de Trevyse' in 1495, which apparently contained the 'first example of music printed in this country', proving, *The Times* argued, that 'England in the 15th century was an eminently musical country'.[31]

Edinburgh's score collection was also extensive, although many items appear to have been printed editions, rather than manuscripts. For example, Mozart's *Verzeichnüss aller meiner Werke* was exhibited, but in an 1805 edition by Johann André.[32] The *Official Catalogue* gives little detail of the musical contents of the earliest manuscripts, describing an 'Antiphonarium' of 'Ancient Church Music with words' entirely by its bindings and physical properties, without date or musical information.[33] Particular Scottish interests were also represented in the display of both the Straloch and Skene Manuscripts,[34] yet most attention went to the 'Dublin' copy of Handel's *Messiah* by J.C. Smith (1712–95) with many additions in Handel's hand, and the 1575 'Song in Forty Parts' by Thomas Tallis (1505–85) in a copy with English words 'in praise of Charles I., and probably written about 1630'.[35]

Both the London and Edinburgh Loan Collections were primarily considered educational and not, like the modern instruments in the exhibitions, to be assessed in terms of commercial value, practical functionality, or modern aesthetic considerations. As *The Times* reported of London, it was a place in which the music student could 'examine the rarest treasures', while in Edinburgh the *Musical World* argued that 'no institution whose curriculum includes the art of music can be considered complete' without the 'object lessons' provided by the Exhibition.[36] Yet these exhibits also embodied meaning beyond the educational, and an examination of their reception shows two conflicting narratives emerge – one progressive, one Romantic – demonstrating what has been described

---

[30] 'The Musical Loan Collection at South Kensington', *The Times*, 25 Jul. 1885, p. 3.
[31] *Ibid*.
[32] Bapty, *Official Catalogue*, p. 164.
[33] *Ibid*, p. 163.
[34] *Ibid*, p. 164.
[35] *Ibid*, p. 165. This was presumably the adaptation sung at the investiture ceremonies of Henry as Prince of Wales in 1610 and his brother Charles in 1616. It had been previously proposed that this version was sung at Charles I's coronation. See Ian Woodfield, '"Music of Forty Several Parts": A Song for the Creation of Princes', *Performance Practice Review*, 7:1 (1994), 54–64.
[36] 'The Musical Loan Collection at South Kensington', *The Times*, 1 Jun. 1885, p. 12; 'The Historic Musical Collection at the Edinburgh Exhibition', *Musical World*, pp. 734–5.

as the most significant, but 'diametrically opposed philosophies' present in late-nineteenth-century conceptions of the past.[37]

A progressivist outlook, underscored by increasing awareness of Darwinian evolutionary theories and Hegelian philosophy, considered studies of the past to demonstrate progress through time. From this perspective the importance of history lay in its capacity to help understand the present, as society repeatedly 'manifested itself in increasingly perfect forms'.[38] Thus, the art of the past could be appreciated, but should be understood as less-developed, and requiring adaptation 'to cater to the cultural requirements of a modern audience'.[39] Promoting this interpretation seems to have been the overarching aim of most exhibitions' engagement with the past. Yet, a contrasting interpretative narrative also emerged, with proponents of the Romantic school appreciating the past for its own sake. In a century filled with war and bloody revolutions, and a society supposedly left increasingly materialist and morally degenerate by the Industrial Revolution, the distant past could represent a 'mythical golden age'.[40] This despair at the present was typified in the work of the European Romantic circle of poets, including August Wilhelm Schlegel (1767–1845), whose assertions that 'our future must be founded on the past! I shall not support the stifling present, I shall bind myself to you, eternal artists', epitomised such a view.[41] In Britain, similar ideas were expounded by figures and movements such as John Ruskin (1819–1900) and the Gothic Revival, the Oxford Movement, and Pre-Raphaelite Brotherhood which were all, 'at heart, nostalgic escapes from a disagreeable present to an agreeable but imaginary past'.[42] At the exhibitions, the 'ancient' instruments represented an idealised past, full of meaning seen to be lacking in the displays of new and industrialised instruments in the exhibition-proper.

From 'Ancient' to 'Modern': Exhibitions and the Discourses of Progressivism and Romanticism

Perhaps the most straightforward interpretation of the displays of 'ancient' instruments, appropriate to the international exhibition ethos, was an evolutionary narrative illustrating the 'progress' of musical history. Although the

---

[37] Elaine Kelly, 'Evolution versus Authenticity: Johannes Brahms, Robert Franz, and Continuo Practice in the Late Nineteenth Century', *19th-Century Music*, 30:2 (2006), 182–204, at p. 182.
[38] *Ibid.*
[39] *Ibid.*, p. 183.
[40] William Vaughan, *German Romantic Painting* (New Haven, 1980), p. 2, quoted in Kelly, 'Evolution versus Authenticity', p. 183.
[41] A.W. Schlegel, as quoted in Pellisov [Karl Emil Schafhäutl], 'Ueber die Kirchenmusik des katholischen Cultus', *Allgemeine musikalische Zeitung*, 36 (1834), p. 744. Quoted in James Garratt, *Palestrina and the German Romantic Imagination: Interpreting Historicism in Nineteenth-Century Music* (Cambridge, 2002), p. 21.
[42] Auerbach, *The Great Exhibition of 1851*, p. 171.

museum showcases at both exhibitions were not chronologically arranged – grouped instead by type, maker, or country – the mixture of 'beautiful' instruments 'of all ages and countries' was nonetheless considered explicitly diachronic, demonstrating 'the gradual development of art manufacture'.[43] The displays were therefore taken by some to demonstrate an evolutionary narrative, particularly in comparison to the modern instruments shown in the exhibitions' industrial divisions.[44] Such a contrast would have been even more pronounced when considered in the context of the exhibitions' overall emphasis on 'progress'.

As *The Times* said of London, the 'development of the art' of music itself could be gauged in 'its visible means of expression' through such a survey 'from its early beginnings to the present day'.[45] Similarly, the *Art Journal* noted the importance of the juxtaposition of a 'collection of the latest developments in the manufacture of musical instruments' with those that could 'serve to illustrate its progressive history'.[46] The manuscripts, too, were described as illustrating 'almost the entire history of music from the early Middle Ages to the present time'.[47] Thus, these displays were interpreted as progressive, showing an evolution of music, in terms of the art, instrumental manufacture, and printing, leading directly to the modern instruments and music on display in the larger exhibitions. This developmentalist narrative was further compounded by the inclusion of non-Western instruments in the displays. Showing non-Western instruments in a space dedicated to the 'ancient', implied that these instruments – despite being, in many cases, in contemporary use – belonged at the less-developed end of a linear, universal music history (as will be discussed further in Chapter Eight).

In contrast to this lineally progressive narrative, others interpreted the displays from a Romantic perspective, championing the 'revival of the art of the distant past' as a means of 'breaking free from more recent tradition'.[48] The dramatic social and cultural shifts of the 1880s and '90s were strongly related to the seismic social changes that came with the Second Industrial Revolution, where people looked to history as a way of making sense of their new world.[49] This perspective was reflected in much of the nineteenth century's Romantic and revivalist culture across many art-forms, prompted both by 'nostalgia

---

[43] 'Music at the International Inventions Exhibition', *Musical World*, 63:8 (21 Feb. 1885), p. 124.
[44] Harry Haskell describes a similar paradox being reinforced by historical survey concerts of this period, see Haskell, *The Early Music Revival: A History* (New York, 1988), p. 21.
[45] 'The Musical Loan Collection at South Kensington', *The Times*, 1 Jun. 1885, p. 12.
[46] 'Music at the Inventions Exhibition, 1885', *Art Journal*, 47 (May 1885), 153–6, at pp. 153–4.
[47] 'The Musical Loan Collection at South Kensington', *The Times*, 25 Jul. 1885, p. 3.
[48] Garratt, *Palestrina and the German Romantic Imagination*, p. 21.
[49] Claus Uhlig, 'Nostalgia for Organicism: Art and Society in Ruskin and Pater', in *John Ruskin: Werk und Wirkung* (Zürich; Berlin: Gebr. Mann, c.2002), pp. 102–19, at p. 103.

for a golden age' and 'repulsion by their own modern times'.[50] As such, the instruments on display at London and Edinburgh evoked a 'vanished past' as relics of an idyllic period holding greater cultural and artistic significance than the productions of modern industry.[51] It is perhaps not surprising, then, that at exhibitions explicitly extolling technological 'progress' – the very things rejected by this movement – that many writers and musicians would be drawn to the exhibits that represented the past with a sense of nostalgia.

A particularly striking example of such an interpretation appears in an 1885 review of the London display by Hermann Smith (1824–1910). Rather than describing any sort of progressive narrative through the exhibit, Smith concentrates on individual objects, imagining their human history, and suggesting their makers were capable of 'speak[ing] to us in their works'.[52] As Smith continued:

> My eyes fall upon an instrument handled by common clay. A neglected thing of no account, battered, and broken, and black with age; a silent hurdy-gurdy, no voice, song, or sound in it these hundred years or more. Whose was it? Why was it kept? The hard brown hand that turned it, the shrivelled bony fingers that wearily earned a living for the player, gone to dust, along with Caesar's; and this time-charred relic remains, the last testament of some one of the common folk without a name, and without a history. Forlorn as it is, someone has cherished it, and found some pathos in its remembered music, or may be – such virtue is in human touch – it has been prized for memory of another who held it dear. [53]

A perceived contrast between an idealised, romanticised past and the apparently unfeeling and materialistic nineteenth century was also highlighted in this description, as Smith asks explicitly, 'to how many lives has it not been a joy-bringer. It lies here dumb and despised. What has the nineteenth century to do with it?'[54]

Similar sentiments were expressed by a *Musical World* critic, who thanked time – 'the destroyer' – for sparing so many 'things so fragile' while 'works of stone and brass have fallen to pieces and crumbled into dust'.[55] Unable to hear the instruments, the critic stated that 'one might in fancy call back from the land of shadows the very artists who once made these noiseless things eloquent, who made them the mediums for expressing the thoughts, feelings, and

---

[50] John Haines, 'Antiquarian Nostalgia and the Institutionalization of Early Music', in Caroline Bithell and Juniper Hill (eds), *Oxford Handbook of Music Revival* (New York, 2014), pp. 3–42, at p. 4.

[51] Edmond Johnson, 'The Death and Second Life of the Harpsichord', *Journal of Musicology*, 30:2 (2013), 180–214, at p. 182.

[52] Hermann Smith, 'A Ramble about the Historic Music Loan Collection at the Inventions Exhibition', *Musical Opinion and Music Trade Review*, 8:94 (1 Jul. 1885), 485–6, at p. 485.

[53] *Ibid.*

[54] *Ibid.*

[55] 'Historical Loan Collection of Musical Instruments, Books, and Manuscripts', *Musical World*, 63:24 (13 Jun. 1885), 395–6, at p. 369.

passions which agitated their restless, frail humanity'. This review concludes by quoting John Keats's *Ode on a Grecian Urn*, 'heard melodies are sweet, but those unheard are sweeter'.[56]

While Smith and the *Musical World* critic were enthralled by the evocation of anonymous players from a romanticised past, for others the most important instruments were those that evoked known, historical figures. These could be imaginary associations; as Shaw described, in the 'ancient' display one might 'fancy himself in the very room in which Shakespear [sic] read his sonnets to "the dark lady", and watched her fingers walk with gentle gait over the blessed wood of the virginals, whilst the saucy jacks leapt to kiss the tender inward of her hand'.[57] More importantly, however, instruments owned by famous musicians were displayed at both exhibitions, as well as smaller novelties including a cup and saucer owned by Muzio Clementi (1752–1832), a watch owned by Beethoven and a piece of his hair, a copy of Handel's will and a 'lace ruffle' he wore, and a music desk decorated by Mendelssohn, along with a cast of his hand.[58] The London collection also contained many instruments once owned by European royalty, including a cello used by George IV (1762–1830), a harpsichord once owned by Empress Maria Theresa (1717–80), a *Clavecin Brisé* or folding harpsichord supposed belonging to Frederick II of Prussia (1712–86, sometimes called 'the Great'), and a set of bagpipes owned by Prince Charles Edward Stuart (1720–88).[59]

The most prominent instruments in this respect were a lute and a virginal believed to have been owned by Elizabeth I, despite contemporary reports doubting the provenance of both. The lute was supposedly left at Helmingham Hall in Suffolk in 1584 'to commemorate Her Majesty having stood sponsor' to the infant Sir Lyonel Tollemache.[60] While the *Musical Times* called this 'a very pretty story … unsupported by evidence', they found the instrument interesting in itself as the work of luthier John Rose.[61] The *Art Journal* thought the importance lay less in the 'plausibility' of the story than in 'the preservation of this lute in the Tollemache family, and the tradition that has been treasured for centuries'.[62] The virginal was exhibited in one of the 'historic rooms', yet despite drawing much attention it had only a speculative connection with the

---

[56] *Ibid.*

[57] [George Bernard Shaw, unsigned], 'Historical Instruments', *Dramatic Review*, 19 Sep. 1885, repr. in Dan H. Laurence (ed.), *Shaw's Music: The Complete Musical Criticism in Three Volumes*, vol. 2 (London, 1981), p. 358.

[58] Hipkins, *Guide to the Loan Collection*, pp. 17, 38, 57–8.

[59] *Ibid*, pp. 21, 42.

[60] *Ibid*, pp. 33–4. This instrument is now classified as an orpharion or bandora and remains at Helmingham Hall, see Andrew Hartig, 'Orpharion or Bandora by John Rose, London, 1580', *Renovata Cythara: The Renaissance Cittern Site*, ed. Andrew Hartig, 13 Aug. 2017 <http://www.cittern.theaterofmusic.com/old/rose.html> [accessed 19 Feb. 2021]; and Robert Hadaway, 'An Instrument-Maker's Report on the Repair and Restoration of an Orpharion', *Galpin Society Journal* 28 (1975), 37–42.

[61] 'The Historic Loan Collection (Concluded)', *Musical Times*, 26:511 (1 Sep. 1885), pp. 517–19.

[62] 'Music at the Inventions Exhibition, 1885', *Art Journal*, 47 (Oct. 1885), 305–8, at p. 308.

Queen.[63] The 'potency of the myth', however, was enough to give this exhibit an important place in both the Exhibition display and the public imagination.[64] This was evidently the case with all of the instruments displayed as musical relics of historical figures: the romantic notion of their associations were far more important than reliability of provenance.

This phenomenon was most obviously demonstrated by the exhibition of autographs and letters by musicians. As the *Musical Times* noted, at London, 'the handwriting of almost every well-known composer may be studied'.[65] Julian Marshall (1836–1903) – writer and owner of one of the most substantial contemporary music libraries in England – exhibited many such items, including letters by Chopin, Auber, Christoph Willibald Gluck (1714–87), Verdi, Haydn, and Louis Spohr (1784–1859).[66] Felix Moscheles (1833–1917, the son of Ignaz, 1794–1870) sent scores by his father, Luigi Cherubini (1760–1842), Clementi, and Theodor Döhler (1814–56), as well as Mendelssohn's 'Certificate of Doctor's Degree, Leipzig, 1836'.[67] At Edinburgh manuscripts and autographs were very prominent, with the *Magazine of Music* reporting that 'an enumeration of their names' would suffice 'to give some indication of their value'. The long list they provided included continental composers such as Bach, Beethoven, Mozart, Wagner, Chopin, Berlioz, and Clara Schumann (1819–96), British composers such as William Croft (1678–1727), Samuel Wesley (1766–1837), and Henry Bishop (1787–1856), and performers, conductors, critics, and publishers such as Chorley, Anton Rubinstein (1829–94), Pablo de Sarasate (1844–1908), Hans von Bülow (1830–94), and Vincent (1781–1861) and Alfred Novello (1810–96).[68] Most amusing among these was an autograph by Liszt inscribed 'against albums, autograph collections, and such like, strenuously protests Franz Liszt'.[69]

Elizabeth I's virginal appeared in one of three 'Historic Rooms' at London: spaces that were an example of the 'period rooms' popular in late-nineteenth-century museums, with interiors reconstructed in a manner supposedly representative of a particular period or region.[70] Instead of the common practice of grouping objects by their material, these spaces emphasised the

---

[63] Hipkins, *Guide to the Loan Collection*, p. 111; Johnson, 'The Death and Second Life of the Harpsichord', p. 195.

[64] This instrument is now in the V&A. See 'The Queen Elizabeth Virginal', *Victoria and Albert Museum* <http://collections.vam.ac.uk/item/O70511/the-queen-elizabeth-virginal-spinet-baffo-giovanni-antonio/> [accessed 18 Feb. 2021].

[65] 'The Historic Loan Collection (Concluded)', *Musical Times*, p. 518.

[66] Arthur Searle, 'Julian Marshall and the British Museum: Music Collecting in the Later Nineteenth Century', *British Library Journal*, 11 (1985), 67–87, at p. 67; Hipkins, *Guide to the Loan Collection*, pp. 26, 63.

[67] Hipkins, *Guide to the Loan Collection*, p. 60.

[68] 'The Historic Musical Collection at the Edinburgh Exhibition', *Magazine of Music*, p. 219.

[69] [no title], *Musical Times*, 31:570 (1 Aug. 1890), p. 467.

[70] Julius Bryant, 'Museum Period Rooms for the Twenty-first Century: Salvaging Ambition', *Museum Management and Curatorship*, 24:1 (2009), 73–84, at p. 75.

cultural history and use of the objects by exhibiting them in context.[71] London's three 'historic' rooms – decorated by George Donaldson (1845–1925), the art and furniture dealer and collector – contained instruments, furniture, paintings, and tapestries, arranged 'in illustration of the surroundings in which consecutive generations of our ancestors worshipped at the shrine of music'.[72] The eighteenth-century room (Figure 15) contained many string and woodwind instruments, an English spinet made by John Hitchcock (c.1725–74), and a 'quartet music desk'.[73] The room was arranged, as the *Art Journal* stated, to encourage viewers to imagine 'the conclusion of a small music party', with the chairs 'hastily pushed aside, having on them, or nearby, the instruments which have just been used'.[74] The sixteenth-century room was distinguished for holding Elizabeth's virginal, as well as a number of Italian lutes and harps (Figure 16). The Louis XVI Salon contained a Dutch harpsichord 'painted with scenes from the period of Louis XIV by Van der Meulen' and 'said to have belonged to Marie Antoinette', as well as lutes, harps, and guitars (Figure 17).[75]

These rooms encouraged the use of imagination, placing the instruments into physical, yet unreal space: a romanticised, idealised context. A report in the *Musical World* reinforced this interpretation by describing how by:

> placing a set of instruments in association with furniture of the same epoch the character of the music practised might even be partially divined. The old desk suggests the spinet, as the lute conjures up the high-backed chair upon which the performer rests, and one step more brings us, as it were, within sound of the subdued strains.[76]

In all, the period rooms were perhaps the most marked manifestation of a romanticising impulse in the display of 'ancient' instruments. Rather than placing the instruments in the clinical museum display case – where 'progress' could be gauged by quick comparison with nearby objects, all stripped of context – the period rooms were 'at once empathetic, aesthetic, spiritual, and sensual', as their 'human scale' promoted a closer connection to the objects they held.[77] Seeing the instruments, even though they remained silent, in a context that evoked their human usage, prompted a particular sense of nostalgia in the viewer for the past.

---

[71] Dianne H. Pilgrim, 'Inherited from the Past: The American Period Room', *American Art Journal*, 10:1 (1978), 4–23, at p. 6.

[72] '"The Musical Loan Collection at South Kensington", *The Times*, 1 Jun. 1885, p. 12; Hipkins, *Guide to the Loan Collection*, p. 110.

[73] Hipkins, *Guide to the Loan Collection*, p. 110; 'The Historic Loan Collection', *Musical Times*, p. 453.

[74] 'Music at the Inventions Exhibition, 1885', *Art Journal*, 47 (Aug. 1885), 229–32, at p. 232.

[75] Hipkins, *Guide to the Loan Collection*, p. 111.

[76] L.T. 'Historical Loan Collection of Musical Instruments, Books and Manuscripts', *Musical World*, 63:26 (27 Jun. 1885), pp. 395–6.

[77] Marjorie Schwarzer, 'Literary Devices: Period Rooms as Fantasy and Archetype', *Curator: The Museum Journal*, 51:4 (2008), 355–60, at p. 359.

Figure 15. 'The English Eighteenth-Century Music Room', in 'Music at the Inventions Exhibition, 1885', *Art Journal*, 47 (Aug. 1885), 229–32, at p. 231. The instruments depicted here are an eighteenth-century English oboe by Milhouse in Newark (on the quartet music stand, left), a 1723 viola d'amore by Johannes Blasius Weigert in Linz (face down on chair, centre), a 1610 Venetian chitarrone by Michael Atton (far corner, right) and a spinet by John Hitchcock (serial no.1630, right). © British Library Board, shelfmark 1733.459000.

But being 'one step' away from the sounds of the instruments – as the *Musical World* had described it – was one of the great disappointments associated with these displays. 'The pity is', *The Times* stated, 'that these splendid instruments must of necessity remain mute – that we cannot have an orchestra of Joachims, Sarasates, and Piattis to make them sound in harmonious concord'.[78] As in the displays of modern instruments, which required demonstration recitals to fully engage visitors, so too were there limits on how much could be learnt from silently displayed historic instruments. For this reason, a number of concerts of 'ancient music' were organised in association with the Loan Collection at London in 1885.

---

[78] 'The Musical Loan Collection at South Kensington', *The Times*, 1 Jun. 1885, p. 12.

Figure 16. 'A Sixteenth-Century Room', in 'Music at the Inventions Exhibition, 1885', *Art Journal*, 47 (Nov. 1885), 349–52, at p.351. The instruments depicted here are a sixteenth-century Italian archlute (far left), a sixteenth-century Italian cetera (on chair, centre-left), an Italian lute by Tieffenbrucker (centre), another sixteenth-century Italian lute (on coffer, obscured by chair, centre-right) and 'Queen Elizabeth's Virginal' (right). © British Library Board, shelfmark 1733.459000.

❧ *Concerts of 'Ancient Music'*

The physical separation between old and new seen in the exhibits of 'ancient' and modern instruments also appeared in performance at London 1885. Recitals of 'ancient' music were held through June and July and were received in the musical press as an important educational corrective to the Exhibition's other commercial musical offerings. The series began with three recitals of English glees and madrigals given by the Round, Catch, and Canon Club comprising works by Thomas Ford (1580–1648), Thomas Weelkes (1576–1623), Samuel Webbe (1740–1816), and William Horsley (1774–1858), and the other eighteenth- and nineteenth-century composers shown in the third concert's programme (Table 3). The following week, three concerts by students and teachers of the Brussels Conservatoire led by Mahillon played the same programme each time (Table 4). A single concert of English and Italian madrigals by the Bristol Madrigal Society presented 'the very finest examples of the Elizabethan writers'

Figure 17. 'The Louis XVI Music Room', in 'Music at the Inventions Exhibition, 1885', *Art Journal*, 47 (Oct. 1885), 305–8, at p.307. The instruments depicted here are a French mandoline (face-down on table, left), a guitar, inlaid with pearl with perforated sides (centre-left, at rear), French harp (centre-left), a 1586 Venetian lute by Jacob Hesin (centre), a 1612 clavecin or harpsichord, by Hans Ruckers of Antwerp, restored 1773 by Taskin (centre), a cither (cittern), inlaid with silver and pearl (far right). © British Library Board, shelfmark 1733.459000.

the next week (Table 5), before a concert of sacred Italian and English vocal music (Table 6), including the *Missa Brevis* by Giovanni Pierluigi da Palestrina (1525–94) and the *Miserere* by Gregorio Allegri (1582–1652), was conducted by W.S. Rockstro (1823–95).[79] Finally, three recitals were given by a group of Dutch singers performing 'ancient Netherlandish music', as well as organ works by Bach, Handel, and Girolamo Frescobaldi (1583–1643), 'the appropriateness of which' in a Flemish concert, the *Athenaeum* thought 'was not apparent'.[80] Their first concert's programme is given in Table 7.

The glees and madrigals of the Round, Catch, and Canon Club were described as being of 'extraordinary excellence', and exhibiting 'a kind of art

---

[79] 'Historic Concerts at the Inventions Exhibition', *Musical Times*, 26:510 (1 Aug. 1885), 477–9, at p. 478.
[80] 'Music at the Inventions Exhibition', *Athenaeum*, 3012 (18 Jul. 1885), 88–9, at p. 89.

Table 3. Round, Catch, and Canon Club, International Inventions Exhibition, 26 June 1885

Work	Composer
Madrigal 'This Pleasant Month of May'	William Beale (1784–1854)
Glee 'Mark'd You Her Eye'	Reginald Spofforth (1769–1827)
Glee 'Under the Greenwood Tree'	Thomas Arne (1710–78)
Glee 'Queen of the Valley'	John Wall Callcott (1766–1821)
Glee 'The Bee'	James Elliott (1783–1856)
Round 'Wind, Gentle Evergreen'	Henry Harrington (1727–1816)
Glee 'Sleep, Gentle Lady'	Henry Bishop
Catch 'Ah! How Sophia'	John Wall Callcott
Four Part Song 'The Long Day Closes'	Arthur Sullivan

once held in honour by Englishmen'.[81] Along similar lines the Bristol Madrigal Society's performance – which 'sustained the noble character of the Elizabethan period' – was reviewed as 'interesting' and 'enjoyable'.[82] Both concerts were of particular interest as the Exhibition's only explicit demonstration of an English musical tradition, and were lauded as examples of a golden age in England's musical history. As John South Shedlock (1843–1919) wrote in *The Academy*, these performances provided a reminder of 'a time when English composers could more than hold their own against the best foreigners'.[83] In particular, 'Sumer is icumen in' – a 'pure English creation' – performed early in the Bristol programme, was touted as a marker of English musical brilliance, as 'far more melodious and attractive' than 'any music of the corresponding period in the foreign school'. As 'the germ of modern music' it could be regarded as 'the direct and absolute progenitor of the oratorios of Handel, the symphonies of Beethoven, and the opera of Wagner'.[84] While attendance was reportedly small, and the Albert Hall somewhat overwhelming for unaccompanied vocal music, most critics also acknowledged an enthusiastic response from the audience.

Mahillon's concerts with members of the Brussels Conservatoire were also received with 'exceptional interest', and the players regarded as being of 'consummate skill'.[85] Performing in the Music Room, crowds were so large that

---

[81] George Bernard Shaw, 'Art Corner', *Our Corner*, Jul. 1885, repr. in *Shaw's Music*, p. 292; L.T., 'International Inventions Exhibition', *Musical World*, 63:36 (5 Sep. 1885), p. 560.

[82] L.T., 'International Inventions Exhibition', p. 560; 'Historic Concerts at the Inventions Exhibition', *Musical Times*, p. 478.

[83] J.S. Shedlock, 'Music at the Inventions Exhibition', *Academy*, 688 (11 Jul. 1885), p. 34.

[84] 'Bristol Madrigal Society', *Bristol Mercury and Daily Post*, 9 Jul. 1885, p. 8.

[85] 'Recent Concerts', *The Times*, 3 Jul. 1885, p. 4. Peter Holman examines the reception of gamba player Édouard Jacobs (1851–1925) in these concerts in *Life after Death*, pp. 327–8.

Table 4. Members of the Conservatoire Royal, Brussels (Victor Mahillon, conductor), International Inventions Exhibition, 1, 2 and 4 July 1885

Work	Composer
Aria	J.S. Bach
Minuet	Luigi Boccherini (1743–1805)
Fragment of a Concerto	Johann Joachim Quantz (1697–1773)
Song 'Douce Dame Jolie' (1350)	Guillaume de Machaut (c.1300–1377)
Song 'Las! en mon doux printemps' (1560)	Marie Stuart (1542–1587)
'Dans notre village'	Seventeenth Century
Canarie	Jacques Champion de Chambonnières (c. 1601–72)
L'Égyptienne	Jean-Philippe Rameau (1683–1764)
Gigue de la suite en si bémol	J.S. Bach
Sinfonia pastorale 'Eurydice'	Jacopo Peri (1561–1633)
Sonata	Giuseppe Tartini (1692–1770)
Sicilienne	J.S. Bach
Bourrée	G.F. Handel
Minuet	G.F. Handel
Aria 'Hippolyte et Aricie' (1733)	Jean-Philippe Rameau
Cantique 'Alla Trinita beata'	Fifteenth Century
Aria	J.S. Bach
Soeur Monique	François Couperin (1668–1733)
Le Rappel des oiseaux	Jean-Philippe Rameau
La Bourbonnais	François Couperin
Les Papillons	François Couperin
'March of the Lansquenets'	c.1519

many attendees were turned away at the door, and critics noted 'applause as hearty from the chance visitor as from the genuine enthusiast in the art'.[86] A common theme in the response to these performances was the music's capacity to transport the listener through time. Where in the exhibits of 'ancient' instruments, critics longed to hear their sounds to complete their immersion in the past, here, it seems the visual was the missing illusory element. While one critic described how, 'with eyes shut one could almost imagine oneself transported back nearly two centuries,'[87] another argued that the 'ultra-modern' music room

---

[86] 'Historic Concerts at the Inventories', *Musical Opinion and Music Trade Review*, 8:95 (1 Aug. 1885), 546–8, at p. 546.

[87] Shedlock, 'Music at the Inventions Exhibition', p. 34.

Table 5. Bristol Madrigal Society, International Inventions Exhibition, 8 July 1885

Work	Composer
'God Save the Queen' (5 Voices)	arr. William Horsley
'Sumer is icumen in' (6 Voices) c.1228	arr. Robert Lucas Pearsall (1795–1856)
'All Creatures Now' (5 Voices) 1599	John Bennet (c.1575–after 1614)
'When April Deck'd' (6 Voices) 1570	Luca Marenzio (1553/4–99)
'Lady, When I Behold' (6 Voices) 1598	John Wilbye (1574–1638)
'The Nightingale' (3 Voices) 1608	Thomas Weelkes
'When All Alone' (5 Voices) 1575	Girolamo Converso (d.1575)
'Have I Found Her' (5 Voices) 1615	Thomas Bateson (1570–1630)
'Lay a Garland' (8 Voices) 1840	Robert Lucas Pearsall
'I Saw Lovely Phillis' (4 Voices) 1837	Robert Lucas Pearsall
'My Bonny Lass' (3 Voices) 1595	Thomas Morley (1557/8–1602)
'In Dulci Jubilo' (8 Voices) 1834	Robert Lucas Pearsall
'As Vesta Was' (6 Voices) 1601	Thomas Weelkes
'Lady, See! On Every Side' (4 Voices) 1570	Luca Marenzio
'Sweet Honey-Sucking Bees' (5 Voices) 1609	John Wilbye
'The Silver Swan' (5 Voices) 1612	Orlando Gibbons (1583–1625)
'Die Not, Fond Man' (6 Voices) 1613	John Ward (c.1589–1638)
'In Going to My Lonely Bed' (4 Voices) 1560	Richard Edwards (1525–66)
'Sir Patrick Spens' (10 Voices) 1840	Robert Lucas Pearsall
'The Waits' (4 Voices) 1667	Jeremiah Saville (d. c.1667)

Table 6. Concert of Sacred Music (W.S. Rockstro, conductor), International Inventions Exhibition, 14 July 1885

Work	Composer
Missa Brevis (for 4 voices)	Giovanni Pierluigi da Palestrina
Miserere (for 9 voices)	Gregorio Allegri
Harpsichord Solo: Praeludium	John Bull (1562–1628)
Anthem 'Rejoice in the Lord Always'	John Redford (1491–1547?)
Anthem 'If Ye Love Me, Keep My Commandments'	Thomas Tallis
Anthem 'Call to Remembrance'	Richard Farrant (c.1525–30 to 1580)
Anthem 'Almighty and Everlasting God'	Orlando Gibbons

Table 7. Concert of Ancient Netherlandish Music (Daniel de Lange
[1841–1918], conductor), International Inventions Exhibition, 15 July 1885

Work	Composer
Fantasia (for Organ)	Jan Pieter Sweelinck (1562–1621)
Psalm CXXII (4 Voices)	Jan Pieter Sweelinck
Kyrie (4 voices), from the Mass, 'L'homme armé'	Guillaume Dufay (1397–1474)
Kyrie and Christe (4 Voices)	Johannes Ockeghem (1410–97)
Agnus Dei II. (3 Voices) from the Mass 'Fortuna Desperata'	Jacob Obrecht (1457/8–1505)
Psalm CXVIII (6 Voices)	Jan Pieter Sweelinck
Toccata and Fugue in D minor	J.S. Bach
'Douleur me bat' (6 Voices)	Josquin des Prez (c.1450 to 1455–1521)
'Si je suis brun' (4 Voices)	Orlande de Lassus (1530 or 1532–94)
'Entre vous filles de quinze ans' (4 voices)	Jacobus Clemens non Papa (c.1510–1515 to 1555/6)
Old Netherlandish Popular Songs: 'Maximilianus de Bossu'; 'Isser lemant uit Oost Indien Gekomen'; 'Waer dat men sich al keert of wendt'; 'Merck toch'	
'Je ne fus jamais si ayse' (3 Voices)	Nicolas Gombert (c.1495–c.1560)
'Un gay bergier' (4 Voices)	Thomas Crecquillon (c.1505–15 to 1557)
'Tu as tout seul, Jan' (5 voices)	Jan Pieter Sweelinck

could have been better 'calculated' to lend a 'tinge of illusion or sentiment' to the performance, proposing the stage be set like a seventeenth-century drawing room, and the performers costumed.[88]

The instruments themselves drew many comments, particularly the *flauti dolci* (recorders) used in the sixteenth-century 'March of the Lansquenets'. Many found the sound jarring, with *The Times* complaining that 'the "sweet flutes" were not in perfect tune',[89] and comparisons made to 'street organs',[90] with the *Monthly Musical Review* suggesting that 'the only thing lacking to complete the illusion being a monkey with a chain'.[91] Others took the unusual timbre with good humour, with *The Sunday Times* stating that while 'not precisely agreeable to sensitive ears' the sound was 'irresistibly droll and characteristic', and that

---

[88] 'Ancient Music at the Inventions', *The Sunday Times*, 5 Jul. 1885, p. 7.
[89] 'Recent Concerts', *The Times*, 3 Jul. 1885, p. 4.
[90] 'Historic Concerts at the Inventions Exhibition', *Musical Times*, p. 478.
[91] 'Concerts at the Exhibition', *Monthly Musical Record*, 15:176 (1 Aug. 1885), 183–4, at p. 183.

'many historical revivals are funny as well as instructive'.[92] Shaw described the instruments – the worst of which resembling the 'leg of a small stool' – as not deserving the name 'sweet flutes':[93]

> On the same inscrutable principle, in our own day, we have execrable machines made with concertina reeds, fed with bands of perforated paper, and played by turning a handle, advertized as the Dulciana, the Melodina, the Harmonista, and The Cottager's Joy. The 'sweet flute' has an inimitable plaintive silliness that is all its own; but it is not sweet.[94]

Other instruments were regarded more sympathetically. Even Shaw saw the 'common cross flute' – spoken of 'so unkindly' by Mozart – as providing in a performance with harpsichord accompaniment 'a flavor unattainable nowadays with Boehm flutes and Steinway grands'.[95] Other critics were also pleasantly surprised on hearing period music played on period instruments. In a harpsichord performance of works by de Chambonnières, Rameau, and Bach, Shedlock argued the instrument's 'short and delicate tone' helped listeners understand the baroque trills and ornaments, which sound 'fidgetty and meaningless' when played on the piano.[96]

The concert of sacred music conducted by Rockstro opened with Palestrina's *Missa Brevis*, a work 'surrounded by a sacred halo'.[97] The *Musical World* gave a mixed review of the performance overall, arguing that it was a mistake to begin with the Palestrina – a work 'marked by a tenderness that winds itself around the sympathies of the auditor, by a grace that appeals to his fancy, a sadness which adds pathos to the sacred words, by a buoyancy ready for the outstretched wings of hope' – as it left listeners disappointed by the works that followed.[98] Others, however, found the Mass more difficult – 'chaste and solemn' though it was – as modern listeners, 'wearied by masses overladen with counterpoint and ornament' found its 'pure strains' a 'sudden and striking contrast'.[99] The Allegri *Miserere* was less well received, with most critics concentrating on the story of Mozart's supposed secret transcription of the work. Shaw was particularly scathing about the English performers' pitch, suggesting that if the Sistine Chapel choir sang the *Miserere* as Rockstro's choir sang it, a performance 'once a century would be too often'.[100] The English songs that completed the programme were rarely discussed, except for repeated mention of 'Purcell,

---

[92] 'Ancient Music at the Inventions', *The Sunday Times*, p. 7.
[93] [George Bernard Shaw, unsigned], 'Historic Concerts', *Dramatic Review* (4 Jul. 1885), repr. in *Shaw's Music*, p. 301.
[94] Ibid, p. 302.
[95] Ibid, p. 302.
[96] Shedlock, 'Music at the Inventions Exhibition', p. 34.
[97] 'Music at the Inventories', *Musical World*, 63:30 (25 Jul. 1885), p. 465.
[98] L.T., 'Illustrations of Sacred Music of the 16th and 17th Centuries', *Musical World* (18 Jul. 1885), p. 451.
[99] 'Music at the Inventions Exhibition', *Academy*, 689 (18 Jun. 1885), p. 50.
[100] [George Bernard Shaw, unsigned], 'An English Failure and a Dutch Triumph', *Dramatic Review*, 18 Jul. 1885, repr. in *Shaw's Music*, p. 311.

by far the greatest composer of the seventeenth century, being unaccountably absent'.[101] The Music Room was regarded as an unsuitable venue for such delicate music, with the singers being forced to compete with 'the throbbings of neighbouring engines' and 'a harsh and echoless structure of iron'.[102] Acoustic issues aside, the atmosphere of the exhibition seemed incompatible with the music, with the Allegri specifically requiring 'the cathedral of St. Peter's, with altar, priests, intonation, incense' to complete the experience,[103] without which it could not engage the listener.[104]

The final concerts of 'ancient Netherlandish music' were, in contrast, revelatory. Many critics, having never heard the works before, were amazed by 'the quaint phrases' and 'the beautiful and solemn harmonies' that brought 'a pleasure almost unknown' to modern audiences.[105] Although it was reported that, initially 'the grave, solemn strains' were 'too sombre for the butterfly auditors',[106] quickly, the audience – amateurs and professionals alike – became enraptured.[107] Secular songs, including those by Orlande de Lassus and Jacobus Clemens non Papa, were seen as representative of a unique Dutch spirit: 'they breathe a fire, a sea-wind, a hardiness, daring, and weird romance, a stirring, touching, electrifying spirit, going straight to the heart'.[108]

It was, however, the music of Sweelinck, with its 'rugged and quaint strains' that was most highly praised.[109] Shaw found Sweelinck's secular songs, psalms, and organ works to be 'remarkable', with a 'culminating power worthy of Wagner, a freedom and breadth almost worthy of Handel, and a harmonic treatment that would not have discredited Bach'.[110] Sweelinck also drew explicit comparison with Palestrina, perhaps expressing a lingering anti-Catholic sentiment in the response to the Italian sacred music of the previous concert. The *Athenaeum* enjoyed his 'manly vigour' and expressiveness 'which cannot be found in the Italian music of the same period'.[111] The *Musical Times*, in praising Sweelinck's 'masculine vigour and energy', further noted that these were 'the special characteristics of Netherlandish music' compared to an implied effeminate 'school of Palestrina'.[112] Critics painted Sweelinck as the anti-Palestrina, pointing to the 'manly' Dutch music as historically overlooked as a

---

[101] 'Music at the Inventions Exhibition', *Athenaeum*, p. 89.
[102] L.T. 'Illustrations of Sacred Music', p. 451.
[103] 'Music at the Inventions Exhibition', *Academy*, p. 50.
[104] 'Historic Concerts at the Inventories', *Musical Opinion*, p. 546.
[105] 'Ancient Netherlandish Music', *Morning Post*, 16 Jul. 1885, p. 2.
[106] 'Historic Concerts at the Inventories', *Era*, 18 Jul. 1885, p. 16.
[107] 'Historic Concerts at the Inventories', *Musical Opinion*, p. 547.
[108] 'Music at the Inventories', *Musical World*, p. 465.
[109] Shedlock, 'Music', *Academy*, 690 (25 Jul. 1885), p. 66.
[110] [Shaw], 'An English Failure and a Dutch Triumph', p. 312.
[111] 'Music at the Inventions Exhibition', *Athenaeum*, p. 89.
[112] 'Historic Concerts at the Inventions Exhibition', *Musical Times*, p. 479.

consequence of the Council of Trent's 'ban' on polyphonic religious music: the same time that Palestrina 'found favour with the Church of Rome'.[113]

These concerts overall were regarded as being of great educational value to the public and British musical culture broadly.[114] As the *Musical Opinion* reported, 'to hear the actual music of the time preceding Bach and Handel was to experience an advance in education beyond that gained by reading in books'.[115] For many critics, these concerts were one of the few 'worthwhile' musical aspects of the Exhibition, providing a clear – and artistically superior – contrast to the commercial instrumental recitals, or the popular bands and light orchestras providing entertainment in the grounds. The *Athenaeum* thus stated that these concerts were 'in some measure compensating' for the 'shortcomings' of the other music;[116] for Shaw the Dutch singers were so impressive that for them alone 'all the sins against music of the Inventions Council may be forgiven';[117] at the *Musical Times*, the historic concerts were 'the silver lining to the black cloud' of the music at the Exhibition.[118] Many writers hoped that these concerts would lay the groundwork for an increased appreciation of high art music, with 'the works of the primitive masters' appearing in the public consciousness as 'a fertile field that has long lain fallow … now reopening to cultivation'.[119] As the *Musical Times* concluded, 'it must ever be so in the art of music. We have only to scatter seed broadcast, and though some of it will fall on stony ground and perish, some will also take root and bear fruit a hundred-fold'.[120]

Despite such positive reviews, attendance at these concerts was comparably low, unable to compete with the draw of carnival amusements and popular music.[121] In much of the press there was a palpable embarrassment at the public's lack of engagement with such 'worthwhile' music, and Shaw rebuked the 'foolish Philistines' who 'took themselves elsewhere to try their weight, ride in the air car, or smoke in the gardens'.[122] Embarrassment was further extended to the commissioners' 'shabby treatment' of the performers, who were not paid, despite coming 'from far and suffer[ing] many things for the glory, honour, and profit' of the Exhibition. The musicians also complained of a 'most unhandsome personal reception', with no one 'present to introduce them, no one was

---

[113] 'Dutch Music at the International Exhibition', *Musical Standard*, 26:1095 (25 Jul. 1885), p. 52; 'Music at South Kensington', *Musical Times*, 26:509 (Jul. 1885), 387–8, at p. 387.
[114] 'Concerts at the Exhibition', *Monthly Musical Record*, p. 183.
[115] 'Historic Concerts at the Inventories', *Musical Opinion*, p. 547.
[116] 'Music at the Inventions Exhibition', *Athenaeum*, p. 88.
[117] [Shaw], 'An English Failure and a Dutch Triumph', p. 313.
[118] 'Historic Concerts at the Inventions Exhibition', *Musical Times*, p. 478.
[119] 'Music at the Inventories', *Musical World*, p. 465.
[120] 'Historic Concerts at the Inventions Exhibition', *Musical Times*, p. 478.
[121] 'Historic Music at the Inventions', *Daily News*, 25 Jun. 1885, p. 3.
[122] [Shaw], 'An English Failure and a Dutch Triumph', p. 313.

in the chair at their performances, no vote of thanks or decent recognition of any kind was offered them, and – *proh pudor!* – hardly any food.'[123]

Although these concerts may not have been appreciated by large audiences, nor by the organising committees to any great extent, such examples of high art music – in comparison to the commercial and popular music offered elsewhere – necessitated praise from critics who believed themselves to be the 'doorkeepers' of music. This is, in part, an example of Bourdieu's notion of *habitus*, or 'the system of dispositions with which a person is invested by education and upbringing.'[124] Here, 'denial of lower, coarse, vulgar, venal, servile – in a world, natural – enjoyment' by way of the public's delight at the popular music, was distinguished from an assertion of the critics' own superiority for being 'satisfied with the sublimated, refined, disinterested, gratuitous, distinguished pleasures' in their support of such 'high' art.[125] As the middle classes expanded in the nineteenth century, taste – and in particular, ways of demonstrating 'refined' taste – grew in importance as a marker of social standing 'since it was no longer common knowledge who was important.'[126] Writers, therefore, regardless of their actual enjoyment of these concerts, were compelled to review positively, given the cultural associations of the 'ancient' music. But the critical response to the 'ancient' music was also emblematic of the romanticising impulse evident in the reception of the 'ancient' instruments. The sounds of these concerts were experienced by those invested in the pursuit of 'high art' as representative of an idealised past, and an antidote to the modern, commercial, and popular music heard throughout the Exhibition.

International exhibitions were intended to display the accumulated technological and artistic achievements of their era, at a time known 'for its rejection of the past and self-conscious embrace of a newly-defined modernity.'[127] Yet, as the *Era* argued, 'one of the best ideas connected with music at the Inventories' was 'introducing examples of the music of past times to contrast with what has been produced in later days.'[128] The conceptual meeting and disjuncture between old and new seen at both London 1885 and Edinburgh 1890 can illuminate some important aspects of that period's relationship with the musical past where, 'inherent in the idea of modernity' was a constant 'contrast with tradition.'[129] At both London and Edinburgh, this idea was clearly demonstrated by the blatant contrast between the 'ancient' and 'modern' musical objects,

---

[123] 'Bristol Madrigalians at the Inventions', *Bristol Mercury and Daily Post*, 28 Aug. 1885, p. 3.

[124] Derek B. Scott, *Sounds of the Metropolis: The Nineteenth-Century Popular Music Revolution in London, New York, Paris, and Vienna* (Oxford, 2008), p. 85.

[125] Pierre Bourdieu, *Distinction: A Social Critique of the Judgement of Taste*, trans. Richard Nice (London, 1986), p. 7.

[126] Scott, *Sounds of the Metropolis*, p. 85.

[127] Edmond Johnson, 'Revival and Antiquation: Modernism's Musical Pasts' (unpublished Ph.D. dissertation, University of California, Santa Barbara, 2011), p. 2.

[128] 'Historic Concerts at the Inventories', *Era*, p. 16.

[129] Giddens, *The Consequences of Modernity*, p. 36.

and further still at London by the sounds of 'ancient' music. The varied and ambivalent interpretations of the old objects and works only strengthened their contrast.

CHAPTER 5

Performance, Rational Recreation, and Music for 'Progress'

The London Inventions Exhibition of 1885 was the only exhibition of the period to have an entire division devoted to music. Encompassing the historical loan collection of 'ancient' musical instruments, a vast collection of newly manufactured instruments, and concerts given by soloists, early music troupes, orchestras, bands in the gardens, and non-Western musical ensembles, it was by far the most extensive representation of 'music' of any exhibition in this study. But the narratives that developed around the music division, particularly in terms justifying such an immense display, demonstrate two conflicting points of view, both of which were reflected in the speeches given at the Exhibition's opening ceremony. On one hand, music was to be promoted in its own right, as an art-form of value and importance, finally getting the recognition it deserved from the British public. As George Grove (1820–1900) – the Chair of the Executive Committee for Music – stated in his speech, 'at last the time of music has come. Hitherto commerce and practical arts and science have occupied too much of the exclusive attention of the country'.[1] On the other hand, as the Prince of Wales (1841–1910) communicated in his own speech, music could have a greater social and utilitarian role. Based on his interest 'in the advancement of musical education' the Prince hoped that this exhibition would 'have the effect of encouraging the love of that art in this country', expecting 'beneficial results' for the public overall.[2]

The Prince of Wales was not alone in articulating a narrative of public 'improvement' through music at the exhibitions. For all of their commercial implications, exhibitions were, largely, educational endeavours, and at many of those held throughout the 1880s, musical activities were organised with distinctly educational aims. For writers in the musical press, exhibitions appeared the perfect forum to expose large crowds to 'good' music both for the sake of the art itself and to 'improve' the public through its edifying influence. But 'good' music was not just any music; it was specifically 'high art' music. As the *Musical Times* put it, to fulfil its educational purposes, the music heard at the exhibitions must be selected without 'the slightest concession to that vulgarity of taste which is supposed to reign supreme among the masses'.[3]

---

[1] 'The Inventions Exhibition', *Daily News*, 30 Apr. 1885, p. 3.
[2] 'Opening of the Inventions Exhibition', *Daily News*, 5 May 1885, p. 5.
[3] 'Music at South Kensington', *Musical Times*, 26:508 (1 Jun. 1885), 317–19, at p. 317.

While musical performances were common at all the exhibitions of the 1880s, orchestral and choral concerts were particularly promoted for their educational and 'improving' qualities at the exhibitions in the Australian colonies and in Scotland. Sydney 1879 and Melbourne 1888 held some of the most extensive programmes of orchestral music at any exhibition in this study, and both these exhibitions, with the addition of Adelaide 1887 and Edinburgh 1890, also staged significant programmes of oratorio. There was evidently a commercial advantage to hosting such concerts, as changing, large-scale musical events could encourage attendees to visit an exhibition on multiple occasions, which was useful in cities with relatively small populations. Ultimately, however, the aim of such performances – as it was presented by their organisers – was to expose the broader public to art music, particularly the canonic 'great' works, which were considered to be of 'unquestionable value as a refining and educational agency'.[4] Such a goal aligned with that of the contemporary rational recreation movement, into which both the educational use of art music and the exhibitions themselves could fit. In Australia, additionally, organisers hoped first to educate a geographically distant part of the Empire on the musical traditions of Europe, then to use the positive public response to such music to demonstrate the cultural 'progress' of their communities.

The nineteenth-century definition of musical 'high art', as Denise Von Glahn and Michael Broyles explain, was 'predominantly Western … composed by specially trained individuals', and supposedly 'universal because of its transcendence … unparalleled in its complexity, expressivity, originality, and thus meaning'.[5] This definition, and the phrase 'high art' itself is, of course, deeply problematic, particularly when presented in an implied distinction to 'popular culture'. Yet despite twenty-first-century unease with such a dichotomy, a perceived opposition between 'high' and 'low' forms was something clearly and widely understood during the nineteenth century. As intellectuals began to feel 'increasingly alienated from the new industrial society', as John Rickard argues, they came to consider high art as 'something to be defended from the barbarism of the mass market'.[6] Further, while 'high' and 'low' culture cannot be directly mapped onto the 'high' or 'low' classes, they are not unrelated: in many ways the status of 'high art' comes from its longstanding associations with 'the rich and powerful', and particularly in the context of rational recreation, for some 'high art' was certainly seen as aspirational.[7] As we shall see in this and the chapter that follows, these issues are markedly reflected in the press reception of the music at the exhibitions, whether in 'high' or popular forms.

---

[4] [no title], *Sydney Morning Herald*, 26 Sep. 1879, p. 4.
[5] Denise Von Glahn and Michael Broyles, 'Art Music', *Grove Music Online* (2012) <http://www.oxfordmusiconline.com> [accessed 3 Mar. 2021].
[6] John Rickard, 'Cultural History: The "High" and the "Popular"', *Australian Cultural History*, 5 (1986), 32–43, at p. 32.
[7] Derek B. Scott, *Sounds of the Metropolis: The Nineteenth-Century Popular Music Revolution in London, New York, Paris, and Vienna* (Oxford, 2008), p. 85.

❧ Rational Recreation, Taste-Making, and 'Progress'

Musicians, critics, and organisers considered that music could be put to multiple 'improving' uses. The first of these was through a rational recreation framework. Rational recreation was an ideological, mainly middle-class movement developed in Britain over the second half of the nineteenth century, intended to promote public education while 'civilising' the masses.[8] It was established in response to the substantial increases in leisure time following the Industrial Revolution that were afforded to people across the class spectrum.[9] While the ostensible benefits of free-time and leisure were widely accepted, the main beneficiaries of this change – the middle classes – were also 'uneasy' about 'the potentially corrupting effect of leisure' on both themselves and the working classes.[10] Rational recreation was a reaction to this anxiety, and was intended to provide alternative and 'wholesome' distractions from less respectable recreational pursuits 'such as the music hall and pub'.[11] While most highly developed in the United Kingdom and North America, by the end of the nineteenth century rational recreation also existed in the Australian colonies, with similar ethical preoccupations emerging to suggest that the education of the underprivileged was one of the duties of the more fortunate.[12]

International exhibitions – particularly those held in the 1880s – were seemingly the 'perfect exemplars' of the rational recreation movement, providing a combination of education and pleasure to the millions who attended.[13] Their vast buildings, overfilled with objects, were a physical affirmation of the popular pedagogical principle of 'learning by looking': a theory that proposed that people learned initially by observing objects, next through comparison, and only then through 'abstract reasoning'.[14] The combination of education and entertainment was considered central to the ethos of the many exhibitions, and arrangements were often made to make the events as accessible as possible to people of every class. At Sydney 1879, for example, commissioners noted that New South Wales's labour laws, the eight-hour day and half-holiday Saturday, as well as discounted entrance prices on public holidays, would make it 'possible for all classes to have an opportunity of paying the Exhibition several visits'.[15]

---

[8] Christine Garwood, *Museums in Britain: A History* (Oxford, 2014), p. 31.
[9] Peter Bailey, *Leisure and Class in Victorian England: Rational Recreation and the Contest for Control, 1830–1885* (London, 1978), p. 5.
[10] Ibid.
[11] Garwood, *Museums in Britain*, p. 31.
[12] Bryan Jamison, 'Making "Honest, Truthful and Industrious Men": Newsboys, Rational Recreation and the Construction of the "Citizen" in Late Victorian and Edwardian Brisbane', *Journal of Popular Culture*, 33:1 (1999), 61–75, at p. 63; Roger Covell, *Australia's Music: Themes of a New Society* (Melbourne, 1967), p. 16.
[13] John M. MacKenzie, *Propaganda and Empire: The Manipulation of British Public Opinion, 1880–1960* (Manchester, 1984), p. 97.
[14] Graeme Davison, 'Exhibitions', *Australian Cultural History*, 2 (1982/1983), 5–21, at p. 6.
[15] *Official Record of the Sydney International Exhibition, 1879* (Sydney, 1881), p. lxix.

Discounted entry and special rail timetables were also implemented at many British exhibitions, much to the same effect.

Music was also an important aspect of the general rational recreation movement, being in many forms able to assert the key Victorian 'bourgeois value' of 'respectability'.[16] Across Britain, efforts were made to disseminate 'high-status' music amongst the lower classes, including the People's Concert Society,[17] for example, or the prevalence of vocal and instrumental musical instruction in Mechanics' Institutes.[18] Similarly, popular contemporary sight-singing movements – including the Tonic Sol-fa system by John Curwen (1816–80) – helped to spread musical literacy, making large amounts of music available to all classes. Curwen's philosophy suggested that 'good music' (or 'high art') could counter the moral effects of 'bad music' (or, popular forms), and in doing so the 'cultural life of the era' could be generally improved.[19] In Australia, too, Mechanics Institutes, choral societies, and sight-singing methods were established and disseminated, with the intention of building an audience 'capable of responding to the affirmatory messages' of art music.[20] In all, the respectability and moral value of 'high art' music was considered significant enough that most people, 'even scientists who lacked performance skills and rarely attended the concert hall' considered it to be a marker of 'civility, refinement, and culture'.[21]

In Australia, the impulse towards 'improving' the masses through music took on an even broader compass. While organisers remained apparently invested in the education of the public for their individual personal and moral benefit, it was also the cultural reputation of the colonies that such a programme could improve, with these exhibitions giving 'a great impulse to the cultivation of music'.[22] Ultimately, organisers and critics hoped to be able to demonstrate that public taste in the young colonies was equal to that of Europe, and of Britain in particular. Critics in the colonies – 'powerfully influenced by the British gaze' throughout this period – frequently engaged in discourses around the idea of demonstrating the society's 'civilisation' through music, in a manner modelled on British standards.[23] High art music, and oratorio particularly – a central pillar of British musical culture – was widely considered among the

---

[16] Scott, *Sounds of the Metropolis*, p. 59.
[17] This Society intended to bring orchestral music to the working classes of suburban London. See Alan Philip Bartley, *Far from the Fashionable Crowd: The People's Concert Society and Music in London's Suburbs* (Newbury, 2009).
[18] Scott, *Sounds of the Metropolis*, p. 62.
[19] Charles Edward McGuire, *Music and Victorian Philanthropy: The Tonic Sol-Fa Movement* (Cambridge, 2009), p. 32.
[20] Covell, *Australia's Music*, p. 16.
[21] Charles Brotman, 'Alfred Wallace and the Anthropology of Sound in Victorian Culture', *Endeavour*, 25:4 (2001), 144–7, at p. 146.
[22] 'Music at the Melbourne Exhibition', *Manchester Guardian*, 4 May 1888, p. 8.
[23] For an exploration of this discourse see Sarah Kirby, '"The Worst Oratorio Ever!": Colonialist Condescension in the Critical Reception of George Tolhurst's *Ruth* (1864)', *Nineteenth-Century Music Review*, 16 (2019), 199–227, particularly at pp. 202–4 and 211–13.

most enlightening and edifying genres of music, and thus, in the exhibition context, could be used to demonstrate the host cities' 'progress' and 'civilisation' on the global stage. By fostering such a public appreciation of music, a colony could 'demonstrate to the world that the nation was ready for its next stage of development'.[24] Within these concerts music was used as a powerful symbol of 'progress, refinement and the maturation of public taste'.[25]

❧ Orchestral Concerts

Both Sydney 1879 and Melbourne 1888 featured vast programmes of orchestral music. In Sydney, 'orchestral concerts of high class music' were given twice a week, with the intention of giving 'great pleasure to the music-loving portion of the community'.[26] In Melbourne, an even larger series of concerts of works by 'the great masters', 'the best works of modern composers', and 'pieces of a light and agreeable character, yet possessing artistic value' were performed daily.[27] The organisation and reception of these concerts at both exhibitions demonstrates with striking clarity the way they were conceived and understood as a vehicle for the dissemination of art music to a wide audience, while enlightening the general public and proving the 'civilisation' of the colonies. These aims were made explicit by the exhibition commissioners themselves. At Sydney, the *Official Record* published by the commissioners states that, while music could be a means of encouraging 'the public to visit the building and grounds over and over again', this 'satisfying financial result' was matched by the 'legitimate and improving' benefits of 'music of a well selected character' which, 'while amusing', could also 'seek to elevate'.[28] According to the Melbourne commissioners, high art music could certainly be 'a source of pleasure' for audiences, but the main goal of the undertaking was 'the stimulation of a love of good music for its own sake' and a 'consequent elevation of the public taste'.[29]

Both the Sydney and Melbourne exhibitions intended to demonstrate their respective colony's capacity to produce and appreciate music to a European standard. They emphasised this by employing European directors of music, who, in the case of Melbourne, came at considerable expense. In Sydney, Milanese composer Paolo Giorza was appointed musical director, bringing much éclat to the undertaking. Although many local musicians were disappointed that an Australian had not been chosen, politician Geoffrey Eagar (1818–91), defended Giorza, highlighting his European credentials. He asked:

---

[24] Jennifer Royle, '"Preparing to Exhibit": Frederick Cowen in the Public Press Preceding Melbourne's Centennial International Exhibition, 1888–89', *Context: Journal of Music Research*, 14 (1997–8), 53–62, at pp. 54–5.
[25] Ibid.
[26] *Official Record of the Sydney International Exhibition, 1879* (Sydney, 1881), p. lxvii.
[27] *Official Record of the Centennial International Exhibition, Melbourne, 1888–1889* (Melbourne, 1890), p. 259.
[28] *Official Record of the Sydney International Exhibition, 1879*, pp. xxxiii–iv.
[29] *Official Record of the Centennial International Exhibition*, p. 259.

whether any member of the profession here can produce testimonials comparable with those submitted by that gentleman? ... An artist who, among other things, composed a 'cantata' which was performed with great success before the late King of Italy ... whose masses have been performed before Pope Leo XIII, and whose name appears as the composer of 207 pieces of music, of varied character, in the advertising sheet of the great publisher, Lucca, of Milan, presents some claims to our notice beyond those of any local celebrity.[30]

Giorza was immediately given the duty of organising orchestral, choral, and instrumental concerts, conducting many of these himself. But belying the commissioners' apparent 'striving for high European standards', was the meagre budget that they ultimately allocated to music; when attendances were not as high as they had hoped, 'music was said to be failing in its purpose', expenses were reduced and the concerts had to be stopped.[31] While they lasted, however, Giorza's orchestral concerts were very well received.

In Melbourne, Frederic Cowen – recently appointed conductor of London's Philharmonic Society – was employed to fill the post of musical director. Cowen was initially not inclined to take the position, writing in his memoir that he 'did not relish the idea' of being away from home for the six months required. Instead of refusing outright, however, he made his fee 'so prohibitive' that he 'never expected to hear anything more about the matter'.[32] He was greatly surprised when the committee agreed, paying him the exorbitant rate of £5,000 plus expenses (roughly $680,000 in Australian dollars in recent years).[33] Cowen was soon accompanied to Australia by fifteen professional English orchestral players to lead the new seventy-three-piece Centennial Orchestra, established by Alberto Zelman and George Peake (1853–1933) specifically for the Exhibition.[34]

Cowen's engagement was regarded as making a strong statement about the colony's readiness to appreciate European art music on the world stage.[35] The commissioners had heavily promoted the idea of 'cultural progress' to justify Cowen's expense, and he was championed in the local press along the same lines.[36] The British musical press too, perhaps a little paternalistically, described his arrival on similar terms. As the *Manchester Guardian* reported, Cowen

---

[30] Geoffrey Edgar, 'Musical Arrangements for the International Exhibition', *Sydney Morning Herald*, 23 May 1879, p. 7, quoted in Roslyn Maguire, 'Paolo Giorza, Director of Music: The Most Accessible Art', in Peter Proudfoot, Roslyn Maguire, and Robert Freestone (eds), *Colonial City Global City: Sydney's International Exhibition 1879* (Darlinghurst, 2000), pp. 129–47, at pp. 131–2.

[31] Roslyn Maguire, '"Pleasure of a High Order": Paolo Giorza and Music at Sydney's 1879 International Exhibition', *Context: Journal of Music Research*, 22 (2001), 41–50, at p. 45; Maguire, 'Paolo Giorza', p. 140.

[32] Frederic Hymen Cowen, *My Art and My Friends* (London, 1913), p. 151–2.

[33] Calculated at 'How Much is it Worth?', *Thom Blake Historian* <http://www.thomblake.com.au/secondary/hisdata/calculate.php> [accessed 7 Jun. 2019].

[34] Royle, 'Preparing to Exhibit', p. 54.

[35] *Ibid*, p. 62.

[36] *Ibid*, p. 55.

had brought with him so much music that he could not 'but raise the taste of the local public'.[37] Throughout his tenure, Cowen's exhibition concerts were described in hyperbolic language of a kind commonly used when describing Australian demonstrations of European standards, with some performances labelled 'a red-letter day in the history of music in Victoria', regarded as ushering in 'a new era in music', or capable of 'contribut[ing] greatly to the enlightenment of the public as to what is excellent'.[38]

Despite being employed to educate and elevate public taste through a demonstration of 'high art', both Giorza and Cowen's orchestral concerts sat at the intersection between education and entertainment. In Sydney, for example, several 'Festival' concerts were intended to increase familiarity with a single 'great' composer, such as Beethoven or Mozart. But in these programmes, serious works of 'high art' were balanced by 'lighter' pieces. At the Beethoven Festival, following a performance of the Piano Concerto in C major and the overture *Die Weihe des Hauses,* were selections from Benedict's opera *The Brides of Venice*, Waldteufel's 'A Toi' waltz, and an orchestral medley called 'Gems of Scotland'. At the Mozart Festival, a number of arias, the overture to *Don Giovanni,* and one of the symphonies in D, were paired with popular ballads, including 'Alice, Where Art Thou' by Joseph Ascher (1829–69).[39]

At these concerts, many critics highlighted how responsive the audiences were to the 'high art' works, as if to demonstrate the success of the Exhibition's rational recreational endeavour. As the *Sydney Morning Herald* documented proudly, the 'thoroughly attentive audience' was evidence of 'how great an interest is taken in classical music' in the colony.[40] The critic for the *Sydney Mail and New South Wales Advertiser* also praised local comprehension of the music, 'proved by the riveted attention and perfect stillness of the audience'.[41] That these concerts were received as educational and elevating was further demonstrated by the negative reception of the more 'popular' works that also appeared on the programmes. 'Love and War' by Thomas Cooke (1782–1848), for example, heard during the Beethoven Festival, was singled out as sounding 'harshly on our ears', and 'painful to hear' while the 'very air' was still full of the 'elevating influence' of Beethoven.[42]

Many of Cowen's orchestral programmes in Melbourne were similarly intended to educate their audiences in canonic symphonic works. Although

---

[37] 'Music at the Melbourne Exhibition', *Manchester Guardian*, p. 8.
[38] Julius Herz, 'Cowen's Ruth', *Table Talk*, 14 Sep. 1888, p. 11; 'The Cantata and Poem', *Age*, 1 Aug. 1888, p. 13, quoted in Royle, 'Preparing to Exhibit', p. 55; For a discussion of similar language used in the Australian reception of Wagner, see Suzanne Cole and Kerry Murphy, 'Wagner in the Antipodes', *WagnerSpectrum*, 4:2 (2008), 237–68, at p. 239.
[39] 'International Exhibition', *Evening News*, 7 Nov. 1879, p. 3.
[40] 'Music at the Garden Palace', *Sydney Morning Herald*, 31 Oct. 1879, p. 3.
[41] Launcelot, 'Music & Drama', *Sydney Mail and New South Wales Advertiser*, 1 Nov. 1879, p. 762.
[42] Ibid.

many programmes featured only single symphonic movements on programmes made up of shorter works including overtures, gavottes, waltzes, and sections of popular operas and ballets, special concerts were given throughout the season making a feature of a single symphony in its entirety. Over the course of the Exhibition, audiences heard many complete symphonies by Mozart, Haydn, Schubert, and Robert Schumann (1810–56), and all nine Beethoven symphonies were performed at least twice.[43]

The repetition of works was considered important in fostering a public understanding of the music. Beethoven's fifth symphony, noted by the *Argus* as appealing 'on a first hearing to the instinct of even the musically uneducated', was thoroughly familiar by its fourth repetition, allowing listeners to express 'unbounded admiration in the most unmistakable manner'.[44] This, the *Argus* critic felt, was 'the right and proper way of elevating the public taste':

> A work that pleases most on a first hearing is generally the one to get easily tired of, whereas a great work, full of grand and original thoughts ... is with many, on a first hearing, little better than mere jargon. On a second hearing the light begins to dawn, whilst on a third the whole appears in dazzling beauty, and after such an experience the listener cares no more for the tawdry, flimsy manufacturer that originally pleased.[45]

The *Argus* also noted this effect on a Strauss waltz, performed twice several months apart, which by the second hearing was 'so little to the liking of the audience that no more Strauss waltzes were heard in the concert hall'.[46] This demonstrated, apparently, that the 'elevation' of public taste was working. Audiences had rejected the 'lower' work, in favour of repetitions of works of high art.

Overall, the press in both Sydney and Melbourne were impressed with how the exhibitions created opportunities to educate the public in musical 'high art', and the vigour with which these were taken up. In 1879, there was a general optimism that such programming would have a lasting effect on Sydney's cultural life.[47] The *Sydney Morning Herald* noted the intermingling of classes and communities at the concerts, describing the 'nave and transept, galleries and basement' as 'alike thronged' at one of Giorza's concerts by 'all classes of the community – the hardy sons of toil, the men of commons and well-to-do citizens'.[48] The Brisbane *Telegraph*'s Exhibition correspondent also noted with pleasure that the music was:

> calculated to improve the taste and elevate the minds; and that which may be described as of the 'musical fireworks' order being entirely discarded. This fact also speaks well for 'the people' who listen with evident feelings of great pleasure to the strains of Beethoven, Mendelssohn and others of the great masters whose

---

[43] 'The Centennial International Exhibition', *Argus*, 1 Feb. 1889, p. 9.
[44] *Ibid.*
[45] *Ibid.*
[46] *Ibid.*
[47] Maguire, 'Pleasure of a High Order', p. 52.
[48] 'News of the Day', *Sydney Morning Herald*, 29 Sep. 1879, p. 5, quoted in Maguire, 'Paolo Giorza', p. 139.

works are generally supposed to be thoroughly appreciated by those only who have been 'educated' to their thorough enjoyment.[49]

Critics were similarly quick to describe the Melbourne audience's appreciation and understanding of European art music as it was presented by Cowen. While it was believed that Australians inherently possessed the capacity to understand music, as the *Argus* described, just as 'the healthiest plant requires water and sunshine', so too must musical taste be 'nurtured in the atmosphere of art'.[50] The 'nurturing' environment of the Exhibition meant, as the *Centennial Magazine* claimed, that audience members who had 'never been abroad' could 'rapturously' applaud concerts made up entirely of previously unheard works of European high-art music. Such a phenomenon was regarded as clear evidence that 'music has progressed in Australia'.[51]

To prove that such colonial 'progress' in the 'development of taste' had been made, organisers at Melbourne 1888 put their audiences to the test by holding a plebiscite concert towards the end of the Exhibition season. The final programme – selected by a public poll of previously heard works – contained Beethoven's 'Pastoral' symphony, Wagner's overtures to *Tannhäuser* and *Rienzi*, Handel's Largo for Organ, Harp, and Strings, and Liszt's Hungarian Rhapsody no. 1. Other strong contenders included Cowen's own 'Scandinavian' symphony, other Beethoven and Schubert symphonies, and Rossini's *William Tell* overture.[52] This collection of works demonstrates clearly Cowen's influence on public taste. There were, however, reservations about the plebiscite, with the Melbourne correspondent of the *Hamilton Spectator* joking that the process had caused 'misery' among 'lovers of music' – or at least those who 'pretend to know about that art' – by putting them on the spot to name their favourite works. In the *Spectator*'s view, 'not to vote argued ignorance … but to pose as a musician and name something as a symphony which in reality was a gavotte or a nocturne would be worse than awful'.[53]

One of the most striking aspects of the plebiscite programme was the domination of Wagner, with many of his other works – beyond the two that made the final programme – also ranking highly. Wagner's popularity had been growing steadily in Australia over the previous decade, since the first Melbourne performance of *Lohengrin* performed by W.S. Lyster's opera company in 1877.[54] In Australia, Wagner's music did not carry the cultural baggage that it did in parts of Europe, particularly France, where narratives that tied it to German nationalism were accentuated by the political tensions of the aftermath of the

---

[49] 'Sydney Exhibition', *The Telegraph* [Brisbane], 3 Nov. 1879, p. 2.
[50] 'Music at the Exhibition. Grand Plebiscite Concert', *Argus*, 3 Dec. 1888, p. 8.
[51] F.W. Elsner, 'The Progress of Instrumental Music in Australia', *Centennial Magazine*, 1:8 (Mar. 1889), 544–9, at p. 545.
[52] 'Centennial International Exhibition. The Plebiscite Concert', *Argus*, 26 Nov. 1888, p. 8.
[53] 'Melbourne Gossip', *Hamilton Spectator*, 29 Nov. 1888, p. 4.
[54] Cole and Murphy, 'Wagner in the Antipodes', p. 251

Franco-Prussian war.[55] It similarly faced none of the 'critical resistance to the so-called "music of the future"' that it experienced in Victorian England in the previous decades.[56] Indeed, for a colonial Australian audience, 'the idea of the future could not help but dominate the imagination', potentially making audiences even more receptive.[57] In general, however, and despite having a significant German population, the Australian response of Wagner appears not to have engaged deeply in the aesthetic and philosophical discourses that characterised the reception of his music elsewhere: lacking, perhaps, 'the critical or rhetorical privilege' that his works were given in Europe.[58] Equally, the challenge of Wagner's *Zukunftsmusik* could hardly be fully attained through the performance of short excerpts, despite concert performances of operatic excerpts contributing significantly to his establishment in the musical canon.[59] Yet, as Frederick William Elsner (*c*.1857–1901) – surgeon and pioneer of dermatology – wrote in the *Centennial Magazine*, in Australia '*everyone knows* that Wagner thought he had found out the secret of the failure of composers of opera', 'how he wrote, lectured, and composed in support of his doctrines with all the energy and fanaticism of a religious enthusiast', and of the 'blood that is spilt over this never ending controversy'. But these matters were regarded as entirely peripheral to 'how much footing the music of Wagner … has gained in Australasia'.[60]

Nonetheless, Wagner's music was used 'as a yardstick against which the sophistication of Melbourne audiences was being measured', from its first performance in Melbourne to the Exhibition.[61] Although many complete operas – and much of the repertoire Cowen played – had been heard in Melbourne previously, some critics felt that these works 'cannot be said to have been heard before' given how differently they sounded under Cowen's direction.[62] As part of the series, Cowen was also responsible for introducing the all-Wagner programme to Melbourne, on the model of those heard in Britain and America,

---

[55] See Rachel Orzech, *Claiming Wagner for France: Music and Politics in the Parisian Press, 1933–1944* (Rochester, forthcoming), chapter 2. See also for discussion of the nationalist use of Wagner's music in 'the so-called rapprochement activities' of the later 1937 Paris Exposition Universelle. Many thanks to Rachel for allowing me to read her manuscript.

[56] Katherine Fry, 'Music and Character in the London Reception of Wagner', in Sarah Collins (ed.), *Music and Victorian Liberalism: Composing the Liberal Subject* (Cambridge, 2019), pp. 201–19, at p. 201.

[57] Peter Tregear, 'Post-Colonial Tristesse: Aspects of Wagner Down Under', *Context: Journal of Music Research*, 39 (2014), 69–77, at p. 71.

[58] Ibid.

[59] William Weber, *Canonic Repertories and the French Musical Press: Lully to Wagner* (Rochester, 2021), see chapter eight, 'Richard Wagner, Concert Life, and Musical Canon in Paris, 1860–1914', pp. 228–66.

[60] Elsner, 'The Progress of Instrumental Music in Australia', p. 544, my emphasis.

[61] Cole and Murphy, 'Wagner in the Antipodes', p. 251.

[62] 'Orchestral Concert', *Age*, 15 Aug. 1888, p. 9, quoted in Cole and Murphy, 'Wagner in the Antipodes', p. 248.

giving five such performances at the Exhibition. These concerts gave a significant boost to Wagner's popularity: as the author Ada Cambridge (1844–1926) described, the Exhibition was where she 'learned to be a Wagnerite, after several unsuccessful attempts'.[63]

The plebiscite concert was, for many critics, concrete proof that the Australian public had become 'civilised', and now held an accepted 'European' taste. Many reported with pride Cowen's comments that he was 'highly satisfied' with the audience's response, and with his suggestion that taste in Melbourne was in 'general accord' with London and other European capitals.[64] The *Official Record* regarded the poll as 'a valuable indication of the correctness' of Australian musical taste, and the *Age* considered it to be 'in the highest degree creditable' given that 'Beethoven, Handel, Wagner and Liszt are representative of the highest schools of composition'.[65] It was argued that these concerts disproved 'the allegation that the public prefer music of a light, and commonplace description'.[66] When reported in Britain, the *Musical World* joked that English readers were 'astonished' at the programme: the plebiscite concert 'may well surprise those who fondly believe that, however Antipodean Australia may be in other ways, its music taste is as unprogressive as our own', concluding that 'there is something in living at the other end of the world, after all'!'[67]

❧ Choral Music

Amongst the grand orchestral concerts given at Sydney 1879 and Melbourne 1888 were also several performances of complete oratorios. Choral music played an important role in the educational-entertainment programmes of other exhibitions too, with oratorios also heard at Adelaide 1887 and Edinburgh 1890. As a mainstay of nineteenth-century British culture, representing – as Howard Smither describes – 'morality, self-improvement, and social respectability', the importance of oratorio 'is virtually impossible to exaggerate'.[68] The presence of vocal societies capable of presenting such music was regarded in Britain as an essential marker of the nation's musicality, and critics often defended England from hackneyed claims that it was *das Land ohne Musik* by boasting of the 'monumentality' of its oratorio-performing forces.[69] As the art form considered the cultural pinnacle of the metropolitan centre, oratorio was an apt genre for those organising exhibitions – particularly in cities peripheral to London – to demonstrate their society's 'progress'.

---

[63] Ada Cambridge, *Thirty Years in Australia* (London, 1903), p. 186.
[64] 'Centennial International Exhibition. The Plebiscite Concert', *Argus*, p. 8.
[65] 'Orchestral Concerts', *Age*, 3 Dec. 1888, p. 5.
[66] 'Musical Events', *Leader*, 8 Dec. 1888, p. 27.
[67] 'Facts and Comments', *Musical World*, 69:3 (19 Jan. 1889), 36–7, at p. 37.
[68] Howard E. Smither, *A History of the Oratorio*, vol. 4 'The Oratorio in the Nineteenth and Twentieth Centuries' (Chapel Hill, 1987), p. 249.
[69] Smither, *A History of the Oratorio*, p. 253.

Oratorio was therefore of huge importance in the British colonies. In Australia, where Britain's culture and history had a striking effect on thought and practice, musical institutions often replicated those of Britain in 'an atmosphere of excitement and adulation'.[70] As in Britain, choral societies were established across the colonies: in Victoria, for example, the Melbourne Philharmonic Society was founded in 1853, giving the first Melbourne performances of many works by Handel, Haydn, and Mendelssohn, while provincial societies were also instituted across the colony.[71] By the 1860s and '70s many Australian capitals had a 'prospering tradition of oratorio and vocal music', where a substantial number of local singers were supported by touring European artists, conductors, and impresarios.[72] By the exhibitions, then, the Australian public would have been familiar with much oratorio. As with orchestral music, however, on the world stage of an international exhibition, it was important to assert that Australia could equal Britain in the practice of art and music. As such, oratorio performances were considered some of the most important musical events of the exhibitions.

The choral tradition in Scotland, too – which influenced the presentation of oratorio at Edinburgh 1890 – was related to similar activities in England. This is, perhaps, unsurprising, given that during the nineteenth century, Scottish people held multiple inter-related identities, being at once 'citizens of Scotland, the United Kingdom, and the British Empire'.[73] Scotland therefore, in addition to an independent musical tradition, had a similarly long practice of choral singing. While the metropolitan centres of Glasgow and Edinburgh had prestigious Choral Unions, by the 1880s choral societies existed in almost every town, regardless of its size, with members drawn from the local community.[74] Repertoire performed by Scottish societies was relatively similar to that heard in England – dominated by Handel and Mendelssohn – but there is also evidence that they showed a greater interest and inclination towards new music.[75] The overwhelming presence of Handel, however, as in the English tradition, was most distinctly reflected in the exhibition programming.

The repertoire, timing and scale of the oratorios performed at the various exhibitions differed significantly by city. An oratorio was given once a month

---

[70] Richard White, 'The Outsider's Gaze and the Representation of Australia', in Don Grant and Graham Seal (eds), *Australia in the World: Perceptions and Possibilities* (Perth, 1994), pp. 22–8, at p. 24; Thérèse Radic, 'Major Choral Organizations in Late Nineteenth-Century Melbourne', *Nineteenth-Century Music Review*, 2:2 (2005), 3–28, at p. 12.

[71] Janice B. Stockigt, 'A Study of British Influence on Musical Taste and Programming: New Choral Works Introduced to Audiences by the Melbourne Philharmonic Society, 1876–1901', *Nineteenth-Century Music Review*, 2:2 (2005), 29–53, at p. 30.

[72] Kirby, 'The Worst Oratorio Ever', p. 209.

[73] Jane Mallinson, 'Choral Societies and Nationalist Mobilization in the Nineteenth Century: A Scottish Perspective', in Krisztina Lajosi and Andreas Stynen (eds), *Choral Societies and Nationalism in Europe* (Boston, 2015), pp. 70–82, at p. 77.

[74] *Ibid*, p. 76.

[75] *Ibid*, p. 78.

during Sydney 1879, all of which were performed by the Sacred Choral Association, an organisation formed especially for this purpose. The first – Haydn's *The Creation* – was heard in October by over 14,000 people, and similarly large attendances were recorded for those that followed: Handel's *Israel in Egypt* was performed in November, Mendelssohn's *Elijah* in December, *Messiah* in January, *Crown of Thorns* – the first composed in an Australian colony – by Charles Packer (1810–83) in February, and the season concluded with Benedict's *St Peter* in early April.[76] Organisers explicitly referenced the British choral festivals in staging these, with the commissioners hoping that they would be as 'successful' as 'the musical festivals in Britain'.[77]

The oratorio performances given at Adelaide 1887 were organised under quite different circumstances, with *Messiah* and *Judas Maccabaeus* only heard due to public demand. In early November, the Adelaide Musical Association had given an extremely well-received performance of *Judas Maccabaeus* at the Adelaide Town Hall, in response to which many letters appeared in the local press suggesting the performance be repeated at the Exhibition. One letter explained that such a performance could satisfy a 'public taste' for 'something more inspiring and out of the common' than the other music heard at the Exhibition so far.[78] Another suggested, along similar lines, that it could be 'a pleasant relief' from previous 'puerile in the extreme' performances of *Dick Whittington and His Cat*.[79] The organisers and Musical Association agreed to this proposal, but before *Judas Maccabaeus* was heard, a second oratorio – *Messiah* – was announced and given three days before Christmas by the Adelaide Philharmonic Society.[80] The suggestion to present oratorio at the Exhibition was clearly made with an awareness of what the form represented: as an 'enlightening' genre that could 'improve' public taste, but also as a symbol of sophisticated and 'civilised' European culture. As one critic wrote, these works could provide a 'healthy ... encouragement of the appreciation of high class music' to the public. But they could also demonstrate to 'visitors from the other colonies and England that the "Farinaceous Village" can boast of being able to produce besides the "golden grain" the lovely music of the great master of composition [Handel] in a manner that leaves little to be desired'.[81]

In Melbourne, Cowen's concert series contained the largest number of choral works of any of the 1880s exhibitions, with nineteen performances of oratorios or cantatas heard across the season, performed by the Centennial Exhibition choir (depicted in Figure 18 performing at the opening ceremony). Each of these concerts saw the building 'filled to its utmost holding capacity', with many

---

[76] *Official Record* [Sydney], p. lxvii.
[77] Ibid, p. xxxv.
[78] Musicus, 'Music at the Exhibition', *Evening Journal*, 4 Nov. 1887, p. 3.
[79] Veritas, 'Judas Maccabaeus', *South Australian Advertiser*, 10 Nov. 1887, p. 6.
[80] 'Handel's Messiah', *South Australian Register*, 22 Dec. 1887, p. 4.
[81] Ibid.

Figure 18. 'The Opening of the Centennial Exhibition – The Choir Rendering the Cantata', *Illustrated Australian News*, 399 (15 Aug. 1888), p. 145. NLA https://trove.nla.gov.au/newspaper/article/59981080.

thousands of people reportedly turned away at the door.[82] This overwhelming attendance is surprising given the number of times each work was repeated. *Elijah* was heard four times, while *The Creation* and two cantatas – Cowen's *Sleeping Beauty* and Sullivan's *Golden Legend* – were performed twice each. Cowen's *Ruth* was performed five times in the space of five months, in an occurrence the *Argus* believed to be 'unique in the history of oratorios' anywhere in the world.[83] Similarly, Christmas 1888 saw four performances of *Messiah* in Melbourne in one week, with three at the Exhibition followed by a separate

---

[82] 'Grand Choral Concert. Cowen's Ruth', *Argus*, 7 Sep. 1888, p. 6; Andante, 'Music at the Exhibition', *Australasian*, 22 Sep. 1888, p. 35.
[83] 'Grand Choral Concert: Ruth', *Argus*, 8 Oct. 1888, p. 10.

performance by the Philharmonic Society.[84] The press were evidently proud that such a 'unique' undertaking of high-status art had occurred at a colonial exhibition, as this demonstrated the sort of cultural development and progress they were so keen to present to the rest of the world. These oratorio concerts pleased everybody – commissioners included – as they were also extremely profitable, taking over £600 per night, in total more than covering Cowen's fee.[85]

The oratorio performances at all the exhibitions were among the musical events most extensively covered in the contemporary press. Critics praised the music itself, but were particularly positive in their depictions of the audience for demonstrating their refined taste, enthusiastic response, and overall cultural 'progress'. At Sydney, the exhibition building was always filled many hours before a performance began. While some exhibitors complained that their displays were swallowed up by the mass of people – during *Israel in Egypt*, 'the trophies and pagodas stood like islands amidst a sea of faces' – there appears to have been a genuine enjoyment of the music amongst the crowd.[86] Such large attendances were remarkable given reports of the Sydney summer heat, with many critics referencing the uncomfortable conditions as evidence of the audiences' dedication. The *South Australian Register*'s critic described the temperature during *Crown of Thorns* as that 'which makes you feel as though you were being stewed ... as your inner garments clung to you like an extemporized wet-sheet arrangement'.[87] They concluded, however, that the work was worth such discomfort. The *Sydney Morning Herald*, too, described – in reference to *Messiah* – the audience's reverence for the work as visible in the 'the eager, earnest attention with which, score in hand, numbers came long before the hour fixed for commencing', waiting patiently 'for more than four hours to get even so imperfect a reminder of the majestic grandeur of this outpouring of the genius of the mighty Handel'.[88]

Adelaide audiences were similarly praised for their numbers when *Judas Maccabaeus* was finally performed in January 1888, with 'one of the largest attendances of the season' drawn by the 'guarantee' of a good performance.[89] Much like at Sydney, the hall was completely filled, and the adjacent galleries and courts were overcrowded with people attempting to hear the music.[90] Both this performance, and *Messiah* in December the previous year, were very well received, with critics arguing that 'both the educated and uneducated lover of music' had evidently understood and appreciated such works of high art,[91] as they 'testified their approval in loud applause'.[92]

---

[84] 'Music at the Exhibition: The Messiah', *Argus*, 28 Dec. 1888, p. 5.
[85] 'Victoria', *Brisbane Courier*, 10 Jan. 1889, p. 4.
[86] 'Sydney International Exhibition', *Argus*, 11 Nov. 1879, p. 7.
[87] 'Sydney International Exhibition', *South Australian Register*, 1 Mar. 1880, p. 5.
[88] 'Music at the Garden Palace', *Sydney Morning Herald*, 5 Jan. 1880, p. 5.
[89] 'Adelaide Jubilee Exhibition', *South Australian Advertiser*, 6 Jan. 1888, p. 6.
[90] 'The Jubilee Exhibition', *South Australian Register*, 6 Jan. 1888, p. 6.
[91] 'The Messiah', *Evening Journal*, 23 Dec. 1887, p. 3.
[92] 'Adelaide Jubilee Exhibition', *South Australian Advertiser*, p. 6.

Given the general awareness of oratorio as one of the most profoundly enlightening genres, and the framing of Cowen as a bearer of European culture, it is unsurprising that his oratorio *Ruth* was the most favourably reviewed of any presented at an exhibition during this period. Through *Ruth*, Cowen was described as an agent opening up 'a way between the art treasures of the old world and the young continent'.[93] The *Argus* believed *Ruth* was 'ranked high amongst the greatest productions of modern times',[94] while the *Australasian* pronounced it 'the generous outpouring of a mind with apparently inexhaustible inspiration in the matter of graceful tune'.[95] Cowen – as conductor of his own work – also drew appreciation from the performers. Julius Herz (1841–98), writing in *Table Talk*, described the 'privilege and pleasure' felt by the performers in giving 'satisfaction to their distinguished conductor'.[96] *Ruth*'s final performance led to ten minutes of applause 'without cessation', and the women of the choir wore an ear of wheat in their hair, 'obtained from the South Australian Court', as a symbolic gesture of gratitude to Cowen, referencing the character Ruth's work in the wheat and barley harvests.[97]

The Melbourne press, like that of Sydney and Adelaide, were quick to point out how the public response to *Ruth* and the other oratorios signalled a cultured and 'civilised' colonial audience. 'The musical taste of the city' was praised, as was the demand that secured so many repetitions of each work.[98] The *Argus* believed that *Ruth* – relatively unconventional in structure – was not composed to 'tickle the ears of the groundlings', requiring instead a sophisticated audience like that of Melbourne to comprehend it.[99] Cowen's high European standards were also seen as useful for Australian audiences. *Table Talk* noted that after hearing *Messiah* 'under such favourable conditions', people would be able to use the performance as 'a recognised standard of excellence by which they can measure successive performances'.[100]

While successful performances of oratorio in Australia were regarded as representative of the colonial audiences' developing taste and cultural progress, the purpose and reception of the oratorios heard in Scotland at Edinburgh 1890 was quite different. The Exhibition's series began in May with the Greenock Choral Union's performance of *The Creation*, followed two days later by the Dundee Amateur Choral Union's *Judas Maccabaeus*. The Paisley Choral Union gave Handel's *Samson* and the Glasgow Choral Union performed *Messiah* in June. The season then closed in early July with the Portobello Choral Society performing Handel's *Ode for St Cecilia's Day*. With the exception of Glasgow, all these societies came to Edinburgh from smaller towns, and many in the

---

[93] 'Facts and Comments', *Musical World*, 68:13 (30 Mar. 1889), 195–6, at p. 195.
[94] 'Grand Choral Concert. Cowen's Ruth', *Argus*, p. 6.
[95] Andante, 'Music at the Exhibition', p. 35.
[96] Herz, 'Cowen's Ruth', p. 11.
[97] 'The Last Exhibition Concert', *Weekly Times*, 2 Feb. 1889, p. 5.
[98] 'Grand Choral Concert: Ruth', *Argus*, p. 10.
[99] Ibid.
[100] 'The Messiah', *Table Talk*, 28 Dec. 1888, p. 12.

regional press saw their local society's performance as a test of their own town's musical capacity.

Edinburgh – the Scottish metropolis – was known for its particularly critical and unaffected audience. While oratorio was again used as a symbol of musical progress and sophistication, this time it was the performers who had to prove themselves to the audience. Many of the major British musical periodicals made this clear: the *Musical Herald* explained that, in addition to being 'a most pleasant attraction', the exhibition oratorio concerts would give 'people an opportunity, otherwise impossible, of hearing the musical associations of quite a host of different towns, and of judging of the advance of music in the districts represented'.[101] The benefit of raising musical standards across Scotland was also emphasised, with the *Herald* stating that it 'cannot but do incalculable good' for the societies' own development to 'put forth a grand effort to appear to advantage before critical Edinburgh'.[102]

This shift in the direction of who was demonstrating their 'musical progress' to whom can be seen in the disparity of interest in these performances within the different types of press. Although the wider musical press made occasional references to these concerts, the majority of reports came from the various choral societies' own towns. The *Musical Times* substantially reviewed only the already well-regarded Glasgow Choral Union's performance in the 'sister metropolis', whereas the *Greenock Telegraph and Clyde Shipping Gazette* gave many details of their own Union's performance of *The Creation*.[103] The *Musical Times* did, however, briefly note the 'most favourable impression' the Greenock Choral Union made by their 'round body of tone and the good balance of parts'.[104] In Portobello – now a suburb of Edinburgh, but in the nineteenth century its own town – the *Advertiser* was extremely proud of their local society, which was 'pretty well up to the mark' in performing the *Ode for St Cecilia's Day*. They believed it was creditable that their 'local choristers ... exhibited so little nervousness before so large an audience' including 'an encouraging attendance of well-wishers from the district'.[105]

The *Dundee Courier & Argus* gave much detail of their local Union's performance, and of the 'two hundred performers ... accompanied by about an equal number of friends, who ... showed their interest in their fellow townsfolk', giving details of the rail route used to get to Edinburgh and the weather along the way.[106] They were pleased to note that on 'the first occasion on which the members of the Dundee Amateur Choral Union have sung out of Dundee' it was 'gratifying to be able to report that they never sang better, and it was

---

[101] 'News from All Parts', *Musical Herald*, 1 Jul. 1890, p. 441.
[102] *Ibid.*
[103] 'Music in Edinburgh', *Musical Times*, 31:570 (1 Aug. 1890), p. 490; 'Greenock Choral Union', *Greenock Telegraph and Clyde Shipping Gazette*, 26 May 1890, p. 2.
[104] 'Music in Edinburgh', *Musical Times*, 31:569 (1 Jul. 1890), 413–14, at p. 413.
[105] 'Gleanings', *Portobello Advertiser*, 4 Jul. 1890, p. 4.
[106] 'Dundee Amateur Choral Union at the Edinburgh Exhibition', *Dundee Courier & Argus*, 30 May 1890, p. 3.

perhaps even still more pleasant to note the enthusiastic reception with which their efforts were met'.[107] The *Dundee Advertiser* was also excited by the reception in Edinburgh 'accorded to the Choral Union by an audience so critical in musical matters', which they considered to be 'most encouraging'.[108]

Oratorio held a prominent place in the rational recreation movement, exerting what was believed to be a 'powerful moral influence' that could be incorporated into the concerted efforts to 'improve' the lives of the public across the class spectrum.[109] It is entirely appropriate, then, that oratorio also held a prominent place in the exhibitions' musical arrangements, themselves institutions of rational recreation. But oratorio too could be symbolic of other processes. In Australia, the idea of self-improvement was taken on by the population as a whole – perhaps a consequence of the more permeable class boundaries in the colonial society – and it was not just the lower and middle classes expecting to learn from its performance. Oratorio, as a transplanted, seminal British musical institution, used in Britain to 'civilise' the lower classes, was fully supported as a means of demonstrating both the 'civilisation' and 'progress' of the colonies.[110] In Scotland, oratorio was still seen as demonstrative of the highest class of music, with all of its moral and educational overtones. But in the exhibition context it was used not by the hosts – already relatively comfortable with their social position – but by smaller societies attempting to demonstrate the breadth of their musical capabilities to what was widely considered an elite audience.

Ultimately, however, while noting the 'improving' qualities of the music and the audiences' expression of their 'civilisation', in many cases the most overwhelming element of the press coverage was simply a tremendous joy. Ideological narratives aside, musicians, critics, and audiences alike appeared deeply thankful toward the forces that allowed these works to be presented on such a scale, with one critic stating at the end of the Sydney Exhibition, without these regular performances, 'there are people in Sydney who are asking themselves whether there is anything left worth living for'!'[111] The joy of these musical events was summed up in the *South Australian Register*, describing the Sydney performance of *Messiah*'s famous 'Hallelujah' chorus:

> That strain of majestic and glorious music, which has so often lifted up gathered thousands by its ocean swell of exultant song, seemed on the occasion to make every heart beat. If we may judge of the feelings of others by our own feelings, we were conscious of such a quickened pulse, such an electric thrill of excitement that made every nerve to quiver in the pent-up excitement of a great gladness that we could have shouted. And that this was the case was pretty manifest when the crash of the final 'for ever' fell on the ear. Then, like the voice of many waters,

---

[107] *Ibid.*

[108] 'Dundee Amateur Choral Union at the Edinburgh Exhibition', *Dundee Advertiser*, 30 May 1890, p. 5.

[109] Howard Smither, '"Messiah" and Progress in Victorian England', *Early Music*, 13:3 (1985), 329–48, at p. 343.

[110] Scott, *Sounds of the Metropolis*, p. 61.

[111] 'The Exhibition', *Sydney Mail and New South Wales Advertiser*, 24 Apr. 1880, p. 800.

rose the responsive applause of that dense mass. Again, again, and again it rang through the place. And the strain, which might be regarded as worthy to be the Coronation Anthem of the Lord of all when He comes as the King on whose head are many crowns, again rolled forth.[112]

In the examples of both orchestral and choral concerts – all of which were staged with 'improving' or instructive intentions – music was considered to fulfil the educational aims of the exhibition-institution through the edifying influence of 'high art'. Such ideas clearly circulated throughout the Empire, and the music at the exhibitions demonstrates many educational and musical philosophies already present in nineteenth-century critical thought. But these performances were also successful because they captured an attentive audience who appreciated the music on its own terms, regardless of such narratives. This was even more the case in the presentation of 'popular' musical forms. These, however, drew a distinctly different critical response in the musical press.

---

[112] 'Sydney Exhibition', *South Australian Register*, 2 Feb. 1880, p. 6.

CHAPTER 6

Music for Leisure and Entertainment

In a lecture to the Society of Arts in November 1884, Ernest Hart (1835–98) – surgeon and editor of the *British Medical Journal* – reported his observations of the recently closed London International Health Exhibition. 'It was often said by the public scorner', he began, 'when walking through the crowded course of the Exhibition … "This is a Health Exhibition – Where is the health?"'. The popular response to this question, Hart determined, was 'outside in the gardens'.[1] From their inception, exhibitions had been designed to combine education, entertainment, and spectacle. While their educational aspects generally remained confined to the inside of the buildings, by the 1880s the gardens that surrounded them had become hives of entertainment. These outdoor spaces, in layout and function, inherited the traditions of the seventeenth- and eighteenth-century European 'pleasure garden', combining fountains, walkways, grottos, and spectacular lighting effects with a wide variety of refreshments and carnival amusements. The centrepiece of these gardens was the bandstand, and military or brass bands and light orchestras filled the programmes of most exhibitions, playing to a consistently numerous and attentive public. The bands in their impressive garden setting were, for many, the main drawcard of the exhibitions. As the *Illustrated London News* explained in 1886, 'we have heard several honest pleasure-takers avow that they go, year by year … not to inspect the objects displayed there, but to listen to the music'.[2] The *St James's Gazette* concurred; most exhibition visitors only wanted 'to stroll upon the terraces and amongst the flowers and fountains, and to lounge within hearing of good music well played'.[3]

But what constituted 'good' music? For the critical musical press this was the kind of music that could enlighten and 'improve' the public, and was found in the high art of symphonies, oratorios, and the works of the canonic greats. It was certainly not the kind of music curated to popular taste or to make money. The bands in the exhibition gardens were, therefore, categorically *not* good music. The same could be said of the organ recitals that were given inside the exhibitions. While the quasi-religious atmosphere of buildings was heightened by the performance of organ music, critics were frequently frustrated by the organists' supposed pandering to popular taste,

---

[1] Ernest Hart, 'The International Health Exhibition: Its Influence and Possible Sequels', *Journal of the Society of Arts*, 33 (28 Nov. 1884), 35–58, at p. 55.
[2] 'Our Note Book', *Illustrated London News*, 29 May 1886, p. 560.
[3] 'The Lesson of the Health Exhibition', *St James's Gazette*, 25 Jul. 1884, p. 6.

with repertoire more closely resembling the bands in the gardens than the transcendental art expected of them.

Exhibitions were expensive endeavours to run, so it was imperative to encourage as many people to visit as many times as possible if they were to cover their costs. From this perspective, music played a utilitarian role, and bands and organists – performing selections and potpourris extracted from popular works to large and appreciative audiences – were an extremely profitable drawcard. Many in the musical press lamented the explicitly commercial and populist nature of this music, considering it to draw attention away from the 'legitimate' educational aspects of the exhibitions. In contrast, however, many rational recreation and public health advocates from outside the musical community considered 'good' music to be *any* music, if it encouraged people to pursue leisure outdoors. In this sense, if the public came to the gardens, the bands were already a positive influence, regardless of their additional commercial function. As Hart concluded, 'the eagerness of the English people to resort to healthful means of outdoor amusement' at the Exhibition 'was in itself a valuable result'.[4]

Although the music described in this chapter is labelled 'popular' – largely because it *was*: huge crowds came specifically to hear it – this term, when presented in binary opposition to 'art' music, is what Dave Russell calls 'a troublesome concept' without clear definition.[5] Yet, as the arguments in the press make clear, nineteenth-century musical authorities certainly understood there to be a distinction between 'high' and 'popular' art, and the music discussed here was critiqued in these terms. Perhaps a better label might be what Derek Scott defines as 'nonserious music'. This is music perceived as 'not tax[ing] the mind', being 'consumed merely as an amusement, usually alongside the distractions of talking, laughing, or dancing'; a music defined by its 'supposed complicity with acts of effortless consumption'.[6] This definition comes from the behaviour of the audience while engaging with it, and fits with the music given by bands and organists at the exhibitions. Little of this music was performed in traditional concert halls, with the audience focusing purely on its artistic qualities. Instead it was heard alongside conversation, promenading, and other distractions.

❧ Gardens, Lights, and Music in the 'Open Air'

From the Great Exhibition of 1851, through the 1860s and '70s, the success of international exhibitions in London steadily declined. Reinvigorating the institution in the 1880s, organisers adopted a 'more visitor-friendly approach' taking cues from successful public establishments, including leisure palaces, and the recently held and more entertainment-focused American and French

---

[4] Hart, 'The International Health Exhibition', pp. 55–6.
[5] Dave Russell, *Popular Music in England, 1840–1914: A Social History* (Manchester, 1997), p. 1.
[6] Derek B. Scott, *Sounds of the Metropolis: The Nineteenth-Century Popular Music Revolution in London, New York, Paris, and Vienna* (Oxford, 2008), p. 87.

exhibitions.[7] Common to these institutions was the presence of pleasure gardens, filled with music and spectacle. Although the original commercial pleasure gardens of London – including famous examples like Marylebone and Vauxhall – had closed by the 1880s, their influence in combining music and landscaping endured in municipal parks, botanical gardens, and zoos with ubiquitous bandstands and walks.[8] These outdoor spaces sprang from a desire to improve public health in over-crowded cities, but their additional recreational features – particularly music – were added when it was realised that most people 'would not visit parks simply for their own physical well-being'.[9]

Larger scale nineteenth-century leisure palaces, such as the rebuilt Crystal Palace at Sydenham, the Westminster Royal Aquarium and Winter Garden, and the Alexandra Palace, were part of this same tradition. The Sydenham Crystal Palace – initially fitted out with a theatre, concert room, and library – was described in its prospectus as providing 'refined recreation' to 'elevate the intellect, instruct the mind, [and] improve the hearts' of visitors who may 'have no other incentives to pleasure but such as the gin-palace, the dancing saloon and the alehouse can afford them'.[10] This moralistic tone, however, quickly abated and more entertainment attractions were incorporated – including model dinosaurs – while bands and popular organ recitals became increasingly prevalent.[11] The Alexandra Palace, opening in the early 1870s with its company seal reading 'healthy exercise, rational recreation', was designed along similar lines.[12] Alongside much music in diverse indoor and outdoor spaces, other amusements included snake charmers, archery fields, and the chance to observe 'a baby elephant taking its daily bath'.[13]

The London 1880s exhibitions used the gardens of the Royal Horticultural Society, situated between the exhibition building and the Royal Albert Hall. These gardens enclosed two bandstands, with adjacent promenades, refreshment rooms, and large fountains. In the evening, the space was illuminated with newly installed electric lighting (Figure 19). Music was given every afternoon and evening, with bands alternating programmes between the east and west bandstands

---

[7] Wilson Smith, 'Old London, Old Edinburgh: Constructing Historic Cities', in Marta Filipová (ed.), *Cultures of International Exhibitions 1840–1940* (Burlington, 2015), pp 203–30, at p. 206.

[8] Rachel Cowgill, 'Performance Alfresco: Music-Making in London's Pleasure Gardens', in Jonathan Conlin (ed.), *The Pleasure Garden, from Vauxhall to Coney Island* (Philadelphia, 2013), 100–26, at p. 126.

[9] Harriet Jordan, 'Public Parks, 1885–1914', *Garden History*, 22:1 (1994), 85–113, at p. 86.

[10] Ronald S. Ely, *Crystal Palaces: Visions of Splendour* (Ripley, 2004), p. 49, quoted in Colin Eatock, 'The Crystal Palace Concerts: Canon Formation and the English Musical Renaissance', *Nineteenth-Century Music*, 34:1 (2010), 87–105, at p. 91.

[11] Michael Musgrave, *The Musical Life of the Crystal Palace* (Cambridge, 1995), p. 17; Eatock, 'The Crystal Palace Concerts', p. 92.

[12] Paul Watt and Alison Rabinovici, 'Alexandra Palace: Music, Leisure, and the Cultivation of "Higher Civilization" in the Late Nineteenth Century', *Music & Letters*, 95:2 (2014), 183–212, at p. 183.

[13] *Ibid*, p. 193.

Figure 19. Illustration of the illuminated fountain in the gardens at night at London 1885 in John Dinsdale, *Sketches at the Inventories* (London, 1885), [pages not numbered].

(Figure 20 and 21). Across the exhibitions between 1883 and 1886, the gardens and bands grew in popularity until they began to overshadow the exhibitions themselves. The *Saturday Review* reported that, at the 1883 Fisheries Exhibition, 'people who did not care for fisheries came for the bands', and the *Dundee Courier* noted that music drew people to the 1884 Health Exhibition, 'not the desire to study the technical side of the question of health'.[14] *Punch* suggested in 1884 that the best time to see the exhibits was between six and ten in the evening, as with 'your twenty or thirty thousand fellow visitors being away in the grounds listening to the music, you will literally have the whole place to yourself'.[15] By the 1885 Inventions Exhibition, Shaw described the exhibitions' annual success as unrelated to people's interest 'in fishery, in hygiene, or in inventions, but to their love of a crowd, a band, and "a gardens"'.[16] *Punch* concluded that the exhibitions' themes were irrelevant, and the outdoor entertainment all that mattered:

> No doubt a Grand International Walking-Stick Contest, or a Cosmopolitan Collection of Cotton Night-Caps, if wedded to 'bands in the grounds, and

---

[14] 'The Fisheries Exhibition', *Saturday Review of Politics, Literature, Science and Art*, 56:1462 (3 Nov. 1883), p. 559; 'Our London Letter', *Dundee Courier*, 23 Jun. 1884, p. 3.
[15] 'Our Insane-Itary Guide to the Health Exhibition', *Punch*, 30 Aug. 1884, p. 98.
[16] [George Bernard Shaw, unsigned], 'A Substitute for Strauss', *Dramatic Review*, 27 Jun. 1885, repr. in Dan H. Laurence (ed.), *Shaw's Music: The Complete Musical Criticism in Three Volumes*, vol. 2 (London, 1981), p. 273.

Figure 20. 'The Eastern Kiosk', in John Dinsdale, *Sketches at the Inventories* (London, 1885), [pages not numbered].

concerts in the Albert Hall', would do just as well as Fish or Biscuits. Next year we are to have Inventions (with 'bands, &c., &c.') and in 1886 Colonial Exhibits (with 'bands, &c., &c.'), and probably by 1890 we shall have come to Toothpicks (with 'bands, &c., &c.'), and then, most likely it will be time to think of repeating once more Fish and Biscuits.[17]

As bands and gardens became ubiquitous, more and more of the outdoor amusements described in the introduction to this book were added. Melbourne 1888 included an aquarium with daily fish, seal, and sea lion feedings, stalactite caves and grottos, a fernery, a hydraulic lift to the building's dome, and a working dairy.[18] At Liverpool 1886 there was a billiard room, dairy and bakery, a lighthouse in 'exact reproduction of the famous "Eddystone"', and 'the most "captivating" object in the grounds' – a captive balloon – which offered an impressive view to anyone who braved the ascent.[19] Edinburgh 1886 had an archery field and a bowling green, while Glasgow 1888 had a switch-back railway, and gondolas steered by Venetian gondoliers giving rides on the river Kelvin.[20] Edinburgh 1890 included a swimming bath, a shooting gal-

---

[17] 'Our Insane-Itary Guide to the Health Exhibition', *Punch*, 28 Jun. 1884, p. 309.
[18] *Official Daily Programme*, 24 Sep. 1888, NLA SR 607.34945 C397.
[19] *International Exhibition of Navigation, Travelling, Commerce, & Manufacture, Liverpool 1886: Official Guide* (Liverpool, 1886), p. 74; *All About the Liverpool Exhibition, 1886* (Liverpool, 1886), p. 9.
[20] 'Glasgow International Exhibition', *Glasgow Herald*, 10 May 1888, p. 10.

Figure 21. 'Evening Fete: Music in the Gardens', *Illustrated London News*, 2 Aug. 1884, p. 97. © Illustrated London News Ltd/Mary Evans.

lery, a reproduction of the Hampton Court maze, a panorama of the Battle of Trafalgar, and a ride called 'Ye Ocean Wave' that simulated sailing on a rough sea.[21] Such amusements added to the carnival atmosphere of the gardens.

[21] 'Grand Opening Ceremony', *Dundee Courier & Argus*, 2 May 1890, p. 3.

These gardens, however, were not always viewed positively. Complaints were made at Melbourne 1888 about the switch-back railway, as some feared that it and the other amusements interfered with the Exhibition's 'educative potential'.[22] Others felt that the gardens held the dangerous possibility of encouraging classes to mix. Liverpool 1886's closing night – 'patronised by a very mixed class of visitors' – was marred by a violent riot started by gangs of drunk and 'well-dressed young men', causing injuries and property damage following the final band performance.[23] At London 1884, a critic in the Paris *Figaro* noted that the garden's 'real attraction' was the 'opportunity given to persons of both sexes for "agreeable rencontres"',[24] and the *Era* suggested that while 'hundreds of respectable people' came to 'anchor on the lawns and repose to the accompaniment of the music', the 'dark nooks and shady corners' were used by 'some of the most unmistakable members of the frail sisterhood'.[25] These insinuations were not exclusive to London: one entry in the Melbourne 1880 Visitors' Register complains that there was 'too much ladies underclothing shown in the gardens at night'![26] Still, the majority of commentators concerned with the public's social and moral status saw the 'healthful' benefits of the gardens and their musical activities. Music critics, in contrast, disagreed. For the musical press, the effectiveness of rational recreation through music was directly linked to the 'quality' of the works.[27] It was not music in itself that was edifying; it was *good* music, and good music listened to attentively.

❧ Bands

Bands, whether military, factory, or civilian, provided most of the music in the gardens. As a musical manifestation of Victorian modernity, bands were linked to rational recreation, and were often proudly sponsored by middle and upper class factory owners or philanthropists.[28] In addition to providing musical training for many, band repertoire was considered educational, presenting 'the standard classics of the bourgeois musical canon' to audiences unfamiliar with the concert hall.[29] Yet, despite the general approval of rational recreationists,

---

[22] Jennifer Royle, '"Preparing to Exhibit": Frederick Cowen in the Public Press Preceding Melbourne's Centennial International Exhibition, 1888–89', *Context: Journal of Music Research*, 14 (1997–8), 53–62, at p. 59.

[23] 'Serious Riot at the Liverpool Exhibition', *Daily News*, 10 Nov. 1886, p. 6.

[24] 'Correspondance anglaise', *Le Figaro*, 14 May 1884, p. 3.

[25] 'The Health Exhibition', *Era*, 19 Jul. 1884, p. 13.

[26] Visitors' Register of Melbourne International Exhibition, 1880 [manuscript], SLV, MS 9306.

[27] Meirion Hughes, *The English Musical Renaissance and the Press, 1850–1914: Watchmen of Music* (Aldershot, 2002), pp. 29–30.

[28] Trevor Herbert, 'Victorian Brass Bands: Class, Taste and Space', in Andrew Leyshon, David Matless, and George Revill (eds), *The Place of Music* (New York, 1998), pp. 104–28, at p. 105; Scott, *Sounds of the Metropolis*, p. 61.

[29] Duncan Bythell, 'Provinces versus Metropolis in the British Brass Band Movement in the Early Twentieth Century: The Case of William Rimmer and His Music', *Popular Music*, 16:2 (1997), 151–63, at p. 151.

bands 'occupied an uneasy cultural position' between art and popular music.[30] As Trevor Herbert and Arnold Myers argue, there remained 'an element of ambivalence' in their cultural status.[31] As values shifted across the nineteenth century, bands became, for some, synonymous with 'bad musical taste' and a caricatured working class.[32] Bands were both condemned for presenting high-art in 'ruthlessly butchered selections' which destroyed 'the integrity of the work',[33] and were criticised for playing 'trash' including 'marches, dances, show-piece solos and inane descriptive numbers' written specifically for them.[34]

Bands performed daily at nearly every exhibition in the 1880s. In Britain, the most prominent were the Grenadier Guards conducted by Dan Godfrey (1831–1903), who played at every London exhibition between 1883 and 1886. Numerous other military bands, including those of the Coldstream Guards, Royal Artillery, and Royal Marines, also appeared repeatedly across the decade. Continental European bands were often seen as an additional drawcard, with the Pomeranian or Blücher Hussars and the Thuringian regiment of the German Infantry drawing large crowds in London, while the visiting Royal Swedish Värmland Grenadiers and Hungarian 'Blue' National Band – depicted in a painting by John Lavery (1856–1941) at Glasgow 1888 in Figure 22 – received much praise across Scotland. Bands with particular local connections were similarly well received, such as the local Burton Volunteer Band at Liverpool 1886, the Edinburgh City Police Band at Edinburgh 1890, and factory bands like the Black Dyke Mills Band – a Yorkshire wool-mill band and one of the oldest and best-known in Britain – who were admired across northern England and Scotland.

Bands were equally prominent at the Australian exhibitions, and in Australia generally during this period. The Australian tradition developed concurrently with that in Britain through a consistent flow of migrant bandsmen, imported instruments, and a well-established musical network ensuring similar musical standards across the Empire.[35] Although records are scarce for Sydney 1879, it appears many bands performed, including ten or twelve local players – directed by Herr [Arnold Theodore] Kopff (1846–1920) – who performed daily in the basement refreshment rooms, alongside other bands making regular appearances in the gardens. At Melbourne 1880, many local, regional, and international bands played, including groups from Sandhurst (now Bendigo), Horsham, and Kyneton, as well as the visiting Austrian Strauss Band. At

---

[30] Herbert, 'Victorian Brass Bands', p. 106.
[31] Trevor Herbert and Arnold Myers, 'Music for the Multitude: Accounts of Brass Bands Entering Enderby Jackson's Crystal Palace Contests in the 1860s', *Early Music*, 38:4 (2010), 571–84, at p. 571.
[32] Herbert, 'Victorian Brass Bands', p. 125.
[33] Bythell, 'Provinces versus Metropolis', p. 152.
[34] Ibid.
[35] Duncan Bythell, 'The Brass Band in the Antipodes: The Transplantation of British Popular Culture', in Trevor Herbert (ed.), *The British Brass Band: A Musical and Social History* (Oxford, 2000), pp. 217–44, at pp. 226–8.

Figure 22. John Lavery, *The Blue Hungarians* (1888),
courtesy The Fleming Collection, London.

Adelaide 1887 there was public outcry when no bands were initially provided. One letter in the press castigated the commissioners for their 'sin of omission' in 'a crying shame' of 'ill-judged parsimony'.[36] Eventually, instrument sellers Broad & Co. publicly offered 'free use of a complete set of Besson's patent "Prototype" brass and wood instruments' to any band who might play;[37] the commissioners conceded, and by July a full programme of band music was provided.[38] Bands played at Melbourne 1888 every evening inside the building for the first few months, before moving into the grounds in summer. While performing inside, their repertoire was fully listed in the printed daily programme alongside Cowen's orchestra. When they moved outdoors, however, their programme position also moved. The location and time of the performances – with no repertoire details – were listed under 'Variety Entertainments', alongside Spanish students singing in a gondola on the gardens' lake, Mademoiselle Franzini the

[36] Citizen, 'Music at the Exhibition', *South Australian Advertiser*, 12 Jul. 1887, p. 7.
[37] 'An Exhibition Band', *Express and Telegraph*, 1 Jul. 1887, p. 4; 'An Exhibition Band', *South Australian Advertiser*, 4 Jul. 1887, p. 7.
[38] 'The Jubilee Exhibition', *Adelaide Observer*, 30 Jul. 1887, p. 30.

'Champion Bicyclist' who 'dashed' daily 'through pot plants and mazes of bottles' at 'lightning speed', 'Prestidigitateur' Arthur Francis performing 'genuine sleight of hand', and Sylvo the Innovator whose 'Extraordinary Equilibristic Entertainment' made use of 'bottles, plates, pyramids of glasses, globes, hats, swords … Feats of Equation with an ordinary buggy whip; Manipulation of Japanese Block, and all the latest Equipoise novelties'.[39] This change suggests a downgrading of the bands' status alongside their changed venue.

While attempts were made to present music in the grounds at Calcutta 1883, like much at this exhibition, the endeavour was plagued with difficulties. By mid-December the Exhibition's unpredictable electricity connection meant that the gardens were poorly lit, which discouraged visitors from making use of the spaces to the same extent they did elsewhere. Jules Joubert, the notoriously obstreperous head executive commissioner, announced an upcoming performance by a private band that month, but when the appointed afternoon arrived he became involved in an argument with the bandmaster, who then refused to allow his band to play.[40] The bandmaster had asked Joubert to use his influence to stop military bands playing at private functions 'to the detriment of professionals', but he refused.[41] By the end of the month, and perhaps as further insult to the bandmaster, Joubert convinced a military band to perform instead. Attendance figures, however, were reportedly not influenced at all by this additional music.[42]

The bands' repertoire at the exhibitions remained static throughout the 1880s and across the Empire. While there was some regional variation – works based on Walter Scott's novels such as Bishop's *Guy Mannering* overture or Foster's *Rob Roy* Overture were conspicuous at Scottish exhibitions – programmes otherwise consistently reflected a relatively codified repertoire. Programmes generally contained operatic overtures, waltzes, selections, fantasias, and potpourris, as can be seen in tables 8 to 10, showing similar programmes from London, Melbourne, and Edinburgh.

This type of programming was so standardised that *Punch* provided a mock programme for the opening of the 1884 Health Exhibition: a 'Grand Selection of Sanitary Music by the Band of the First Long Life Guards' consisting of:

Potpouri [sic]: 'The Mock Doctor'
Aria: 'In this Bath Chair my Fathers Sat'
Bacchanal Song with Chorus: 'Fill me a Bumper of Cod-Liver Oil'
Zymotic Fantasia: 'Ye Spotted Snakes'
Overture: 'Very Catching'
Hygienic Scherzo with Variations: 'Drain, Drain the Bowl'
Peruvian Barcarole: "Tis Bitter Thus!'
Convalescent Adagio: Beethoven's 'Nightlight Sonata'[43]

---

[39] *Official Daily Programme*, 7 Jan. 1889, 12 Jan. 1889, and 14 Jan. 1889, NLA SR 607.34945 C397.
[40] 'International Exhibition', *Englishman*, 14 Dec. 1883, p. 2.
[41] Ibid.
[42] Ibid.
[43] 'Their Very Good Health!', *Punch*, 12 Apr. 1884, p. 173.

Table 8. Grenadier Guards, International Inventions Exhibition, 5 May 1885

Work	Composer
3:00pm	
March *Glück auf*	Carl Ludwig Unrath (1828–1908)
Overture *Tannhäuser*	Wagner
Selection *Attila*	Verdi
Valse *Hypatia*	May Ostlere (1850–1916)
Aria 'Cujus animam'	Rossini
Overture *Athalie*	Mendelssohn
Valse *Soirée d'été*	Waldteufel
Nocturne *Addio a Napoli*	Carl Bohm (1844–1920)
Entr'acte, Bridal Chorus and Finale *Lohengrin*	Wagner
7:30pm	
Austrian March *d'Banda Kommt*	Theodor Franz Schild (1859–1929)
Overture *Raymond*	Ambroise Thomas (1811–96)
Selection *Stradella*	Friedrich von Flotow (1812–83)
Selection of Lieder	Mendelssohn
Selection *Carlotta*	Carl Joseph Millöcker (1812–83)
Fantasia *Boccaccio*	Franz von Suppé (1819–95)

Table 9. The Band of the 2nd Battalion, U.R., Melbourne International Exhibition, 14 November 1888

Work	Composer
8:00pm	
March *Iolanthe*	Sullivan
Walzer *Olympia-Tänze*	Joseph Lanner (1801–43)
Selection *Faust*	Gounod
Quadrille *Zurich*	Fred Godfrey (1837–82)
Waltz *With the Stream*	Theophilus Marzials (1850–1920)
Overture *Golden Heart*	Louis Antoine St Jacome (1830–98)
Grand March *Alfred Choral*	Julius Siede (1825–1903)
Galop *Tritsch-Tratsch*	Johann Strauss II (1825–99)

Table 10. Royal Horse Guards (Blues), Edinburgh
International Exhibition, 13 September 1890

Work	Composer
3:00pm	
March from Gounod's *Faust*	Charles Godfrey (1790–1863)
Overture *Poet and Peasant*	Franz von Suppé
Walter *Amoretten Tänze*	Joseph Gung'l
Selection from Wagner's *Tannhäuser*	Charles Godfrey, Jr. (1839–1919)
Overture *The Yeomen of the Guard*	Sullivan
Glee 'When Winds Whistle Cold' (*Guy Mannering*)	Bishop
Spanish Valse	Moritz Moszkowski (1854–1925)
Reminiscences of Verdi	Fred Godfrey
Scottish Quadrille *Caledonia*	Crispiniano Bosisio (1807?–58)
7:30pm	
Overture *Zampa*	Ferdinand Hérold (1791–1833)
Piccolo Solo *L'Oiseau du bois*	Charles Le Thière (1859–1929?)
Israelites March *Eli*	Michael Costa (1808–84)
National Fantasia *Scotland's Pride*	Charles Godfrey
Fantasia on Neapolitan Airs	Charles Godfrey
Cornet Solo *Love's Old Sweet Song*	James Lynam Molloy (1837–1909)
Descriptive Piece *Echoes of Killarney*	Charles Godfrey
Nautical Fantasia *A Voyage in a Troopship*	George Miller (1853–1928)

GENERAL RECEPTION OF BANDS

Audiences consistently enjoyed the bands in the exhibition gardens, and commentators outside of the musical press – particularly those involved in rational recreation or public health – were impressed by the receptiveness to outdoor entertainment. As the *St James's Gazette* described in 1884, bands in the gardens were a 'gratifying and instructive' way to relax: 'so innocent, so healthful, so blameless'.[44] They highlighted the 'naturalness' of being outdoors, when so many worked 'between the four walls of shop, office, or factory'.[45] The *Daily News* in 1885 similarly described the bands as performing music 'that is understoodest of the people, awakening pleasant remembrances, touching the finer feelings, and sometimes going straight to the heart'.[46] In using the phrase

---

[44] 'The Lesson of the Health Exhibition', *St James's Gazette*, 25 Jul. 1884, p. 6.
[45] *Ibid*.
[46] 'A Monster Day at the Inventions', *Daily News*, 26 May 1885, p. 5.

'understood of the people' – quoting the twenty-fourth of the Thirty-Nine Articles of Religion in the Book of Common Prayer which states that prayer must be in a language 'understood of the people' – this writer perceives this music as both accessible and edifying. Similarly, the *Ragged School Union Quarterly Record* described the 'instructive and elevating effects' of the bands and gardens on special days of reduced entry prices at London 1886. These days allowed 'working men and their families' and the 'children and their parents of our schools and missions ... to hear the music and witness the illuminations' which 'create[d] joy in not too sunny lives'.[47]

The diary of Elizabeth Lee (1867–?) – a Merseyside teenager who visited the 1884 Health Exhibition and Liverpool 1886 – is a source that gives revelatory descriptions of this music.[48] Aged sixteen in 1884, Lee described the Health Exhibition's 'splendid gardens ... illuminated with every sort of variegated lamps and Japanese lanterns' and the 'splendid Electric light fountain display' as complementing her enjoyment of the Grenadier and Royal Horse Guards.[49] Recalling the 'Nautical Fantasia' – *A Voyage in a Troopship* – she liked the musical representation of a storm and the section entitled 'Calm Evenings on Deck'.[50] At the Liverpool Exhibition, Lee described the bands as 'jolly', finding that the Hungarian band and the Belgian Guides 'charmed' her,[51] while the 'splendid' Royal Horse Guards formed part of 'the jolliest evening I ever had'.[52] She was enthralled by the 'The British Army Quadrilles' – another descriptive piece – involving orchestral imitation of 'musketry firing' and 'a battle'.[53]

Many commentators saw the exhibitions' garden entertainment as a model applicable to other public spaces. As Hart concluded in his lecture, London could 'learn from the success of the music and the lighting' of the Health Exhibition to transform parks currently 'unused' except for 'the worst vices' of 'the lowest dregs of the population' into 'sites of healthful and innocent recreation'.[54] Hart echoed comments made earlier by his wife, who spoke at a meeting of the Popular Ballad Concert Committee on the 'practical moral' demonstrated by the Exhibition's gardens. Alice Hart (1848–1931, née Rowland) – a social reformer and philanthropist who had also studied medicine – explained that she 'would fain every summer night see our beautiful parks illuminated with the electric light, and hear bands playing freely to the people' as at the

---

[47] 'Colonial and Indian Exhibition', *Ragged School Union Quarterly Record*, 11:44 (Oct. 1886), p. 201.

[48] Diary sources can 'reveal much about aspects of everyday life which otherwise are never recorded'. For more information on this particular source, see Colin G. Pooley, Siân Pooley, and Richard Lawton (eds), 'The Diary of Elizabeth Lee: An Introductory Essay', in *The Diary of Elizabeth Lee: Growing up on Merseyside in the Late Nineteenth Century* (Liverpool, 2010), pp. 1–62.

[49] Elizabeth Lee, *Diary of Elizabeth Lee*, p. 116.

[50] *Ibid.*

[51] *Ibid*, p. 205.

[52] *Ibid*, p. 209.

[53] *Ibid*, p. 212.

[54] Hart, 'The International Health Exhibition', p. 56.

Exhibition.[55] The *St James's Gazette* republished these comments, concluding that music in parks would 'add brightness to hundreds of thousands of lives which suffer not so much from work, as from dullness and *ennui* and the want of relaxation', helping to clear out pubs by providing 'plenty of sensible and harmless recreation'.[56]

Similar appreciation of bands was seen in Australia. An initial paucity of outdoor music at Sydney 1879 prompted many letters to the press, including one observing how the absence of bands was 'strange' given the 'attraction to the grounds' they would provide.[57] The Young Australia Band eventually began to perform in the gardens, giving 'excellent music to a large and delighted audience',[58] and other unnamed bands reportedly contributed 'much to the enjoyment of visitors'.[59] Yet, despite their popularity, none of the Sydney bands were part of the 'official' programme. The performers were not paid, and were even required to cover their own daily admission until the owner of a café in the grounds began paying on their behalf, noticing how they attracted people to the gardens.[60] The Young Australia Band was also supported by private patronage from the Austrian Empire's exhibition commissioner, who in an amusing incident was announced as a performer rather than patron, leaving his friends disappointed, having 'hastened to see the instrument he would play'.[61] Similarly, private entrepreneurs Young and O'Connell arranged for Herr Kopff's band to perform 'popular music in capital style during each afternoon' in their refreshment rooms, in a move 'thoroughly appreciated' by patrons.[62] As the *Sydney Morning Herald* proclaimed, at Sydney 1879, 'it is left to private enterprise to provide anything really popular'.[63]

The response to bands at Melbourne 1880 and 1888 was also positive, with high attendances reported on any afternoon that they played.[64] In 1888, the *Illustrated Australian News* reported that the public placed 'a higher estimate upon the value of the brass band' to whose music 'they can promenade in comfort' than they did of Cowen's orchestral concerts.[65] This was also reported in the British press, with a correspondent writing to the *Musical Opinion and Music Trade Review* that Cowen's orchestra was less appreciated by people who hoped to promenade while listening. After a 'considerable amount of

---

[55] 'The Lesson of the Health Exhibition', *St James's Gazette*, 25 Jul. 1884, p. 6.
[56] *Ibid.*
[57] 'To the Editor of the Herald', *Sydney Morning Herald*, 21 Oct. 1879, p. 3.
[58] 'Music at the Garden Palace', *Evening News*, 3 Nov. 1879, p. 3.
[59] 'Sydney International Exhibition', *Sydney Morning Herald*, 17 Nov. 1879, p. 7.
[60] 'Music at the Garden Palace', *Sydney Morning Herald*, 17 Nov. 1879, p. 7.
[61] 'The Music at the Garden Palace', *Sydney Morning Herald*, 15 Dec. 1879, p. 7.
[62] 'International Exhibition', *Evening News*, 21 Jan. 1880, p. 3.
[63] 'International Exhibition', *Evening News*, 20 Nov. 1879, p. 3.
[64] 'Exhibition Notes', *Age*, 11 Oct. 1880, p. 3.
[65] 'Theatres', *Illustrated Australian News*, 15 Sep. 1888, p. 166, quoted in Royle, 'Preparing to Exhibit', p. 59.

grumbling' by those who 'desired to hear lively military music', more bands were engaged to 'infuse a little life into the Exhibition'.[66]

In Scotland, too, bands were greatly enjoyed. The *Dundee Courier* described how the 'flaring incandescent lights with the many-coloured shades seem to inspire every heart with a sense of empyrean happiness' at Edinburgh 1886, while a military band made the audience 'supremely merry ... and one or two whose musical faculties ha[d] been more acutely tickled, vocally illustrate[d] their satisfaction'.[67] Similar responses were recorded in the *Edinburgh Evening Dispatch*, describing the audience at the Royal Horse Artillery's first Scottish performance as obliged to the organisers 'for putting them in the way of hearing such excellent music from so thoroughly good a band'.[68] An interview with the Guards' conductor, Charles Godfrey, recorded how impressed he was with their Edinburgh reception, saying his players were 'extremely gratified' to be 'received with so much enthusiasm'.[69] When the Exhibition ended, the *Evening Dispatch* concluded that 'military bands ... have been sources of great enjoyment to all classes of visitors'.[70]

Occasionally audiences were *too* enthusiastic. At Edinburgh 1890, Axel Svensson, conductor of the Royal Swedish Värmland Grenadiers, was mobbed by 'enthusiastic admirers' following the band's final performance and 'the friendly intervention of a couple of policemen was necessary to help him through the crowd'.[71] Svensson was then 'followed by a cheering crowd right up to the door'.[72] At Glasgow 1888, the Royal Artillery's 'wildly enthusiastic audience' encored every work, then turned so aggressive that the conductor Ladislao Zavertal (1849–1942) also required a police escort to leave the stage.[73] More mildly, at Liverpool 1886, 'enthusiastic' ladies embarrassed the Blue Hungarian Band's conductor by showering him with 'numerous floral offerings' so often that he was apparently relieved to end the engagement.[74]

RECEPTION OF BANDS IN THE MUSICAL PRESS

The positive reception, presented above, was not mirrored in the musical press, where the general consensus of most critics suggested bands were either not playing 'music', or that it was simply not 'good' enough to have any 'improving'

---

[66] 'News from the Melbourne Exhibition', *Musical Opinion and Music Trade Review*, 12:136 (1 Jan. 1889), p. 190.

[67] Jornan, 'Nights in International Exhibition', *Dundee Courier & Argus*, 13 May 1886, p. 3.

[68] 'Exhibition Jottings', *Edinburgh Evening Dispatch*, 19 May 1886, p. 2.

[69] 'The Royal Horse Guards' Band and Their Conductor', *Edinburgh Evening Dispatch*, 9 Oct. 1886, p. 2.

[70] 'The Exhibition Music', *Edinburgh Evening Dispatch*, 30 Oct. 1886, p. 2.

[71] 'Exhibition Notes', *Edinburgh Evening Dispatch*, 29 Aug. 1890, p. 2.

[72] *Ibid.*

[73] 'Glasgow International Exhibition. The Closing Day – Enormous Attendance', *Glasgow Herald*, 12 Nov. 1888, p. 4.

[74] 'The Blue Hungarian Band, A Remarkable Company of Musicians', *Edinburgh Evening Dispatch*, 25 Sep. 1886, p. 2.

effect. The *Musical Times* in 1883 considered that while 'the majority will find some pleasure in a military band' at the Fisheries Exhibition, it was 'gross flattery' to 'tell them that they appreciate instrumental music'.[75] In October 1884, the *Magazine of Music*'s 'Music of the Month' column stated that 'some purists' would argue that 'there has been no music' that month. To imply otherwise – that is, to consider the bands in the gardens of the Health Exhibition as music – would, amongst purists, 'bring down fully-charged vials of wrath upon the luckless one who classed these with serious music'.[76]

Much of this criticism related to the association of bands with the working classes. In 1885 the *Musical Times* assured readers that while there was 'no piece in the *répertoire* of the Grenadier Guards' band' more popular than the *Tannhäuser* Overture, when played by a military band rather than full orchestra it could have no 'refining influences ... on intelligences cultivated or uncultivated'.[77] They continued by arguing that the 'East Ender' should 'have a chance of hearing Wagner', but played by a band such music could not 'work miracles, and supply them with a soul-satisfying religion', as what 'electrifies does not *ex ipso facto* elevate, refine, and purify the intelligence of the hearer'.[78] Shaw also argued in the *Dramatic Review* that music could not be enlightening when presented by bands, concluding that 'transcriptions of overtures ... ballet music, selections from operas, Turkish patrols, and arrangements of *The Lost Chord* for cornet solo' could do nothing but 'afford small satisfaction'.[79] He concluded another article in *Our Corner* by describing Dan Godfrey – the Grenadier Guards' much-loved conductor – as dependent on officers who were 'sure to consider coarse playing and trivial music the best value for their subscriptions', uninterested in 'anything more serious than the overture to *William Tell*'.[80] As Herbert and Myers have argued, the working-class associations of the brass band, despite rational recreationist approval, created a level of critical ambivalence.[81] This is seen clearly in the reception here.

Shaw also suggested that the presence of bands tainted his experience of other aspects of the exhibitions. In 1885 he sarcastically wrote that the ancient music collection in the galleries of the Albert Hall could be viewed 'by gaslight, to military music', and the illusion (quoted previously) of Shakespeare and the 'dark lady' was 'greatly heightened by the band of the Coldstream Guards playing a selection from the *Mikado* outside'.[82]

---

[75] 'Music Halls and Music Schools', *Musical Times*, 24:489 (1 Nov. 1883), 593–4, at p. 593.
[76] 'Music of the Month', *Magazine of Music*, 1:7 (Oct. 1884), p. 17.
[77] 'Music for the People', *Musical Times*, 26:512 (1 Oct. 1885), 579–81, at p. 580.
[78] Ibid.
[79] [Shaw, unsigned], 'A Substitute for Strauss', *Dramatic Review*, 27 Jun. 1885, repr. in *Shaw's Music*, p. 274.
[80] [Shaw, unsigned], 'Art Corner', *Our Corner*, Sep. 1885, repr. in *Shaw's Music*, p. 291.
[81] Herbert and Myers, 'Music for the Multitude', p. 571.
[82] [Shaw, unsigned], 'Historical Instruments', *Dramatic Review*, 19 Sep. 1885, repr. in *Shaw's Music*, p. 358.

Much of the criticism of the bands related to their programmes of selections, potpourris, and fantasias. This was not unique to the exhibitions: from the 1860s, such works were approached with growing hostility by critics who lamented the lack of distinction between 'the sublime and the frivolous, the delicately ideal and the boisterously rowdy'.[83] Critics were uncomfortable with the way these works failed to recognise the apparent 'schism between the "serious" and popular styles', unashamedly blending both.[84] These works were utterly sneered at in an 1885 *Quarterly Musical Review*, where Frederick Corder (1852–1932) described them as constructed by:

> extracting from a large work all the best melodic ideas, as a child collects all the plums from its share of pudding, and putting these in one savoury spoonful before the vulgar public, too impatient and too dull of palate to take its musical food in any save the smallest and strongest of doses.[85]

Corder had conducted a series of concerts at the Brighton Aquarium from 1880 offering 'high art' music on the model of the Crystal Palace Saturday concerts. His programmes, which were 'very lofty' in the context of the kind of music usually heard in leisure palaces, were very poorly attended.[86] While this surely demonstrates a commitment to the ideals he espoused in his essay, it might also account for a little bitterness towards the public who flocked instead to the band concerts given elsewhere in the Aquarium, just like at the exhibitions.

Ultimately, the frustration felt in the musical press was based on a suspicion that the organisers did not genuinely support the supposed high aims of the exhibitions, and were concerned more with making money. As the *Musical Times* concluded in 1885:

> were the Exhibition a commercial speculation and nothing more, we could understand the performers being told to play down to the taste of the mob … But we have always been told that South Kensington is an art centre … Either South Kensington is a centre for art-education or it is not. If it is, the manner in which music is being treated … is nothing short of disgraceful. If it is not, let the veil of pretence and hypocrisy which now hides its doings be ruthlessly torn away, and the truth made manifest to all whom it may concern.[87]

Despite the insinuations of the critics, the repertoire performed by bands was not unrelated to the 'high art' the musical elite expected. While certainly pandering to popular taste, works of the 'great' composers – including operas and symphonic works – *were* presented, and engaged with by the general public.

---

[83] '"Light" and "Heavy"', *Dwight's Journal of Music*, 24:13 (Sep. 1864), p. 310, quoted in Scott, *Sounds of the Metropolis*, p. 94.

[84] Scott, *Sounds of the Metropolis*, p. 95.

[85] Frederick Corder, 'Musical Misrepresentation', *Quarterly Musical Review*, 1:3 (Aug. 1885), 187–92, at p. 190.

[86] Makiko Hayasaka, 'Organ Recitals as Popular Culture: The Secularisation of the Instrument and Its Repertoire in Britain, 1834–1950' (unpublished Ph.D. Thesis, University of Bristol, 2016), pp. 160–1.

[87] 'Music at South Kensington', *Musical Times*, 26:508 (1 Jun. 1885), pp. 318–19.

Yet, presented in band arrangements or as pot-pourris, this music was dismissed by the musical press. Despite their claims to support the dissemination of high art to the masses, the press paradoxically rejected bands: the form of music-making at the exhibitions that engaged the greatest number of people. Bands were one of the easiest ways to disseminate music widely, making this music more accessible and effectively 'democratising' it by welcoming a wider audience.

❧ *Organ Recitals*

With the exception of Calcutta, all the 1880s exhibitions included daily organ recitals. London 1885 – an extreme example – had eight large organs, heard at up to ten recitals per day; Shaw joked that the total number of organists playing at once 'can hardly be computed at less than twenty seven'.[88] But organs played an ambiguous role at these exhibitions. As exhibits, they demonstrated manufacturing skill, and industrial and commercial value. But they were also associated with culture at its highest and most transcendental, with inherent religious connotations through their relationship with sacred music and the church. Organ music at the exhibitions, however, was not church music, and was heard in the midst of general exhibits with audiences not expected to listen actively. The music accompanied promenading and the perusal of displays, and listeners would rarely experience an entire performance from start to finish.

Nineteenth-century secular organ music developed along similar lines to the open-air tradition discussed above. Having been prominent in eighteenth- and early nineteenth-century pleasure gardens, secular organ music also featured in the leisure spaces that formed their legacy.[89] At the Great Exhibition, organs provided background music, holding, as Makiko Hayasaka describes, 'no function as a recital to which an audience might attentively listen'.[90] This carried on as a significant feature of the aural environment in the relaxed atmosphere of the Sydenham Crystal Palace, Alexandra Palace, and aquariums and winter gardens.[91] At the 1880s exhibitions, organ music also fitted this model, fulfilling the same function as the bands outside: a pleasant accompaniment to other leisure activities.

Standard secular organ repertoire was codified from the 1830s through town-hall concerts at which rational recreationalists attempted to harness the organ's apparent morally improving qualities – imbibed through its association with the church – in a broadly secular setting.[92] While sacred works (or sections of works) by Bach, Mendelssohn, and Handel were ever-present at town-hall recitals, transcriptions of orchestral, operatic, and 'lighter' works were added

---

[88] [Shaw, unsigned], 'Pianoforte and Organ', *Dramatic Review*, 25 Jul. 1885, repr. in *Shaw's Music*, p. 316.
[89] Hayasaka, 'Organ Recitals as Popular Culture', p. 7.
[90] *Ibid*, pp. 105, 142.
[91] *Ibid*.
[92] *Ibid*, pp. 2, 66.

to cater to popular taste, and over the following decades, secular organ repertoire began to resemble that of the bands discussed above.[93] This convention can be seen in the repertoire presented at the exhibitions. Both well-known performers – such as Henry Charles Tonking (1863–1926), Edwin Lemare (1865–1934), James Turpin (1840–96), William Stevenson Hoyte (1844–1917), William Spark (1823–97), and even a young Henry Wood (1869–1944) – and amateurs alike performed overtures and selections from operas by Wagner, Weber, and Meyerbeer, alongside Mendelssohn and Handel, and even sections of Mozart symphonies.

Although organ recitals at the Australian exhibitions were generally well liked, the organ at Melbourne itself (Figure 23) – built by George Fincham (1828–1910) – seems to have divided opinion, and the 1880 Visitors' Register is full of conflicting comments. In November 1880, neighbouring entries state 'would like to see the organ performed on every afternoon' (Henry J. Francis, Sydney), followed by 'rather too much music of an afternoon' (Robert Taylor, Warrnambool). Later in December, R. Ogden of Sandridge proclaimed the 'organ a great failure', while Charles Henry Daniel of Geelong believed the 'organ is grand'. Thomas Tregear of Long Gully called the 'organ splendid', while a Maurice of Fitzroy felt the 'organ spoils it'. By the Exhibition's end one commenter thought the organ was 'improving', while another on the same day called it 'worse than ever'.[94] This organ was used much less at Melbourne 1888. Cowen, on his arrival, instructed that its pitch be lifted to match the instruments of the orchestral players accompanying him from England. This retuning, however, was done in winter, and by summer the pitch had risen so much that the organ became completely unusable.[95]

In Scotland, organ recitals were given in the buildings' concert halls. This made them more like traditional concerts, away from the exhibitions' overall bustle, but they maintained some aspects of a relaxed atmosphere with visitors coming and going as they pleased. At Edinburgh 1886 more than 300 recitals were given, but as the *Edinburgh Evening News* explained, the lack of any real selection process (and that the positions were unpaid) meant that the organ was 'open practically to all comers', and performances were 'occasionally more excruciating than entertaining'.[96] While the Executive Committee hoped to create opportunities for 'young and inexperienced players', what resulted, according to the *Edinburgh Evening Dispatch*, was 'wearisome tootle', played by organists unused to an instrument of the size or calibre of that provided:

---

[93] For analysis of this repertoire see both John Henderson, 'UK Recitals and Their Repertoire 1880–1930,' in *A Directory of Composers for Organ* (Swindon, 1996), and *Ibid*, p. 75.

[94] Visitors' Register of Melbourne International Exhibition, 1880 [manuscript], SLV, MS 9306, *passim*.

[95] Simon Purtell, '"Musical Pitch ought to be One from Pole to Pole": Touring Musicians and the Issue of Performing Pitch in Late Nineteenth- and Early Twentieth-century Melbourne', *Context: Journal of Music Research*, 35/36 (2010/2011), 111–25, at pp. 117–18.

[96] 'The International Exhibition', *Edinburgh Evening News*, 1 Nov. 1886, p. 2.

Figure 23. 'The Great Organ at the Melbourne Exhibition', *Australasian Sketcher*, 28 Aug. 1880, p. 137. SLV Accession no: A/S28/08/80/209.

The performer, whose previous experience has probably been limited to a small organ ... usually succeeded, while endeavouring to master the four manuals and fifty stops of the Exhibition organ, to produce a sort of musical chaos that never failed to empty the chairs with remarkable rapidity. One could not hear the tortuous strains of some of these aspiring musicians without feeling that the managers of a church in the Far West exercised a wise discretion in giving prominence to a notice board bearing the legend 'Please don't shoot the organist; he is doing his best'.[97]

There was similar backlash at Edinburgh 1890 where organists' only payment was what might today be described as playing 'for exposure'. As the *Musical Opinion and Music Trade Review* argued, 'only second rate players'

[97] 'The Exhibition Organ', *Edinburgh Evening Dispatch*, 23 Oct. 1886, p. 2.

would accept such an offer.[98] The same publication attacked these players for disregarding 'the dignity of the organ' by sending 'through its pipes stuff not good enough to be ground out by handle'.[99] This was a common criticism, with the musical press responding to these recitals much as they did to the bands. At Glasgow 1888, while professional organists were employed, attracting 'large and attentive audiences',[100] most were accused by the *Musical World* of offering 'routine' performances 'of vulgar sensationalism'.[101] Yet, they conceded, it was probably 'wise, in this democratic age, in making concession to the popular taste' to 'make both ends meet'.[102]

Organ recitals at the London exhibitions received even more damning criticism. The *Musical Times* was disappointed by the repertoire choices of the organists at the 1884 Health Exhibition, believing they 'should have known better':

> Once more has there been superstitious worship of the ugly idol known as 'popular taste', and that in a manner peculiarly disgraceful. Some excuse may be found for public caterers who fear the pecuniary loss which might befall them by aiming 'above the heads of the people' … But nothing whatever can be urged in palliation of those who drag their art through the mire for the sake of merely winning applause from hearers too vulgar to appreciate recitals of genuine organ music.[103]

The *Musical Times* concluded that it was 'insufferable' that 'the divinest of the arts should receive injury at the hands of those who ought most jealously to guard its interests'.[104] At the 1885 Inventions Exhibition, the *Musical Times* found the 'indignation' of the previous year to 'again bubble up', as programmes were similarly filled with 'operatic pot pourris and other selections'.[105] In reviewing a recital by organist John Jeffreys (1857–c.1940) they noted that 'the oddest feature' of his programme was that it 'did not include a single piece of genuine organ music', questioning whether his object had been 'to prove that the capacity of the organ is limited. If so, he succeeded admirably, for the effect … was supremely ridiculous'.[106]

Considering the debates surrounding music as an exhibited object that surrounded the exhibitions, it is striking that, despite many organisers best efforts to 'exhibit' examples of high-art music, it was popular music that came closest to becoming a static object. Programmes by bands, orchestras of 'light' music,

---

[98] 'Music in Scotland', *Musical Opinion and Music Trade Review*, 13:155 (1 Aug. 1890), p. 465.
[99] 'Music in Scotland', *Musical Opinion and Music Trade Review*, 13:156 (1 Sep. 1890), 497–8, at p. 497.
[100] 'Music in Glasgow', *Musical Times*, 29:545 (1 Jul. 1888), p. 425.
[101] 'Glasgow – Dr. Spark's Exhibition Recitals', *Musical World*, 67:30 (28 Jul. 1888), p. 598.
[102] *Ibid.*
[103] 'Occasional Notes', *Musical Times*, 25:501 (1 Nov. 1884), 631–3, at p. 632.
[104] *Ibid.*
[105] 'Music at South Kensington', *Musical Times*, 26:508 (1 Jun. 1885), 317–19, at p. 318.
[106] *Ibid.*

MUSIC FOR LEISURE AND ENTERTAINMENT 149

and organists remained remarkably consistent, and audiences clearly appreciated the reliability of familiar music that they knew they would enjoy. The band and organ recitals were something one could *go* to see, like a painting, or sculpture, and have a fair idea of what to expect. If not always the same works, similar styles and works that fulfilled the same function were consistent. At these exhibitions, visitors were even able to hear the repetition of a popular work several times in one day. Shaw illustrates this in an exaggerated account of the 1885 Inventions Exhibition, worth quoting at length, demonstrating the way in which an individual work could became static:

> A visitor enters the exhibition from Kensington Gore. A deafening jangle in the Albert Hall causes him to refer to his program, where he finds that he is listening to War March of the Priests – Athalie – Mendelssohn. When he has had enough of it, he passes through the conservatory, where he hears majestic strains from the Guards' band. A contrivance resembling a date rack informs him that item No. 6 in the list is being performed. Consulting his program, he ascertains that No. 6 is Mendelssohn's War March from Athalie. Proceeding to the Central Gallery ... he is overpowered by a flood of harmony from Messrs Willis and Sons' organ. Greatly struck by the grandeur and dignity of the music, he turns again to his program and reads 'March of the Priests, Athalie, Mendelssohn-Bartholdy'. Having heard this composition before, he does not wait ... He is recalled by a trumpet-like fanfare from Messrs Brindley and Foster's organ. Something in the melody stirs vague associations with the past. The program seems to swim before his eyes, and his hand is not steady; but he succeeds in deciphering 'March, Athalie, Mendelssohn'. He hears it to the end; has a turn in the aquarium; and wanders to where Mr. H. Wedlake's organ is discoursing a vigorous and lofty theme. He recognizes it as something he has heard before; but he cannot think of its name, unless it be the Hallelujah Chorus. He determines to put a cross in the margin of his program, so that he will remember to speak to his wife of the majesty of Handel when he gets home. On attempting to do so, he finds, not Handel, but Mendelssohn. It is not the Hallelujah Chorus, but the march from Athalie. Uttering a slight imprecation, he retires, and watches the fountains playing until a ravishing air, wafted into the grounds from Messrs Bryceson Brothers' electric organ, brings him back full of delight and curiosity. Again referring to the program, he learns that the organist is busy with the march from Athalie. He is a little surprised, but finds the march growing on him. When it is over he endeavors to *encore* it; but the crowd does not applaud sufficiently, and he is disappointed until another look at the program informs him that the march will be played again later in the evening on Messrs J.W. Walker and Sons' organ. Whilst in search of this instrument he stumbles upon a gentleman who is trying the vocalion in the Siamese court. Charmed by the rhythmic character of the *morceau*, he waits, and asks the gentleman what he has been playing. 'Oh, a march' says the gentleman, 'Mendelssohn's, you know, from Athalie, you must have heard it often'. He admits that he has and withdraws. On his way to Messrs Walkers' exhibit, he is arrested by the now almost familiar fanfare from Messrs Henry Jones and Sons' organ, upon which Mr. Trego is just striking up the War March of the Priests. Finally, when the organs are shut up for the night, he thinks of home, and goes out to take a last look at the illuminated gardens. The band breaks forth into a wellknown tune. This time he needs no program to tell him that he is listening to Mendelssohn's splendid war march. 'But why' he asks 'are

the people taking off their hats?' 'Because' replies the policeman, 'the band is playing God Save the Queen!'[107]

The conflicting reception of the 'popular' music at these exhibitions – loved by the public and hated by the musical press – is symptomatic of wider contemporary discussions around appropriate contexts and uses of music. Educating the public on industrial progress and high art may have been the exhibitions' aim, but the manner in which organisers attempted to broaden access to 'high' culture was not particularly well managed. With a few exceptions, the music organised directly by the commissioners was commercial, would encourage attendance, and lead to more ticket sales. However, as the exhibition institution was strongly linked to the rational recreation movement, organisers and commentators from outside the musical sphere were clearly impressed by the public's willingness to engage with music within spaces considered to be healthy and morally encouraging. Yet, the musical press were evidently uncomfortable with the intermingling of art and commerce. As Derek Scott argues, negative nineteenth-century associations with music that appeared commercial abounded:

> When Schumann writes of the gold rattling in Strauss Sr.'s pocket as he conducts, he is not making any comment on the quality of the music; he is indicating his disgust at the intermingling of music and commerce. The rupture between art and entertainment was caused primarily by an intense dislike of the market conditions that turned art into a commodity. Entertainment music was regarded as hand-in-glove with business entrepreneurs for whom popular music was a mere commodity and profits the main concern.[108]

Given that the kinds of music discussed here were evidently popular within the commercial context of the exhibitions, critics were almost by default required to disapprove of them for their obvious commodity status.[109] Invested in an ideological struggle to promote art music without compromising its integrity, the press's attacks on the exhibition bands and organists are less criticism of the works and performers than on commercialism itself. Just as the musical press were compelled to write positively of concerts in esoteric genres to maintain their sense of cultural superiority (as discussed in previous chapters), they were equally compelled to criticise music that did not conform to their rigid ideas of cultural status.

---

[107] [Shaw], 'Pianoforte and Organ', *Dramatic Review*, 25 Jul. 1885, repr. in *Shaw's Music*, pp. 317–18.
[108] Scott, *Sounds of the Metropolis*, p. 87.
[109] *Ibid*, p. 93.

CHAPTER 7

Nationalism and Music

International exhibitions were – supposedly – universal displays of human achievement. From the Great Exhibition onwards, the language used in many official publications grandly reinforced themes of universalism, cosmopolitanism, and monogenism. It was Prince Albert's speech at a Mansion House banquet in 1850 that first codified this narrative. Albert espoused a 'confident brand of internationalism', that saw 'the distances which separated the different nations and parts of the globe ... gradually vanishing before the achievements of modern invention'.[1] According to Albert, the Great Exhibition would provide 'a living picture of the point of development at which the whole of mankind has arrived'.[2] Yet within the structures of the Great Exhibition and those that followed, was an inherent paradox: universalism might have been the aim, but objects were displayed in explicitly national terms.

Despite the official narratives, exhibitions were intrinsically nationalistic. With almost total control over the content, layout, and programme of an exhibition, the host nation unfailingly curated the presentation of different cultures in a hierarchy for its own benefit. The competitive aspects similarly contrasted art, technological developments, and manufactured products by country in a way that highlighted the achievements of the host. Thus, while exhibitions were presented as 'microcosms that would summarize the entire human experience', their hierarchies of display were 'carefully articulated' to portray different nations as occupying fixed places in a supposed global order.[3] These nationalistic tendencies in representation are equally present in the British and colonial exhibitions studied here. In Britain, avowals of peace, progress, and universalism came only alongside the assertion of Britain's position as 'the first industrialized nation' and 'most powerful and advanced state'.[4] In Australia, commissioners consciously constructed self-promotional narratives

---

[1] David Raizman and Ethan Robey, 'Introduction', in David Raizman and Ethan Robey (eds), *Expanding Nationalisms at World's Fairs: Identity, Diversity, and Exchange, 1851–1915* (London, 2018), pp. 1–14, at p. 4; 'The Exhibition of All Nations', *The Times*, 22 Mar. 1850, p. 5.
[2] 'The Exhibition of All Nations', *The Times*, p. 5.
[3] Zeynep Çelik and Leila Kinney, 'Ethnography and Exhibitionism at the Expositions Universelles', *Assemblage*, 13 (1990), 34–59, at p. 36.
[4] Jeffery A. Auerbach, *The Great Exhibition of 1851: A Nation on Display* (New Haven, 1999), p. 1.

about 'striding forward on the world stage', presenting an Australian national identity that conjured images of 'a wealth of resources and progressive ideals'.[5]

The age of exhibitions in the second half of the nineteenth century also coincided with the peak of European musical nationalism: a phenomenon often described as an attempt at 'emancipation from the cultural hegemony of Teutonicism',[6] culminating in efforts to create individual, locally idiomatic, politically functional national musics.[7] While this manifested in various ways – through the elevation of folk music, or the assertion that certain composers' works were imbued with a 'national spirit' – many scholars argue that there is, in fact, rarely anything inherently national in music: that the discourse surrounding a work is often divorced from its creation.[8] Thus, the location of 'nation' within a musical work is generally the product of extrinsic markers, rather than elements within music, and national musics are largely defined by how they are employed, rather than what they contain.[9]

It might be expected, given the nationalistic underpinnings of exhibitions as an institution, occurring at the height of European musical nationalism, that the musical content of the events considered here would also have a nationalist focus. This was certainly the case at the contemporary French Exposition Universelle held in Paris in 1889: an event steeped in Republican rhetoric, commemorating the centenary of the 1789 revolution. A Commission des Auditions musicales was convened specifically to showcase French musical achievements, organising five orchestral concerts with the aim of displaying 'the immense superiority' of French music.[10] As Annegret Fauser describes, these performances were heard alongside other concerts of national musics, which created a context in which critics could engage in 'essentialist stereotyping' of different countries: 'music from abroad was received first and foremost as picturesque

---

[5] Kate Darian-Smith, '"Seize the Day": Exhibiting Australia', in Kate Darian-Smith, Richard Gillespie, Caroline Jordan, and Elizabeth Willis (eds), *Seize the Day: Exhibitions, Australia and the World* (Clayton, 2008), pp. 01.1–01.14, at p. 01.4. While Australia was not technically a federated 'nation' during the nineteenth century, there was most certainly a collective sense of an 'imagined community' within Australia as distinct from Britain and the rest of the world.

[6] Jeremy Dibble, 'Grove's Musical Dictionary: A National Document', in Harry White and Michael Murphy (eds), *Musical Constructions of Nationalism: Essays on the History and Ideology of European Musical Culture, 1800–1945* (Cork/Corcaigh, 2001), pp. 3–50, at p. 33.

[7] Richard Taruskin, 'Nationalism', *Grove Music Online* <http://www.oxfordmusiconline.com/> [accessed 8 Mar. 2021].

[8] Carl Dahlhaus, *Nineteenth-Century Music*, trans. J. Bradford Robinson (Berkeley, 1989), p. 38; Annegret Fauser, *Musical Encounters at the 1889 Paris World's Fair* (Rochester, 2005), p. 56; see also Marina Frolova-Walker, 'Against Germanic Reasoning: The Search for a Russian Style of Musical Argumentation', in White and Murphy (eds), *Musical Constructions of Nationalism*, pp. 104–22.

[9] Dahlhaus, *Nineteenth-Century Music*, p. 39.

[10] Fauser, *Musical Encounters*, p.16, quoting Alfred Bruneau, 'Musique', *La Revue indépendante*, Aug. 1889, p. 204.

and always lacking substance when compared to that of France'.[11] Strangely, however, in the exhibitions held at the same time in the British Empire, this was rarely the case.

In the British and Australian exhibitions of the 1880s, in general, discussion of nation was avoided in the musical departments when it came to Western art music (non-Western music was a different matter). While national rivalries emerged in the display of instruments manufactured in different countries (particularly when it came to awarding prizes), in performed music, musicians from across Europe played diverse repertoire, and the press made little judgement based specifically on national origins. At an organisational level – where there was an official plan regarding music – there even seems to have been a deliberate avoidance of making art music a nationalist matter. In London, as has already been shown, the 1885 Inventions Exhibition was not considered explicitly a forum to show off British music, but an opportunity to educate the public in music overall.[12] In Australia, at Sydney 1879, it was initially suggested that only works by Australian composers be heard, based on the suspicion – the *Official Record* noted – that as 'Australians have asserted a pre-eminence over their British brethren in the physical pastimes of cricket and rowing' they might also succeed in music.[13] This proposal, however, was rejected on the grounds that music was 'not alone a universal language', making it 'unwise to restrict the musical performances' to any local idiom.[14] Yet the *Official Record* also cautiously noted that an Australian school of composition was noticeably limited, presenting perhaps the real reason for the proposal's dismissal.

Nationalism, where it does arise in the reception of music at these exhibitions, appears almost exclusively in the critical response to the bands and light orchestras that provided entertainment, playing 'popular' rather than educational or illustrative music. This was especially the case when large sums of money were spent on employing these musicians; organisers, aware of the public's enjoyment of bands in the gardens, invested heavily in bringing bands from abroad. While the public appears to have enjoyed the visiting bands – one need only think of the Royal Swedish Värmland Grenadiers' conductor being mobbed by adoring fans at Edinburgh 1890[15] – in the musical press, many critics and letter-writers regarded the employment of 'foreign' bands as an offensive lack of investment in local music. Three case studies demonstrate this particularly clearly: the reception of the orchestra of Eduard Strauss (1835–1916) at London 1885; of the 'Austrian Strauss Band' – the first European professional band to tour Australia – at Melbourne 1880;[16] and the Viennese Ladies' Orches-

---

[11] *Ibid*, pp. 57–8.
[12] See the speeches given at the opening ceremony by the Prince of Wales and chair of the musical committee, George Grove, discussed in Chapter Five.
[13] *Official Record of the Sydney International Exhibition, 1879* (Sydney, 1881), p. xxxiv.
[14] *Ibid*, p. xxxiv.
[15] 'Exhibition Notes', *Edinburgh Evening Dispatch*, 29 Aug. 1890, p. 2.
[16] Graeme Skinner, 'Austrian Strauss Band', *Australharmony* <https://sydney.edu.au/paradisec/australharmony/register-organisations-from-1861-A-Z.php> [accessed 8

tra at Liverpool 1886. The press, public, and musical community reacted to these bands – interestingly, all from Austria – in different ways. While Strauss's London employment was criticised as being purely commercial, in Melbourne a competing Australian Band was 'spurred into temporary cohesion' to 'avenge the supposed indignity' of 'the importation of a foreign band'.[17] In Liverpool, the tensions arising from the employment of a non-British orchestra were further complicated by issues of gender.

As we have seen, the repertoire of the bands and light orchestras at the exhibitions was relatively codified. Most ensembles played similar works in similar genres and styles, with only a small amount of individual variation (such as a greater density of waltzes in the Strauss Orchestra's programmes).[18] There was, equally, nothing inherently 'British' or 'Australian' in the works played – Wagner, Meyerbeer, and Rossini were as popular as Sullivan – but the reception of continental European bands at times brought out an aggressive strain of nationalism. This nationalism was of the kind that Dahlhaus has described as emerging 'as an expression of a politically motivated need', appearing 'when national independence is being sought, denied, or jeopardized rather than attained or consolidated'.[19] For many critics, the employment of foreign bands in the context of an exhibition – for all the universalist rhetoric, a supposedly 'national' institution – was considered an attack on their own local musicians, and in a sense, denying their nation's musical independence. Thus, while the press were generally critical of bands at the exhibitions overall, they jumped to the defence of those that could be considered British (or Australian), when they were presented in juxtaposition with foreign bands.[20]

Outrage at the employment of non-British bands appears throughout most of the British exhibitions. During the 1883 Fisheries Exhibition, parliament even became involved in the debate around the employment of non-British musicians, with one member suggesting that it was unfair that visiting bands were given 'posts of honour' in prominent positions such as the conservatory and main building, while 'the English were relegated to obscure positions in the garden grounds' where crowds may not immediately notice them.[21] In 1884, at the Health Exhibition, the British bands were seen to have been placed in

---

Mar. 2021].

[17] 'Exhibition Notes', *Argus*, 18 Oct. 1880, p. 6; 'Music at the Exhibition', *Sydney Morning Herald*, 25 Oct. 1880, p. 6.

[18] The only exception was perhaps the Blue Hungarian Band, who played at Liverpool and Edinburgh in 1886 and Glasgow in 1888, making use of several 'czimbalom' or dulcimers, and performing 'distinctive airs of a distinctive race'. See 'Music at Glasgow International Exhibition', *Magazine of Music*, 5:7 (Jul. 1888), p. 162; 'Musical Notes', *Liverpool Mercury*, 12 Aug. 1886, p. 7.

[19] Dahlhaus, *Nineteenth-Century Music*, p. 38.

[20] Trevor Herbert and Arnold Myers, 'Music for the Multitude: Accounts of Brass Bands Entering Enderby Jackson's Crystal Palace Contests in the 1860s', *Early Music*, 38:4 (2010), 571–84, at p. 571.

[21] T.L. Southgate, 'Foreign Musical Produce', *Musical Standard*, 25:991 (28 Jul. 1883), 52–3, at p. 52.

direct competition with those visiting from France and Germany. The *Musical Times* – so often critical of military bands – here blamed a lack of government funding for the limited public awareness of their own musical institutions.[22] In continental Europe, they reported, such bands were state funded rather than supported by private subscriptions, and therefore had better resources and were more frequently heard by the public: 'the Health Exhibition, by importing bands from abroad, has made contrast easy in this respect'.[23]

Despite this supposed lack of government investment, many publications also openly considered the British bands to be simply better than their continental European counterparts. Also during the Health Exhibition, the *Musical World* proudly stated, 'we may congratulate ourselves that the German and French military bands ... have not eclipsed those associated with our own Coldstream and Grenadier Guards'.[24] In the lead up to the Inventions Exhibition the following year, *The Times* argued that military bands 'from all parts of England' could, as they had at the Health Exhibition, be 'expected to show a standard of popular musical culture at least equal to that of the French "orphéonistes" and "fanfares" and, at any rate, greatly superior to the terrible visitation which the country of Beethoven sends to our shores in the shape of the typical German band'.[25] Further still, when finally it was decided, at the Colonial and Indian Exhibition of 1886, that no non-British bands would perform, the *Musical Standard* received at least one letter suggesting that this was 'a pity' as it was a lost opportunity to favourably compare British bands to those from other parts of Europe.[26] Non-British bands also became the subject of derision in the satirical press, with *Punch*, for example, openly mocking the German bands in 1884, describing 'Bismarck's Cuirassiers defiantly blowing their own trumpets' by performing 'music written for the sweetest of strings upon the brassiest of brass'.[27] They concluded that if an audience member – having grown so 'accustomed to ... [the] tours de force' of German bands – were told that the bands 'were just going to imitate on a couple of dozen trombones the bleating of a lamb or the warbling of a nightingale, he would receive the intelligence without the faintest soupçon of astonishment'.[28]

While much of this discourse centred on the employment of continental European bands at exhibitions in England, in Scotland the mood was quite different. Bands, wherever they were from, were consistently positively received in the daily press surrounding the Edinburgh and Glasgow exhibitions, and even the musical press found little to criticise. The Blue Hungarian Band, for example, was described in 1886 by the *Edinburgh Evening Dispatch* as ranking

---

[22] 'Military Bands', *Musical Times*, 25:498 (1 Aug. 1884), pp. 452–3.
[23] Ibid.
[24] Phosphor, 'Facts in Fragments', *Musical World*, 62:41 (11 Oct. 1884), p. 644.
[25] 'Music at the International Inventions Exhibition', *The Times*, 17 Feb. 1885, p. 8.
[26] Thomas Hopkinson, 'Music at the Colonial and Indian Exhibition', *Musical Standard*, 31:1144 (3 Jul. 1886), p. 11.
[27] 'Our Insane-Itary Guide to the Health Exhibition', *Punch*, 21 Jun. 1884, p. 290.
[28] Ibid.

among 'the most attractive musical entertainments provided during the run of the Exhibition'.[29] At Edinburgh 1890, the Royal Swedish Värmland Grenadiers were equally described as 'so popular' that management arranged an extension of their engagement, providing 'a genuine musical treat' for the Exhibition's visitors.[30] Where nationalist sentiments occasionally appeared in the Scottish reception of bands, it was not in response to continental bands, but instead, those from England. For, example, a correspondent for the *Musical Opinion and Music Trade Review* reported on the local musicians' frustration at Edinburgh 1890 that 'no expense' had been 'spared in bringing military and other bands from across the border, even when these are at least not superior to our own', concluding that, while the Exhibition 'cannot do without the English bands' they 'might engage our own more freely'.[31]

In all, however, the most spectacularly nationalistic musical criticism at any exhibition came from a single individual – albeit one supposedly speaking on behalf of many others and given a platform in one of the most prominent musical journals of the era.[32] In a series of letters to the *Musical World*, Thomas Reynolds (1848–1919) – a viola player of the Hallé orchestra, and frequent correspondent with the *World* – protested the engagement of 'foreign' bands at London 1885. Only two ensembles out of the thirteen bands employed at London were not from Britain: the 5th Pomeranian Blücher Hussars and the Strauss Orchestra. Discounting the remaining eleven, Reynolds expressed his 'astonishment and disgust' that German and Austrian bands were to be employed at 'that essentially national institution' of the Exhibition, given a lack of available work in London for English performers.[33] He then turned to argue that the visiting performers might choose to stay in England after their engagement, taking up 'their residence permanently in this country – as invariably happens on such occasions – thereby still further reducing the daily diminishing incomes of English musicians'.[34] Concluding with a call-to-arms for British musicians, Reynolds essentially suggests that to support the employment of foreign musicians was treasonous:

> I have heard a great outcry about the want of patriotism of those few individuals who dare to rejoice in the successes gained by the brave and patriotic Arabs of the Soudan; yet, surely, even such conduct cannot be compared with that of these

---

[29] 'The Blue Hungarian Band, A Remarkable Company of Musicians', *Edinburgh Evening Dispatch*, 25 Sep. 1886, p. 2.

[30] 'International Exhibition Notes', *North British Advertiser & Ladies' Journal*, 30 Aug. 1890, p. 4.

[31] 'Music in Scotland', *Musical Opinion and Music Trade Review*, 13:153 (1 Jun. 1890), 394–5, at p. 394.

[32] Richard Kitson, 'The Musical World', *Répertoire international de la press musicale / Retrospective Index to Music Periodicals* <https://www.ripm.org/?page=JournalInfo&ABB=MWO> [accessed 4 Jun. 2020].

[33] Thomas Reynolds, '"General Depression" and the Inventions Exhibition', *Musical World*, 63:9 (28 Feb. 1885), p. 140.

[34] *Ibid*.

high-born and intellectual Englishmen (most of whom are supported by the contributions of English taxpayers), to whom have been confided the arrangements for an English national exhibition, but who not merely neglect the fine opportunity thus afforded them of providing a little extra employment for their not over-wealthy fellow-countrymen, but put themselves to a deal of trouble (and probably extra expense) to bring over a body of foreigners to compete with English musicians.[35]

Several months later, Reynolds wrote again to the *Musical World*, angered that his suggested protest had not been carried out. While he assured readers that many other musicians 'fully concurred' with his opinions, 'not being bricklayers' labourers, or journeymen carpenters' they would not stage a public demonstration.[36] Using intensely militaristic language, he went on to state that the present 'painful results' were due to the 'apathy and dilatoriness of British musicians' who had left the 'press to fight their battles for them' having first 'allowed the enemy to march into the citadel unopposed'.[37] The 'painful results' to which Reynolds referred was the employment of the Strauss Orchestra, whose performances formed one of the most talked about aspects of music at the Inventions Exhibition in 1885.

THE STRAUSS ORCHESTRA

Popular music and nationalism reached a notable juncture in the reception of the Strauss Orchestra at London 1885. This band, conducted by Eduard Strauss – brother of Johann II and Josef (1827–70), and son of Johann I (1804–49) – was employed to perform twice daily for two months between June and August. The orchestra occupied an interesting midpoint on the continuum between the 'high art' performed by the early music ensembles in the Albert Hall and the military and brass bands in the grounds. Using both string and wind instruments, they performed a mixture of the waltzes and quadrilles associated with the Strauss name, and less-typical orchestral versions of 'high art' works (including Josef Strauss's arrangement of Beethoven's 'Moonlight' Sonata; see selected programmes in Table 11). As Shaw wrote, 'a musically endowed man may be either a Richter or a Christy Minstrel ... Strauss holds an intermediate position between the two extremes'.[38]

Some in the press approached this engagement with nostalgia, remembering Johann Strauss I's successful British tour of 1838.[39] Others, like Reynolds, were horrified by the salary Strauss was awarded – apparently £6,000 for two

---

[35] Ibid.
[36] Thomas Reynolds, 'The Engagement of Foreign Orchestras', *Musical World*, 63:25 (20 Jun. 1885), p. 380.
[37] Ibid.
[38] [George Bernard Shaw, unsigned], 'Art Corner', *Our Corner*, Sep. 1885, repr. in Dan H. Laurence (ed.), *Shaw's Music: The Complete Musical Criticism in Three Volumes*, vol. 2 (London, 1981), p. 290.
[39] 'International Inventions Exhibition: The Musical Section', *Glasgow Herald*, 14 Feb. 1885, p. 5.

Table 11. Selected Programmes, Strauss Orchestra,
International Inventions Exhibition, 1885

Work	Composer
9 June 1885	
Overture *Das Spitzentuch der Königin*	Johann Strauss II
Valse *Landeskinder*	Eduard Strauss
Funeral March	Fryderyk Chopin
Polka *Annen*	Johann Strauss II
An der schönen blauen Donau	Johann Strauss II
Entr'acte and Pizzicato Polka *Sylvia*	Léo Delibes (1815–1910)
Valse *Neu Wien*	Johann Strauss II
Ave Maria	Franz Schubert
Polka Mazurka *Liebeszeichen*	Eduard Strauss
Old English Song 'Once I Loved a Maiden Fair'	
Quick Polka *Jugendfeuer*	Eduard Strauss
16 June 1885	
Overture *Der Freischütz*	Carl Maria von Weber
Valse *Wo die Zitronen blühen*	Johann Strauss II
Adagio Bis [sic] Moll Sonata	Ludwig van Beethoven
Polka *Vergnugungsanzeiger*	Eduard Strauss
Air *Rinaldo*	G.F. Handel
Concert March	Elias Parish Alvars (1808–49)
Old English Song 'Once I Loved a Maiden Fair'	
Valse *Lagunen*	Johann Strauss II
Nocturne	Fryderyk Chopin
Quick Polka *Free of Duty*	Eduard Strauss
29 June 1885	
Overture *Athalie*	Felix Mendelssohn
Valse (on English Airs) *Greeting*	Eduard Strauss
Air and Recitative *Rinaldo*	G.F. Handel
Polka *The Postillion of Love*	Eduard Strauss
Overture *Das Spitzentuch der Königin*	Johann Strauss II
Valse *Fledermaus*	Johann Strauss II
Moment Musical	Franz Schubert
Quick Polka *Steeplechase*	Johann Strauss II

months of performances (or roughly £660,000 as of 2020) – taking exception to such an expense being granted to a foreign band. A writer in the *Musical Opinion and Music Trade Review* was particularly indignant about the cost, questioning the importation of 'instrumentalists who are admitted – even when their speciality of dance music is concerned – to be no better than, if so good as, our home musicians'.[40]

The generalised outrage in the press about the significant expenditure on 'foreign' music prior to Strauss's first performance set the tone for the orchestra's overall critical reception. Their initial concert, in a bandstand in the gardens, was very poorly received in the musical press: as the *Musical Times* wrote, 'they came, they saw, but it can scarcely be said that they conquered'.[41] They received so much criticism in their first few weeks that the organisers questioned whether the outdoor venue was to blame, and their concerts were quickly relocated into the Albert Hall. The *Musical World* reported that, despite the official reason for the venue change being the supposed inadequacy of the outdoor performance conditions, 'the fundamental reason' was really 'the adverse opinions passed'.[42] The move to the Albert Hall only encouraged more critical scrutiny, with the *Musical Times* reporting that never before had critics been 'called together to pronounce a serious verdict' in such a way.[43] Strauss's first indoor programme, containing many of his signature waltzes, but also transcriptions of Wagner, Schubert, English songs, and 'a most cruel distortion of Chopin's Marche Funèbre', was regarded by the *Musical World* as a direct 'challenge to criticism', but also 'a vindication', as their assessments – and those of many other critics – did not change.[44]

Shortly after their first Albert Hall concert, Strauss (whose energetic conducting, violin in hand, is depicted in Figure 24) was interviewed by the *Musical Opinion*. While he was immensely pleased with his public reception, describing the applause he received as not 'equalled, even in sunny Italy',[45] he was evidently unhappy with the way his band had been described in the musical press. He suggested that the negative reactions were due to mistaken expectations – that many thought he would be presenting 'classical music' – something that he had never considered his orchestra to play. He also returned fire on the critics themselves, stating that he should never have tried playing Wagner to British audiences who – unlike those in continental Europe – 'had not learned to appreciate this great master'.[46] This only caused many writers to double down on their criticism, with the *Musical Times* retaliating by 'paraphras[ing] the

---

[40] 'Contemporary Opinion: Foreign versus English Musicians', *Musical Opinion and Music Trade Review*, 8:94 (1 Jul. 1885), 501–3, at p. 501.
[41] 'Music at South Kensington', *Musical Times*, 26:509 (1 Jul. 1885), 387–8, at p. 387.
[42] J.B., 'Strauss' band at the Inventions Exhibition', *Musical World*, 63:24 (13 Jun. 1885), p. 372.
[43] 'Music at South Kensington', *Musical Times*, p. 387.
[44] *Ibid*; J.B., 'Strauss' Band at the Inventions Exhibition', p. 372.
[45] 'Contemporary Opinion: Foreign versus English Musicians', *Musical Opinion*, p. 501.
[46] *Ibid*.

Figure 24. 'Musical Recollections' [Strauss at centre], in John Dinsdale, *Sketches at the Inventories* (London, 1885), [pages not numbered].

answer given by Claude Melnotte in "The Lady of Lyons," when Damas accuses him of not understanding his own language – "Not as you play it".[47]

Despite the venom of much of the musical press's attacks on Strauss, even by their own reports, audiences greatly enjoyed the Orchestra, and even the *Musical Times* admitted that Strauss gave 'pleasure to an enormous number of people'.[48] Although audiences were consistent, class once again pervaded the critical response. Shaw noted that a large crowd was not an achievement in itself: the same 'number of heads', he stated, could be attracted by a 'Christy Minstrel show, a variety entertainment, or a prizefight', the only difference being their 'character and class'.[49] The fervent public reception was particularly lamented by the musical press in comparison to the small audiences at the concurrent 'ancient music' concerts. Shaw also mocked a 'substantial British Matron' who, during the Bristol Madrigal Society's performance:

> walked proudly into the amphitheatre with her daughter, hesitated, and said in a distinct and audible voice 'This isn't Strauss, is it?' Her daughter looked suspiciously at melodious Bristol, and replied doubtfully 'I don't think it can be'. 'Then come out of this' said the matron, and retired somewhat indignantly.[50]

---

[47] 'Music at South Kensington', *Musical Times*, p. 387.
[48] Ibid.
[49] [Shaw], 'A Substitute for Strauss', *Dramatic Review*, 27 Jun. 1885, repr. in *Shaw's Music*, p. 276.
[50] [George Bernard Shaw, unsigned], 'Brasses and Pipes', *Dramatic Review*, 11 Jul. 1885, repr. in *Shaw's Music*, p. 309.

For many, Strauss's orchestra was purely entertainment, and thus purely commercial. *The Times* described the engagement as 'agreeable to the public and useful to the *entrepreneur*', but hoped that 'the educational purpose' of the exhibitions would 'not be thrown into the shade by them'.[51] *Musical Times* editor Henry Lunn similarly suggested that, though 'music was made a prominent feature in the prospectus' no 'important results to the art' had yet been achieved. While Strauss 'may have greatly added to the profits of the Exhibition, assuredly neither of the advertised objectives of the undertaking – "No. 1, Inventions; No. 2, Music" – can have been in the slightest degree benefited by this excessive outlay'.[52]

THE AUSTRIAN AND AUSTRALIAN BANDS

In Melbourne several years earlier, the employment of another 'Strauss' Band caused another nationalistic response. The Melbourne 1880 engagement of the Austrian Strauss Band (Military and Orchestral) conducted by Alois F. Wildner began inauspiciously, when the ship they were travelling on was seriously delayed and their concerts had to be postponed. While waiting for their arrival, the *Exhibition Visitors' Daily Programme* – a newspaper printed by the organisers – regularly updated readers on the ship's location, and provided facts and information about the band, building a sense of anticipation. The 'celebrated' band of fifty-five players, who laid 'claim to a repertoire even more extensive' than the 'famous Coldstream guards', were considered to give 'the most brilliant examples of military music in the world'.[53] On arrival, the Band played first at the Flemington Racecourse and the Melbourne Town Hall in performances of 'unqualified success', and their first concert at the Exhibition saw its highest attendance since opening day.[54]

Public and press alike were thrilled by the Austrians' opening Exhibition performance (see programme, Table 12), and the overwhelmingly positive response to their 'very choice' selection of works prompted 'no feeling but that of the highest admiration'.[55] The band performed some of their programme in a military band formation, and some as an orchestra, and the *Argus* reported how 'finely' their repertoire choices brought out their 'dual character'.[56] The band was so well-received and drew so much attention from the public that 'the specific business of the Exhibition languished decidedly when the music was on', leaving large sections of the building empty as the majority of visitors crowded to hear the music. It was reported that 'the great bulk of the visitors

---

[51] 'The Musical Loan Collection at South Kensington', *The Times*, 25 Jul. 1885, p. 3.
[52] Henry C. Lunn, 'The London Musical Season', *Musical Times*, 26:510 (1 Aug. 1885), 449–53, at p. 451.
[53] 'Melbourne International Exhibition', *Exhibition Visitors' Daily Programme*, 3 (2 Oct. 1880), p. 1.
[54] 'Exhibition Notes', *Age*, 16 Oct. 1880, p. 5.
[55] *Ibid*.
[56] 'Exhibition Notes', *Argus*, 16 Oct. 1880, p. 8.

Table 12. Austrian Strauss Band, Melbourne International Exhibition, 15 October 1880

Work	Composer
Grand March *Le Prophète*	Giacomo Meyerbeer
Festival Overture	Jacopo Foroni (1825–58)
Waltz *The Beautiful Blue Danube*	Johann Strauss II
Awakening of Spring	Carl Philipp Emanuel Bach (1714–88)
Overture *William Tell*	Gioachino Rossini
Overture *Pique Dame*	Franz von Suppé
Polka *Special Correspondence*	Franz von Suppé
Selection *Lucrezia Borgia*	Gaetano Donizetti
Chorus of Pages *Princess of Trebizonde*	Jacques Offenbach (1819–80)
Fantasia on the Austrian Military Signal Retraite	Béla Kéler (1820–82)
Austrian National Anthem	
'God Save the Queen'	

came just about the time the music was to commence, and that they left when it ceased'.[57]

Although the public response to the Austrian Band in Melbourne was extremely favourable, the response among local musicians was one of outrage and a response from the community was swift. A sense of rivalry created by the fervent anticipation of the Austrian Band quickly compelled Melbourne musicians into forming a competing 'Australian Band', conducted by Leon Caron, a French migrant, and a composer already prominent within the Exhibition, having composed the cantata *Victoria* for its opening ceremony. The *Sydney Morning Herald* described the formation of the competing Australian band as entirely related to the 'proverbial' 'susceptibilities and jealousies of musicians':

> the arrival of the Austrian Strauss Band, and the enthusiasm with which the performances have been received, seem to have disturbed and aroused every morsel of envy and jealousy which exists in the breasts of the musicians of Victoria; and all petty rivalries sank into insignificance in the resolve to avenge the supposed indignity put upon them by the importation of a foreign band.[58]

The ninety members of the Australian band – as the *Sydney Morning Herald* was quick to note, most of whom were migrants and therefore 'Australian in name only' – included 'every local player of repute', and attempted to match the Austrians in both military and orchestral formations.[59] The sense of rivalry was so strong that all players performed throughout the entire Exhibition

---

[57] *Ibid*.
[58] 'Music at the Exhibition', *Sydney Morning Herald*, 25 Oct. 1880, p. 3.
[59] *Ibid*; 'Exhibition Notes', *Age*, 18 Oct. 1880, p. 5.

voluntarily.[60] Giving its first performance the day after the Austrian Band's debut, the Australians performed some of the same repertoire (including Rossini's *William Tell* Overture, the Grand March from Meyerbeer's *Le Prophète*, and selections from operas by Donizetti, see programme, Table 13), in an act the *Sydney Morning Herald* described as being in 'bad taste, and worse discretion'.[61]

The Australian Band's reception was mixed. The *Sydney Morning Herald* noted how 'humiliating' it was to hear well-respected local musicians engaging in such parochialism and making remarks 'against the invasion of the strangers'.[62] The *Argus*, too, described their 'regretful feeling' that the band had been 'spurred into temporary cohesion' in a display of something like 'trade unionism' rather than 'for the sake of art'.[63] Audiences seem to have enjoyed the performances, but the *Argus* noted that the band demonstrated a 'want of practising together' that 'barred the way to an artistic finish' which was particularly noticeable in comparison to the Austrians 'amongst whose members perfect drill has produced complete subjection of the individual members to the will of the conductor'.[64] The *Age* was also conciliatory, stating that while the Australians were not 'altogether perfect' they showed 'a most creditable sample of what can be produced by effective organisation'.[65]

Both bands, Austrian and Australian, also occasionally performed with pianists; the Australians working with James Ure (1855–1917) and the Austrians with French pianist Henri Ketten (1848–83). In this, the Austrians were once again far more popular. Following performances at both the Exhibition and

Table 13. Caron's Australian Band, Melbourne International Exhibition, 16 October 1880

Work	Composer
Overture *Der Freischütz*	Carl Maria von Weber
Potpourri of Tunes from Donizetti's Operas	Gaetano Donizetti
Waltz *My Best Day in Berlin*	Joseph Gung'l
Overture *William Tell*	Gioachino Rossini
Overture *Zampa*	Ferdinand Hérold
Turkish March	Theodor Michaelis (1831–87)
Polka *Pizzicato*	Johann Strauss II
Quadrille *Covent Garden*	Charles Coote Jr. (1831–1916)
Grand March *Le Prophète*	Giacomo Meyerbeer
'God Save the Queen'	

[60] 'Music at the Exhibition', *Sydney Morning Herald*, 25 Oct.1880, p. 3.
[61] *Ibid.*
[62] *Ibid.*
[63] 'Exhibition Notes', *Argus*, 18 Oct. 1880, p. 6.
[64] *Ibid.*
[65] 'Exhibition Notes', *Age*, 18 Oct. 1880, p. 5.

the Town Hall, public demand for further performances led Ketten to delay his departure from Melbourne in December.[66] Ada Cambridge's novel *The Three Miss Kings* – set during the Melbourne 1880 Exhibition – includes a description of a joint recital by Ketten and the Austrian Band.[67] Much of her depiction of the concert centres on the Australian public's capacity to appreciate European music, explaining that while 'Australians may not have such an enlightened appreciation of high-class music as, say, the educated Viennese, who live and breathe and have their being in it', this was not due to 'indifference', but rather 'inexperience'.[68] Cambridge continues that the Austrian Band were always playing to a full and attentive audience, and 'no city in Europe (according to his own death-bed testimony) ever offered such incense of loving enthusiasm to Ketten's genius' as Melbourne.[69] This passage illustrates further some of the insecurity the colonial musical public felt, with a similar need to demonstrate their understanding and prove themselves equal to European musical standards as was demonstrated in the reception of orchestral and vocal 'high art'.

VIENNESE LADIES' ORCHESTRA

At Liverpool 1886, the press was once again filled with angry letters decrying the employment of a 'foreign' band, this time further compounded by contemporary arguments about gender and music, and women's capacity to perform to the same standard as men. The Viennese Ladies' Orchestra (Figure 25), conducted by Marie Schipek (c.1841–?), played regularly at the Exhibition between May and July, where delays in construction of the building's concert hall forced the Orchestra outside onto a bandstand in the gardens. The Orchestra's programmes appear similar to those of the military bands alongside which they played, made up of potpourris, selections, overtures, and quadrilles, as well as many waltzes by Strauss II and Waldteufel. It is difficult, however, to discuss their musical choices in detail, as no printed programmes appear to have survived, and full programmes are rarely mentioned in the press. Instead, when not describing the women's appearance, reviews were largely filled with outrage at the band's employment and £2,000 payment (approximately £214,000 as of 2019).[70] As the *Liverpool Review* commented, 'at the end of their sojourn here they will return well satisfied to their native haunts, having ... lined their pockets pretty thickly with British gold'.[71] The *Liverpool Mercury* was indignant that an 'orchestra whose members are permanently resident in England' had not been employed, given, as the critic believed, there were better qualified performers 'in our own country, in our own city', capable of more than 'an occasional operatic selection and a string of polkas, waltzes, and quadrilles'.[72]

---

[66] 'Amusements', *Sydney Morning Herald*, 23 Feb. 1881, p. 6.
[67] Ada Cambridge, *The Three Miss Kings* (1891; repr. London, 1987), p. 121.
[68] Ibid.
[69] Ibid, p. 122.
[70] 'Musical Notes', *Liverpool Mercury*, 27 May 1886, p. 6.
[71] [no title], *Liverpool Review*, 22 May 1886, p. 13.
[72] 'Musical Notes', *Liverpool Mercury*, 22 May 1886, p. 7.

Figure 25. 'The Viennese Lady Orchestra', *Magazine of Music*, 4:38 (May 1887), p. 26. Image published with permission of ProQuest. Further reproduction is prohibited without permissions. Image produced by ProQuest as part of *British Periodicals*. www.proquest.com.

At London 1885, critics had legitimised their anger at the employment of Strauss and his orchestra by undermining the performers' abilities and harshly criticising performance elements and repertoire choices. In the case of a women's orchestra, discussion of music was almost unnecessary, as critics could use the performers' gender to undermine their professional status. During the nineteenth century, women who encroached on the traditionally masculine concert hall (or here, the even more decidedly masculine bandstand) were often met with open hostility. Despite a growing trend in the formation of dedicated women's orchestras and bands towards the turn of the century,[73] these organisations encountered a great deal of resistance, as women continued to be routinely and overwhelmingly excluded from professional orchestras.[74] 'Ladies' Orchestras', both professional and amateur, playing in theatres, tea shops and at other exhibitions, were important institutions offering training and employment to many women performers.[75] But their existence further fuelled ongoing debates about the 'professional' and 'amateur' status of women's music-making,

---

[73] See for example, Greta Kent's illustrative *A View from the Bandstand* (London, 1983) a memoir filled with images of the women musicians from her family album.

[74] Judith Tick, 'Women in Music', *Grove Music Online* <http://www.oxfordmusiconline.com/> [accessed 8 Mar. 2021].

[75] Sophie Fuller, 'Women Musicians and Professionalism in the Late-Nineteenth and Early-Twentieth Centuries', in Rosemary Golding (ed.), *The Music Profession in*

heightened here by the comparison implicit in the lucrative employment of a band both 'foreign' and female, in contrast to other local – and it might be assumed, male – bands.

Throughout the reception of the Viennese Ladies' Orchestra, many critics focused their attention on the performers' bodies and appearance, and particularly on details of their clothing. This was common to the reception of women instrumentalists at the time, who were often regarded 'as women first and artists second',[76] and where even the most highly successful performers remained 'caught in a web of conflicting ideas' about the relative value of the works they performed and 'problematic notions of the use of the body'.[77] For example, the *Liverpool Courier*'s only comment on the Orchestra's first performance was that, 'attired in blue and white, these fair musicians looked charming'.[78] The *Liverpool Review*, too, gave no details of the music, describing only the 'striking effect' of their 'white dresses and tri-coloured sashes'.[79] The *Liverpool Mercury* gave a lengthy description of the women's appearance, sexualising the performers as 'nymphs'. It described them as:

> a well-figured body of ladies ... [that] look like the prospective mothers of a military nation. There is something martial in their costumes of ruby satin bodices, slashed across the breast after military fashion with silver braid, to which are subjoined their handsomely-made short white muslin skirts. They soon settled down in the orchestra, and after a few, premonitory twangs from recalcitrant violins, the fraulein who leads the band stepped forward, and, with earnestness in her face and energy in her arms, waved on her attended nymphs. The music proceeded with occasional interludes of rest for a couple of hours, until, indeed, one began to wonder how these blonde musicians, hatless and in thin attire, could endure the chill night air.[80]

This same review extended its discussion of appearances to women in the audience, contrasting the orchestra's 'nymphs' with the 'Lancashire witches settled down recumbently'[81] to listen while engaged 'in the hopelessly impossible task of inducing the abbreviated skirts of fashion to hide the persistently obtrusive and disobedient ankles of nature'.[82]

Britain, 1780–1920: New Perspectives on Status and Identity (Abingdon, 2018), pp. 149–69, at p.163.

[76] Elizabeth Kertesz, 'Perceptions of Women as Composers and Instrumental Performers in the Allgemeine Wiener Musik-Zeitung (1841–48)', *Context: Journal of Music Research*, 4 (1992/1993), 10–15, at p. 14.

[77] Katharine Ellis, 'Female Pianists and Their Male Critics in Nineteenth-Century Paris', *Journal of the American Musicological Society*, 50:2/3 (1997), 353–85, at p. 355.

[78] 'Liverpool International Exhibition', *Liverpool Courier*, 18 May 1886, p. 4.

[79] [no title], *Liverpool Review*, 26 Jun. 1886, p. 13.

[80] 'Saturday Night at the Exhibition', *Liverpool Mercury*, 24 May 1886, p. 5.

[81] Potentially referencing the Pendle witches, popularly depicted as hag-like old women, and well-known in the nineteenth century through William Harrison Ainsworth's extraordinarily popular *The Lancashire Witches: A Romance of Pendle Forest* (London, 1854).

[82] 'Saturday Night at the Exhibition', *Liverpool Mercury*, 24 May 1886, p. 5.

When the music itself was addressed, it was rarely reviewed positively, despite the press's own reports of large and engaged audiences who were 'charmed by the strains of the delightful music'.[83] Reviewers instead placed frequent emphasis on perceptions of physical strength or weakness. These were concepts often raised in nineteenth-century discussions of women's musical abilities, and as such it is therefore not unusual to see women performers criticised for a perceived lack of strength and power.[84] As the *Porcupine* described the Orchestra, they produced a 'musical effect [that] would be reckoned weak even for a second-rate "spa band"', although the reviewer apparently enjoyed the 'charm of novelty in seeing a number of girls in pretty uniforms fiddling through a set of German waltzes'.[85] The *Liverpool Review* also described their tone as 'thin and scratchy', and 'not up to the standard we have a right to expect, considering the excellent local material we have ready to be utilized'.[86]

Letters to the editor also often discussed the Orchestra in similar terms: one writer to the *Liverpool Mercury* – using the pseudonym 'Bagpipes' and describing himself as 'a Scotchman' who 'delight[s] in really good and powerful instrumental music' – was disappointed at an apparent lack of power in the women's playing. He suggested that the performers were probably very good, but for their own wellbeing, should not be playing outdoors. This letter ends by adding that 'a lady friend' had drawn the author's attention to the performers' lack of hats, and asked that the Exhibition provide them with 'suitable covering for their heads' during the cold nights.[87] Others commentators made pointed mention of the need to 'strengthen' the Exhibition's musical programme through the employment of British military bands instead of foreign women: 'when you have a good article at home it is better to employ it than travel farther afield on the plea that an imported article must be superior'.[88]

The Strauss Orchestra at London 1885, the Austrian Band at Melbourne 1880, and the Viennese Ladies' Orchestra at Liverpool 1886 were all critiqued, either by the musical press or local musical communities, in nationalistic terms, and critics argued that their place (and often, their salaries) should have been given instead to British or Australian performers. They were not, however, the only 'foreign' performers who appeared at these exhibitions. Dutch and Belgian early music ensembles appeared to glowing receptions at London 1885, and much prestige was given to the Sydney Exhibition by the appointment of Milanese

---

[83] 'The Exhibition', *Liverpool Courier*, 27 May 1886, p. 4; 'Liverpool International Exhibition', *Liverpool Mercury*, 20 May 1886, p. 6.

[84] Paula Gillett, *Musical Women in England, 1870–1914: 'Encroaching on All Man's Privileges'* (New York, 2000), p. 21.

[85] 'Musical Notes', *The Porcupine*, 22 May 1886, p. 5.

[86] [no title], *Liverpool Review*, 22 May 1886, p. 13; [no title], *Liverpool Review*, 26 Jun. 1886, p. 13.

[87] Bagpipes, 'Music at the Shipperies', *Liverpool Mercury*, 25 May 1886, p. 6.

[88] F.N., 'Music at the Shipperies', *Liverpool Mercury*, 25 May 1886, p. 6.

conductor Paolo Giorza, or to Melbourne 1888 by engaging British conductor Frederic Cowen.

It appears that musical communities were willing to accept the expertise of outsiders performing 'high art', or lending higher status to the event, essentially bringing with them 'cultural capital' in its embodied state.[89] These musicians, it was felt, could provide something previously unavailable to the local musical community, and were widely accepted in the hope of transferring some of their capital to the community itself in line with the aims of the exhibitions to exert an 'improving' influence over the public. When their music held a lower status – for example, light orchestral or band music – those invested in local music felt the importation of performers was degrading to their own capabilities: an admission or capitulation that they might require help in even these 'lesser' forms.

This is largely related to the musical and cultural insecurities of both British and Australian society. Throughout the nineteenth century, Britain is considered to have had something of an 'inferiority complex' or identity crisis in regard to their musical culture, culminating in a constant need to re-assert that they were *not* the 'land without music'.[90] In the Australian colonies, there was a strong desire for recognition of Australia's cultural capabilities as equal to those of Britain, and of the major cities of Melbourne and Sydney as equal to London, in a climate of assumptions of British cultural superiority.[91] This Australian cultural insecurity can be seen in both the disproportionate response to the employment of a single foreign band at Melbourne 1880, but equally in the employment of Cowen at Melbourne 1888. Cowen was not an Australian, but from the 'home' country, Britain, which added an additional element of imperial sentiment in the prestige he brought to the undertaking, and suggests a lack of confidence in the available local musicians' capabilities.[92]

As has been shown in the previous chapters, in the context of the 'universal' display of exhibitions, the musical press were compelled to write positively of concerts of more esoteric genres to maintain their sense of cultural superiority, particularly when such music was placed in direct comparison with the new, modern, and popular; they were equally compelled to criticise music that did not conform to their rigid ideas of cultural status. When any music other than high art was provided by foreign musicians, the criticism was further compounded, as it brought out the insecurities the critics held of their own national musical capabilities. This resulted in a surprisingly defensive and nationalistic reception.

---

[89] Pierre Bourdieu, 'The Forms of Capital', in J. Richardson (ed.), *Handbook of Theory and Research for the Sociology of Education* (New York, 1986), 241–58, at p. 244.

[90] Colin Eatock, 'The Crystal Palace Concerts: Canon Formation and the English Musical Renaissance', *Nineteenth-Century Music*, 34:1 (2010), 87–105, at pp. 89–91.

[91] Jennifer Royle, 'Musical (Ad)venturers: Colonial Composers and Composition in Melbourne, 1870–1901', *Nineteenth-Century Music Review*, 2:2 (2005), 133–59, at p. 135.

[92] Thérèse Radic, 'The Victorian Orchestra 1889–1891: In the Wake of the Centennial Exhibition Orchestra, Melbourne', *Australasian Music Research*, 1 (1996). 13–101, at p. 20.

The non-British or non-Australian bands discussed in this chapter still performed music in genres familiar to British and Australian audiences, and could thus be critiqued in direct comparison to local music and musicians. As the next chapters show, however, musical performances and objects from non-Western traditions – entirely unfamiliar to the host countries' cultures – were received in a strikingly different way.

CHAPTER 8

Curating Non-Western Musics

Alongside the three 'period' rooms of the ancient music display at the London 1885 Inventions Exhibition stood a fourth: the 'Oriental Room'. Less conspicuous than its historical neighbours, the 'curious collection' it housed included, according to the *Monthly Musical Record*, 'a vast number of quaintly-shaped instruments of all kinds, stringed, wind, and pulsatile'.[1] International exhibitions provided many different avenues for encounters between Western and non-Western cultures, and their musical displays were no exception. These encounters were, of course, highly curated, as the organisational practices that governed the exhibitions were deliberately constructed to perpetuate cultural and racial hierarchies. Narratives of Western 'progress' could be strengthened by contrasting objects of the Western musical tradition with 'barbarous' and 'savage' non-Western equivalents, in a space that took no account of these objects' differing cultural and social uses and contexts. Yet, despite this one-sided mode of display, these exhibitions provided some of the first large-scale public forums for Western audiences to experience music from beyond Western Europe, not through 'the imaginary world of European exoticism' but head on, as the 'real thing'.[2]

The exhibitions of the 1880s provided two different forums for the display of non-Western musical instruments. At Sydney 1879, Melbourne 1880, Calcutta 1883, Adelaide 1887, and several of the London exhibitions, non-Western instruments were exhibited in the competitive, general sections, in the same space as newly manufactured Western instruments. Here, they were placed in direct competition with instruments by Western makers and were interpreted explicitly through a Western organological framework. Although some of these exhibits were contributed by British colonial agencies – as occurred at the 1886 Colonial and Indian Exhibition – in a few cases, objects were sent by members of the exhibiting cultures. However, even Abu Bakar the Maharajah of Johor (1833–95), Sourindro Mohun Tagore of Bengal, and the representatives of the Tokyo Institute of Music – three of the most prominent non-Western exhibitors – presented their displays in ways that emphasised a specific interpretive narrative, informed by their individual and complex relationships with the West.

In contrast to these 'competitive' exhibits, at London 1885 and Edinburgh 1890, many non-Western instruments were shown amongst museum-displays of 'ancient' or historical instruments, where they were presented as

---

[1] 'Music and Inventions', *Monthly Musical Record*, 15:176 (1 Aug. 1885), 169–70, at p. 170.
[2] Annegret Fauser, *Musical Encounters at the 1889 Paris World's Fair* (Rochester, 2005), p. 139.

anthropological or 'ethnographic' objects. These instruments came from royal, university, and private collections, and were curated without the input of any member of the cultures that they supposedly represented. Displayed in the context of 'ancient' Western music, these exhibits physically manifested a developmentalist racism common to the period, which viewed non-Western music as representative of an earlier stage in human evolution; it was not 'living and evolved', but rather a precursor to Western music: a part of ancient history.[3] In both these modes of display – 'competitive' or museum – exhibits of non-Western instruments were curated with a Western audience's expectations in mind.

Throughout this chapter and the next, I use the term 'Western' to describe British and Australian (and in a few cases, Anglo-Indian) audiences, and 'non-Western' for a wide variety of musical cultures and traditions from India to China, Japan, Siam, Burma, and many Malay states. These terms are clearly problematic. First, neither term has a definite meaning: 'West', in binary opposition to 'East', depends largely – to quote Hon-Lun Yang – on 'the person defining these words, on the purpose(s) for the definitions, and especially on when the distinctions' were made.[4] Second, these words imply an Orientalist dichotomy that defines one in terms of, or in distinction from the other.[5] Still, I use both terms here partly because there are few succinct alternatives available, but also because – while the terms are metonymic and oppositional – the 'Western' audiences of the nineteenth-century exhibitions whose responses are considered here really did seem to view the 'non-West' as a kind of singular entity. London audiences and critics show a marked simplification in understanding different non-Western cultures, often conflating many into one monolithic 'Oriental' whole. To give just one example, the *World* described Chinese musicians who performed at London 1884 as acknowledging their audience 'with the deepest and gravest salaams'.[6] The term 'salaam' – an Arabic greeting – in the context of a performance by Chinese musicians, was presumably not deployed as a nuanced indicator of the critic's awareness of a Chinese-Muslim minority (there is no evidence that the visiting musicians were a part of this) but instead as a marker of generic 'Eastern-ness'.[7]

Orientalism and Exhibiting Non-Western Music

Although international exhibitions purported to display objects and ideas from across the world, exhibits from non-Western cultures were generally few in number. This is perhaps unsurprising, given that exhibitions were products

---

[3] Bennett Zon, *Representing Non-Western Music in Nineteenth-Century Britain* (Rochester, 2007), p. 9.
[4] Hon-Lun Yang, 'Music, China, and the West: A Musical-Theoretical Introduction', in Hon-Lun Yang and Michael Saffle (eds), *China and the West: Music, Representation, and Reception* (Ann Arbor, 2017), pp. 1–18, at p. 1.
[5] Edward W. Said, *Orientalism* (London, 2003), p. 7.
[6] 'Chinese Music', *World*, repr. *Coventry Herald*, 25 Jul. 1884, p. 4.
[7] Ibid.

of wider Western social and communication networks. While the organisers may have espoused internationalism and universalism, invitations to exhibit were usually issued through government channels, meaning that before they had even begun, exhibitions were limited by both the breadth of the diplomatic networks they employed and political decisions regarding who was invited. In organising Melbourne 1880, for example, the *Weekly Times* reported that the colony of Victoria had issued an 'invitation' to the world, 'asking all the *civilised* nations to join her in making an Exhibition'.[8] This invitation was taken up by only thirty-three governments, mostly from Western European countries, other British colonies, and the United States. Equally, due to these mostly Western organisational networks, when non-Western exhibits were curated they were usually arranged by Western agents, and rarely involved members of the exhibited cultures. The objects selected and narratives foregrounded were then often based on whether they would appeal to or interest local attendees.

Even once invitations to exhibit were accepted, exhibitions were designed to show the economic and cultural power of the host nation and so, accordingly, exhibits were deliberately arranged to give the impression of a hierarchy of 'civilisation' with the hosts at the top.[9] These hierarchies could be seen in the layout of the buildings: at the Great Exhibition, for example, Britain showed its apparent industrial dominance by occupying half of the Crystal Palace, allocating the building's other half to the entire rest of the world.[10] French exhibitions, too – including the 1867 Exposition Universelle – reinforced power relationships through architecture, placing non-Western cultures' displays in the 'picturesque' areas of the surrounding parks and gardens, away from the main industrial exhibits.[11] Examination of the floorplans of many of the 1880s exhibitions reveals similar hierarchies in their layout: at Melbourne 1880, small displays from Fiji, Jamaica, Ceylon, and the Straits Settlements are tucked away between enormous sections dedicated to the United States and Belgium; at the Scottish exhibitions, many non-Western exhibits were contained in separate pavilions in the grounds; Calcutta 1883 was starkly divided, with goods from outside of India housed in a permanent brick building, while a temporary iron building holding 'native' manufactures (seen in Figure 26) was accessible via a bridge across the busy Chowringhee (now Jawaharlal Nehru) Road.[12]

---

[8] 'The Melbourne International Exhibition', *Weekly Times*, 9 Oct. 1880, p. 1. My emphasis.

[9] Peter H. Hoffenberg, *An Empire on Display: English, Indian, and Australian Exhibitions from the Crystal Palace to the Great War* (Berkeley, 2001), p. xxii. See also Maurizio Peleggi, *Lords of Things: The Fashioning of the Siamese Monarchy's Modern Image* (Honolulu, 2002), p. 144.

[10] Ewan Johnston, '"A Valuable and Tolerably Extensive Collection of Native and Other Products": New Zealand at the Crystal Palace', in Jeffrey A. Auerbach and Peter H. Hoffenberg (eds), *Britain, the Empire, and the World at the Great Exhibition of 1851* (Aldershot, 2008), pp. 77–92, at p. 78.

[11] Zeynep Çelik and Leila Kinney, 'Ethnography and Exhibitionism at the Expositions Universelles', *Assemblage*, 13 (1990), 34–59, at p. 36.

[12] Thomas Prasch, 'Calcutta 1883–1884', in John E. Findling and Kimberly D. Pelle (eds), *Encyclopedia of World's Fairs and Expositions* (Jefferson, 2008), pp. 75–7, at p. 76.

Figure 26. 'The Indian Annex', in 'The Calcutta Exhibition', *Art Journal*, 46 (Apr. 1884), p. 97. The temporary 'Indian Annex' is shown here behind a bandstand and the lake, which has a display of Indian 'agricultural implements' along its edge. The permanent Indian Museum building that housed the Western displays can be seen at the far left. Periodicals Collection, SLV.

These organisational hierarchies affected the public interpretation of non-Western exhibits as can be seen in their descriptions in everything from official publications to the press. In Britain, and indeed, in Australia, displays from non-Western cultures were almost always illustrated in terms of what the objects 'comprised' rather than what they 'signified', stripped of their historical and cultural contexts and quantified only by their raw materials.[13] It was only once pared back to composite parts – materials that might be recognisable or seen as useful in Western society – that they were given meaning. Exhibitions, then, in their displays of objects from non-Western cultures, were large-scale manifestations of the Orientalist 'systems of representation' that Edward Said describes as used to bring Othered cultures into 'Western learning, Western consciousness, and later, Western empire'.[14]

All of these aspects – hierarchies of space, control by Western agents, and the decontextualisation of objects – can be seen clearly in the exhibition of non-Western musical instruments at the 1886 Colonial and Indian Exhibition in London. Here, instruments from many British colonies and dominions were presented as part of larger collections designed to give an overview of daily life in the cultures from which they were taken. These displays were curated by government or British agents. Sinhalese instruments were sent by the government of Ceylon; several non-specified collections of 'musical instruments',

[13] Paul Young, 'Mission Impossible: Globalization and the Great Exhibition', in Jeffrey A. Auerbach and Peter H. Hoffenberg (eds), *Britain, the Empire, and the World at the Great Exhibition of 1851* (Aldershot, 2008), pp. 3–25, at p. 16.
[14] Said, *Orientalism*, pp. 202–3.

including some used by 'Aboriginal Native Tribes', were sent by Dudley Francis Amelius Hervey (1849–1911), Resident Councillor of Malacca;[15] exhibits from government agents in British North Borneo included a 'Bornean Jewsharp' and a number of flutes and string instruments;[16] a drum, trumpets, and flutes were sent from British Guiana by the colonial government.[17] The largest department, India, was also filled with wind, string, and percussion instruments sent by various British government agents from across the subcontinent. In a few exceptions, a collection was sent by Sourindro Mohun Tagore (discussed below), and two others sent by 'Native Princes and Nobles'.[18]

Instruments, as only a small part of much larger 'ethnographic' displays, drew little attention or comment in the press surrounding this exhibition. Descriptions of the instruments in the *Official Catalogue* – a publication also compiled by government officials – however, followed many of the tropes outlined above. The authors emphasised the raw or natural materials used in making these instruments: from Tibet there was 'a flute made of human bone'; from Punjab 'a pipe with a gourd air-chamber'; and the authors acknowledged the 'considerable art and ingenuity' shown in the use of ostrich egg shells and gourds in the construction of sitars from Lucknow.[19] These descriptions are quite different from those given of Western instruments – such as pianos and harmoniums sent to the same exhibition from Canada – which emphasised beauty, craftsmanship, and function. In other cases, the non-Western instruments were openly dismissed. A general catalogue entry of 'musical instruments' was all that was given from Hyderabad, for example, of which the authors deemed 'no remarks necessary'.[20]

Said considers the 'implicit and powerful difference' between the Orientalist and the Oriental to be that 'the former writes about, whereas the latter is written about'.[21] At the exhibitions, this might be paraphrased: the former exhibits, whereas the latter is exhibited. There were, however, some exceptions. In the display of musical objects at the 1880s exhibitions, three exhibitors were also members of the 'exhibited' non-Western cultures: the Maharajah Abu Bakar of Johor, the Bengali musicologist Sourindro Mohun Tagore, and representatives of the Tokyo Institute of Music. All three of these exhibitors had complex personal or cultural relationships with the West; Abu Bakar and Tagore might be considered almost auto-Orientalists, while Japan – having recently 'opened up' to Western influence – had a conflicted relationship with Western cultural

---

[15] *Colonial and Indian Exhibition, 1886: Official Catalogue* (London, 1886), p. 357
[16] *Ibid*, pp. 346, 376.
[17] *Ibid*, p. 392.
[18] *Empire of India: Special Catalogue of Exhibits by the Government of India and Private Exhibitors* (London, 1886), p. 224.
[19] *Ibid*, pp. 248, 242.
[20] *Ibid*, p. 291.
[21] Said, *Orientalism*, p. 308.

institutions.[22] Considering the relationships these figures and institutions had with the West, and specifically the British Empire, can help to contextualise their displays within the wider Orientalist practice of exhibiting.

ABU BAKAR, MAHARAJAH OF JOHOR

Abu Bakar, the Maharajah of Johor, sent musical instruments to Sydney 1879, Melbourne 1880, Adelaide 1887, and the 1886 Colonial and Indian Exhibition.[23] He provided at each – among wider collections of clothing, craft, weapons, and specimens of local plants and woods – a *rebana* (a frame drum with jingles) and a *gendang* (double-headed drum). These were described as 'native drums and tambourines', and Abu Bakar was awarded certificates of honourable mention at Sydney, Melbourne, and Adelaide.[24] At the Australian exhibitions, these instruments were donated to the local cities after the exhibitions closed and so, when they were described in the press, it appears that more interest was taken in them as gifts to the state than for their musical qualities.[25] In 1886, however, Abu Bakar's instruments are not mentioned in any British press at all.

Abu Bakar had a close relationship with the British monarchy, and his unusual titles – 'Temenggong Seri Maharaja' assumed in 1862, shortened to 'Maharaja' in 1868, and 'Sultan' in 1886 – were adopted with Victoria's sanction. He was extremely well-travelled, making extended trips to India and the rest of Asia, and was the first Malay ruler to visit Europe. He was given many imperial honours, including being made an Honorary Knight Commander of the Star of India (KCSI) and was awarded a Grand Cross of St Michael and St George (GCMG) in 1876 for 'services to the British Government'.[26] A visit to London in 1885 and 1886 – which saw the signing of a treaty in which he was officially recognised as Sultan – concluded with his attendance at the

---

[22] Auto-Orientalism is common in other contexts of international 'display', particularly noticeable in the twentieth and twenty-first centuries in, for example, the Eurovision song contest where not traditionally 'Western' cultures present what might be described as the 'fantasy of seeing the East through the eyes of the West'. See Matthew Gumpert, '"Everyway That I Can": Auto-Orientalism at Eurovision 2003', in Ivan Raykoff and Robert Deam Tobin (eds), *A Song for Europe: Popular Music and Politics in the Eurovision Song Contest* (Aldershot, 2007), pp. 147–57, at p. 150.

[23] It was reported that Abu Bakar intended to personally visit the Adelaide 1887 exhibition, but he instead sent a governmental representative, the 'canny old Scotch resident of Johore – "Dato" James Meldrum'. See 'Adelaide Jubilee Exhibition', *Queenslander*, 20 Aug. 1887, p. 307.

[24] *Straits Settlement Court: International Exhibition Sydney 1879, Official Catalogue of Exhibits* (Sydney, 1879), p. 13; 'Miscellaneous Instruments', *Official Record Containing Introduction, History of Exhibition, Description of Exhibition and Exhibits, Official Awards of Commissioners and Catalogue of Exhibits* (Melbourne, 1882), pp. 54–5.

[25] *Official Catalogue of the Exhibits* (Adelaide, 1887), p. 104; *Official Record* [Melbourne 1880], pp. 339, 362.

[26] Rahman Tang Abdullah, 'Sultan Abu Bakar's Foreign Guests and Travels Abroad, 1860s–1895: Fact and Fiction in Early Malay Historical Accounts', *Journal of the Malaysian Branch of the Royal Asiatic Society*, 84:1 (2011), 1–22, at pp. 1, 3, 7.

Colonial and Indian Exhibition. While the Exhibition is not mentioned in any official Johor documents – indeed, the Johor official chronicle never explained the purpose of his extended stay in Britain after the treaty was signed[27] – his attendance at the Exhibition is confirmed by numerous reports in the British press which describe his appearance at the opening ceremony, 'as usual, blazed with diamonds'.[28]

Abu Bakar was evidently attuned and open to adopting other customs and cultures to influence others' perception of Johor and himself. In Europe, he adopted Western dress and customs 'to gain prestige' and as a means of impressing officials, while in Japan he similarly adopted Japanese traditions and dress.[29] Abu Bakar's image was thus highly curated, and 'calibrated' to gain respect, 'modernising or westernising in some areas whilst also maintaining many Malay traditions'.[30] The same could be said for the exhibits he sent to the exhibitions. Within the largely European exhibition tradition, Abu Bakar displayed objects that were specifically curated to demonstrate to a European (or Australian) audience a sense that he and his Sultanate were simultaneously part of and distinct from Western culture. Malay traditions were represented by displays of objects such as the musical instruments he sent; new manufactures showed his modernising impulse, while natural resources showed how useful trade relationships might be formed in the future.

SOURINDRO MOHUN TAGORE

Tagore was renowned for distributing musical instrument collections as gifts to international governments, heads of state, and to international exhibitions in a sustained effort to promote Bengali music. The collection he sent to Melbourne 1880 – which now resides at Monash University – saw him awarded an honourable mention 'for having furnished such an interesting collection'.[31] At Calcutta 1883, his exhibits in the Indian section were far more prominent than any other exhibitor's,[32] and at London 1886, his 'complete collection' was described in the *Official Catalogue* as the best of all the Indian instrument exhibits.[33]

Like Abu Bakar, Tagore had a polarised relationship with the British Empire, and his work was infused with both 'Hindu nostalgia' and 'contemporary

---

[27] *Ibid*, p. 10.
[28] 'The Colonial and Indian Exhibition', *Birmingham Daily Post*, 5 May 1886, p. 5.
[29] Abdullah, 'Sultan Abu Bakar's Foreign Guests', pp. 16–17.
[30] Jenny McCallum, 'Sound, Authority and the Malay Sultanate: 19th-Century Transformations under Sultan Abu Bakar of Johor', unpublished paper (quoted with permission), p. 1.
[31] *Official Record* [Melbourne 1880], pp. 54–5. Tagore also provided a number of papers on Indian music that were read at the Social Science Congress held in Melbourne at the same time as the Exhibition.
[32] 'Bengal', *Official Report of the Calcutta International Exhibition, 1883–84. Vol. 2 Catalogue of Exhibits from the Indian Empire* (Calcutta, 1885), p. 8.
[33] *Colonial and Indian Exhibition, 1886: Official Catalogue*, p. 18.

British imperialism'.[34] Trained in Hindustani, Bengali, and Germanic musical traditions, Tagore promoted traditional musical training by establishing music schools, while also accumulating many European titles and honours. Scholars are conflicted in their interpretation of these efforts: Gerry Farrell describes Tagore's musicological work – documenting and disseminating Hindustani music – as a response to British imperialism in a nationalist attempt to 'fight the British on their own ground';[35] Richard Williams, however, argues that this nationalist reading is misplaced as there is little to suggest that he was 'dissatisfied with colonial rule', openly parading his European awards and honours and writing reverentially of royal and colonial officials.[36] Williams considers Tagore's distribution of instruments to foreign governments as asserting his 'authority over his own cultural domain' for a European audience. Many of the objects in his collections were not usable, contemporary instruments, but are instead non-functional and highly decorated, illustrating both Tagore's 'archaizing impulses' and 'European tastes for the exotic'.[37] The collections sent to the various Australian exhibitions demonstrate these qualities strikingly, including among more traditional instruments a number that are clearly experimental.[38]

Despite cultivating relationships with Western dignitaries, Tagore's exhibits were still received critically by the press and the musical juries. In Melbourne 1880, the 'Report of the Juries' provided taxonomical and organological descriptions of his 'Hindoo' instruments based heavily on comparisons with Western instruments and technologies.[39] The Jury included: French composer Leon Caron; German-born church organist Gustav Gerlach (c.1843–?); composer Julius Siede; Italian flautist, tenor, and composer Antonio Giammona (c.1842–1890); Irish organist and chemist Charles Plunket (c.1827/31–1902); and local piano-tuner Thomas Morant (c.1830–95), all of whom were no doubt talented musicians, but none appear to have any particular knowledge of non-Western musics. The report concluded that while 'in Europe, makers have become clever by dint of studying the laws that regulate the emission of sound', in India – as supposedly demonstrated by these instruments – manufacture is 'left to cabinetmakers, who are generally ignorant of the simplest elements of music, and have no means of finding proper proportions'.[40] Descriptions emphasise the instruments' 'primitiveness' as well as their raw materials, including drums 'covered with sheepskin, new and unprepared', and flutes of bamboo 'such as

---

[34] Richard Williams, 'Hindustani Music between Awadh and Bengal, c.1758–1905' (unpublished Ph.D. thesis, King's College London, 2015), p. 270.
[35] Gerry Farrell, *Indian Music and the West* (Oxford, 1997), p. 67.
[36] Williams, 'Hindustani Music between Awadh and Bengal', p. 270.
[37] Ibid, p. 271.
[38] See Reis W. Flora, 'The Tagore Collection of Indian Musical Instruments in Melbourne', *TAASA Review* (Journal of The Asian Arts Society of Australia), 6:2 (1997), p. 20.
[39] *Official Record* [Melbourne], p. 54.
[40] Ibid.

nature has formed them'.[41] While the jury conceded that they were 'finished in better style than many we have seen', this again suggested that the standard of instrument manufacture – even of traditional instruments – in India was lower than in Europe or the colonies.

The Melbourne jury's limited engagement with Tagore's instruments was still greater than that received by his collection at the Colonial and Indian Exhibition. Displayed with instruments from other parts of India, none of these instruments were considered anything beyond 'ethnographic' illustrations, and were not assessed by any official. Even the official report on the musical instruments displayed there, written by John Stainer (1840–1901), did not acknowledge these instruments. Stainer considered the Exhibition's representation of music to consist 'entirely of pianofortes and organs' in a display from Canada.[42]

TOKYO INSTITUTE OF MUSIC

In contrast to the traditional instruments sent from Johore and India, representatives from the Tokyo Institute of Music in Japan sent both instruments and displays documenting the Japanese music education system to the 1884 London Health Exhibition. The Tokyo Institute of Music was described in the Japanese Exhibition catalogue – a document compiled for Western audiences – as established 'to make inquiries into musical matters in general, to select and compile songs and their notes for schools, to examine the methods of teaching them, and to undertake the improvements of popular music'.[43] Most of these exhibits were representative of the educational reforms implemented by Isawa Shūji (1851–1917) during the Meiji period, and demonstrate a hybrid Japanese–Western educational culture.

Isawa's reforms to music education were influenced by his training in the USA.[44] His goals, then, in addition to the overall ambition of 'improvement' described in the Japanese Exhibition catalogue, showed a distinct Western influence and strong parallels with the rational recreation movement.[45] While there were a few examples of traditional Japanese music and instruments, the majority of the display contained books and scores, many of which were translations of standard European texts. These included the *National Music Reader* by Luther Mason (1818–96) and *A Musical Grammar* by John Wall Callcott.[46] Mason – an American 'renowned music educationalist' – had met Isawa in the

---

[41] *Ibid*, p. 55.
[42] H. Trueman Wood (ed.), *Reports on the Colonial Sections of the Exhibition: Issued under the Supervision of the Council of the Society of Arts* (London, 1887), p. 491.
[43] *A Catalogue with Explanatory Notes of the Exhibits from the Department of Education, Empire of Japan, in the International Health and Education Exhibition, Held in London, 1884* (London, 1884), p. 29.
[44] Takenaka Toru, 'Isawa Shūji's "National Music": National Sentiment and Cultural Westernisation in Meiji Japan', *Itinerario*, 34:3 (2010), 97–118, p. 99.
[45] *Catalogue with Explanatory Notes*, p. 29; *Ibid*, p. 100.
[46] *Catalogue with Explanatory Notes*, p. 30.

United States, and was invited to Tokyo to work at the Tokyo Imperial University between 1880 and 1882.[47]

The Japanese exhibits attracted some press attention, most of a positive character, particularly when assessed in comparison with the Chinese music heard at the same Exhibition. These reports seem to deliberately set one 'Oriental' culture against another, declaring the one with the most recognisably Western aspects as superior. As the *Morning Post* stated, the Japanese section 'completely overshadows' the music of the Chinese musicians 'in an intellectual' sense.[48] *The Times* noted that the strength of the Japanese display – and one of the reasons it was highly praised in the press – was because Japan had demonstrated a 'surprising readiness' to adopt 'Western ideas of education and methods of instruction'.[49] The *Morning Post* continued, 'no Oriental nation has hitherto allowed Western civilisation to influence it as has the Japanese'.[50] The more traditionally Japanese aspects of the exhibits were, the *Morning Post* argued, a manifestation of 'the fact that whilst European civilisation is penetrating hour by hour with gigantic strides amongst this intelligent people, they still retain much of their artistic originality'.[51] It appears that the 'fundamental dislocation in the country's socio-cultural life', regarded by modern scholars as the result of Japan's relatively recent opening up to Western influence, was exactly the thing that the British press found most interesting.[52]

In the case of the Japanese educational exhibits, it was not Japan, or Japanese culture in itself that impressed the press, but an apparent demonstration of the strength of their own Western culture in influencing Japanese practice. Similarly, in the reception of non-Western musical instruments from other parts of the world – even those by figures such as Abu Bakar and Tagore who appear to have been personally respected by powerful British and Imperial figures – both juries and press interpreted and critiqued these objects in ways that emphasised what they saw as the 'superiority' of their own cultural objects through direct comparison. This kind of critique was further developed and even institutionalised in the display of non-Western music, not as competitive exhibits, but in museum spaces, as exhibits of 'ancient' instruments.

❧ *Museum Exhibits*

While only a few non-Western musical instruments were displayed in the general, competitive sections of the exhibitions, at the London Inventions Exhibition of 1885, and at Edinburgh in 1890, there was another space where non-Western instruments abounded. These exhibitions separated their musical exhibits into two distinct categories, ancient and modern, and it was within

---

[47] Takenaka, 'Isawa Shūji's "National Music"', p. 102.
[48] 'International Health Exhibition', *Morning Post*, 25 Aug. 1884, p. 6.
[49] 'Japan at the Health Exhibition', *The Times*, 28 Aug. 1884, p. 2.
[50] 'International Health Exhibition', *Morning Post*, p. 6.
[51] Ibid.
[52] Takenaka, 'Isawa Shūji's "National Music"', p. 97.

the 'ancient' sections that more non-Western instruments could be found. In London, these instruments were housed in an 'Oriental Room', with 'Indian decoration' by Wardle & Co., alongside the other 'period-room' exhibits; in Edinburgh they were scattered throughout the main historical display.

The instruments in these exhibits were borrowed from institutional and private collections, meaning they represented not their own contextual origins, but rather the 'structures of domination' constructed by their collectors through the Orientalist impulse to collect, codify, and catalogue other cultures.[53] As such, many exhibits at London also came from colonial government representatives, explorers, or people who had travelled widely. For example, a number of wind instruments from China, the Pacific islands, South America, Borneo, and Madagascar were exhibited by James Veitch (1792–1863) and his family: horticulturalists who travelled the world sourcing plants for their nurseries, and frequently exhibited exotic plants at international exhibitions.[54] Politician Harry Verney (1801–94) exhibited a collection of Javanese instruments that had belonged to Stamford Raffles (1781–1826), the British colonial official responsible for establishing modern Singapore.[55] Other exhibits demonstrated long institutional traditions of collecting, such as the Persian, African, and Malagasy instruments sent to London from Stonyhurst College – a Jesuit school with global links – or the many Japanese, Burmese, Indian, and Chinese instruments sent to both Edinburgh and London by Professor Herbert Oakley (1830–1903) and the University of Edinburgh.[56]

In the competitive exhibition space – in which Abu Bakar, Tagore, and the Tokyo Institute of Music displayed their objects – visitors were encouraged to view instruments in direct comparison with each other in terms of commercial, aesthetic, and functional value. In the non-competitive museum space, non-Western instruments were instead explicitly shown for the education and curiosity of a Western audience. Yet similar narratives to those discussed above also emerged in the discourse around their representation here. For example, many instruments shown at London were described only vaguely in the *Official Catalogue*, compiled by Alfred Hipkins. Among objects from the royal collections came a 'flageolet', a nondescript 'percussion instrument', a 'pair of cymbals', and a 'tom-tom', all presented without any contextual information about which musical culture they supposedly represented. This practice was repeated in the catalogue of instruments sent to the Edinburgh Exhibition

---

[53] Ting Chang, *Travel, Collecting, and Museums of Asian Art in Nineteenth-Century Paris* (Burlington, 2013), p. 5.
[54] Alfred J. Hipkins, *Guide to the Loan Collection of Musical Instruments, Manuscripts, Books, Paintings, and Engravings, Exhibited in the Gallery and Lower Rooms of the Albert Hall* (London, 1885), pp. 114, 117–18; See Shirley Heriz-Smith, 'James Veitch & Sons of Exeter and Chelsea, 1853–1870', *Garden History*, 17:2 (1989), 135–53.
[55] C.M. Turnbull, 'Raffles, Sir (Thomas) Stamford Bingley (1781–1826)', *Oxford Dictionary of National Biography* (Oxford, 2004); Hipkins, *Guide to the Loan Collection*, pp. 113–14.
[56] Hipkins, *Guide to the Loan Collection*, pp. 113, 117–18.

from the University of Edinburgh, which included vague, and often anglicised, descriptions of Indian 'tom toms', Burmese 'gongs', and Chinese 'fiddles' and 'oboes'. As with the non-Western instruments in the competitive exhibits, descriptions of many instruments in the museum section were also reduced to their raw or material properties rather than their social or cultural function. At London, several dozen gourd instruments were shown, including a 'cane musical instrument, with resonance gourd' from West Africa.[57] Among the Indian 'tom-toms' shown at Edinburgh, there was one 'made of burnt clay', as well as two Chinese 'fiddles', one with a body made of a gourd, and another of a 'cocoa-nut'.[58]

Some instruments were catalogued in a way that emphasised conquest narratives, demonstrating imperial power and perpetuating stereotypes of violence in relation to non-Western cultures. At London, the royal collection included the war drum of the King of Ashantee [Ashanti] – presumably taken during the Anglo-Ashanti Wars – which was described as 'carved from a tree trunk, perforated by musket shots' with 'two human jaws attached to it'.[59] A brass gong 'taken from Tippoo Sahib's tent' was also part of the royal display. Tipu (1750–99) was the eighteenth-century Sultan of Mysore, killed during the Anglo-Mysore wars at the siege of Seringapatam in 1799.[60] Both these instruments, through their situation in the museum exhibit, became more symbolic of British power than of Ashanti or Mysuru musical culture. Strangely, in the same collection was a guitar 'made from the head of the Duke of Schomberg's horse, killed at the battle of the Boyne, 1690'.[61] This instrument – unless Ireland was considered 'the Orient' – appears quite out of place in the 'Oriental Room'. This perhaps demonstrates a wider conflation of 'conquest' contexts where, despite Schomberg fighting on the side of William of Orange, both the 'battle' context and use of bone made the 'Oriental Room' appear a more appropriate display space.

In all of these museum exhibits, attribution and credit was given to their Western collectors, not to any members of the non-Western cultures the objects were intended to represent. This – in the case of two of the largest institutional collections shown at London 1885 – led to an accidental and striking misattribution of one culture as metonymic for many others. Two vast collections of Indian instruments were exhibited by the Brussels Conservatoire and its curator Victor Mahillon, and from the Royal College of Music (RCM) in London. Although not mentioned in the catalogue, both of these collections were sent to each institution by Tagore, as part of his efforts to distribute Bengali music

---

[57] *Ibid*, p. 113.
[58] Samuel Lee Bapty (ed.), *International Exhibition of Electrical Engineering, General Inventions and Industries, Edinburgh 1890: Official Catalogue*, 2nd ed. (Edinburgh, 1890), pp. 158, 160.
[59] Hipkins, *Guide to the Loan Collection*, p. 117. This instrument remains in the Royal Collections Trust (RCIN 69929).
[60] *Ibid*, p. 121; Zareer Masani, 'The Tiger of Mysore', *History Today*, 66:12 (2016), 11–16.
[61] Hipkins, *Guide to the Loan Collection*, p. 118.

around the world. The RCM collection had been donated a year earlier, following which Tagore was created a Knight Bachelor 'in recognition of his services to the cause of education and the advancement of the art of music'.[62] The Brussels Conservatoire collection had been similarly donated in 1876.[63] Yet Tagore's name only appears once in the catalogue of these exhibits, in reference to a photograph of 'the private band of Rajah Sourindro Mohun Tagore'.

Comparison between the RCM and Brussels collections show them to be almost identical, and the information provided about the instruments is equally similar, suggesting that the printed catalogue descriptions also came from Tagore. This means that the public, on visiting the 'Oriental Room', would have seen many instruments at least twice over, attributed to different institutions. Viewers, therefore, might have assumed these objects to be broadly representative of Indian culture overall. What they were encountering, however, were actually only Hindustani instruments, and beyond that, instruments curated by Tagore to demonstrate a highly specific image of Indian culture. To that extent, both collections even included some of Tagore's modern, hybrid instruments such as the nadesvara vina, a European violin body fitted with the neck of a kachchapi vina.[64]

The attribution of these collections to the institutions lending them separated them from their cultural context, reinforcing their status as artefacts or curiosities, and erased the contributions of their original makers. In the case of Tagore, however, while having no involvement with the London 1885 Exhibition himself, he appears to have had an enormous influence on the portrayal of Indian music. This shows, in fact, that his donations had a far more wide-reaching impact in the period immediately following their distribution than perhaps first thought.

THE RECEPTION OF MUSEUM DISPLAYS OF NON-WESTERN INSTRUMENTS

The position of non-Western instruments amongst the 'ancient' instrument museum-spaces at London and Edinburgh played an important role in how they were received. In London, displaying all non-Western instruments in the 'Oriental Room' off the main galleries meant that the displays were easily passed over. Consequently, while many reviewers produced lengthy articles on the historic collection overall, the 'Oriental Room' was rarely discussed in detail. The *Musical Times*, concluding a series of articles on the wider collection, described the non-Western instruments only as 'a curious collection … on the left of the

---

[62] Paul Banks, *Sir Sourindro Mohun Tagore and the Tagore Medal: A Centenary History* (London, 1999), p. 8.

[63] Nazir Ali Jairazbhoy, 'The Beginnings of Organology and Ethnomusicology in the West: V. Mahillon, A. Ellis and S.M. Tagore', *Selected Reports in Ethnomusicology*, 8 (1990), 67–80, p. 68.

[64] Jonathan Katz, 'Raja Sir Sourindro Mohun Tagore (1840–1914)', *Popular Music*, 7:2 (1988), 220–1, at p. 220.

staircase from the conservatory'.[65] Similarly, the *Monthly Musical Record* gave little detail of the 'curious collection of Indian musical instruments' (it seems the enormity of Tagore's two collections overshadowed any other cultures represented), beyond the 'vast number of quaintly-shaped instruments', and a 'kind of dulcimer, the oldest ancestor of the piano'.[66]

Where critics did discuss non-Western instruments, most were dismissive. The *Globe* referred to the 'remarkable collection' as being 'musically speaking ... of little value', but suggested instead that 'the quaintness of their forms, and the richness of their decoration' would 'attract and repay attention'.[67] While this was partly because the instruments could not be heard, given that the average exhibition visitor would have had little idea how to make music with them anyway, the instruments' musical functions were dismissed as valueless. Instead, displayed primarily for the Western gaze, their chief function became their visual aesthetic qualities.

The situation of non-Western instruments – many of which were recently built and still in contemporary use – alongside 'ancient' Western instruments implied that they belonged within a linear, universal music history. Such developmentalist racism, both in curatorial approach and reception, aligned with a contemporary theoretical movement from a polygenic understanding of human populations, to one of monogenism, seeking 'universal traits' in human culture and implying that variation came from one's relative 'progress' along a linear developmental timeline.[68] In nineteenth-century British musical discourses, early written representations of non-Western music came largely from travel writings, but as comparative anthropological studies became established, 'concepts of universalism' in music also emerged.[69] Thus, William Stafford's 1830 *A History of Music*, for example – one of the earliest music histories of the nineteenth century – could easily group in one chapter 'the music of the ancients and non-Western nations'.[70] Similarly, John Frederick Rowbotham's *A History of Music* from 1885 could situate 'primitive music within the chronological context of ancient', or what he called 'prehistoric music'.[71] Indeed, the fact that many of the exhibited non-Western instruments were contributed by the same individual collectors who had sent 'ancient' European instruments suggests that the conflation of historic and non-Western instruments reflected wider ideologies and collecting practices of the time.

---

[65] 'The Historic Loan Collection (Concluded)', *Musical Times*, 26:511 (1 Sep. 1885), 517–19, at p. 519.
[66] 'Music and Inventions', *Monthly Musical Record*, p. 170.
[67] 'The Musical Exhibition', *Globe*, 1 Jun. 1885, p. 3.
[68] Jann Pasler, 'The Utility of Musical Instruments in the Racial and Colonial Agendas of Late Nineteenth-Century France', *Journal of the Royal Musical Association*, 129:1 (2004), 24–76, at p. 24.
[69] Zon, *Representing Non-Western Music*, p. 78.
[70] *Ibid*, p. 95.
[71] *Ibid*, p. 104.

The characterisation of non-Western music as a precursor to even 'ancient' Western music was prominent in the reception of non-Western instruments at these exhibitions. Indian instruments were described at London as the 'ancestors' of modern Western equivalents,[72] and at Edinburgh, 'strange as they may appear to a European', as the 'obvious precursors of the products of western civilisation'.[73] The *Musical World* described the Chinese instruments at Edinburgh in similar terms, with the 'curious Chinese trumpet, or "La-pa," with sliding tube' particularly singled out as the precursor to the trombone.[74] This article described the entire display in explicit terms of a developmental lineage, 'from the primitive tam-tam of the African savage ... to the highly-developed violin made at Naples in 1736 by "Januarius Gagliano, alumnus Antonii Stradivarii"'.[75] This developmentalist narrative in the reception of the museum displays of non-Western instruments was also compounded by the same tropes that appeared in the reception of instruments in the competitive sections, and in the official catalogues. Many in the press emphasised the instruments' material properties – particularly in relation to raw or natural materials used in their construction – demonstrating a problematic assertion that 'savages' are 'inherently more imitative of, or steeped in, nature'.[76]

Bennett Zon argues, in discussing nineteenth-century writing on non-Western music, that while some authors demonstrate a striking 'incomprehension', condemning such music aesthetically, or 'simply omitting any reference to it', many did 'accept its historiographical legitimacy' even if they subordinated it to 'a Western musical hegemony'.[77] Such tendencies were present in both the curation and reception of non-Western musical instruments at the international exhibitions of the 1880s, whether these instruments were placed in direct competition with Western instruments, or seen as their historical precursors. Yet, as Zon also notes, this reaction was not always universal: some writers and critics made 'a truly benign effort to replace incomprehension with some form of intellectual or cultural meaning' even if that was 'unintentionally deprecatory and subordinating'.[78] In the reception of these exhibitions, there were some legitimate attempts to understand the instruments displayed, even if these were limited in scope or still situated in comparisons to Western instruments. For example, the *Musical World* made a specific example of 'a remarkably fine pair of Chinese cymbals' in the Edinburgh collection, describing them as 'very

---

[72] 'Music and Inventions', *Monthly Musical Record*, pp. 169–170.
[73] 'The Historic Musical Collection at the Edinburgh Exhibition', *Musical World*, 70:37 (13 Sep. 1890), 734–5, at p. 734.
[74] *Ibid*.
[75] *Ibid*.
[76] Zon, *Representing Non-Western Music*, p. 6.
[77] Bennett Zon, 'From "Incomprehensibility" to "Meaning" Transcription and Representation of Non-Western Music in Nineteenth-Century British Musicology and Ethnomusicology', in Rachel Cowgill and Julian Rushton (eds), *Europe, Empire, and Spectacle in Nineteenth-Century British Music* (Aldershot, 2006), pp. 185–199, at p. 187.
[78] *Ibid*, p. 189.

superior in quality and tone to the average European specimens of this instrument'.[79] The *Art Journal*, too, in summary of the London Exhibition suggested that the collection of Indian instruments:

> will either strengthen or finally dispel the idea perhaps which prevails in the minds of not a few who have visited India, that there is a method and beautiful science in that music which although not yet apparent to us, may yet be so when we have had an opportunity of being sufficiently educated up to it.[80]

Similar assessments – admitting that non-Western musics might require a level of familiarity or education to understand – while in the minority, were also apparent in the reception of non-Western music when it was performed at some of these exhibitions. As we shall see, the critical tropes and modes of assessment took on quite a different dimension when applied to music that could actually be *heard*.

---

[79] 'The Historic Musical Collection at the Edinburgh Exhibition', *Musical World*, p. 734.
[80] 'Music at the Inventions Exhibition, 1885', *Art Journal*, 47 (May 1885), 153–6, at p. 154.

CHAPTER 9

Performing Non-Western Musics

The 1884 London Health Exhibition was held, its organisers said, to demonstrate the concept of health in the 'widest possible sense'. As its *Official Catalogue* noted, the displays would illustrate 'all the conditions of healthful life, as regards the food of the people, their clothing, and the dwellings in which they live'.[1] The South Kensington buildings were filled with exhibits of 'healthy' building materials, examples of public and industrial hygiene, and aspects of education and gymnasia. Dress also made up a large proportion of the display, with fabrics and manufacturing techniques shown next to morbid exhibits of the effects of 'poisonous dyes' on the skin and 'displaced viscera' produced by tightly-laced corsets.[2] The majority of the exhibits, however, related to food. As *Punch* wryly remarked, it seemed the 'great object of nine-tenths of the Exhibitors ... to excite the appetite of the passer-by'.[3] Throughout the Exhibition, visitors could examine different methods of food preparation and preservation, see exotic international foods, and even taste these for themselves in the many restaurants inside the building. It was here that the first Chinese restaurant in London could be found, extending out over an artificial ornamental lake in the grounds. And, for diners in this restaurant, as *The Times* noted, 'no Chinese banquet is considered complete without music'.[4]

Every day of the Health Exhibition, visitors to the Chinese restaurant heard music by a band of Chinese musicians. But this band was not the only non-Western ensemble to appear at exhibitions in the British Empire during this period. A year earlier, at Calcutta 1883, a Burmese troupe performed daily with an orchestra in a theatre constructed on the far side of the Exhibition grounds. Also in London, the year after the Health Exhibition, the Court Band of the King of Siam appeared at the Inventions Exhibition where they performed three times per week in the Albert Hall. Live performances given by visiting musicians, unlike the depersonalised and decontextualised exhibits of non-Western instruments, allowed audiences to engage with the sonic realities of their respective musical traditions. For many audience members, these performances may have provided a first encounter with the sound of any

---

[1] *International Health Exhibition, 1884: Official Catalogue* (London, 1884), pp. xlvii–xlviii.
[2] Douglas Galton, 'The International Health Exhibition', *Art Journal*, 46 (May 1884), 153–6, at p. 156.
[3] 'Our Insane-Itary Guide to the Health Exhibition', *Punch*, 21 Jun. 1884, p. 290.
[4] 'The Health Exhibition', *The Times*, 29 Mar. 1884, p. 5.

non-Western music, beyond its representation in European exotic opera or operetta.[5] Despite these performances being specifically curated with a Western audience in mind, they were largely viewed as curiosities by the press and public. They projected narratives designed to fulfil Western expectations, and reinforced the notions of social and racial hierarchies inherent to the exhibitions more broadly. The reception of Burmese music by Westerners in Calcutta is illustrative of many common tropes in the reception of non-Western music at exhibitions. Further demonstrating these tropes, the comparative reception of the Chinese and Siamese bands in London makes for a compelling case study into the influence of race, class, and social hierarchy in the late Victorian British national consciousness.

'Exhibiting' People, Exhibiting Music

The Burmese, Chinese, and Siamese bands that performed in 1883, 1884, and 1885 were the only non-Western performers who were specifically engaged to provide music at any exhibition in this study. The official programmes of the other British exhibitions were filled with Western art or popular musics, even in cases like the Colonial and Indian Exhibition, which could have easily provided opportunities to present music from across the Empire. Officially, however, the only music offered was by military bands, continuing the most popular (and profitable) tradition of the previous exhibitions. This, according to James Richards, 1886 superintendent for music, 'proved sufficient, and was highly satisfactory'.[6]

That is not to say that there was no other non-Western music in these spaces. There was almost certainly music-making in the 'native villages' erected at some exhibitions, notably Calcutta 1883, and the Colonial and Indian Exhibition and Liverpool, both in 1886. These 'living ethnological exhibits' – among the most horrific and exploitative anthropological exhibitionary practices of the nineteenth century – placed human beings 'on display' in artificially constructed environments.[7] Also common at continental European and American exhibitions, such villages were usually situated in the grounds, alongside carnival amusements, placing them firmly within the exhibitions' 'entertainment' rather than 'educational' remit. This went hand-in-hand with the way such displays were viewed by the public, as few 'intellectualised what they saw', looking instead through a romanticised lens, rather than at the obvious exploitation.[8]

---

[5] Gilbert and Sullivan's *The Mikado*, for example, was premiered in March 1885, between the two London exhibitions discussed here.

[6] *Report of the Royal Commission for the Colonial and Indian Exhibition* (London, 1887), p. 219.

[7] See, for example, Saloni Mathur, 'Ethnological Exhibits: The Case of 1886', *Cultural Anthropology*, 15:4 (2000), 492–524.

[8] Paul Greenhalgh, *Ephemeral Vistas: The Expositions Universelles, Great Exhibitions and World's Fairs, 1851–1939* (Manchester, 1988), p. 84.

'Exhibited' people were brought to the exhibitions by agencies or individuals, although records are often limited in describing the practices used to induce – or force, as at London 1886 where prisoners were transported to the Exhibition from an Agra jail – them to come.[9] As Monier Monier-Williams (1819–99) described of Calcutta 1883, 'living specimens of the various frontier tribes' were sent 'under the charge of trustworthy Europeans'.[10] These Europeans included Justus Brainerd Vinton (1840–87) of the well-known American Baptist missionary family, who 'brought most singular specimens of Karens', and Maurice Vidal Portman (1860–1935) – the British naval 'officer in charge of the Andamanese' – who brought a group of people from the Andaman and Nicobar islands, whose 'only idea of music is striking a kind of wooden sounding-board, placed on the ground, with one foot'.[11] While music was often part of the 'pageants' given by the people in these villages, a lack of documentation of their day-to-day activities makes it difficult to uncover the extent of music's presence. Further, in describing these villages, the press seemed mainly concerned with the visual, illustrating the people's appearance, dress, and surroundings, rather than providing details of their performances. This lack of reference to music possibly relates to the fact that these villages had no 'recognizable forum', such as a stage, for music performance, leading viewers to either ignore any music making, or perceive it as 'environmental sound'.[12]

The grounds of the Liverpool Exhibition contained three 'living ethnological' displays. The first, a Lapland village, housed two Sámi families, with reindeers, dogs, hunting, and fishing apparatus and sledges, to give an impression of 'the habits and customs of those dwellers in the great frozen north'.[13] Nearby was an African Ashanti 'palace', 'completely appointed according to native taste', but designed and built by 'a Birkenhead firm of architects'.[14] Music was clearly played here, though press references to it are fleeing, and largely disparaging. The *Wigan Observer* described what the 'natives ... choose to regard as music' as produced by a single musician, 'who sat on the floor knocking away at an instrument' with sounds that 'very much resembled cracked pots'.[15] Most prominent at Liverpool was the Indian Pavilion, arranged by the theatrical animal trader William Cross (1840–1900) – sometimes described as the English Barnum – which held animals from Cross's menagerie and at least fifty Indian

---

[9] Mathur, 'Ethnological Exhibits: The Case of 1886', pp. 504–7.
[10] Monier Monier-Williams, 'Royal Asiatic Society. Proceedings of the Sixty-First Anniversary Meeting of the Society, Held on the 19th of May, 1884', *Journal of the Royal Asiatic Society of Great Britain and Ireland*, 16:4 (1884), 144–53, at p. 146.
[11] Satadru Sen, 'Savage Bodies, Civilized Pleasures: M.V. Portman and the Andamanese', *American Ethnologist*, 36:2 (2009), 364–7, at p. 364; *Ibid*, p. 146.
[12] Annegret Fauser describes a similar phenomenon at Paris 1889, see Annegret Fauser, *Musical Encounters at the 1889 Paris World's Fair* (Rochester, 2005), pp. 246–8.
[13] 'Liverpool International Exhibition', *Crewe Guardian*, 1 May 1886, p. 2.
[14] *Ibid*.
[15] 'Liverpool International Exhibition', *Wigan Observer and District Advertiser*, 4 Jun. 1886, p. 8.

people.[16] The *Liverpool Courier*, at the Pavilion's opening, focused mainly on its 'handsome domes, cupolas, and minarets' and 'artistic' interior decorations. The Indians who performed in this ceremony, they noted, had 'never appeared in public before', having been recently brought to England by Federigo Salva (c.1853–1920), an agent for Cross who had 'penetrated far into the interior of India' and faced 'almost insurmountable difficulties in inducing' them to leave their homes.[17] While a pamphlet put together by Cross described the Indian music performed here as having 'undeniably a certain charm' despite not being 'in conformity with our ideas of melody', it argued that the music 'gives us an excellent idea of the kind of vocal and instrumental concerts which the native Hallés or Carl Rosas perform in India'.[18] The *Courier*, too, reported a 'curious musical item' in this ceremony, consisting of 'a drumming sort of chant descriptive of their voyage to Liverpool' reminiscent of 'penillion singing'; however, little further detail was given.[19]

In contrast to these English exhibitions, the Australian colonial exhibitions – particularly Sydney and Melbourne – showed limited engagement with non-Western cultures in any capacity. This was particularly true for the local Indigenous traditions, musical or otherwise.[20] The reasons for this silence were twofold.[21] First, the self-representation of the Australian colonies at their own exhibitions aimed to demonstrate that they were prosperous, 'civilised', and an 'egalitarian and classless' society.[22] This depiction jarred considerably with white Australia's treatment of Indigenous people, making it difficult for organisers to represent Aboriginal Australians without contradicting this narrative. Where

---

[16] Alexander Scott, 'The "Missing Link" Between Science and Show Business: Exhibiting Gorillas and Chimpanzees in Victorian Liverpool', *Journal of Victorian Culture*, 25:1 (2020), 1–20, at p. 13.

[17] 'The Exhibition. Opening of the Indian Pavilion', *Liverpool Weekly Courier*, 5 Jun. 1886, p. 3.

[18] William Cross, *Liverpool International Exhibition, 1886, the Indian Village, North-East Corner of the Grounds: 50 Natives of India, Together with Elephants, Camels, Zebras, Brahmin Bulls &c. Imported Specially for this Exhibition by William Cross* (London, 1886), p. 11.

[19] 'The Exhibition. Opening of the Indian Pavilion', *Liverpool Weekly Courier*, p. 3.

[20] Lynette Russell, '"An Unpicturesque Vagrant": Aboriginal Victorians at the Melbourne International Exhibition 1880–1881', *La Trobe Journal*, 93–94 (2014), 77–81, at p. 77; Peter Hoffenberg, *An Empire on Display: English, Indian, and Australian Exhibitions from the Crystal Palace to the Great War* (Berkeley, 2001), p. 228.

[21] Hoffenberg, *An Empire on Display*, p. 149.

[22] Linda Young, '"How Like England We Can Be": The Australian International Exhibitions in the Nineteenth Century', in Kate Darian-Smith, Richard Gillespie, Caroline Jordan, and Elizabeth Willis (eds), *Seize the Day: Exhibitions, Australia and the World* (Clayton, 2008), 12.1–12.19, at p. 12.2; Louise Douglas, 'Representing Colonial Australia at British, American and European International Exhibitions', *reCollections: Journal of the National Museum of Australia*, 3:1 (2008), <https://recollections.nma.gov.au/issues/vol_3_no_1/papers/representing_colonial_australia> [accessed 10 Mar. 2021].

Indigenous cultural objects were displayed, they were presented, not as part of contemporary Australia, but as ethnographic curiosities of 'ancient' history, alongside 'prehistoric' objects from Europe and the Americas. Second, colonial Australia faced growing international criticism through the latter half of the nineteenth century for their deliberate and appalling treatment of Indigenous people. In this light, colonial exhibition representatives exhibited Indigenous cultural objects defensively, specifically emphasising weapons to purposely present Indigenous Australians as dangerous and war-like, and the objects 'signifiers of the threat under which heroic settlers lived'.[23]

The only Australian exhibition that engaged with Indigenous music-making was Adelaide 1887, where groups of Ngarrindjeri and Narungga people from the Point McLeay and Point Pearce missions gave a pageant in the Exhibition grounds during September.[24] This performance began with an illustration of 'savage life', showing mat-making and fire-starting techniques, accompanied by traditional songs. A contrasting second part then demonstrated – through hymns, recitations, and popular songs – 'how "civilised" the Aboriginal people had become' under the mission's influence.[25] After singing 'God Save the Queen', the men then moved to the grounds and staged a mock battle. This event was so popular that a second series of performances were given in November, where the Narungga people performed hymns and parts of Talbot Erle and William Abel's *The Musical Robinson Crusoe* – a highly didactic work intended to build character by presenting 'morally uplifting aspirations'[26] – and the Ngarrindjeri people gave a 'more polished performance' of the original display.[27]

The critical response to these performances was generally enthusiastic; however, critics focused almost entirely on the 'civilising' influence of the missions – represented through the performance of Western music – rather than on the traditional songs and dances. When traditional music was discussed at all, it was considered amusing, rather than serious. As one critic wrote, 'covered in evergreens and their bodies painted they looked most comical', while 'the manner in which they danced … beat time with their sticks, and expressed themselves in language unintelligible to the audience, created a great deal of fun'.[28] Other critics quickly reminded readers that the performers themselves, 'under the influence of civilization', objected to traditional performance, apparently feeling that it was 'degrading to resort to their old bush life'.[29] As the

---

[23] Douglas, 'Representing Colonial Australia'.
[24] Tom Gara, 'Aboriginal Participation in the Adelaide Jubilee International Exhibition', in Christine Garnaut, Julie Collins, and Bridget Jolly (eds), *Adelaide's Jubilee International Exhibition: The Event, the Building, the Legacy* (Darlinghurst, 2016), pp. 157–69, at p. 162.
[25] *Ibid*, p. 163.
[26] Andrew O'Malley, *Children's Literature, Popular Culture, and Robinson Crusoe* (London, 2012), p. 45.
[27] Gara, 'Aboriginal Participation in the Adelaide Jubilee International Exhibition', p. 164.
[28] 'An Aboriginal Entertainment', *Evening Journal*, 23 Nov. 1887, p.3.
[29] 'Aboriginal Entertainment', *Adelaide Observer*, 10 Sep 1887, p. 30.

Evening Journal concluded, while they 'enjoy the fun' as much as their audience, they 'would rather not resort to their primitive customs'.[30] This reception represents another instance of Indigenous voices and music being 'absorbed into narratives of progress and praised for assimilating'.[31]

Tropes in the Reception of Non-Western Music at Exhibitions

While non-Western music may not, officially, have played a large role at many exhibitions in the British Empire, other Western exhibitions of the late nineteenth century had significantly more varied programmes. At the 1889 Paris Exposition Universelle, Eastern European, Middle Eastern, and gypsy folk music could be heard in the cafés along the Champ de Mars, while traditional music from the French colonies including Algeria, Tunisia, Vietnam, and Java could be found in the 'native villages' of the colonial section. In the US, the 1893 World's Columbian Exhibition in Chicago had a similar range of different musics, mostly heard on the 'Midway', an area containing the Exhibition's carnival amusements, including ethnographic villages on the model of Paris. Nations and cultures represented here included the South Sea Islands, Java, Turkey, Algeria, Tunisia, Dahomey, and China, as well as a 'Street in Cairo' exhibit, a Persian Palace, and an East Indian Bazaar.[32]

The critical response to this music in Paris and Chicago has been studied in detail, and common tropes uncovered in these studies also appear in the reception of non-Western music at exhibitions in the British Empire. These tropes – largely infused with the same developmentalist racism common to other contemporary writing about non-Western music – were formed by critics trying to make sense of musics that 'redrew the boundaries of musical experience', while shattering preconceived ideas formed through Western musical exoticism.[33] This 'reality check', as Fauser describes it, proved unsettling for many and elicited a range of responses. Some critics attempted to draw meaning from theoretical paradigms such as Darwinism, suggesting that these musics were representative of less-evolved cultures, on par with pre-historic Western traditions. Others contrasted the 'civilized West and barbaric East', suggesting that the musics were a product of a lack of cultural refinement.[34]

In all these descriptions, there was a 'recurring theme of comparison', considering non-Western music in terms of familiar Western ideas or experiences.[35]

---

[30] 'An Aboriginal Entertainment', *Evening Journal*, p. 3.
[31] As has also been documented at exhibitions in New Zealand. See Inge Van Rij, '"Walking Backwards Into the Future": Music, Museum Culture, and the New Zealand and South Seas Exhibition (1889–1890), *Music & Letters*, 99:2 (2018), 224–59, at p. 225.
[32] David M. Guion, 'From Yankee Doodle Thro' to Handel's Largo: Music at the World's Columbian Exposition', *College Music Symposium*, 24:1 (1984), 81–96, at p. 94.
[33] Fauser, *Musical Encounters*, pp. 139–44.
[34] *Ibid*, p. 145.
[35] *Ibid*.

This was a manifestation of one of the central tenets of Orientalism: the polarisation of Self and Other, or 'us' Europeans against 'those' non-Europeans.[36] Comparative language is particularly common in articles by authors who were not musicians, or those reports written for generalist audiences who may have lacked a vocabulary to discuss unfamiliar music using specific musical language. Such reports often described the instruments in terms of Western equivalents – using instrument names such as 'violin', 'zither', or 'banjo' to describe non-Western stringed instruments – or attempted to illustrate the sounds through comparisons to sound-experiences more familiar to their audiences.

Critical responses were frequently negative, and 'derogatory remarks' often pervaded accounts.[37] In many cases, critics used the musics 'merely as a source of cheap laughs',[38] to the extent that some reviews give the impression that the authors were 'entering a competition as to who could write the most outrageous condemnation'.[39] Here – and alongside numerous other racist stereotypes – one particular method of description was through ludicrous catalogues of comparisons, depicting the sounds, not as music, but as noise. Fauser examines French critics at Paris 1889 describing the music in the Vietnamese theatre as sounding like 'saucepan solos accompanied by drums, cymbals and tramway horns', 'lunatic amateurs', and 'shouting', while David Guion quotes a Chicago writer describing the music on the Midway as a 'queer, droning, shrieking clamor, now loud now soft, now emitting screams like a calliope'.[40]

Although many reviews were mocking or disparaging, some critics did seek to understand the music in its cultural and intellectual context, even if, in pursuing that understanding, they came to still 'deprecatory or subordinating' conclusions.[41] Even the Chicago critic quoted by Guion, above, follows by arguing that 'what we want is not a funny article in which adjectives and nouns are lugged in to amuse, but a learned disquisition on barbaric musical systems'.[42] However, critics who were less derisive tended to view the performances with a detached, anthropological eye. By considering the music not

---

[36] Edward W. Said, *Orientalism* (London, 2003), p. 7.
[37] Kiri Miller, 'Americanism Musically: Nation, Evolution, and Public Education at the Columbian Exposition, 1893', *19th-Century Music*, 27:2 (2003), 137–55, at p. 151.
[38] Guion, 'From Yankee Doodle Thro' to Handel's Largo', p. 94.
[39] Fauser, *Musical Encounters*, p. 189.
[40] Hyppolyte Lemaire, 'Théâtres', *Le Monde illustré*, 15 Jun. 1889, pp. 398–9; Jules Lemaître, 'Le Théâtre Annamite', *Le Figaro*, 8 Jul. 1889, p. 1, quoted in Fauser, *Musical Encounters*, pp. 189–90; *Chicago Evening Post*, 30 Jul. 1893, quoted in Guion, 'From Yankee Doodle Thro' to Handel's Largo', p. 94.
[41] As is similarly seen in contemporary general histories of music that deal with non-Western music. Bennett Zon, 'From "Incomprehensibility" to "Meaning" Transcription and Representation of Non-Western Music in Nineteenth-Century British Musicology and Ethnomusicology', in Rachel Cowgill and Julian Rushton (eds), *Europe, Empire, and Spectacle in Nineteenth-Century British Music* (Aldershot, 2006), pp. 185–99, at p. 189.
[42] *Chicago Evening Post*, 30 Jul. 1893, quoted in Guion, 'From Yankee Doodle Thro' to Handel's Largo', p. 94.

as *music* understood in a Western sense, but as an artefact to be observed and studied, they further embodied an Orientalist role, seeing the non-Western music and musicians as fixed, passive, and 'in need of investigation'.[43]

The tropes described above can be seen in the press and other written responses to Burmese music at Calcutta 1883, where daily performances by a Burmese theatre troupe represent the only consistent programme of non-Western music at an exhibition outside of England in this study. In fact, they were the only consistent performers of any music at this exhibition overall, long outlasting the short-lived piano recitals organised by Brinsmead, or the sporadic band concerts in the grounds. Despite many reports indicating that a large proportion of the Exhibition's attendees were Indian, surviving sources that respond to the Burmese theatre tend to be in the English-language press: targeted towards the Anglo-Indian community, or written by visitors from Britain or Australia. This reception, therefore, reflects only how this music was received by Western audiences.

The Burmese theatre, constructed on the far side of the lake in the grounds, hosted a daily *zat pwe*. *Zat pwe* – a large-scale classical form combining drama, music, and dance – would traditionally last all night; restricted by the Exhibition's opening hours, at Calcutta it became an all-day undertaking.[44] Music was integral to this style of performance, and a *hsaing waing* orchestra – made up of drum and gong circles, cymbals, and wind instruments – accompanied throughout. The theatre was a wooden structure enclosing the roofless performance space, with a large tree branch standing upright in the centre: a common feature in Burmese drama, used to represent the forest that was integral to many plays' narratives.[45] There was no 'backstage', and the performers moved about freely, making 'no attempt to stay in character' when not participating in the action.[46] This was another important aspect of this dramatic style: the performers acknowledged the audience, prepared in their full view, and expected the audience to move around, leading to the performance being perceived both for its story, and for the immediate experience of observing the play.[47]

While there is little documentation of the Calcutta performances in any official exhibition reports, an account of a performance was given by Monier-Williams – an Indian-born British linguist and Boden Professor of Sanskrit at Oxford – in his book *Buddhism, in its Connexion with Brāhmanism and Hindūism, and in its Contrast with Christianity*. He described the play as depicting part of the Hindu epic *Ramayana*, during which the musicians' 'noisy performances appeared to constitute an important element in the proceedings':

---

[43] Said, *Orientalism*, p. 308.
[44] Kirstin Pauka, 'Zat pwe', *Oxford Encyclopedia of Theatre and Performance* (2003) <https://www.oxfordreference.com> [accessed 12 Mar. 2021].
[45] Noel F. Singer, *Burmese Dance and Theatre* (Kuala Lumpur, 1995), p. 43.
[46] A.L. Becker, 'Journey through the Night: Notes on Burmese Traditional Theatre', *Drama Review*, 15:2 (1971), 83–7, at p. 85.
[47] *Ibid*, p. 84.

The chief musician sat on the ground in the middle of a circular frame-work – about two or three feet high – hung round with drums of different sizes, which he struck with his hands ... The hero and heroine of the drama – Rāma and Sītā – kept up a tedious colloquy, interspersed with jokes, for hours ... every now and again Sītā, in spite of a tight dress, varied the monotony of the dialogue by executing a slow dance, characterized by strange contortions, twistings, and wrigglings of the limbs. Hideous masks were at intervals assumed by the actors, and, of course, by the demons who intervened at odd moments with much ludicrous gesticulation.[48]

The *Ramayana* was a popular subject in Burmese theatre from the eighteenth century onwards, potentially attributable to Thai influence following the 1767 Burmese attack on Ayutthaya, which bought back many cultural traditions to Burma.[49] Others, however, argue that there is evidence to suggest earlier engagement, meaning the story of Rama may have been 'acquired direct from India'.[50] A traditional Burmese performance of the *Ramayana* could last between forty-five and sixty-five nights,[51] and Monier-Williams reported that the Calcutta performance lasted between ten and twenty-eight days.[52] Such lengthy performances – running for up to twelve hours per day – seemed to greatly perplex several authors who reported on the Exhibition. One used the length to engage directly with discourses of 'civilisation', suggesting that the Burmese should 'adapt their own peculiar customs considerably so as to suit the habits and convenience of the civilized west'.[53]

Most of the Australian press responded to the Burmese theatre with a kind of bemused interest, if also laced with a sense of supremacy, and some occasional derogatory comments. The *pat waing* – the circular set of tuned drums described above – was essential to the orchestra, and it – alongside the *kyi waing*, a similar set of gongs – drew much attention. One author described a musician as 'seated in a thing like a bath with bells all round him'.[54] Tropes about the 'noisiness' of the music were also employed to joke about the position of the theatre in the grounds. Writers suggested that, because the 'din of their national instruments was something infernal,' and 'their ideas of music and operatic performance differ considerably from those formed by Europeans' the Burmese had 'been relegated to the furthermost corner of the enclosure'.[55] Ultimately, one writer concluded 'the performance is about the most imbecile

---

[48] *Ibid*, pp. 348–9.
[49] Robert Garifas, 'The Development of the Modern Burmese Hsaing Ensemble', *Asian Music*, 16:1 (1985), 1–28, at p. 5.
[50] Singer, *Burmese Dance and Theatre*, p. 23.
[51] *Ibid*.
[52] Monier-Williams, *Buddhism*, p. 349; 'Professor Monier Williams on India', *The Times*, 2 Jun. 1884, p. 5.
[53] 'The Calcutta Exhibition', *Adelaide Observer*, 29 Dec. 1883, p. 33.
[54] 'Theatrical Gossip', *Adelaide Observer*, 15 Mar. 1884, p. 26.
[55] 'The Calcutta Exhibition', *Argus*, 25 Jan. 1884, p. 10; 'The Calcutta Exhibition', *Sydney Morning Herald*, 31 Jan. 1884, p. 5.

and absurd that mortal man ever witnessed'.[56] While the Burmese performers in Calcutta were received with limited interest – perhaps because they were less of a novelty in this geographic context – non-Western music at two exhibitions in London in the years that followed drew far more sustained attention.

China at the International Health Exhibition

Through the 1870s and '80s China participated in numerous international exhibitions across Europe and the United States. Each time, the Chinese government entrusted the organisation to a Western agent, Robert Hart (1835–1911), who was Inspector General of the Chinese Imperial Maritime Customs in Peking [Beijing]. For the 1884 London Health Exhibition, Hart worked in conjunction with James Duncan Campbell (1833–1907) – his London-based non-resident secretary – in undertaking what he termed 'the herculean task of mounting at such great distance' exhibits to introduce China 'to a Western public that was all too uninformed about her'.[57]

The 1884 Chinese section (Figure 27), located in the Exhibition Road wing of the building, opened out through its restaurant and tea rooms onto the central gardens. The decorations on the walls included paintings of 'wisteria and a bamboo tree … with birds flying about among the leaves', lit by porcelain lanterns.[58] Exhibits included musical instruments, books, ornamental soapstone, clothing, shoes, and weapons. Room displays illustrated Chinese interiors, with an 'an official Cantonese reception room' containing 'handsome furniture' of marble and inlaid wood, and the 'sleeping room of a Ningpo house' containing two beds in red-tasselled winter and summer hangings, and 'a Chinese lady's toilet table' with 'rouge-pot and powder-puff'.[59] Four shops, with fronts of carved wood, were also arranged to 'represent a Chinese street'.[60] The Peking shop sold 'curios and bronzes', the Hankow, tobacco and pipes, while the Canton and Kiukiang shops sold porcelain, enamel, and 'miscellaneous fancy goods', some 'old, rare, and costly', others 'modern and cheap'.[61] The largest exhibits in the section included ceremonial bridal and sedan chairs, horse and mule carts, and a catafalque and model crematory.[62]

On a visual level, this section was received well by the British press, who seemed impressed by the apparently 'faithful reproductions' of Chinese buildings, 'charmingly decorated by a Pekin artist' and 'characteristically florid in

---

[56] 'The Calcutta Exhibition', *Argus*, p. 10.
[57] John King Fairbank, Katherine Fros Bruner, and Elizabeth MacLeod Matheson (eds), *The I.G. in Peking: Letters of Robert Hart, Chinese Maritime Customs, 1865–1907* (Cambridge, 1975), p. 99, fn. 6.
[58] 'Lunch with the Celestials', *Pall Mall Gazette*, 5 Jul. 1884, p. 4.
[59] 'The Chinese Court at the Health Exhibition', *The Times*, 10 Jul. 1884, p. 6.
[60] *Illustrated Catalogue of the Chinese Collection of Exhibits for the International Health Exhibition* (London, 1884), p. 140.
[61] *Ibid*; 'The Chinese Court at the Health Exhibition', *The Times*, p. 6.
[62] *Illustrated Catalogue of the Chinese Collection*, pp. 26, 56, 62.

appearance'.[63] In reality, however, the display was curated for London audiences, and many decisions were made with aesthetics rather than veracity in mind (the flower arrangements, for example, were designed by Hart's wife).[64] The English-language press in China was critical of the display, describing it as 'something of a fraud' that 'convey[ed] a very false impression'. The *North-China Herald* suggested that, while the decoration and furniture gave an idea of the 'gorgeousness of colour and elaborateness of detail' in Chinese design, the displays did not illustrate 'the squalor, and the tinsel, and the flimsiness, and the dirt'.[65] Hart, too, admitted that the displays needed to be altered for British audiences, particularly in the case of food and drink. When Campbell initially proposed the restaurant – arguing that 'a few good cooks and some Chinese boys to act as waiters' would make the Chinese section 'the chef d'oeuvre of the Exhibition'[66] – Hart initially disagreed:

> The English idea of the Chinese Tea-House and Chinese Restaurant has nothing corresponding to it in China except the fact that there are buildings in which people can buy and eat food and drink tea: if we could supply you with one of them bodily, you would indeed have a slice out of the real life of China, but English sight-seers would neither eat in it nor sit in it, and the Committee would very soon beg us to move them, that and the other.[67]

The shops and restaurants were staffed, and the exhibits built and decorated, by a delegation of Chinese cooks, musicians, shopkeepers, painters, masons, and carpenters who had been sent from China. Although all professionals – and in the case of the shopkeepers, established merchants – the power-relationship between these workers and the English organisers was remarkably skewed. As Hart wrote to Campbell, 'they will be under strict control and without your permission will not be at liberty to do anything'.[68] This lack of autonomy was strikingly demonstrated in reports that in 'tak[ing] care of' the group, the organisers had them vaccinated, on noticing that many appeared to have smallpox scars.[69] Despite this, Hart did seem to want the Exhibition to be a process of cultural exchange, advising Campbell to 'arrange for the Chinese … to see the sights and hear music', wanting them to return with 'lots to tell about our public amusements in London'.[70] In December, on their return, Hart reported that they were 'all well and delighted with their trip and treatment and English

---

[63] 'The Food of the "Celestials"', *Western Mail*, 5 Jul. 1884, p. 3.
[64] 'Lunch with the Celestials', *Pall Mall Gazette*, p. 4.
[65] 'The English-Mail Papers', *North-China Herald and Supreme Court & Consular Gazette*, 22 Aug. 1884, p. 209.
[66] Robert Ronald Campbell, *James Duncan Campbell: A Memoir by His Son* (Cambridge, 1970), p. 54.
[67] Robert Hart to James Duncan Campbell, 14 Jan. 1884, in *The I.G. in Peking*, p. 517.
[68] Hart to Campbell, 17 Feb. 1884, in *Ibid*, p. 524; Hart to Campbell, 8 Mar. 1884, in *Ibid*, p. 532.
[69] 'Lunch with the Celestials', *Pall Mall Gazette*, p. 4.
[70] Hart to Campbell, 20 Apr. 1884, in *The I.G. in Peking*, p. 540.

Figure 27. 'The Chinese Court', *Illustrated London News*, 2 Aug. 1884, p. 96. © Illustrated London News Ltd/Mary Evans.

experiences, including the pleasure of treating girls to gin and being invited everywhere to "kissee-kissee!".[71]

By far the most popular part of the Chinese display was the restaurant, wherein visitors 'amused themselves' by 'trying to manipulate the pretty carved ivory metal-tipped chopsticks'.[72] The food drew comments about flavours and ingredients unusual to British palates; as one critic wrote, 'the Chinese eat many things which we do not eat', including some dishes demonstrating 'the skilful manner in which they utilize treasures of the deep which we waste'.[73] Others questioned the size of the dishes, suggesting that 'the beef-eating Britisher' might find 'the endless array of dishes scarcely make[s] an honest meal', with one 'gentlemen at the table … after conscientiously partaking of 28 different things, confessed that he began to long for something to eat'.[74] But it was the music that accompanied the meal that drew the most attention.

In allowing Campbell to establish the restaurant – modified to cater to British tastes – Hart had revelled in the idea of including music, hoping to 'induce a Chinese string band' to 'torture the London ear with the delights of Chinese daily life'.[75] Despite this quip, Hart was a great lover of music, and a self-styled intermediary between Chinese and British musical cultures.[76] This influenced the decisions he made in representing China at exhibitions, and meant that the Customs Service made efforts to present Chinese music in a way that demonstrated its cultural and social meaning. One such attempt was through issuing an *Illustrated Catalogue of the Chinese Collection*, of which nearly a quarter is dedicated to a 'Short Account of Chinese Music'.[77] This included examples of songs and scales, a brief history of Chinese music, depictions of instruments with explanations of their use, and discussions of ritual and popular music.[78] While this document still shows some of the deprecatory tendencies towards non-Western music that litter contemporary Western academic literature, by discussing popular music – describing 'music halls' with pun-filled comic songs met by 'candid frank laughter' – it also situates this music in the present, rather than as a relic of the musical past.[79] The 'Short Account' also ends with a reminder that, despite Western tastes, 'the Chinese – and they are some three hundred millions – understand and appreciate the beauties of their own tunes'.[80]

---

[71] Hart to Campbell, 13 Dec. 1884, in *Ibid*, p. 581.
[72] 'The Chinese Court at the Health Exhibition', *The Times*, p. 6.
[73] 'Lunch with the Celestials', *Pall Mall Gazette*, p. 4.
[74] 'The Food of the "Celestials"', *Western Mail*, p. 3.
[75] Hart to Campbell, 14 Jan. 1884, in *The I.G. in Peking*, p. 519.
[76] Han Kuo-huang, 'J.A. Van Aalst and His Chinese Music', *Asian Music*, 19:2 (1988), 127–30, at p. 127.
[77] This 'short account' is an abridged version of *Chinese Music* by J.A. Van Aalst (1858–c.1914), also published in 1884. Although Van Aalst is not credited in the catalogue, he was the Postal Secretary of the Chinese Imperial Maritime Customs at the time, and the account reproduces sections of *Chinese Music* verbatim.
[78] *Illustrated Catalogue of the Chinese Collection*, pp. 150–1.
[79] *Ibid*, p. 156.
[80] *Ibid*, p. 157.

Chinese music was occasionally heard in London before 1884[81] – including reports of informal performances at the 1851 Great Exhibition – but the Chinese restaurant band was the first large-scale and regular public demonstration of its kind.[82] Despite the Customs Service's efforts to provide context for the music, both the daily and musical press's assessments were filled with outlandish and negative criticism. Reports generally made no effort to account for the music in real terms – as the question mark after the word 'music' in the depiction of the band in Figure 27 makes clear – and the press provide little information on what works the six musicians might have played.[83] Instead, many critics jumped immediately to the tropes described above. Several use the 'health' and food-related theme of the Exhibition as the basis of their jokes, questioning the effect of the music on 'digestion', or, as the London correspondent of the *Dundee Courier* asked, 'how such a triumph of cacophony can in any way conduce to health'. This critic proceeded with racist stereotypes, suggesting the music depicts 'feelingly the ravages of indigestion' on a 'mandarin who has supped on puppie-dog … who dreams that he is being torn to pieces by a yelping multitude of his victims'.[84]

Reports frequently included comparisons to Western equivalents, employing Western musical terminology and organological frameworks. The *Pall Mall Gazette* listed banjos, fiddles, horns, clarinets, and flutes, while employing a developmentalist paradigm to describe the sheng as 'the embryo' of the Western organ.[85] Other comparisons were explicitly racist, once again providing ridiculous lists of noises. One critic styled the music as sounding like 'all the dishes and saucers' of the restaurant 'being smashed at once',[86] while for another it was an 'army of bagpipes, the squallings of maltreated babies, the whistling of locomotives, the foghorns of a steamer, the clashing of cymbals, the beating of drums'.[87] Supposedly quoting a 'well-known critic', the *Pall Mall Gazette* labelled the sounds as a combination of 'half a dozen children from four to eight years of age provided with a coal-scuttle, a kettle, a whistle, a most vile fiddle, a pumpkin, and a couple of drumsticks', set 'in a field to chase the rooks away'.[88] The *Daily News* described the orchestra as breaking out 'with crashes,

---

[81] David Clarke, 'An Encounter with Chinese Music in Mid-18th-Century London', *Early Music*, 38:4 (2010): 543–58.
[82] 'Chinese Exhibition', *The Times*, 30 Apr. 1851, p. 5.
[83] *Illustrated Catalogue of the Chinese Collection*, p. 142.
[84] 'Chinese Music at the Health Exhibition', *Dundee Courier*, 22 Jul. 1884, p. 5.
[85] 'Chinese Music at the Exhibition', *Pall Mall Gazette*, 10 Jul. 1884, p. 6. Fétis made a similar claim in his *Histoire générale de la musique*, see François-Joseph Fétis, *Histoire générale de la musique depuis les temps les plus anciens jusqu'à nos jours* (Paris, 1869), p. 70. *Grove* also notes that the free-reed organ may have been developed in Europe in the eighteenth century using sheng technology. See Barbara Owen, Peter Williams, and Stephen Bicknell, 'Organ', *Grove Music Online* <http://www.oxfordmusiconline.com> [accessed 12 Mar. 2021].
[86] 'Lunch with the Celestials', *Pall Mall Gazette*, p. 4.
[87] 'Chinese Music at the Exhibition', *Pall Mall Gazette*, p. 6.
[88] Ibid.

cries of pain, and miscellaneous din', with the singer emulating 'a well-known member's "Yah, yah," in the House of Commons'.[89] 'Horrible, barbarous, deafening, and meaningless', concluded the *World*, and the performance 'a *souvenir de Bedlam*'.[90]

The apparent 'dissonance' of Chinese music led the press to invoke comparisons with Wagner, describing it variously as 'ultra-Wagnerian'[91] and putting Wagner 'quite into the shade' for its 'discordancy'.[92] The *Daily News* felt the performances 'suggested Wagner done by village school children, with cats in the rear, and a bull in a crockery shop'.[93] The *Pall Mall Gazette* noted their anonymous 'well-known' critic was 'a profound admirer of Wagner', as if to suggest that he had a relatively high tolerance for dissonance.[94] Although Wagner's reception was often polarised – and informed by extra-musical philosophical debates beyond aesthetic considerations – by his death in 1883 his music was widely accepted in Britain.[95] But these comments suggesting Wagnerian qualities in the Chinese musical aesthetic do not engage with his music in any nuanced way. They rather use him as an emblem of a polarising figure, representative of an understood limit to chromatic tonality.

Much to the surprise of many a critic, the Chinese band also performed Western music, including 'God Save the Queen', 'God Bless the Prince of Wales', and 'Rule Britannia'. According to the *Pall Mall Gazette*, they were taught these songs by a local 'unfortunate professor', who 'slowly and sadly' repeated each piece 'until by dint of enormous stubborn perseverance' the band learnt the works.[96] Campbell's son recalled in his memoir that these rehearsals were held at the Campbell family home, and the 'unfortunate professor' was Henry Wylde (1822–90), head of the London Academy of Music.[97] The *Gazette* also published an extract of 'Rule Britannia' 'in a species of bastard notation' (Figure 28).[98] While it is impossible to say who transcribed this, it does match clearly with the standard notation of 'Rule Britannia' (Figure 29).

The performance of Western music on Chinese instruments was Campbell's idea, and Hart advised against it, writing, 'I don't agree with you in getting those musicians to play English airs: I fear they'll only get laughed at!'[99] It seems he was correct in judging the British reaction, at least as far as it was reported in the press. The *Coventry Herald* noted that, while the audience applauded 'vociferously' with 'a broad grin of amusement on every countenance', the band's

---

[89] 'The Food of the "Celestials"', *Western Mail*, p. 3.
[90] 'Chinese Music', *Coventry Herald*, 25 Jul. 1884, p. 4.
[91] 'The Health Exhibition', *The Times*, p. 5.
[92] 'Chinese Music at the Exhibition', *Pall Mall Gazette*, p. 6.
[93] 'The Food of the "Celestials"', *Western Mail*, p. 3.
[94] 'Chinese Music at the Exhibition', *Pall Mall Gazette*, p. 6.
[95] Anne Dzamba Sessa, *Richard Wagner and the English* (London, 1979), p. 37.
[96] 'Chinese Music at the Exhibition', *Pall Mall Gazette*, p. 6.
[97] Campbell, *James Duncan Campbell*, p. 55.
[98] 'Chinese Music at the Exhibition', *Pall Mall Gazette*, p. 6.
[99] Hart to Campbell, 14 Sep. 1884, in *The I.G. in Peking*, p. 565.

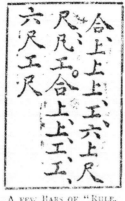

Figure 28. 'A Few Bars of "Rule Britannia"', in 'Chinese Music at the Exhibition', *Pall Mall Gazette*, 10 Jul. 1884, p. 6. Newspaper image © The British Library Board. All rights reserved. With thanks to The British Newspaper Archive (www.britishnewspaperarchive.co.uk).

Figure 29. 'A Few Bars of "Rule, Britannia"', transcribed from the *Pall Mall Gazette* by François Picard (April 2017) and reproduced with permission.

rendition of 'God Save the Queen' was met with 'deafening' laughter.[100] While this could certainly have been a laughter of surprised recognition on the part of the audience, many in the press framed it as one of ridicule. *Punch* even joked that this performance of the National Anthem, 'played in several different keys all at once' and met with 'roars of laughter' was rather suspicious: 'Could these Chinese Musicians be Irish Fenians disguised? Detectives, shut your ears, but keep your eyes open'.[101]

---

[100] 'Chinese Music', *Coventry Herald*, p. 4.
[101] 'Our Insane-Itary Guide to the Health Exhibition', *Punch*, 19 Jul. 1884, p. 34.

🌿 Siam at the International Inventions Exhibition

The following year, the Court Band of the King of Siam, along with a display of Siamese instruments, was sent to the 1885 Inventions Exhibition. Far from the semi-formal restaurant setting of the Chinese band's 1884 performances, the Siamese band performed several times per week in the Exhibition's Music Room and the Royal Albert Hall. Siam's participation in nineteenth-century exhibitions was part of a wide-ranging effort to project a modernised, Westernised image to the world. Chulalongkorn, Rama V (1853–1910), the King of Siam at the time, was known as 'a fervent anglophile', and his reign saw a deliberate refashioning of the Siamese court on a Western European model.[102] As such, like many representatives of non-Western cultures, Siam's exhibition participation was conflicted between publicly presenting an image of a modernising country, and representing themselves through their own distinct material culture: between 'pandering to Western curiosity for the exotic' or 'producing evidence of their accomplishments' on a Western framework.[103] Exhibitions were also used as a means of cultural diplomacy, as Chulalongkorn, and his father Mongkut (1804–68, Rama IV), often sent collections of instruments to such events, before donating them as state gifts.[104]

The Siamese exhibit at the Inventions Exhibition was on a smaller scale than that mounted by China the year before. Located in the East Central Gallery of the main building, Siam could be found between the Japanese, Swiss, and German displays, next to a slightly incongruous exhibit of Baillie Hamilton's Vocalion (discussed in Chapter 2). The only objects sent from Siam were musical instruments, which arrived well after the Exhibition was opened and were left out of the *Official Catalogue*.[105] The *Official Guide*, published later, however, described the display as 'occupied by many curious musical instruments',[106] and as if grasping for something else to add, noted that 'some of the cases contain beautiful specimens of native textile fabrics'.[107] The display itself was presented under an eye-catching 'tent', with an 'awning of red and white stripes, with the white elephant stamped around the border'.[108]

---

[102] Maurizio Peleggi, *Lords of Things: The Fashioning of the Siamese Monarchy's Modern Image* (Honolulu, 2002), p. 61.

[103] *Ibid*, pp. 143–4.

[104] Nineteen instruments, for example, were presented to the US government during the 1876 Philadelphia World's Fair, and a similar collection was sent to the Paris Exposition Universelle in 1867. See Paul Michael Taylor and William Bradford Smith, 'Instruments of Diplomacy: 19th Century Musical Instruments in the Smithsonian Collection of Thai Royal Gifts', *Journal of the Siam Society*, 105 (2017), 245–72.

[105] Alfred Hipkins, *Guide to the Loan Collection and List of Music Instruments, Manuscripts, Books, Paintings, and Engravings: Exhibited in the Gallery and Lower Rooms of the Albert Hall* (London, 1885), p. 127.

[106] These instruments are also illustrated in Alfred Hipkins, *Musical Instruments: Historic, Rare and Unique* (Edinburgh, 1888).

[107] *Official Guide: International Inventions Exhibition of 1885* (London, 1885), p. 52.

[108] 'A Siamese Band', *Bismarck Daily Tribune*, 31 Jul. 1885, p. 4.

Siamese involvement with the Exhibition was arranged largely through diplomatic means, with the organisers working closely with the Siamese ambassador to the United Kingdom Prince Nares Varariddhi (1855–1925), and the Siamese Legation. The press reported, before the Exhibition opened, that the organisers had offered the ambassador £1,000 to cover the costs of bringing the musicians to London. However, they also reported, 'with Oriental generosity', the Siamese Court refused the payment, covering the costs themselves.[109] The Siamese exhibits were also accompanied by a publication – along the lines of the 'Short Account of Chinese Music' described above – written by the English secretary to the Siamese Legation in London, Frederick Verney (1846–1913).[110] Titled *Notes on Siamese Musical Instruments*, this work gave details and illustrations of the exhibited instruments.

While at many points, Verney defers to Alexander Ellis[111] for technical information regarding the instruments and the music played on them, his own comments give interesting context to the way the Legation intended the music to be understood. Verney explained that the 'stumbling-block' to appreciating different musical cultures lay in education, suggesting that taste was learned, and that 'in order justly to appreciate the music of the East it would be necessary to forget all that one has experienced in the West, and *vice versa*'.[112] In recognising a lack of understanding as issuing from both sides, Verney is considered 'one of the first to see past the problem of ethnocentrism and come to understand Siamese music on its own terms'.[113] As in the 'Short Account of Chinese Music', Verney is also careful to remind readers that:

> numerically speaking, there is a large preponderance of humanity in opposition to the music of the West. That in fact by far the greater number of human beings on this earth are indifferent to the sweetest melodies of Strauss, of Verdi, or of Gounod … It never seems to occur to the minds of modern musical critics that perhaps there may be something to be said in favour of music which has the power of arousing the passions of the Eastern world. They take up their pens in splendid ignorance of the origin, or the effects, of the music they criticise, and at once condemn the performance because it is not consonant with their own training and experience.[114]

---

[109] 'London Gossip', *Evening Telegraph*, 2 May 1885, p. 2.

[110] Frederick Verney was the son of Harry Verney who was credited as exhibiting Raffles' collection of Javanese instruments in the Oriental Room of this exhibition. He was also, incidentally, Florence Nightingale's nephew.

[111] Alexander Ellis (1814–90), philologist and mathematician, was noted for his work on musical pitch.

[112] Frederick W. Verney, *Notes on Siamese Musical Instruments* (London, 1885), p. 5.

[113] Terry E. Miller and Jarenchai Chonpairot, 'A History of Siamese Music Reconstructed from Western Documents, 1505–1932', *Crossroads: An Interdisciplinary Journal of Southeast Asian Studies*, 8:2 (1994), 1–192, at p. 29.

[114] Verney, *Notes on Siamese Musical Instruments*, pp. 6–7.

Verney also situates Siamese music in the present, describing the role of music in contemporary religious services, and 'comic singing' in theatres which 'enjoys the applause of something akin to a Western music-hall audience'.[115]

The Siamese band's performances began in late June – two months into the Exhibition – and occurred two to three times per week throughout the season. These concerts were received in the press far more positively than the Chinese band the previous year. While their tone remained occasionally patronising, the music was described as 'on the whole pleasing as well as interesting'.[116] The visual elements drew initial attention, and the stage, instruments, and the performers clothing was often described in great detail. The *Daily News* presented the musicians as 'intelligent, imperturbable little people squatting on the carpet', who 'like most of their fellow countrymen abroad, wear ordinary European costume'.[117] Shaw, in the *Dramatic Review*, also described the performers as 'grave foreigners squatting cross-legged before their strange instruments' in clothing 'which, in delicate compliment to western habits in general, and our great railway companies in particular, is closely copied from the uniform of the English ticket collector'.[118] The instruments, too, placed on stage before each concert began, were often described in grand terms, highlighting the craftsmanship and beauty of the instruments as objects, 'exquisitely ornamented and inlaid'.[119]

The music itself, the *Musical Times* concluded – albeit a little hesitantly – was 'singular in the extreme' but 'by no means unpleasing'.[120] Shaw, while noting that many would 'find no whistleable tunes', made a point of suggesting that a sophisticated 'western European' could 'enjoy it and even partly appreciate' the music, as the performers were 'unmistakeably skilful and artistic'.[121] The *Liverpool Mercury*, responding to a comment published in *The Times* that described 'Eastern music' as 'difficult for Europeans to appreciate', concluded that 'though we might not appreciate the music itself, it was impossible not to admire the manner of its performance'.[122] In the same way, the *Globe* argued that 'Oriental music has great charms for those who understand it', doubting whether attendance at 'a first-rate performance' of European music 'at the opera house or a concert room' would impress the performers themselves.[123] 'The ear of a Mozart or a Beethoven', they concluded, 'if treated from earliest infancy with the music of the East, might be incapable of imagining an improvement upon it'.[124]

---

[115] *Ibid*, p. 11.
[116] 'Siamese Music at the Inventions', *Daily News*, 23 Jun. 1885, p. 3.
[117] *Ibid*.
[118] [George Bernard Shaw, unsigned], 'The Conference on Musical Pitch', *Dramatic Review*, 27 Jun. 1885, repr. in Dan H. Laurence (ed.), *Shaw's Music: The Complete Musical Criticism in Three Volumes*, vol. 2 (London, 1981), p. 282.
[119] 'Siamese Music at the Inventions', *Daily News*, p. 3.
[120] 'Music at South Kensington', *Musical Times*, 26:509 (1 Jul. 1885), 387–8, at p. 387.
[121] [Shaw], 'The Conference on Musical Pitch', *Shaw's Music*, p. 282.
[122] 'Musical Notes', *Liverpool Mercury*, 25 Jun. 1885, p. 6.
[123] 'Oriental Music', *Globe*, 26 Nov. 1885, p. 1
[124] *Ibid*.

On several occasions, critics tried to describe the Siamese music in terms of more familiar Western examples. Shaw argued that the piece called *Sensano* – translated as 'Sweet Melody' – 'would have delighted Berlioz', then described how Berlioz might reproduce its sounds, perhaps in an oblique reference to his treatise on instrumentation, but largely through a list reminiscent of the mocking catalogues used by critics for comic effect. Shaw's list, however, is more flattering and includes musical instruments, containing 'a combination of muted violins, trills on the low notes of two flutes playing in thirds, an inverted pedal sustained by an English horn, a worn-out Collard pianoforte, and a kitchen clock out of order and striking continually in consequence'.[125] Elsewhere Shaw also argued, though perhaps less convincingly, that while in part a work entitled 'Krob Chakewarn, or The Glory of the Universe' was 'genuine Siamese' some in the audience had noticed 'after a pause of incredulous astonishment' that 'the glory of the universe' was in fact the Soldiers' Chorus from Gounod's *Faust*.[126]

Like the Chinese band in 1884, the Siamese band also closed their performances by performing 'God Save the Queen', but to a strikingly different press reception. When the Siamese musicians played, there was no suggestion of mocking audience laughter, and most critics appear impressed by the effort. The *Daily News* remarked that even though the National Anthem was given 'curiously', by 'the nature of the instruments' it was done 'cleverly'.[127] Shaw was the only critic who appeared less impressed, arguing that the 'conspicuous exception of the leading note' in the Siamese scale rendered the work 'impossible', while pointing to the 'excruciating effect ... in the second bar' of performing the Anthem with a minor seventh in place of the leading note.[128]

In addition to their on-stage performance of the National Anthem, the musicians appear to have shown an interest in Western music. The Siamese embassy where the band stayed was, in the 1880s, at the corner of Ashburn Gardens and Courtfield Road in South Kensington.[129] And it was here, Shaw believed, the band had 'succumbed to a mad ambition' to perform popular local repertoire.[130] As he explained in another *Dramatic Review* article, residents of Courtfield Road had become 'painfully aware' of the musicians' 'ungovernable fancy for attempting to execute popular music hall and other London melodies on their instruments', illustrating particularly 'Wait til the Clouds Roll By' 'practised on a powerful stone dulcimer without the leading note, in a quiet road every evening after dinner!'[131]

---

[125] [Shaw], 'The Conference on Musical Pitch', *Shaw's Music*, p. 282.
[126] [Shaw, unsigned], 'The Grave Trombone', *Dramatic Review*, 8 Aug. 1885, repr. in *Shaw's Music*, p. 334.
[127] 'Siamese Music at the Inventions', *Daily News*, p. 3.
[128] [Shaw], 'The Conference on Musical Pitch', *Shaw's Music*, p. 283.
[129] 'The Alexander Estate', *British History Online* <http://www.british-history.ac.uk/survey-london/vol42/pp168-183> [accessed 12 Mar. 2021].
[130] [Shaw], 'The Grave Trombone', *Shaw's Music*, p. 334.
[131] *Ibid*, p. 335.

Apart from Shaw's idiosyncratic cynicism in some aspects of the band's reception, in general most commentators were positive, and if they did not like the music exactly, they openly put this down to their own lack of understanding. Verney, in *Notes on Siamese Musical Instruments*, seemed surprised by this, stating that 'the press, which in these days employs men of great experience and culture, spoke of the band in accents of compassionate good-nature', but suggested that this may have caused the public to flock 'to each performance with the highest expectations' only to leave with the 'impression that they had listened to the capricious volubility of a strange confusion of sound'.[132]

The Comparative Reception of the Chinese and Siamese Bands

While Chinese and Siamese musics come from different traditions with unique histories, London audiences and critics of the 1880s showed a marked conflation of different 'Eastern' cultures. When the Siamese band appeared in 1885, they were therefore inevitably received in direct comparison with the Chinese musicians heard the previous year. The *Daily News* made this explicit, writing in 1885 that while it may take some time 'before the unaccustomed listener gets fairly into the swing of the Siamese style', it was evident that the performers 'must be ranked mountains higher than the Chinese sound-torturers of last year'.[133]

That the two bands received such a strikingly different response despite the general conflation of Asian cultures, was based largely on British perceptions of social hierarchy. As David Cannadine argues in *Ornamentalism*, while one way the British historically understood the world was in terms of racial 'superiority and inferiority', more important to their own social structure was 'a carefully graded hierarchy of status'.[134] Royalty in one society was comparable with royalty in their own, and the working classes were of equally low status, regardless of race or ethnicity.[135] The reception of the Chinese and Siamese bands at the exhibitions shows this distinctly: this 'shared recognition of high social rank' commanded that the King of Siam's 'royal' band could not possibly be criticised harshly.[136] Although the British may not have liked the music – and many of the reviews imply that the critics had reservations about the overall sound world – their immobile class hierarchy compelled them to respect it. In the same vein, if court musicians deserved respect, Chinese restaurant-workers-cum-musicians could be openly mocked.

---

[132] Verney, *Notes on Siamese Musical Instruments*, p. 9.
[133] 'Siamese Music at the Inventions', *Daily News*, p. 3.
[134] David Cannadine, *Ornamentalism: How the British Saw Their Empire* (London, 2001), p. 5.
[135] *Ibid*, p. 8.
[136] *Ibid*, p. 9.

This becomes even clearer in the occasional instances when critics do respond negatively to the Siamese band, which are always coupled with attempts to delegitimise their royal status. A critic in the *Musical Times* described the instruments as 'strange and primitive' and making 'odd noises not in the least degree resembling western music'. They supported their argument by asserting that they had heard a rumour that the musicians had 'no claim to the title of "Court Band"', being 'merely a miscellaneous collection of players sent over by the Siamese Government to represent the music of the country'.[137] In contrast, in defending the band against negative comments regarding their appearance, a correspondent in the *St James's Gazette* stated that it was in 'execrable taste to comment upon the personal appearance' of musicians 'sent over here by the King of Siam entirely at his own expense'.[138]

The respective positive and negative tone of responses to the Siamese and Chinese bands extended even to occasions when they were compared to the same, more familiar musical contexts: in particular, in reference to Scottish music which appeared repeatedly in the critical reception of both. Associations between non-Western and Scottish music were common at this time, as a symptom of a widespread European conceptualisation of Scottish people (and Highlanders specifically) as a sort of European primitive Other.[139] Such comparative discourses were codified through the seventeenth and eighteenth centuries – particularly within the work of Charles Burney and after Jean-Jacques Rousseau[140] – and often used pentatonicism as a framework to associate Scotland with primitivist and exoticist ideas regarding other non-Western cultures.[141] At the London exhibitions, the Chinese band was described by various critics as sounding like 'an army of bagpipes', 'a drunken Highlander with bagpipes' and holding 'more charms for Gaelic than for Southern ears'.[142] Another critic argued, in making such a comparison, that while 'the bagpipe at home creates a divided opinion; the Chinese instrument, we should imagine, would not'.[143] In the case of the Siamese band, these comparisons took on a more flattering tone. The *Daily News* noted that Siamese music 'has at times just a suspicion of jig, reel, and strathspey about it' with a 'gentle bagpipey effect',[144] while Shaw singled out the work entitled 'The Pegu Affliction' as afflicting 'countries further

---

[137] 'Music at South Kensington', *Musical Times*, p. 387.
[138] 'Notes', *St James's Gazette*, 26 Jun. 1885, p. 4.
[139] Matthew Gelbart, *The Invention of 'Folk Music' and 'Art Music': Emerging Categories from Ossian to Wagner* (Cambridge, 2007), p. 11. Of Rousseau's pivotal reproduction of an 'air chinois' in his *Dictionnaire de musique* see also Nathan John Martin, 'Rousseau's air chinois', *Eighteenth-Century Music*, 18:1 (2021), 41–64.
[140] See Thomas Irvine, *Listening to China: Sound and the Sino-Western Encounter 1770–1839* (Chicago, 2020).
[141] Gelbart, *Invention of 'Folk Music' and 'Art Music'*, p. 114.
[142] 'Chinese Music at the Exhibition', *Pall Mall Gazette*, p. 6; 'Chinese Music', *Coventry Herald*, p. 4; 'Conversazione at the Health Exhibition', *Morning Post*, 10 Jul. 1884, p. 3.
[143] 'The Food of the "Celestials"', *Western Mail*, p. 3.
[144] 'Siamese Music at the Inventions', *Daily News*, p. 3.

west than Pegu ... for it is nothing but Auld Lang Syne powerfully treated as a declamatory recitative'.[145]

All of this stems from the same European monolithic Orientalist perspective that allowed London critics and audiences of the Chinese and Siamese bands – or those at Calcutta and at other exhibitions who viewed non-Western music more broadly – to make direct and often generic comparisons between 'Eastern' instruments and sound worlds with their own. For even positive comparisons to Scottish music, such as was the case with the Siamese band at 1885, the approval was of a limited kind, implying – in David Gramit's words – that even the 'most sophisticated of Asian musics reaches only the level of the most primitive of Europeans'.[146] Overall, the lack of discrimination between different musical cultures was clearly reflected at these exhibitions, and the only instances in which distinctions are really made is in the reception of the Siamese band as a *royal* band, and, therefore of a higher status.

One of the issues that influenced this broad dismissal of non-Western music – not only in the reception of performance, but the response to and placement of objects, too – was the difficulty in translating musical meaning between distinct cultures. Such difficulty relates directly to music's ephemerality, and is a consequence of the same struggle to conceptualise music within a physical environment as discussed repeatedly in the musical press in relation to exhibitions more broadly. Music – though termed a 'universal language' – cannot be 'translated' in the manner of a text with words. As Frank Ll. Harrison argues, given music's 'semiotic element lies primarily in its use', there are few circumstances where 'a specific music in its original form' can be 'meaningfully transferable without some transference of its contexts of occasion and their social significance'.[147] This is the crux of the British press's difficulty with non-Western music at the London exhibitions. Although local audiences understood restaurant music, the alien quality of the Chinese restaurant and the sounds created by the Chinese musicians could only be interpreted in relation to more familiar food, and more familiar musics. In the case of the Siamese musicians, the royal hierarchy was a context that, if not fully, could be at least partly understood, and this translated into a slightly more favourable, or at least more open-minded reception.

---

[145] [Shaw], 'The Conference on Musical Pitch', *Shaw's Music*, p. 282.

[146] David Gramit, *Cultivating Music: The Aspirations, Interests, and Limits of German Musical Culture, 1770–1848* (Berkeley, 2002), p. 59.

[147] Frank Ll. Harrison: 'Observation, Elucidation, Utilization: Western Attitudes to Eastern Music, ca.1600–ca.1830', in Malcolm Hamrick Brown and Roland John Wiley (eds), *Slavonic and Western Music: Essays for Gerland Abraham* (Oxford, 1985), pp. 5–31, at p. 13.

Conclusion:
Exhibitions and Their Musical Legacies

The way music was experienced at international exhibitions in the late nineteenth century British Empire mirrored many aspects of wider musical life. Exhibitions, through their intention to represent every industrial and artistic achievement of the world, highlighted and brought into focus, in microcosm, issues and debates relating to the role and function of music across the societies that held them. They underlined ongoing debates about the place of 'art' music, the materiality of the instruments that facilitated music's realisation, and the relative values of commercial music, popular music, and music from non-European cultures. The exhibitions discussed here did this in many ways: through the taxonomic ordering and exhibiting of commodified instruments and the subsequent advertisement of these by performance; through the exhibition of instruments as museum-objects for their cultural and historical importance or curiosity value; through the presentation of 'high art' musical works as a means of educating the public and demonstrating cultural 'progress'; through the debates about attracting large audiences by way of 'popular' music, and subsequent arguments about public health and outdoor leisure; and finally, through providing opportunities for Western audiences to engage with music from non-Western cultures. Music was able to play so many roles within the exhibitions because, as an ephemeral, temporal art, within an institution that sought – above all else – to order, codify, and catalogue objects, its resistance to material classification allowed it to fit multiple categories of display and fulfil many different functions.

These exhibitions also had a lasting physical and philosophical impact on the societies that held them in general, and in specific relation to music. There are obvious architectural and institutional legacies. In London, the Victoria & Albert Museum and many of the surrounding South Kensington museums are the direct institutional descendants of the exhibitions, in terms of both their establishing collections and language of display. In Australia, the building for Adelaide 1887 quickly became the Technological Museum, which existed from 1889 to 1963. In Melbourne, the building used for both 1880 and 1888 (although not the vast sheds that housed many of the exhibits) remains the only Australian non-Aboriginal cultural site to receive UNESCO World Heritage status, and is the only remaining original nineteenth-century exhibition building in the world.[1] In Glasgow, the profits of the 1888 Exhibition were used to build the

---

[1] 'Royal Exhibition and Carlton Gardens World Heritage Management Plan Review', *Museums Victoria* <https://museumsvictoria.com.au/reb/royal-exhibition-and-carlton-gardens-world-heritage-management-plan-review/> [accessed 26 Mar. 2021].

Kelvingrove Art Gallery and Museum as the Exhibition's 'permanent memorial', which now holds one of Scotland's most significant art collections.[2]

Just as these exhibitions left architectural legacies, they also, frequently, had important musical consequences. Again from an institutional perspective, the proceeds of the Great Exhibition and the purchase of the Kensington Gore estate in South Kensington facilitated the building of the Royal Albert Hall. Further, the National Training School for Music (the precursor to the Royal College of Music, opened in 1876) was also funded and established with the oversight of the Royal Commission for 1851.[3] The RCM – as well as Imperial College and the Science Museum – were all built on site of the 1880s London exhibitions. In Melbourne, the orchestra assembled for the 1888 Exhibition and conducted by Cowen was maintained to form the Victorian Orchestra. While this first 'permanent' orchestra in the colony only survived two years, as Thérèse Radic notes, it nonetheless 'kept alive the public interest in orchestral music roused by Cowen long enough for [G.W.L.] Marshall-Hall to grasp his opportunity' and begin his pivotal and long-running orchestral concert series.[4] Similarly, the consequences of some exhibitions have allowed for ongoing engagement with non-Western musics. The Monash University Tagore collection of Indian instruments, shown at Melbourne 1880, is a prominent example.

Beyond these larger-scale architectural or institutional relics of the exhibitions there also remain more ephemeral traces of the immediate influence of the exhibitions on musical life. One example is the vast quantity of commercial sheet music published on the theme of exhibitions. The Great Exhibition, for example, inspired hundreds of pieces of music by composers capitalising on the event's popularity, either for music hall or domestic use. As one letter to the editor of *Reynolds's Weekly News* put it, 'musical parasites have rushed into "Great Exhibition Quadrilles" and "Crystal Palace Polkas", and eulogic strains arise in every drawing-room'.[5] While the Great Exhibition prompted the most related compositions, there are works written about almost all the exhibitions considered in this book, from a Fisheries Polka to a song commemorating the switchback railway at Glasgow 1888.[6] Some were souvenirs with highly decorative covers but little engagement with the exhibitions in their lyrical or musical content. Others were comedic or satirical songs for public and music hall performance, while others still commemorated the exhibitions and lauded the achievements of their organisers. Instrumental works, usually for solo

---

[2] Perilla Kinchin and Juliet Kinchin, *Glasgow's Great Exhibitions: 1888, 1901, 1911, 1938, 1988* (Wendlebury, 1988), p. 55.

[3] Guy Warrack, *Royal College of Music: The First Eighty-Five Years 1883–1968* (London, 1977), p. 5.

[4] Thérèse Radic, 'The Victorian Orchestra 1889–1891: In the Wake of the Centennial Exhibition, 1888', *Australasian Music Research*, 1 (1997), pp. 13–101, at p. 47.

[5] 'The Albert Snare: To The Editor of Reynolds's Weekly Newspaper', *Reynolds's Weekly News*, 12 Jan. 1851, p. 5.

[6] Arthur F. Bare, *The Fisheries Polka* (London, 1883); Grosvenor Cross, *The Switchback: New Song and Chorus* (Glasgow, 1888).

piano, sometimes attempted to present musical representations of the various nations in attendance, sonically depicting a passage through the various courts through a medley of different national songs.

On a social level, the exhibitions also had an influence on the musical life of the cities that held them. As we saw in the Introduction to this book, music hall and theatre managers in 1884 and 1885 were concerned about the exhibitions drawing audiences away from their business. This was not only the case for the Health and Inventions Exhibition, but a recurring theme in the musical press throughout all the exhibitions. Before the 1851 Great Exhibition opened, proprietors argued that the Exhibition would have a detrimental effect on their attendances and ticket sales, and the musical press debated and amplified these fears, suggesting that the Exhibition would divert the public's attention, and more importantly, money, away from the regular concert season.

On one hand, some argued that the mass of people entering London to attend the Exhibition would create a larger concert-going public, and attract important performers from elsewhere. The *Illustrated London News*, for example, listed a number of continental musicians who had supposedly 'signified their intention of visiting London in 1851' to take advantage of the crowds of exhibition-visitors who would require further entertainment. These included:

> Liszt, Henselt, Dohler, Thalberg, Leopold de Meyer, Ernst, Sivori, Madame Pleyel, Spohr, Meyerbeer, Auber, Halèvy, Adam, Berlioz, Flotow, Thomas, David, Onslow, Lindpaintner, Staudigl, Pischek, Fétis, Wagner, Dreyschock, De Beriot, Alard, Batta, Franchomme, Hallé, Elwart, Clapisson, Labarre, Mdlle. Puget, Grisar, Musard, Labitzky, Moscheles, Tilmant, Vieuxtemps, Madame Wartel, Rosenhain, Prudent, Blumenthal.[7]

They also reported that several opera companies from Italy would be coming. However, as the *Musical World* argued, perhaps catastrophising, with the Exhibition on, would there be need or even space for these performers?

> Where will they give their concerts? – where find their pianos? Ay, and where find their audiences? When they come, if they come, they will find [venues] … already engaged for entertainments of various kinds, well nigh up to the end of September … Unless inclined to exhibit themselves as '*échantillons*' of modern mechanical skill, at the Exhibition, [they] would be compelled to walk about London with their hands in their pockets.[8]

In the end, Thalberg was the only one of the promised musicians who arrived, bringing with him 'the score of an Opera, instead of a new fantasia for the piano' and having 'staid [sic] away from the arena of public exhibition'.[9] Berlioz also came to London, but as a French representative on the international jury examining the musical instrument displays, not necessarily to promote his own work.

---

[7] 'Music', *Illustrated London News*, 21 Dec. 1850, p. 481.
[8] 'Prospects for Pianists', *Musical World*, 26:3 (18 Jan. 1851), pp. 33–4.
[9] 'The Musical Season of 1851', *Musical World*, 26:24 (14 Jun. 1851), 369–70, at p. 369.

Despite these early criticisms, there is little evidence that such fears were fully warranted, and reports about the overall impact of the Great Exhibition on musical life in London are conflicting. The *Musical World* stated that 'the theatres have not fared so ill for many years past' as the Exhibition had 'absorbed both the curiosity and the money of the public, and there was nothing left to remunerate artists, foreign or native'.[10] Yet only a fortnight later, *John Bull* was arguing that the 'complaint ... that the Great Exhibition was ruining the places of public amusement' was 'without foundation', reporting increased attendance at theatres across the city, including 'crowds of strangers from all parts of the world'.[11] Reports from correspondents published in the New York musical press also regarded the Exhibition 'which threatened destruction to all other attractions' to have, in fact, been 'the efficient means of producing a musical season of unparalleled brilliancy'.[12] In other parts of the world, it seems external musical organisations were able to take deliberate advantage of the exhibitions. In Melbourne, for example, the Victorian Tonic Sol-fa Association specifically gave a series of concerts during the 1880 Melbourne Exhibition season to promote their methods (which were also displayed in the building), advertising in official publications and organising their timetables around the other events of the Exhibition.[13]

One of the most exciting aspects of the study of exhibitions and music is how much work there is left to be done. This book has considered music at the international exhibitions held in the British Empire during the 1880s. But in this decade alone there were other international exhibitions held in Austria-Hungary, Belgium, France, Germany, the Netherlands, and the United States; national exhibitions held in – among others – Spain, Ireland, Italy, Japan, Venezuela, and other parts of the British Empire including New Zealand and South Africa; and larger continental exhibitions, such as the South American Exhibition in Argentina in 1882 and the Nordic Exhibition of 1888 in Denmark. This is to say nothing of the decades that followed, as exhibitions continued to proliferate across the world well into the twentieth century. Many of these events would undoubtedly have had significant musical aspects and historical musicological work is only just beginning to uncover the depth and variety of musical experiences, contexts, and stories that exhibitions can provide.

One of the reasons that the study of music at exhibitions has been previously overlooked in musicology is, perhaps, exactly why they can be so illuminating: exhibitions were not, in themselves, musical events. There was, categorically – and as this book has shown – much music at exhibitions, all of which was important, interesting, and participatory in larger aesthetic, social, and economic discourses. However, the people in charge of them were not really all that interested in music. As was the purview of the institution, the organisers had

---

[10] *Ibid.*
[11] 'Theatres and Music', *John Bull*, 28 Jun. 1851, p. 415.
[12] 'London Season of 1851', *Saroni's Musical Times*, 3:21 (16 Aug. 1851), p. 222.
[13] 'Victorian Tonic Sol-Fa Association', *Tonic Sol-Fa Reporter*, Nov. 1880, p. 248.

the entirety of the world's art, industry, and culture to attempt to represent, and music was just one of many hundred things they had to consider. As a result of this, musical arrangements were often outsourced to invested individuals, partnerships with other institutions, or provided in a largely utilitarian manner.

Thus, for the most part, the majority of music at exhibitions ended up being exactly what might have been expected at a large event of the time. It fulfilled what the largest audience wanted and caused the least amount of contention. For this reason 'light entertainment' prevailed with brass and military bands and secular organ recitals consistently drawing crowds, and creating enjoyable experiences. But in other cases, efforts by groups or individuals gave different or less expected types of music more prominence. It may have been the commercial imperative to demonstrate exhibited instruments that led manufacturers to employ musicians to give recitals at many exhibitions, but the result was a forum in which visitors could hear both prominent and lesser-known performers in a regular and accessible way. Indeed, at exhibitions like Calcutta 1883, it was only through the efforts of Horace Brinsmead that any Western music was regularly performed at all. The displays of 'ancient instruments' at London and Edinburgh were both the result of efforts by a small number of dedicated people. But their influence was far-reaching for the individuals who experienced them, introducing early music to a range of future practitioners, such as John Fuller-Maitland who described the concerts of 'ancient' music at London as the thing that initially fired his 'antiquarian zeal'.[14] The performances by non-Western bands in London were similarly the work of a few independent agents. But their presence had a defining impact on the history of ethnomusicology, with, for instance, experiments conducted by Alexander Ellis, Alfred Hipkins, and the Chinese musicians at the Health Exhibition, providing the foundation for much of Ellis's work on pitch.[15]

Even large-scale musical events within these exhibitions were often the work of individual members or small groups from the local musical community. In Melbourne, for instance, Cowen's appointment at 1888, and the subsequent explosion of orchestral music afforded to Australian audiences, only came about after George Clark Allan (1860–1934, the son of George Leavis Allan, 1826–97, the music warehouse founder) convinced the vice-president of the Exhibition, Frederick Sargood (1834–1930), to feature orchestral music.[16] Once Cowen was appointed, many of the organisers had little interest in or control over what he did; Cowen attended only a single commissioners' meeting, and was given 'carte blanche thereafter' with his advice 'acted upon without question'.[17] Although Cowen's fee of £5,000 sounds exorbitant, this figure made up

---

[14] John Fuller-Maitland, *A Door-Keeper of Music* (London, 1929), p. 107.
[15] 'On the Musical Scales of Various Nations', *Journal of the Society of Arts*, 33:1688 (1885), 485–527. See also Jonathan P.J. Stock, 'Alexander J. Ellis and His Place in the History of Ethnomusicology', *Ethnomusicology*, 51:2 (2007), 306–25.
[16] Peter Game, *The Music Sellers* (Melbourne, 1976), p. 83; Radic, 'The Victorian Orchestra', p. 20.
[17] Radic, 'The Victorian Orchestra', p. 20.

less than 1.5% of the Exhibition's overall expenses, (to give some perspective, approximately 1% of the overall budget was spent on flags). The musical expenses in total, including Cowen's fee, paying all the orchestra members, and all of the popular musical entertainments, came to only roughly 8% of the Exhibition's budget.[18] The profit was, however, as we have seen, both economically and culturally vast.

That exhibitions were not inherently musical events meant that their actual musical aspects, and the debates that arose from music's inclusion, developed almost organically from the surrounding environment in interaction with the wider ideologies of the exhibition-institution. To present any one of music's manifestations – whether genres, objects, or performance styles – within the exhibitions was to suggest that it was somehow representative of 'music' as a whole, by virtue of its representation in a show ostensibly summarising all the world's art and industry. The debates and discussions surrounding the meaning, importance, and function of music at the exhibitions then, were not only about music *at* the exhibitions, but about music's meaning, importance, and function in society overall. Invested individuals and parties could attempt to shape the presentation and representation of music according to their own beliefs, but ultimately, the most successful aspects across the decade and Empire were those vocally supported by the public. The exhibition-institution, then, became a kind of mediating factor in some of the broader debates of the time. As such, the study of music and exhibitions can provide a wider-lens view of the social and cultural role of music in the places where exhibitions were held. This book, I hope, has provided such an insight into music in Victorian Britain, the Australian colonies, and perhaps even parts of India and the broader Empire.

---

[18] See *Centennial International Exhibition, Melbourne, 1888: Report of the Executive Commissioners for the Centennial International Exhibition of 1888, Together with an Account of Income and Expenditure* (Melbourne, 1891).

Bibliography

❧ Manuscript and Archival Collections

British Library, United Kingdom.
[A Collection of Miscellaneous Printed and MS. Material Relating to Pianofortes. Compiled by J.L. Stephen]. General Reference Collection 07902.b.1/9.
Hipkins Papers. Vol. 2. Brit. Mus. Additional MS. 41,637.

National Art Library, London, United Kingdom.
[Collection of Documents Relating to the Colonial and Indian Exhibition Held in London in 1886]. SH.99.0023.

National Library of Australia, Canberra, Australia.
Official Daily Programme / Centennial International Exhibition, Melbourne, 1888–89, NLA SR 607.34945 C397.

Royal Commission for 1851 Archive, London, United Kingdom.
Correspondence RC/H/I/B/14, RC/A/1851/144, RC/A/1851/211, RC/A/1851/221, RC/A/1851/222, RC/A/1851/231, RC/A/1851/232, RC/A/1851/233, RC/A/1851/234, RC/A/1851/235, RC/A/1851/236, RC/A/1851/240.
A Special Report on the Annual International Exhibitions of the Years 1871, 1872, 1873 and 1874 by Henry Cole, C.B. (London, 1875).
Seventh Report of The Commissioners for the Exhibition of 1851 to the Right Hon. Henry Matthews, &c., &c., One of Her Majesty's Principal Secretaries of State (London, 1889).

Senate House Library, University of London, United Kingdom.
A.J. Hipkins Papers: Research Notebooks MS943/1/1, MS943/1/14, MS943/1/2.
South Kensington Music Exhibitions 1872 & 1885 MS943/3/6.
Lectures MS943/2/1, MS943/2/2.
Scrapbooks MS943/4/2, MS943/4/3.
The International Inventions Exhibition: Daily Programme, Musical and Other Arrangements, May 4th–November 9th 1885. London: William Clowes, 1885. Music Library Locked Cupboard [International].

State Library of Victoria, Melbourne, Australia.
Visitors' Register of Melbourne International Exhibition, 1880. [manuscript]. Accession no: MS 9306.
The Exhibition Visitors' Daily Programme (Melbourne, 1880–1). Rare Books RARELTF 606.49451 M48.

University of Cambridge Archives, United Kingdom.
Official Daily Programme [Edinburgh 1890] edited by Robert A. Marr 1891.8.279 UL.

216   BIBLIOGRAPHY

University of Glasgow Library, United Kingdom.
Views of Glasgow International Exhibition, 1888 (Glasgow, [1888]). Wylie Collection, Sp Coll Bh11-a.8.
Special Programme of Music and Sports. International Exhibition of Industry, Science and Art [Glasgow, 1888]. Sp Coll Mu22-c.8.
[Collection of Official Daily Programmes; Grand Opening Ceremony; Programme]. Sp Coll Mu25-a.25.

Victoria and Albert Museum Archives, United Kingdom.
United Kingdom, Edinburgh: International Exhibition, 1890: MA/35/86.
United Kingdom, Glasgow: International Exhibition, 1888: MA/35/87.
United Kingdom, London: International Health Exhibition, 1 May 1884: MA/35/95.
United Kingdom, London: International Inventions Exhibition, 1885: MA/35/96.
United Kingdom, London: Colonial & Indian Exhibition, 1886: MA/35/98.
Australia, Sydney: International Exhibition, 1879; Australia, Melbourne: International Exhibition of Arts, Manufactures, & Agricultural & Industrial Products of All Nations, 1 Oct 1880–30 Apr 1881; Australia, Melbourne: Melbourne Centennial Exhibition, 1888: MA/35/2.

ぺ *Primary Printed Sources*

OFFICIAL DOCUMENTS AND PUBLICATIONS

London Exhibitions 1851–1874
The Crystal Palace, and its Contents: Being an Illustrated Cyclopaedia of the Great Exhibition of the Industry of All Nations, 1851: Embellished with Upwards of Five Hundred Engravings, with a Copious Analytical Index (London, 1852).
Ellis, Robert (ed.), *Official Descriptive and Illustrated Catalogue of the Great Exhibition, by Authority of the Royal Commission*, 4 vols (London, 1851).
Illustrated Catalogue of the International Exhibition, 1862 (London, 1863).
London International Exhibition of 1871: Official Catalogue, Industrial Department (London, 1871).
London International Exhibition of 1872: Official Catalogue, Industrial Department (London, 1872).
London International Exhibition of 1873: Official Catalogue (London, 1873).
London International Exhibition of 1874: Official Catalogue (London, 1874).
Science and Art Department: South Kensington Museum. Catalogue of the Special Exhibition of Ancient Musical Instruments MDCCCLXXII (London, [1872?]).

Sydney 1879
Official Record of the Sydney International Exhibition, 1879 (Sydney, 1881).
Straits Settlement Court: International Exhibition Sydney 1879: Official Catalogue of Exhibits (Sydney, [1879?]).
Sydney International Exhibition, 1879: Visitors' Companion (Sydney, 1879).

Melbourne 1880

Official Catalogue of the Exhibits: With Introductory Notices of the Countries Exhibiting (Melbourne, 1880).
Official Record Containing Introduction, History of Exhibition, Description of Exhibition and Exhibits, Official Awards of Commissioners and Catalogue of Exhibits (Melbourne, 1882).
Report of the Royal Commission for the Australian International Exhibitions to the Queen's Most Excellent Majesty (London, 1882).
Straits Settlements Court, International Exhibition, Melbourne, 1880: Catalogue of Exhibits (Singapore, 1880).

Calcutta 1883

Calcutta International Exhibition 1883-1884: Official Catalogue (Calcutta, 1883).
Official Report of the Calcutta International Exhibition, 1883-84: Compiled under the Orders of the Executive Committee (Calcutta, 1885).

London Health Exhibition 1884

Catalogue with Explanatory Notes of the Exhibits from the Department of Education, Empire of Japan, in the International Health and Education Exhibition, Held in London, 1884 (London, 1884).
The Health Exhibition Literature (London, 1884).
Illustrated Catalogue of the Chinese Collection of Exhibits for the International Health Exhibition (London, 1884).
International Health Exhibition, 1884: Official Catalogue (London, 1884).
Official Guide: International Health Exhibition, 1884 (London, 1884).
Special Catalogue of the Education Division (London, 1884).

London Inventions Exhibitions 1885

Awards of the International Juries, Confirmed and Issued by the Jury Commissioners: International Inventions Exhibition of 1885 ([London], 1885).
Dale, William (ed.), *Brief Description of Spinets, Virginals, Harpsichords, Clavichords, and Pianos, Shown in the Loan Collection of the International Inventions Exhibition, 1885* (London, 1885).
Hipkins, Alfred, *Guide to the Loan Collection and List of Music Instruments, Manuscripts, Books, Paintings, and Engravings: Exhibited in the Gallery and Lower Rooms of the Albert Hall* (London, 1885).
International Inventions Exhibition, 1885: Official Catalogue (London, 1885).
Official Guide: International Inventions Exhibition of 1885 (London, 1885).
The International Inventions Exhibition: Daily Programme, Musical and Other Arrangements, May 4th-November 9th 1885 (London, 1885).
Weale, W.H. James, *A Descriptive Catalogue of Rare Manuscripts & Printed Books, Chiefly Liturgical* (London, 1885).

London Colonial and Indian Exhibition 1886

Colonial and Indian Exhibition: Daily Programme (London, [1886]).
Colonial and Indian Exhibition: Official Guide (London, 1886).
Colonial and Indian Exhibition, 1886: Official Catalogue (London, 1886).
The Colonial and Indian Exhibition 1886: Supplement to the Art Journal (London, 1886).
Cundall, Frank (ed.), *Reminiscences of the Colonial and Indian Exhibition Illustrated by Thomas Riley* (London, 1886).

Empire of India: Special Catalogue of Exhibits by the Government of India and Private Exhibitors (London, 1886).
Report of the Royal Commission for the Colonial and Indian Exhibition, London, 1886 to the Right Hon. Henry Matthews, M.P. &c., One of Her Majesty's Principal Secretaries of State (London, 1887).
Wood, Henry Trueman (ed.), *Reports on the Colonial Sections of the Exhibition* (London, 1887).

Edinburgh 1886
Dunlop, J.C., *Official Penny Guide to the Old Edinburgh Street in the International Exhibition, Edinburgh, 1886* (Edinburgh, [1886]).
International Exhibition of Industry, Science and Art, Edinburgh 1886: The Official Catalogue (Edinburgh, 1886).
Official Guide to the Exhibition, with Notes of What to See in Edinburgh (Edinburgh, 1886).
Women's Industries: Edinburgh 1886 International Exhibition of Industry, Science & Art (Edinburgh, 1886).

Liverpool 1886
All About the Liverpool Exhibition, 1886 (Liverpool, 1886).
Cross, William, *Liverpool International Exhibition, 1886, the Indian Village, North-East Corner of the Grounds: 50 Natives of India, Together with Elephants, Camels, Zebras, Brahmin Bulls &c. Imported Specially for this Exhibition by William Cross* (London, 1886).
International Exhibition of Navigation, Travelling, Commerce, & Manufacture, Liverpool 1886: Official Catalogue (Liverpool, 1886).
International Exhibition of Navigation, Travelling, Commerce, & Manufacture, Liverpool 1886: Official Guide (Liverpool, 1886).
'The Shipperies': International Exhibition of Navigation, Travelling, Commerce & Manufacture, Liverpool, 1886 (Liverpool, 1886).

Adelaide 1887
Adelaide Jubilee International Exhibition, 1887 (Adelaide, 1886).
Adelaide Jubilee International Exhibition, 1887: Reports of Juries and Official List of Awards (Adelaide, 1889).
Official Catalogue of the Exhibits (Adelaide, 1887).

Glasgow 1888
Glasgow International Exhibition, 1888. Views of Glasgow International Exhibition, 1888 (Glasgow, 1888).
Glasgow International Exhibition: Official Guide (Glasgow, 1888).
Glasgow International Exhibition: The Official Catalogue (Glasgow, 1888).

Melbourne 1888
Centennial International Exhibition, Melbourne, 1888: Report of the Executive Commissioners for the Centennial International Exhibition of 1888, Together with an Account of Income and Expenditure (Melbourne, 1891).
Official Catalogue of Exhibits: Centennial International Exhibition, Melbourne, 1888-9 (Melbourne, 1888).

Official Record of the Centennial International Exhibition, Melbourne, 1888–1889 (Melbourne, 1890).
Popular Guide to the Centennial Exhibition: With which is Incorporated the Strangers' Guide to Melbourne (Melbourne, 1888).

Edinburgh 1890

Bapty, Samuel Lee (ed.), *Official Catalogue: International Exhibition of Electrical Engineering, General Inventions and Industries* (Edinburgh, 1890).
Graphic Guide to Edinburgh, the Forth Bridge, and the International Exhibition (Glasgow, 1890).

CONTEMPORARY BOOKS AND ARTICLES

Aalst, Jules A. Van, *Chinese Music* (Shanghai, 1884).
Ainsworth, William Harrison, *The Lancashire Witches: A Romance of Pendle Forest* (London, 1854).
Bare, Arthur F., *The Fisheries Polka* (London, 1883).
Berlioz, Hector, 'Exposition Universelle: Les Instrumens de musique à l'Exposition universelle', *Journal des Débats*, 9 Jan. 1856, p. 3, repro. at *The Hector Berlioz Website* <http://www.hberlioz.com/feuilletons/debats560109.htm> [accessed 1 Apr. 2021].
——, *Les Soirées de l'orchestre* (Paris, 1854), trans. and repr. as 'Berlioz in London: Crystal Palace–1851 Exhibition' at *The Hector Berlioz Website* <http://www.hberlioz.com/London/BL1851Exhibition.html/> [accessed 2 Feb. 2021].
Burney, Charles, 'Chinese Music', *Rees' Cyclopaedia*, vol. 7 (1802–19).
Cambridge, Ada, *The Three Miss Kings* (1891; repr. London, 1987).
——, *Thirty Years in Australia* (London, 1903).
Comettant, Oscar, *In the Land of Kangaroos and Gold Mines* [Au pays des kangourous et des mines d'or], trans. Judith Armstrong (1890; repr. Adelaide, 1980).
Corder, Frederick, 'Musical Misrepresentation', *Quarterly Musical Review*, 1:3 (Aug. 1885), 187–92.
Cowen, Frederic Hymen, *My Art and My Friends* (London, 1913).
Cross, Grosvenor, *The Switchback: New Song and Chorus* (Glasgow, 1888).
Davison, T. Raffles, *Pen-and-Ink Notes at the Glasgow Exhibition: A Series of Illustrations* (1888, repr. London, 2015).
Dinsdale, John, *Sketches at the Colonial and Indian Exhibition* (London, 1885).
——, *Sketches at the 'Inventories'* (London, 1885).
Ellis, Alexander, 'On the Musical Scales of Various Nations', *Journal of the Society of Arts*, 1688:33 (1885), 485–527.
Elsner, Frederick William, 'The Progress of Instrumental Music in Australia', *Centennial Magazine*, 1:8 (Mar. 1889), 544–9.
Engel, Carl, *Musical Myths and Facts* (London, 1876).
Fairbank, John King, Katherine Fros Bruner, and Elizabeth MacLeod Matheson (eds), *The I.G. in Peking: Letters of Robert Hart, Chinese Maritime Customs, 1865–1907* (Cambridge, 1975).
Fétis, François-Joseph, *Histoire générale de la musique depuis les temps les plus anciens jusqu'à nos jours* (Paris, 1869).
Fuller-Maitland, John Alexander, *A Door-Keeper of Music* (London, 1929).
Gurney, Edmund, *The Power of Sound* (London, 1880).

Hart, Ernest, 'The International Health Exhibition: Its Influence and Possible Sequels', *Journal of the Society of Arts*, 33 (28 Nov. 1884), 35–58.
Heine, Heinrich, *Letters on the French Stage*, trans. Charles Godfrey Leland (New York, 1892–1905).
Hipkins, Alfred J., *List of John Broadwood & Sons' Exhibits, International Inventions Exhibition, Division – Music* (London, 1885).
——, *Musical Instruments: Historic, Rare and Unique* (Edinburgh, 1888).
Hoffmann, Ernst Theodor Amadeus, 'Beethoven's Instrumental Music (1813)', in Leo Treitler (rev. ed.), Ruth Solie (ed.), *Source Readings in Music History*, vol. 6 (New York, 1998), pp. 151–6.
Joubert, Jules, *Shavings and Scrapes from Many Parts* (Dunedin, 1890).
Kierkegaard, Søren, *Either/Or*, trans. David F. Swenson and Lillian Marvin Swenson (1843, repr. Princeton, 1972).
Landon, Letitia Elizabeth, *The Works of L.E. Landon in Two Volumes*, vol. 1 (Philadelphia, 1838).
Laurence, Dan H. (ed.), *Shaw's Music: The Complete Musical Criticism in Three Volumes* (London, 1981).
Lee, Henry, *Sea Monsters Unmasked* (London, 1883).
Maccann, John Hill, *The Concertinist's Guide* (London, 1888).
Machell, Thomas, 'On a New Musical Instrument', *Proceedings of the Royal Philosophical Society of Glasgow*, 15 (1884–5), 185–8.
Marr, Robert A., *Music and Musicians at the Edinburgh International Exhibition 1886* (Edinburgh, 1887).
——, *Music for the People: A Retrospect of the Glasgow International Exhibition, 1888. With an Account of the Rise of Choral Societies in Scotland* (Edinburgh, 1889).
Monier-Williams, Monier, 'Royal Asiatic Society. Proceedings of the Sixty-First Anniversary Meeting of the Society, Held on the 19th of May, 1884', *Journal of the Royal Asiatic Society of Great Britain and Ireland*, 16:4 (1884), 144–53.
——, *Buddhism, in its Connexion with Brāhmanism and Hindūism, and in its Contrast with Christianity* (New York, 1889).
Pater, Walter, *The Renaissance: Studies in Art and Literature* (London, 1888).
Pellisov [Karl Emil Schafhäutl], 'Ueber die Kirchenmusik des katholischen Cultus', *Allgemeine musikalische Zeitung*, 36 (1834), 744.
Rimbault, Edward Francis, *Historical Notes on Queen Elizabeth's Virginal on Exhibition at the Historic Musical Loan Collection Inventions Exhibition 1885* (London, 1885).
——, *The Pianoforte, its Origin, Progress, and Construction* (London, 1860).
Verney, Frederick W., *Notes on Siamese Musical Instruments* (London, 1885).
Wheatley, Henry B., 'Decorative Art in London', *The Decorator and Furnisher*, 5:5 (Feb. 1885), 166.
Yapp, George Wagstaffe, *Art Education at Home and Abroad* (London, 1852).

NEWSPAPERS AND PERIODICALS

Australia
Adelaide Observer 1883–7.
Advocate [Melbourne] 1880.
Age [Melbourne] 1880–8.

Argus [Melbourne] 1879–89.
Australasian 1888.
Australian Town and Country Journal 1879.
Brisbane Courier 1889.
Evening Journal [Adelaide] 1887.
Evening News [Sydney] 1879–80.
Express and Telegraph [Adelaide] 1887.
Hamilton Spectator 1888.
Horsham Times 1888.
Illustrated Australian News 1879–88.
Illustrated Sydney News 1879–87.
Leader [Melbourne] 1880–8.
Queenslander 1887.
South Australian Advertiser 1887–8.
South Australian Register 1880–8.
Sydney Mail and New South Wales Advertiser 1879–80.
Sydney Morning Herald 1879–88.
Table Talk 1888.
Telegraph [Brisbane] 1879.
Weekly Times [Melbourne] 1880–9.

China
North-China Herald and Supreme Court & Consular Gazette 1884.

India
Englishman 1883–4.
Friend of India & Statesman 1883.
Indian Mirror 1883.

United Kingdom
Academy: A Weekly Review of Literature, Science, and Art 1885–8.
Athenaeum 1885.
Art Journal 1881–6.
Birmingham Daily Post 1886.
Bristol Mercury and Daily Post 1885.
British Architect 1883–9.
Coventry Herald 1884.
Crewe Guardian 1886.
Daily News [London] 1851–86.
Daily Telegraph 1885.
Decorator and Furnisher 1885.
Dramatic Review 1885.
Dundee Advertiser 1890.
Dundee Courier & Argus 1884–90.
Edinburgh Evening Dispatch 1886–90.
Edinburgh Evening News 1886.
Era 1872–85.
Evening Standard 1885.
Evening Telegraph 1885.
Examiner 1851.
Glasgow Herald 1885–8.

Globe 1885.
Graphic 1871–85.
Greenock Telegraph and Clyde Shipping Gazette 1890.
Illustrated London News 1851–90.
John Bull 1851.
The Key 1871–3.
Lady's Pictorial 1885.
Liverpool Courier 1886.
Liverpool Mercury 1885–6.
Liverpool Review 1886.
Liverpool Weekly Courier 1886.
Lloyd's Weekly Newspaper 1851.
London and Provincial Music Trades Review 1881–5.
Magazine of Music 1884–90.
Manchester Guardian 1888.
Monthly Musical Record 1872–87.
Morning Chronicle 1851.
Morning Post 1851–84.
Musical Herald 1890.
Musical Opinion and Music Trade Review 1880–90.
Musical Standard 1871–90.
Musical Times and Singing Class Circular 1851–90.
Musical World 1851–90.
North British Advertiser & Ladies' Journal 1890.
Orchestra Musical Review 1871–85.
Our Corner 1885.
Pall Mall Gazette 1884.
Penny Illustrated Paper and Illustrated Times 1884–5.
Piano, Organ and Music Trades Journal 1885–8.
Porcupine [Liverpool] 1886.
Portobello Advertiser 1890.
Punch 1884–5.
Ragged School Union Quarterly Record 1886.
Reynolds's Weekly News 1851.
Saturday Review of Politics, Literature, Science and Art 1883–8.
St James's Gazette 1884–5.
Standard [London] 1851.
Telegraph 1879–85.
The Times 1850–90.
The Sunday Times 1871–85.
Tonic Sol-Fa Reporter 1880.
Western Mail 1884.
Wigan Observer and District Advertiser 1886.

United States
Bismarck Daily Tribune 1885.
Chicago Evening Post 1893.
Dwight's Journal of Music 1864–71.
Saroni's Musical Times 1851.

Secondary Sources

Abdullah, A. Rahman Tang, 'Sultan Abu Bakar's Foreign Guests and Travels Abroad, 1860s–1895: Fact and Fiction in Early Malay Historical Accounts', *Journal of the Malaysian Branch of the Royal Asiatic Society*, 84:1 (2011), 1–22.

Abell, Lesley, 'Travellers, Tourists, and Visitors to the Adelaide Jubilee International Exhibition', in Garnaut, Collins, and Jolly (eds), *Adelaide's Jubilee International Exhibition*, pp. 129–39.

Anderson, Lara, 'Adelaide 1887–1888', in Findling and Pelle (eds), *Encyclopedia of World's Fairs and Expositions*, pp. 92–4.

Adams, Annmarie, *Architecture in the Family Way: Doctors, Houses, and Women, 1870–1900* (Kingston, 1996).

———, 'London: The Healthy Victorian City: The Old London Street at the International Health Exhibition of 1884', in Çelik, Favro, and Ingersoll (eds), *Streets: Critical Perspectives on Public Space*, pp. 203–12.

Allen, Jasmine, '"Why are the Painted Windows in the Industrial Department?": The Classification of Stained Glass at the London and Paris International Exhibitions, 1851–1900', in Nichols, Wade, and Williams (eds), *Art versus Industry?*, pp. 61–80.

Anderson, Benedict, *Imagined Communities: Reflections on the Origin and Spread of Nationalism* (London, 2006).

Asquith, Mark, '"Wagner Mania": The Early Reception of Wagner's Aesthetics in England', *Wagner*, 23:2 (2002), 65–80.

Atlas, Allan W., 'The "Respectable" Concertina', *Music & Letters*, 80:2 (1999), 241–53.

Auerbach, Jeffry A., *The Great Exhibition of 1851: A Nation on Display* (New Haven, 1999).

Auerbach, Jeffry A., and Peter H. Hoffenberg (eds), *Britain, the Empire, and the World at the Great Exhibition of 1851* (Aldershot, 2008).

Bailey, Peter, 'Custom, Capital and Culture in the Victorian Music Hall', in Storch (ed.), *Popular Culture and Custom*, pp. 180–208.

———, *Leisure and Class in Victorian England: Rational Recreation and the Contest for Control, 1830–1885* (London, 1978).

Bandyopadhyay, Deb Narayan, Paul Brown, and Christopher Conti (eds), *Landscape, Place and Culture: Linkages between Australia and India* (Newcastle Upon Tyne, 2011).

Bandyopadhyay, Deb Narayan, 'Return of the Revenant: Re-Imagining Calcutta International Exhibition (1883) through Australian Newspapers', in Bandyopadhyay, Brown, and Conti (eds), *Landscape, Place and Culture*, pp. 124–35.

Banks, Paul, *Sir Sourindro Mohun Tagore and the Tagore Medal: A Centenary History* (London, 1999).

Barringer, Tim, and Tom Flynn (eds), *Colonialism and the Object: Empire, Material Culture and the Museum* (London, 1998).

Bartley, Alan Philip, *Far from the Fashionable Crowd: The People's Concert Society and Music in London's Suburbs* (Newbury, 2009).

Bashford, Christina, and Roberta Montemorra Marvin (eds), *The Idea of Art Music in a Commercial World, 1800–1930* (Woodbridge, 2016).

Becker, A.L., 'Journey through the Night: Notes on Burmese Traditional Theatre', *Drama Review*, 15:2 (1971), 83–7.

Benjamin, Walter, 'Paris, the Capital of the Nineteenth Century', *The Arcades Project*, trans. Howard Eiland and Kevin McLaughlin (Cambridge, 1999).
Bennett, Tony, 'The Exhibitionary Complex', in Greenberg, Ferguson, and Nairne (eds), *Thinking About Exhibitions*, pp. 58–80.
Bennett, Susan, 'Glasgow 1888', in Findling and Pelle (eds), *Encyclopedia of World's Fairs*, pp. 95–7.
Bird, Louise, 'Making the Right Impression: The Jubilee Exhibition Ornamental Grounds', in Garnaut, Collins, and Jolly (eds), *Adelaide's Jubilee International Exhibition*, pp. 101–14.
Bourdieu, Pierre, *Distinction: A Social Critique of the Judgement of Taste*, trans. Richard Nice (London, 1986).
——, 'The Forms of Capital', in Richardson (ed.), *Handbook of Theory and Research for the Sociology of Education*, pp. 241–58.
Brake, Laurel, and Julie Codell (eds), *Encounters in the Victorian Press: Editors, Authors, Readers* (Basingstoke, 2004).
Brotman, Charles, 'Alfred Wallace and the Anthropology of Sound in Victorian Culture', *Endeavour*, 25:4 (2001), 144–7.
Brown, Malcolm Hamrick, and Roland John Wiley (eds), *Slavonic and Western Music: Essays for Gerald Abraham* (Ann Arbor, 1985).
Bryant, Julius, 'Museum Period Rooms for the Twenty-First Century: Salvaging Ambition, *Museum Management and Curatorship*, 24:1 (2009), 73–84.
Bush, Douglas E., and Richard Kassel (eds), *The Organ: An Encyclopedia* (New York: 2004).
Buzard, James, Joseph W. Childers, and Eileen Gillooly (eds), *Victorian Prism: Refractions of the Crystal Palace* (Charlottesville, 2007).
Bythell, Duncan, 'The Brass Band in the Antipodes: The Transplantation of British Popular Culture', in Herbert (ed.), *The British Brass Band*, pp. 217–44.
——, 'Provinces versus Metropolis in the British Brass Band Movement in the Early Twentieth Century: The Case of William Rimmer and His Music', *Popular Music*, 16:2 (1997), 151–63.
Campbell, Robert Ronald, *James Duncan Campbell: A Memoir by His Son* (Cambridge, 1970).
Cannadine, David, *Ornamentalism: How the British Saw Their Empire* (London, 2001).
Cantor, Geoffrey, 'Science, Providence, and Progress at the Great Exhibition', *Isis*, 103:3 (2012), 439–59.
Capwell, Charles, 'Sourindro Mohun Tagore and the National Anthem Project', *Ethnomusicology*, 31:3 (1987), 407–30.
——, 'Marginality and Musicology in Nineteenth-Century Calcutta: The Case of Sourindro Mohun Tagore', in Nettl and Bohlman (eds), *Comparative Musicology and Anthropology of Music*, pp. 228–43.
Carls, Ken, 'Edinburgh 1886', in Findling and Pelle (eds), *Historical Dictionary of World's Fairs*, pp. 93–4.
——, 'Glasgow 1888', in Findling and Pelle (eds), *Historical Dictionary of World's Fairs*, pp. 103–4.
Çelik, Zeynep, and Leila Kinney, 'Ethnography and Exhibitionism at the Expositions Universelles', *Assemblage*, 13 (1990), 34–59.
Çelik, Zeynep, Diane Favro, and Richard Ingersoll (eds), *Streets: Critical Perspectives on Public Space* (Berkeley, 1994).

Chandler, James, and Maureen N. McLane (eds), *The Cambridge Companion to British Romantic Poetry* (Cambridge, 2008).
Chang, Ting, *Travel, Collecting, and Museums of Asian Art in Nineteenth-Century Paris* (Burlington, 2013).
Clarke, David, 'An Encounter with Chinese Music in Mid-18th-Century London', *Early Music*, 38:4 (2010), 543–58.
Cole, Suzanne, and Kerry Murphy, 'Wagner in the Antipodes', *WagnerSpectrum*, 4:2 (2008), 237–68.
Colligan, Mimi, and David Dunstan, 'A Musical Opening', in Dunstan (ed.), *Victorian Icon*, pp. 107–14.
Colligan, Mimi, 'More Musical Entertainments', in Dunstan (ed.), *Victorian Icon*, pp. 214–18.
Collins, Julie, 'An Architectural Ornament: The Adelaide Jubilee International Exhibition Building', in Garnaut, Collins, and Jolly (eds), *Adelaide's Jubilee International Exhibition*, pp. 67–81.
Collins, Sarah (ed.), *Music and Victorian Liberalism: Composing the Liberal Subject* (Cambridge, 2019).
Conlin, Jonathan (ed.), *The Pleasure Garden: From Vauxhall to Coney Island* (Philadelphia, 2013).
Covell, Roger, *Australia's Music: Themes of a New Society* (Melbourne, 1967).
Cowgill, Rachel, 'Performance Alfresco: Music-Making in London's Pleasure Gardens', in Conlin (ed.), *The Pleasure Garden*, pp. 100–26.
——, 'The London Apollonicon Recitals, 1817–32: A Case-Study in Bach, Mozart and Haydn Reception', *Journal of the Royal Musical Association*, 123:2 (1998), 190–228.
Cowgill, Rachel, and Julian Rushton (eds), *Europe, Empire, and Spectacle in Nineteenth-Century British Music* (Aldershot, 2006).
Crisp, Deborah, 'The Piano in Australia, 1770 to 1900: Some Literary Sources', *Musicology Australia*, 18:1 (1995), 25–38.
Dahlhaus, Carl, *Nineteenth-Century Music*, trans. J. Bradford Robinson (Berkeley, 1989).
Dalton, Laurie, 'Edinburgh 1886', in Findling and Pelle (eds), *Encyclopedia of World's Fairs*, pp. 87–8.
Darian-Smith, Kate, Richard Gillespie, Caroline Jordan, and Elizabeth Willis (eds), *Seize the Day: Exhibitions, Australia and the World* (Clayton, 2008).
Davies, James Q., and Ellen Lockhart (eds), *Sound Knowledge: Music and Science in London, 1789–1851* (Chicago, 2016).
Davis, John R., *The Great Exhibition* (Stroud, 1999).
Davison, Graeme, 'Exhibitions', *Australian Cultural History*, 2 (1982/3), 5–21.
Delannoy, Manuelle. 'La facture instrumentale espagnole aux expositions universelles parisiennes de 1855 a 1900', *Nassarre: Revista aragonesa de musicología*, 10:2 (1994), 9–17.
De Visscher, Eric, 'Sight and Sound: From a Museum of Instruments to a Museum of Music', *Music in Art: International Journal for Music Iconography*, 39:1–2 (2014), 237–41.
Dibble, Jeremy, 'Grove's Musical Dictionary: A National Document', in White and Murphy (eds), *Musical Constructions of Nationalism*, pp. 3–50.
Dohmen, Renate, 'A Fraught Challenge to the Status Quo: The 1883–84 Calcutta International Exhibition, Conceptions of Art and Industry, and the Politics

of World Fairs', in Nichols, Wade, and Williams (eds), *Art versus Industry?*, pp. 199–216.

Dunstan, David (ed.), *Victorian Icon: The Royal Exhibition Building, Melbourne* (Kew, 1996).

Dunstan, David, 'Melbourne 1880–1881', in Findling and Pelle (eds), *Encyclopedia of World's Fairs*, pp. 67–70.

——, 'Melbourne 1888–1889', in Findling and Pelle (eds), *Encyclopedia of World's Fairs*, pp. 97–9.

Eatock, Colin, 'The Crystal Palace Concerts: Canon Formation and the English Musical Renaissance', *Nineteenth-Century Music*, 34:1 (2010), 87–105.

Edwards, Anthony David, *The Role of International Exhibitions in Britain, 1850–1910: Perceptions of Economic Decline and the Technical Education Issue* (Amherst, 2008).

Edwards, Steve, 'The Accumulation of Knowledge or, William Whewell's Eye', in Purbrick (ed.), *The Great Exhibition of 1851*, pp. 26–52.

——, 'Photography; Allegory; and Labor', *Art Journal*, 55:2 (1996), 38–44.

Ehrlich, Cyril, *The Piano: A History* (Oxford, 1990).

Ellis, Katharine, 'Female Pianists and Their Male Critics in Nineteenth-Century Paris', *Journal of the American Musicological Society*, 50:2/3 (1997), 353–85.

——, *Interpreting the Musical Past* (Oxford, 2005).

——, 'Olivier Halanzier and the Operatic Museum in Late Nineteenth-Century France', *Music & Letters*, 96:3 (2015), 390–417.

Ely, Ronald S., *Crystal Palaces: Visions of Splendour* (Ripley, 2004).

Farrell, Gerry, *Indian Music and the West* (Oxford, 1997).

Fauser, Annegret, *Musical Encounters at the 1889 Paris World's Fair* (Rochester, 2005).

Ffrench, Yvonne, *The Great Exhibition: 1851* (London, 1950).

Filipová, Marta (ed.), *Cultures of International Exhibitions, 1840–1940: Great Exhibitions in the Margins* (Farnham, 2015).

Findling, John E., and Kimberly D. Pelle (eds), *Encyclopedia of World's Fairs and Expositions* (Jefferson, 2008).

——, *Historical Dictionary of World's Fairs and Expositions, 1851–1988* (New York, 1990)

Finger, Stanley, *Doctor Franklin's Medicine* (Philadelphia, 2006).

Finkenbeiner, Gerhard, and Vera Meyer, 'The Glass Harmonica: A Return from Obscurity', *Leonardo*, 20:2 (1987), 139–42.

Flora, Reis W., 'Melbourne and Indian Music', *Australia India Society of Victoria Newsletter*, 19:9 (1996), 1–3.

——, 'Raja Sir Sourindro Mohun Tagore (1840–1914): The Melbourne Connection', *South Asia: Journal of South Asian Studies*, 27:3 (2004), 289–313.

——, 'The Tagore Collection of Indian Musical Instruments in Melbourne', *TAASA Review*, 6:2 (1997), 20.

France, Peter (ed.), *The Oxford Guide to Literature in English Translation* (Oxford, 2000).

Frolova-Walker, Marina, 'Against Germanic Reasoning: The Search for a Russian Style of Musical Argumentation', White and Murphy (eds), *Musical Constructions of Nationalism*, pp. 104–22.

Fry, Katherine, 'Music and Character in the London Reception of Wagner', in Collins (ed.), *Music and Victorian Liberalism*, pp. 201–19.

Fuller, Sophie, 'Women Musicians and Professionalism in the Late-Nineteenth and Early-Twentieth Centuries', in Golding (ed.), *The Music Profession in Britain*, pp. 149–69.
Game, Peter, *The Music Sellers* (Melbourne, 1976).
Gara, Tom, 'Aboriginal Participation in the Adelaide Jubilee International Exhibition', in Garnaut, Collins, and Jolly (eds), *Adelaide's Jubilee International Exhibition*, pp. 157–69.
Garifas, Robert, 'The Development of the Modern Burmese Hsaing Ensemble', *Asian Music*, 16:1 (1985), 1–28.
Garnaut, Christine, Julie Collins, and Bridget Jolly (eds.), *Adelaide's Jubilee International Exhibition: The Event, the Building and the Legacy* (Darlinghurst, 2016).
Garratt, James, *Palestrina and the German Romantic Imagination: Interpreting Historicism in Nineteenth-Century Music* (Cambridge, 2002).
Garwood, Christine, *Museums in Britain: A History* (Oxford, 2014).
Gelbart, Matthew, *The Invention of 'Folk Music' and 'Art Music': Emerging Categories from Ossian to Wagner* (Cambridge, 2007).
Geppert, Alexander C.T., *Fleeting Cities: Imperial Expositions in Fin-de-Siècle Europe* (New York, 2010).
Giddens, Anthony, *The Consequences of Modernity* (Cambridge, 1991).
Gillett, Paula, *Musical Women in England, 1870–1914: 'Encroaching on All Man's Privileges'* (New York, 2000).
Goehr, Lydia, *The Imaginary Museum of Musical Works: An Essay in the Philosophy of Music* (Oxford, 1992).
Gould, Marty, 'Anticipation, Transformation, Accommodation: The Great Exhibition on the London Stage', *Victorian Review*, 29:2 (2003), 19–39.
Gramit, David, *Cultivating Music: The Aspirations, Interests, and Limits of German Musical Culture, 1770–1848* (Berkeley, 2002).
Grant, Don, and Graham Seal (eds), *Australia in the World: Perceptions and Possibilities* (Perth, 1994).
Greenberg, Reesa, Bruce W. Ferguson, and Sandy Nairne (eds), *Thinking about Exhibitions* (London, 1996).
Greenhalgh, Paul, 'The Art and Industry of Mammon: International Exhibitions, 1851–1901', in MacKenzie (ed.), *The Victorian Vision*, pp. 265–79.
——, *Ephemeral Vistas: The Expositions Universelles, Great Exhibitions and World's Fairs, 1851–1939* (Manchester, 1988).
Griffiths, John, *Imperial Culture in Antipodean Cities, 1880–1939* (Basingstoke, 2014).
Groom, Nick. 'Romantic Poetry and Antiquity', in Chandler and McLane (eds), *The Cambridge Companion to British Romantic Poetry*, pp. 35–52.
Guion, David M., 'From Yankee Doodle Thro' to Handel's Largo: Music at the World's Columbian Exposition', *College Music Symposium*, 24:1 (1984), 81–96.
Gumpert, Matthew, '"Everyway That I Can": Auto-Orientalism at Eurovision 2003', in Raykoff and Tobin (eds), *A Song for Europe*, pp. 147–57.
Hadaway, Robert, 'An Instrument-Maker's Report on the Repair and Restoration of an Orpharion', *Galpin Society Journal*, 28 (1975), 37–42.
Harrison, Frank Ll., 'Observation, Elucidation, Utilization: Western Attitudes to Eastern Music, ca.1600–ca.1830', in Brown and Wiley (eds), *Slavonic and Western Music*, pp. 5–31.

Haskell, Harry, *The Early Music Revival: A History* (London, 1988).
Hawkins, Stan (ed.), *Critical Musicological Reflections: Essays in Honour of Derek B. Scott* (Farnham, 2012).
Henderson, John, *A Directory of Composers for Organ* (Swindon, 1996).
Herbert, Trevor, and Arnold Myers, 'Music for the Multitude: Accounts of Brass Bands Entering Enderby Jackson's Crystal Palace Contests in the 1860s', *Early Music*, 38:4 (2010), 571–84.
Herbert, Trevor (ed.), *The British Brass Band: A Musical and Social History* (Oxford, 2000).
Herbert, Trevor, 'Victorian Brass Bands: Class, Taste and Space', in Leyshon, Matless, and Revill (eds), *The Place of Music*, pp. 104–28.
Heriz-Smith, Shirley, 'James Veitch & Sons of Exeter and Chelsea, 1853–1870', *Garden History*, 17:2 (1989), 135–53.
Hill, Jennifer, 'Crossing a Divide? Maud Fitz-Stubbs as Amateur then Professional Musician in Late Nineteenth-Century Sydney', *Context: Journal of Music Research*, 19 (2000), 35–42.
Hobhouse, Christopher, *1851 and the Crystal Palace: Being an Account of the Great Exhibition and its Contents, of Sir Joseph Paxton, and of the Erection, the Subsequent History and the Destruction of His Masterpiece* (London, 1950).
Hoffenberg, Peter H., *An Empire on Display: English, Indian and Australian Exhibitions from the Crystal Palace to the Great War* (Berkeley, 2001).
——, 'Photography and Architecture at the Calcutta International Exhibition', in Pelizzari (ed.), *Traces of India*, pp. 174–95.
——, *A Science of Our Own: Exhibitions and the Rise of Australian Public Science* (Pittsburgh, 2019).
Holman, Peter, *Life After Death: The Viola da Gamba in Britain from Purcell to Dolmetsch* (Woodbridge, 2010).
Holub, Robert C., *Reception Theory: A Critical Introduction* (New York, 1984).
Hughes, Meirion, *The English Musical Renaissance and the Press, 1850–1914: Watchmen of Music* (Aldershot, 2002).
Ingarden, Roman, *The Work of Music and the Problem of Its Identity*, trans. Adam Czerniawski, ed. Jean G. Harrel (Basingstoke, 1986).
Irvine, Thomas, *Listening to China: Sound and the Sino-Western Encounter 1770–1839* (Chicago, 2020).
Jairazbhoy, Nazir Ali, 'The Beginnings of Organology and Ethnomusicology in the West: V. Mahillon, A. Ellis and S.M. Tagore', *Selected Reports in Ethnomusicology*, 8 (1990), 67–80.
Jameson, Frederic, *A Singular Modernity: Essay on the Ontology of the Present* (New York, 2002).
Jamieson, Alasdair, *The Music of Hamish MacCunn* (Bloomington, 2013).
Jamison, Bryan, 'Making "Honest, Truthful and Industrious Men": Newsboys, Rational Recreation and the Construction of the "Citizen" in Late Victorian and Edwardian Brisbane', *Journal of Popular Culture*, 33:1 (1999), 61–75.
Jane, Philip, 'Music in Christchurch during the 1882 International Exhibition', *Journal of New Zealand Studies*, 17 (2014), 21–38.
Jauss, Hans Robert, *Toward an Aesthetic of Reception*, trans. Timothy Bahti (Minneapolis, 1982).
Jenkins, Geraint H. (ed.), *A Social History of the Welsh Language: Language and Community in the Nineteenth Century* (Cardiff, 1998).

Johnson, Edmond, 'The Death and Second Life of the Harpsichord', *The Journal of Musicology*, 30:2 (2013), 180–214.
Johnson, James H., *Listening in Paris: A Cultural History* (Berkeley, 1995).
Johnston, Ewan, '"A Valuable and Tolerably Extensive Collection of Native and Other Products": New Zealand at the Crystal Palace', in Auerbach and Hoffenberg (eds.), *Britain, the Empire, and the World at the Great Exhibition of 1851*, pp. 77–92.
Jones, Emrys, 'The Welsh Language in England c.1800–1914', in Jenkins (ed.), *Language and Community in the Nineteenth Century*, pp. 231–260.
Jordan, Harriet, 'Public Parks, 1885–1914', *Garden History*, 22:1 (1994), 85–113.
Katz, Jonathan, 'Raja Sir Sourindro Mohun Tagore (1840–1914)', *Popular Music*, 7:2 (1988), 220–1.
Kelly, Barbara L., and Kerry Murphy (eds), *Berlioz and Debussy: Sources, Contexts and Legacies: Essays in Honour of François Lesure* (Aldershot, 2007).
Kelly, Elaine, 'Evolution versus Authenticity: Johannes Brahms, Robert Franz, and Continuo Practice in the Late Nineteenth Century', *19th-Century Music*, 30:2 (2006), 182–204.
Kennerley, David, 'Debating Female Musical Professionalism and Artistry in the British Press, c.1820–1850', *The Historical Journal*, 58:4 (2015), 987–1008.
Kent, Greta, *A View From the Bandstand* (London, 1983).
Kertesz, Elizabeth, 'Perceptions of Women as Composers and Instrumental Performers in the Allgemeine Wiener Musik-Zeitung (1841–48)', *Context: Journal of Music Research*, 4 (1992/1993), 10–15.
Kirby, Sarah, 'Prisms of the Musical Past: British International Exhibitions and "Ancient Instruments", 1885–1890', *Early Music*, 47:3 (2019), 393–407.
——, '"Sweet Music Discoursed in Distant Concert Halls": The Telephone Kiosk at the 1890 Edinburgh International Exhibition', *Context: Journal of Music Research*, 44 (2019), 51–9.
——, '"The Worst Oratorio Ever!": Colonialist Condescension in the Critical Reception of George Tolhurst's Ruth (1864)', *Nineteenth-Century Music Review*, 16:2 (2019), 199–227.
Kinchin, Perilla, and Juliet Kinchin, *Glasgow's Great Exhibitions: 1888, 1901, 1911, 1938, 1988* (Wendlebury, 1988).
Kuo-huang, Han, 'J.A. Van Aalst and His Chinese Music', *Asian Music*, 19:2 (1988), 127–30.
Kwint, Marius, Christopher Breward, and Jeremy Aynsley (eds), *Material Memories: Design and Evocation* (Oxford, 1999).
Lajosi, Krisztina, and Andreas Stynen (eds), *Choral Societies and Nationalism in Europe* (Leiden, 2015).
Langley, Leanne, 'The Musical Press in Nineteenth-Century England', *Notes*, 46:3 (1990), 583–92.
Lee, Elizabeth, *The Diary of Elizabeth Lee: Growing Up on Merseyside in the Late Nineteenth Century*, ed. Colin G. Pooley, Siân Pooley, Richard Lawton (Liverpool, 2010).
Leppert, Richard, 'Material Culture and Decentred Selfhood (Socio-Visual Typologies of Musical Excess)', in Hawkins (ed.), *Critical Musicological Reflections*, pp. 101–24.
Leydecker, Karl, 'E.T.A. Hoffmann', in France (ed.), *The Oxford Guide to Literature in English Translation*, p. 331.

Leyshon, Andrew, David Matless, and George Revill (eds), *The Place of Music* (New York, 1998).
Lightman, Bernard, 'Science and Culture', in O'Gorman (ed.), *The Cambridge Companion to Victorian Culture*, pp. 12–42.
Loesser, Arthur, *Men, Women and Pianos: A Social History* (New York, 1990).
Lovell, Percy, '"Ancient" Music in Eighteenth-Century England', *Music & Letters*, 60:4 (1979), 401–15.
Machor, James L., and Philip Goldstein (eds), *Reception Study: From Literary Theory to Cultural Studies* (New York, 2001).
MacKenzie, John, 'Empire and Metropolitan Cultures', in Porter (ed.), *The Oxford History of the British Empire*, pp. 270–93.
——, *Propaganda and Empire: The Manipulation of British Public Opinion, 1880–1960* (Manchester, 1984).
MacKenzie, John (ed.), T*he Victorian Vision: Inventing New Britain* (London, 2001).
Mactaggart, Peter, and Ann Mactaggart (eds), *Musical Instruments in the 1851 Exhibition: A Transcription of the Entries of Musical Interest from the Official Illustrated Catalogue of the Great Exhibition of the Art and Industry of All Nations, with Additional Material from Contemporary Sources* (Welwyn, 1986).
Maguire, Roslyn, 'Paolo Giorza, Director of Music: The Most Accessible Art', in Proudfoot, Maguire, and Freestone (eds), *Colonial City Global City*, pp. 129–47.
——, '"Pleasure of a High Order:" Paolo Giorza and Music at Sydney's 1879 International Exhibition', *Context: Journal of Music Research*, 22 (2001), 41–50.
Mallinson, Jane, 'Choral Societies and Nationalist Mobilization in the Nineteenth Century: A Scottish Perspective', in Lajosi and Stynen (eds), *Choral Societies and Nationalism in Europe*, pp. 70–82.
Martin, Nathan John, 'Rousseau's *air chinois*', *Eighteenth-Century Music*, 18:1 (2021), 41–64.
Marvin, Roberta Montemorra, *The Politics of Verdi's Cantica* (Farnham, 2014).
Marx, Karl, *Capital: A Critique of Political Economy*, trans. Ben Fowkes (London, 1981–90).
Marx, Karl, and Friedrich Engels, *Werke*, 26:1 (Berlin, 1959).
Masani, Zareer, 'The Tiger of Mysore', *History Today*, 66:12 (2016), 11–16.
Mathur, Saloni, 'Ethnological Exhibits: The Case of 1886', *Cultural Anthropology*, 15:4 (2000), 492–524.
McCallum, Jenny, 'Sound, Authority and the Malay Sultanate: 19th-Century Transformations under Sultan Abu Bakar of Johor', unpublished paper.
McCarthy, Conal, 'Dunedin 1889–1890', in Findling and Pelle (eds), *Encyclopedia of World's Fairs*, pp. 108–10.
McGuire, Charles Edward, *Music and Victorian Philanthropy: The Tonic Sol-Fa Movement* (Cambridge, 2009).
Miège, Bernard, 'The Cultural Commodity', trans. Nicholas Garnham, *Media, Culture and Society*, 1:3 (1979), 297–311.
Miller, Kiri, 'Americanism Musically: Nation, Evolution, and Public Education at the Columbian Exposition, 1893', *19th-Century Music*, 27:2 (2003), 137–55.

Miller, Terry E., and Jarenchai Chonpairot, 'A History of Siamese Music Reconstructed from Western Documents, 1505–1932', *Crossroads: An Interdisciplinary Journal of Southeast Asian Studies*, 8:2 (1994), 1–192.

Moon, Krystyn R., 'The Quest for Music's Origin at the St Louis World's Fair: Frances Densmore and the Racialization of Music', *American Music*, 28:2 (2010), 191–210.

Murphy, Kerry, 'Berlioz and the Piano at the Great Exhibition: The Challenge of Impartiality', in Kelly and Murphy (eds), *Berlioz and Debussy*, pp. 67–80.

——, 'Henri Kowalski (1841–1916): A French Musician in Colonial Australia', *Australian Historical Studies*, 48:3 (2017), 346–62.

Musgrave, Michael, *The Musical Life of the Crystal Palace* (Cambridge, 1995).

Nettl, Bruno, and Philip V. Bohlman (eds), *Comparative Musicology and Anthropology of Music: Essays on the History of Ethnomusicology* (Chicago, 1991).

Nettl, Bruno, *Nettl's Elephant: On the History of Ethnomusicology* (Urbana, 2010).

Nichols, Kate, Rebecca Wade, and Gabriel Williams (eds), *Art versus Industry?: New Perspectives on Visual and Industrial Cultures in Nineteenth-Century Britain* (Manchester, 2016).

Oates, Jennifer, *Hamish MacCunn (1868–1916): A Musical Life* (New York, 2016).

Ogata, Amy F., 'Viewing Souvenirs: Peepshows and the International Expositions', *Journal of Design History*, 15:2 (2002), 69–82.

O'Gorman, Francis (ed.), *The Cambridge Companion to Victorian Culture* (Oxford, 2010).

O'Malley, Andrew, *Children's Literature, Popular Culture, and Robinson Crusoe* (London, 2012).

Orr, Kirsten, 'Sydney 1879–1880', in Findling and Pelle (eds), *Encyclopedia of World's Fairs*, pp. 65–7.

Orzech, Rachel, *Claiming Wagner for France: Music and Politics in the Parisian Press, 1933–1944* (Rochester, forthcoming).

Pasler, Jann, 'Listening to Race and Nation: Music at the Exposition universelle de 1889', in Florence Gétreau (ed.), 'La musique aux expositions universelles: Entre industries et cultures', *Musique, images, instruments: Revue française d'organologie et d'iconographie musicale*, 13 (2012), 52–74.

——, 'The Utility of Musical Instruments in the Racial and Colonial Agendas of Late Nineteenth-Century France', *Journal of the Royal Musical Association*, 129:1 (2004), 24–76.

Pearce, Susan, *On Collecting: An Investigation into Collecting in the European Tradition* (Florence, 2007).

Peleggi, Maurizio, *Lords of Things: The Fashioning of the Siamese Monarchy's Modern Image* (Honolulu, 2002).

Pelizzari, Maria Antonella (ed.), *Traces of India: Photography, Architecture, and the Politics of Representation, 1850–1900* (Montréal, 2003).

Pettitt, Clare, 'Shakespeare at the Great Exhibition of 1851', in Gail Marshall and Adrian Poole (eds), *Victorian Shakespeare*, vol. 2 (London, 2003), pp. 61–83.

Pevsner, Nikolaus, *High Victorian Design: A Study of the Exhibits of 1851* (London, 1951).

Pilgrim, Dianne H., 'Inherited from the Past: The American Period Room', *The American Art Journal*, 10:1 (1978), 4–23.

Piotrowski, Andrzej, 'Architecture and the Evolution of Commercial Culture', *International Journal of the Constructed Environment*, 1:1 (2011), 51–63.

——, 'The Spectacle of Architectural Discourses', *Architectural Theory Review*, 13:2 (2008), 130–44.

Plantinga, Leon, 'The Piano and the Nineteenth Century', in R. Larry Todd (ed.), *Nineteenth-Century Piano Music*, pp. 1–15.

Porter, Andrew (ed.), *The Oxford History of the British Empire, Volume 3: The Nineteenth Century* (Oxford, 1999).

Powell, John, 'Calcutta 1883–1884', in Findling and Pelle (eds), *Historical Dictionary of World's Fairs*, pp. 82–3.

——, 'Melbourne 1880–1881', in Findling and Pelle (eds), *Historical Dictionary of World's Fairs*, pp. 74–5.

Prasch, Thomas, 'Calcutta 1883–1884', in Findling and Pelle (eds), *Encyclopedia of World's Fairs*, pp. 75–7.

——, 'London 1886', in Findling and Pelle (eds), *Encyclopedia of World's Fairs*, pp. 88–92,

Proudfoot, Peter, Roslyn Maguire, and Robert Freestone (eds), *Colonial City Global City: Sydney's International Exhibition 1879* (Darlinghurst, 2000).

Purbrick, Louise (ed.), *The Great Exhibition of 1851: New Interdisciplinary Essays* (Manchester, 2001).

Purtell, Simon, '"Musical Pitch Ought to be One from Pole to Pole": Touring Musicians and the Issue of Performing Pitch in Late Nineteenth- and Early Twentieth-Century Melbourne', *Context: Journal of Music Research*, 35/36 (2011), 111–25.

Qureshi, Regula Burckhardt, 'Mode of Production and Musical Production: Is Hindustani Music Feudal?', in Qureshi (ed.), *Music and Marx*, pp. 81–105.

Qureshi, Regula Burckhardt (ed.), *Music and Marx: Ideas, Practice, Politics* (New York, 2002).

Radic, Thérèse, 'Major Choral Organizations in Late Nineteenth-Century Melbourne', *Nineteenth-Century Music Review*, 2:2 (2005), 3–28.

——, 'The Victorian Orchestra 1889–1891: In the Wake of the Centennial Exhibition, 1888', *Australasian Music Research*, 1 (1997), 13–101.

Raizman, David, and Ethan Robey (eds), *Expanding Nationalisms at World's Fairs: Identity, Diversity, and Exchange, 1851–1915* (London, 2018).

Raykoff, Ivan, and Robert Deam Tobin (eds), *A Song for Europe: Popular Music and Politics in the Eurovision Song Contest* (Aldershot, 2007).

Richards, James Howard, 'Baillie-Hamilton, James (John Buchanan) (1837– After 1926)', Bush and Kassel (eds), *The Organ: An Encyclopedia*, pp. 46–7.

Richards, Jeffrey, *Imperialism and Music: Britain 1876–1953* (Manchester, 2001).

Richards, Thomas, *The Commodity Culture of Victorian England: Advertising and Spectacle, 1851–1914* (Stanford, 1990).

Richardson, John G. (ed.), *Handbook of Theory and Research for the Sociology of Education* (New York, 1986).

Rickard, John, 'Cultural History: The "High" and the "Popular"', *Australian Cultural History*, 5 (1986), 32–43.

Roberts, Gwyneth Tyson, '"At Once Illogical and Unfair": Jane Williams (Ysgafell) and the Government Report on Education in Mid Nineteenth-Century Wales', *Women's Writing*, 24:4 (2017), 451–65.

Roche, Maurice, 'Mega-Events, Culture and Modernity: Expos and the Origins of Public Culture', *International Journal of Cultural Policy*, 5:1 (1998), 1–31.

Royle, Jennifer, 'Musical (Ad)venturers: Colonial Composers and Composition in Melbourne, 1870–1901', *Nineteenth-Century Music Review*, 2:2 (2005), 133–59.
——, '"Preparing to Exhibit": Frederic Cowen in the Public Press Preceding Melbourne's Centennial International Exhibition, 1888–1889', *Context: Journal of Music Research*, 14 (1997), 53–62.
——, '"Turning the Wilderness into Flowers": Music as Triumph at Australia's International Exhibitions (1879–1888)', *Context: Journal of Music Research*, 22 (2001), 51–60.
Russell, Dave, *Popular Music in England 1840–1914: A Social History* (Manchester, 1987).
Russell, Lynette, '"An Unpicturesque Vagrant": Aboriginal Victorians at the Melbourne International Exhibition 1880–1881', *La Trobe Journal*, 93–94 (2014), 77–81.
Said, Edward, *Culture and Imperialism* (New York, 1993).
——, *Orientalism* (London, 2003).
Schwarzer, Marjorie, 'Literary Devices: Period Rooms as Fantasy and Archetype', *Curator: The Museum Journal*, 51:4 (2008), 355–60.
Scott, Derek B., *Sounds of the Metropolis: The Nineteenth-Century Popular Music Revolution in London, New York, Paris, and Vienna* (Oxford, 2008).
Scott, Alexander, 'The "Missing Link" Between Science and Show Business: Exhibiting Gorillas and Chimpanzees in Victorian Liverpool', *Journal of Victorian Culture*, 25:1 (2020), 1–20.
Searle, Arthur, 'Julian Marshall and the British Museum: Music Collecting in the Later Nineteenth Century', *British Library Journal*, 11 (1985), 67–87.
Sen, Satadru, 'Savage Bodies, Civilized Pleasures: M.V. Portman and the Andamanese', *American Ethnologist*, 36:2 (2009), 364–7.
Sessa, Anne Dzamba, *Richard Wagner and the English* (London, 1979).
Singer, Noel F., *Burmese Dance and Theatre* (Kuala Lumpur, 1995).
Sladek, Elisabeth (ed.), *John Ruskin: Werk und Wirkung* (Zürich, c.2002).
Smith, Wilson, 'Old London, Old Edinburgh: Constructing Historic Cities', in Filipová (ed.), *Cultures of International Exhibitions*, pp. 203–30.
Smither, Howard E., '"Messiah" and Progress in Victorian England', *Early Music*, 13:3 (1985), 329–48.
——, *The Oratorio in the Nineteenth and Twentieth Centuries*, vol. 4 of *A History of the Oratorio* (Chapel Hill, 1987).
Solie, Ruth A., 'Music', in O'Gorman (ed.), *Cambridge Companion to Victorian Culture*, pp. 101–18.
Steele, Murray, *Liverpool on Display* (Great Britain, 2012).
Stock, Jonathan, 'Alexander J. Ellis and His Place in the History of Ethnomusicology', *Ethnomusicology*, 51:2 (2007), 306–25.
Stockigt, Janice B., 'A Study of British Influence on Musical Taste and Programming: New Choral Works Introduced to Audiences by the Melbourne Philharmonic Society, 1876–1901', *Nineteenth-Century Music Review*, 2:2 (2005), 29–53.
Storch, Robert D. (ed.), *Popular Culture and Custom in Nineteenth-Century England* (London, 1982).
Szuster, Julja I., 'Music of and at the Time of the Jubilee Exhibition', in Garnaut, Collins, and Jolly (eds), *Adelaide's Jubilee International Exhibition*, pp. 173–83.

Talusan, Mary, 'Music, Race, and Imperialism: The Philippine Constabulary Band at the 1904 St Louis World's Fair', *Philippine Studies*, 52:4 (2004), 499–526.

Taylor, Paul Michael, and William Bradford Smith, 'Instruments of Diplomacy: 19th Century Musical Instruments in the Smithsonian Collection of Thai Royal Gifts', *Journal of the Siam Society*, 105 (2017), 245–72.

Taylor, Timothy D., 'The Commodification of Music at the Dawn of the Era of "Mechanical Music"', *Ethnomusicology*, 51:2 (2007), 281–305.

Todd, R. Larry (ed.), *Nineteenth-Century Piano Music* (New York, 2004).

Toru, Takenaka, 'Isawa Shūji's "National Music": National Sentiment and Cultural Westernisation in Meiji Japan', *Itinerario*, 34:3 (2010), 97–118.

Tregear, Peter, 'Post-Colonial Tristesse: Aspects of Wagner Down Under', *Context: Journal of Music Research*, 39 (2014), 69–77.

Turnbull, C.M., 'Raffles, Sir (Thomas) Stamford Bingley (1781–1826)', in *Oxford Dictionary of National Biography* (Oxford, 2004).

Uhlig, Claus, 'Nostalgia for Organicism: Art and Society in Ruskin and Pater', in Sladek (ed.), *John Ruskin: Werk und Wirkung*, pp. 102–19,

Vamplew, Wray, 'Adelaide 1887–1888', in Findling and Pelle (eds), *Historical Dictionary of World's Fairs*, pp. 98–9.

Van Rij, Inge, '"Walking Backwards Into the Future": Music, Museum Culture, and the New Zealand and South Seas Exhibition (1889–1890)', *Music & Letters*, 99:2 (2018), 224–59.

Vaughan, William, *German Romantic Painting* (New Haven, 1980).

Walker, Alan, *Franz Liszt: The Virtuoso Years 1811–1947* (Ithaca, 1987).

Warrack, Guy, *Royal College of Music: The First Eighty-Five Years 1883–1968* (London, 1977).

Watt, Paul, and Alison Rabinovici, 'Alexandra Palace: Music, Leisure, and the Cultivation of "Higher Civilization" in the Late Nineteenth Century', *Music & Letters*, 95:2 (2014), 183–212.

Weber, William, *Canonic Repertories and the French Musical Press: Lully to Wagner* (Rochester, 2021).

White, Harry, and Michael Murphy (eds), *Musical Constructions of Nationalism: Essays on the History and Ideology of European Musical Culture 1800–1945* (Cork, 2001).

White, Richard, 'The Outsider's Gaze and the Representation of Australia', in Grant and Seal (eds), *Australia in the World: Perceptions and Possibilities*, pp. 22–8.

Whitehead, Christopher, *The Public Art Museum in Nineteenth-Century Britain: The Development of the National Gallery*, (Aldershot, 2005).

Willson, Flora, 'Hearing Things: Musical Objects at the 1851 Great Exhibition', in Davies and Lockhart (eds), *Sound Knowledge*, pp. 227–45.

Woodfield, Ian, '"Music of Forty Several Parts": A Song for the Creation of Princes', *Performance Practice Review*, 7:1 (1994), 54–64.

Yang, Hon-Lun, and Michael Saffle (eds), *China and the West: Music, Representation, and Reception* (Ann Arbor, 2017).

Yengoyan, Aram A., 'Sydney 1879–1880', in Findling and Pelle (eds), *Historical Dictionary of World's Fairs*, pp. 72–3.

Young, Linda, '"How Like England We Can Be": The Australian International Exhibitions in the Nineteenth Century', in Darian-Smith, Gillespie, Jordan, and Willis (eds), *Seize the Day*, pp. 12.1–12.19.

Young, Paul, *Globalization and the Great Exhibition: The Victorian New World Order* (Basingstoke, 2009).
——, 'Mission Impossible: Globalization and the Great Exhibition', in Auerbach and Hoffenberg (eds), *Britain, the Empire, and the World at the Great Exhibition of 1851*, pp. 3–25.
Yuen, Karen, 'Fashioning Elite Identities: Dante Gabriel Rossetti, Edward Burne-Jones, and Musical Instruments as Symbolic Goods', *Music in Art*, 39:1–2 (2014), 145–58.
Zon, Bennett, 'From "Incomprehensibility" to "Meaning" Transcription and Representation of Non-Western Music in Nineteenth-Century British Musicology and Ethnomusicology', in Cowgill and Rushton (eds), *Europe, Empire, and Spectacle*, pp. 185–99.
——, *Representing Non-Western Music in Nineteenth-Century Britain* (Rochester, 2007).

Unpublished Theses

Hayasaka, Makiko, 'Organ Recitals as Popular Culture: The Secularisation of the Instrument and Its Repertoire in Britain, 1834–1950' (Unpublished Ph.D. thesis, University of Bristol, 2016).
Johnson, Edmond, 'Revival and Antiquation: Modernism's Musical Pasts' (Unpublished Ph.D. dissertation, University of California, Santa Barbara, 2011).
Skinner, Graeme, 'Toward a General History of Australian Musical Composition: First National Music 1788–c.1860' (Unpublished Ph.D. thesis. University of Sydney, 2011).
Williams, Richard, 'Hindustani Music between Awadh and Bengal, c.1758–1905' (Unpublished Ph.D. thesis, King's College London, 2015).

Web-Based Sources

Boalch, Donald Howard, and Peter Williams, 'Claviorgan', *Grove Music Online*, <http://www.oxfordmusiconline.com> [accessed 5 Feb. 2021].
British History Online, 'The Alexander Estate', <http://www.british-history.ac.uk/survey-london/vol42/pp168-183> [accessed 12 Mar. 2021].
Douglas, Louise, 'Representing Colonial Australia at British, American and European International Exhibitions', *reCollections*, 3:1 (2008), http://recollections.nma.gov.au/issues/vol_3_no_1/papers/representing_colonial_australia [accessed 12 Mar. 2021].
Ehrlich, Cyril, 'Hipkins, Alfred', *Grove Music Online*, <http://www.oxfordmusiconline.com> [accessed 1 Apr. 2021].
Hartig, Andrew, 'Orpharion or Bandora by John Rose, London, 1580', *Renovata Cythara: The Renaissance Cittern Site*, ed. Andrew Hartig, <http://www.cittern.theaterofmusic.com/old/rose.html> [accessed 19 Feb. 2021].
Hoffenberg, Peter H., '1871–1874: The South Kensington International Exhibitions', *BRANCH: Britain, Representation and Nineteenth-Century History*, ed. Dino Franco Felluga, <http://www.branchcollective.org> [accessed 2 Feb. 2021].

Kitson, Richard, 'The Musical World', *Répertoire international de la press musicale / Retrospective Index to Music Periodicals,* <https://www.ripm.org/?page=JournalInfo&ABB=MWO> [accessed 4 June 2020].

Merris, Randall C., 'Marie Lachenal: Concertinist', *Concertina Library* (2005), <http://www.concertina.com/merris/marie-lachenal/index.htm> [accessed 17 Feb. 2021].

Museum of New Zealand, 'The 1885 New Zealand Industrial Exhibition', <https://collections.tepapa.govt.nz/topic/864> [accessed 24 Mar. 2021].

Museums Victoria, 'Royal Exhibition and Carlton Gardens World Heritage Management Plan Review', <https://museumsvictoria.com.au/reb/royal-exhibition-and-carlton-gardens-world-heritage-management-plan-review/> [accessed 26 Mar. 2021].

——, 'Significance, Item NU 35421 Medal: Australian Juvenile Industrial Exhibition, Ballarat, Victoria, Australia, 1878', <https://collections.museumvictoria.com.au/items/273850> [accessed 26 Mar. 2021].

Owen, Barbara, Peter Williams, and Stephen Bicknell, 'Organ', *Grove Music Online,* <http://www.oxfordmusiconline.com/> [accessed 12 Mar. 2021].

Pauka, Kirstin, 'Zat pwe', *Oxford Encyclopedia of Theatre and Performance* (2003), <https://www.oxfordreference.com> [accessed 12 Mar. 2021].

Samson, Jim, 'Reception', *Grove Music Online,* <http://www.oxfordmusiconline.com/> [accessed 24 Mar. 2021].

Skinner, Graeme, 'Austrian Strauss Band', *Australharmony,* <https://sydney.edu.au/paradisec/australharmony/register-organisations-from-1861-A-Z.php> [accessed 8 Mar. 2021].

Taruskin, Richard, 'Nationalism', *Grove Music Online,* <http://www.oxfordmusiconline.com/> [accessed 1 Mar. 2021].

Tick, Judith, Margaret Ericson, and Ellen Koskoff, 'Women in Music', *Grove Music Online,* <http://www.oxfordmusiconline.com/> [accessed 8 Mar. 2021].

Victoria and Albert Museum, 'The Queen Elizabeth Virginal', <http://collections.vam.ac.uk/item/O70511/the-queen-elizabeth-virginal-spinet-baffo-giovanni-antonio/> [accessed 18 Feb. 2021].

Von Glahn, Denise, and Michael Broyles, 'Art Music', *Grove Music Online,* <http://www.oxfordmusiconline.com/> [accessed 3 Mar. 2021].

Index

Page numbers in bold type refer to illustrations and their captions

Aalst, J.A. Van   198 fn.77
Abel, Frederick   9
Aboriginal people (Australia) *see* Indigenous Australia
Abu Bakar, Maharajah of Johor   170, 174, 175–6, 179, 180
Adelaide Jubilee International Exhibition 1887   7, 12, 14, 22–4, 60, 79, 190–1
    Indigenous music at *see* Indigenous Australia
    legacy   209
    piano manufacturers at   63
    see also under bands (brass and military), non-Western musical instruments, oratorio
Adelaide Liedertafel   24
Adelaide Musical Association   121
Adelaide Philharmonic Society   121
Albert Edward, Prince of Wales (later Edward VII)   73, 109
Albert, Prince of Saxe-Coburg and Gotha   46, 58, 151
Alexandra Palace (London)   130, 145
Allan, George Clark   213
Allegri, Gregorio   99, 102, 104, 105
Allison & Co. (piano manufacturer)   69
Amati (violin maker)   87
America *see* United States
ancient instruments   18, 26, 84–5, 86, 87–98, 101, 103, 107, 109, 143, 170, 171, 179–80, 182, 183–4, 213 *see also* Special Exhibition of Ancient Musical Instruments *under* London International Exhibition 1872
ancient music   98–108, 109, 160, 213
Andaman and Nicobar Islands   188
antiquity   85
anthropology   183, 187, 192–3
art manufactures   55, 57, 92
art objects   27, 30–1, 32, 34, 37, 39, 49, 55, 56, 57
Ascher, Joseph   115
Ascherberg (piano manufacturer)   74, 78, **79**, 79
Ashanti people   181, 188
Ashwell, Thomas   89

Auber, Daniel   35, 38, 95
Australia
    band tradition in *see under* bands (brass and military)
    cultural identity   2, 51, 65–8, 112, 120, 152–3, 164, 168
    development of public taste   110, 112–13, 114–17, 119, 121, 123–4, 164
    Indigenous peoples *see* Indigenous Australia
    Australian-made musical instruments *see under* Musical Instruments
Australian Band   16, 154, 162–4
    Ure, James   163
Austria   42, 141, 153–4, 212
Austrian Strauss Band   16, 135, 153–4, 161–4, 167
    Ketten, Henri   163–4
    Wildner, Alois F.   161

Bach, Johann Sebastian   37, 38, 46, 69, 95, 99, 101, 103, 104, 145
Baillie-Hamilton, James *see* vocalion
Band of the 2nd battalion, U.R. (Melbourne) *see under* bands (brass and military)
bands (brass and military)   40–1, 131, 134, 149, 154–6, 167, 213
    in Australia   135–6, 138, 141–2, 161–4
    Austrian Strauss Band *see* Austrian Strauss Band
    Band of the 2nd Battalion, U.R. (Melbourne)   138–9
    Belgian Guides   46, 140
    Black Dyke Mills Band   135
    Burton Volunteer Band   135
    class associations   47, 134–5, 143, 168
    Coldstream Guards   46, 135, 143, 155
    Edinburgh City Police Band   135
    Godfrey, Charles (Jr)   139, 142
    Godfrey, Dan   135, 143, **160**
    Grenadier Guards   46, 135, 138, 140, 143, 155
    Garde républicaine   46
    Hungarian 'Blue' National Band   135, **136**, 140, 142, 154 n.18, 155–6

bands (brass and military) (cont'd)
  in India   17, 137
  Kopff, Arnold Theodore   135, 141
  Pomeranian or Blücher Hussars   135, 156
  reception   139–42
  reception in the musical press   47, 142–5
  repertoire   45–7, 134–5, 137–9, 140, 143–5, 148–9, 154, 164
  Royal Artillery Band   46, 135, 142
  Royal Horse Artillery Band   142
  Royal Horse Guards (Blues) Band   47–8, 139, 140
  Royal Marines Band   135
  Royal Swedish Värmland Grenadiers   135, 142, 153, 156
  in Scotland   135, 137, 139, 142, 155–6
  Svensson, Axel   142
  Thuringian Regiment (German Infantry) Band   135
  Young Australia Band   141
  Zavertal, Ladislao   142
bandstands   128, 130, **132**, **133**, **136**, 165, **173**
banjo   72, 89
Barnby, Joseph   37
Bechstein (piano manufacturer)   74, 76
Beethoven, Ludwig van   38, 80, 94, 95, 115, 116–17, 119
  'Moonlight' Sonata, arr. Josef Strauss   157, 158
Belgian Guides see under bands (brass and military)
Belgium   74, 75, 80, 172, 212 see also Brussels Conservatoire
Bellini, Vincenzo   76, 79
Benedict, Julius   80, 115, 121
Benjamin, Walter   52
Benn, John   9
Bennett, William Sterndale   34, 35, 36
Berlioz, Hector   6, 43, 44 n.93, 95, 205, 211
Berry, Graham   9
Besson (instrument manufacturer)   50, 72, 136
Best, William Thomas   38, 46
Betts, John (luthier)   89
Bishop, Henry   95, 100, 137, 139
Black Dyke Mills Band see under bands (brass and military)
Blagrove, Richard see concertina
Blüthner (piano manufacturer)   62, 69, 74, 75, 79
Böhmer (instrument manufacturer)   69

Bonawitz, Johann Heinrich   75
Boosey (instrument manufacturer)   50, 72
Bord (piano manufacturer)   74
Bourdieu, Pierre   56, 107, 168
brass instruments   50, 87, 136
Brighton Aquarium   144
Brinsmead & Sons (piano manufacturer)   63, 67, 75, 76, 78, 80, 81, **82**
Brinsmead, Horace   76, 213
Bristol Madrigal Society   98, 100, 102, 160
Broadwood & Sons (piano manufacturer)   42, 44, 64–5, 67, 75
Brussels Conservatoire   88, 98, 100–1, 167, 181–2
Bülow, Hans von   95
Burma   171, 194
  Karen people   188
  Burmese music   186–7, 193
  musical instruments from   180, 181, 193
  reception of Burmese music at Calcutta 1883   193–5
  theatre tradition of   193–4
Burnand, Francis Cowley see Punch Magazine
Burney, Charles   207
Burton Volunteer Band see under bands (brass and military)
Burvett, Alice Sydney   76

Calcutta International Exhibition 1883   12, 16–17, 59, 186, 187–8, 208, 213
  bands at see in India under bands (brass and military)
  building and grounds   16–17, 137
  Burmese music at see under Burma
  Indian exhibits   16, 172, **173**, 176
  see also under non-Western musical instruments, piano recitals
Cambridge, Ada   119, 164
Campbell, James Duncan   195–6, 198, 200
Campo (piano manufacturer)   75
Canada   174, 178
carnival attractions   3, 24, 47, 106, 128, 130–33, 136–7, 187, 191
Caron, Leon   16, 162, 163, 177
Centennial Exhibition Choir see under Melbourne Centennial International Exhibition 1888
Centennial Orchestra (Melbourne)   114

ceremonial music   13–14, 16, 20, 22, 34–37, 121, **122**, 162
Chambonnières, Jacques Champion de   101, 104
Charbonnet, Alice   75–6
Cherubini, Luigi   95
Chickering (piano manufacturer)   74, 80
Chidley, Edward *see* concertina
Chidley, Amy *see* concertina
China   171, 191
  exhibits   195–6, **197**
  food   186, 196, 198
  Imperial Maritime Customs Service *see* Hart, Robert
  musical instruments   180, 181, 184, 199
  Chinese music (Health Exhibition)   18, 179, 186–7, 198–201
  musicians   171, 196, **197**, 213
  performance of Western music   200–1
  reception in London   199–201, 206–8
Chopin, Fryderyk   64–5, 79, 95, 158, 159
choral music *see* oratorio
Chorley, Henry   34, 95
Chulalongkorn, Rama V (King of Siam)   202
civilisation   29, 111, 112–13, 119, 121, 124, 126, 172, 179, 189, 190–1, 194
class   11, 21, 24, 29, 47, 63, 77, 86, 107, 110, 111–12, 116, 126, 134–5, 143, 160, 168, 189, 206–8
classification systems   20, 31–2, 49–50, 52, 57–60, 70–1, 180–1, 209
Clarke, William John   9
Clemens non Papa, Jacobus   103, 105
Clementi, Muzio   94, 95
Cognetti, Luisa   75
Coldstream Guards *see under* bands (brass and military)
Cole, Henry   31
Collard & Collard (piano manufacturer)   44, 62
Colonial and Indian Exhibition 1886   3, 9, 12, 13, 20–1, 155, 173, 178, 187
  see also under bands (brass and military), ethnographic displays, non-Western musical instruments
Columbian Exposition, *see* World's Columbian Exposition 1893
Comettant, Oscar   51
commercialism   10, 29, 45, 49–51, 53, 55, 62, 73–4, 76–8, 81, 82–3, 89, 106–7,
110, 129, 144, 150, 153–4, 159, 161, 209, 210
commissioners   3, 8–9, 12, 21, 23, 25, 27, 31, 34–5, 36–7, 40–1, 44–5, 46, 55, 73, 106, 110, 111–4, 121, 123, 129, 136, 144, 148, 150, 151, 172, 189, 210, 213
commodity culture   13, 49–50, 53, 54–8
  cultural commodities   56–7, 64–5, 83
  musical commodities   37, 50, 55–7, 58, 63, 73–4, 78–81, 83, 150, 209
  performers as commodities   81–2
  spectacularised commodities   49, 52–5
concertina   72–3
Cooke, Thomas   115
Cooper, John Thomas   46
Corder, Frederick   144
Cowen, Frederic   6, 22, 25, 114–16, 117, 118–19, 121–3, **122**, 124, 136, 141, 146, 168, 210, 213–14
critics, music *see* press, musical
Croft, William   95
Cross, William   188–9
Crosthwaite Museum (Keswick)   88
Crystal Palace (Sydenham)   130, 144, 145
  see also under Great Exhibition of the Works of Industry of All Nations 1851
cultural commodities *see under* commodity culture
cultural diplomacy   172, 196–7, 203
cultural progress   8, 18, 20, 45, 65–7, 84, 85, 91, 106, 109–10, 111–17, 119, 123–4, 125, 209
Cunliffe-Owen, Edward   9
Cunliffe-Owen, Phillip   3, **5**, 9, 89
curiosities   24, 51, 68–70, 89, 182, 209
Curwen, John   112

dance   31, 190, 193–4
Darwinism   20, 91, 191
Debenham, Madame Marie *see* concertina
Debussy, Claude   6
Deichmann, Carl   37
demonstration recitals   60, 72–4, 77, 82–3, 97, 213 *see also* piano recitals
Dilke, Charles Wentworth   31
Döhler, Theodor   95
Donaldson, George   96
Donizetti, Gaetano   38, 162, 163
Duboin, Olga   74
Dundee Amateur Choral Union   124, 125–6

Dutch Singers (Inventions Exhibition) *see under* Netherlands, the

early music *see* ancient music
Edinburgh, Scotland   124, 125
Edinburgh City Police Band *see under* bands (brass and military)
Edinburgh International Exhibition of Industry, Science, and Art 1886   12, 21, 26, 60, 132, 142, 146, 154 n.18, 155-6
  Old Edinburgh Street   21, 86
  see also bands (brass and military), *see also under* organ recitals
Edinburgh International Exhibition of Electrical Engineering, General Inventions, and Industries 1890   2, 9, 12, 14 n.44, 60, 26, 84-5, 87, 89-91, 93, 95, 107, 110, 120, 132-3, 139, 142, 147, 153, 156, 170, 179-80, 184, 213
  see also ancient instruments, bands (brass and military), museum displays *under* non-Western musical instruments, *see also under* oratorio, organ recitals
Edinburgh, University of   89, 90, 180-1
Edison, Thomas Alva   9, 26
education   18, 29, 45, 58-60, 90, 98, 106, 109-10, 111-13, 115-16, 119, 121, 123, 127, 126, 128-9, 134, 144, 150, 161, 178-9, 180, 203
Elizabeth I, Queen, instruments owned by   94, 95, 96, **98**
Ellis, Alexander   203, 213
Elsner, Frederick William   118
Engel, Carl   86
England, United Kingdom   11, 35, 36, 41, 90, 99-100, 118, 120, 156
  Das Land ohne Musik   119, 168
entertainment   3, 15, 17, 18, 21, 24, 26, 27-8, 45-8, 86, 106, 111, 115, 129-34, 136-7, 139-40, 150, 153, 160-1, 187, 213, 214
Érard (piano manufacturer)   42, **43**, 65, 74, 75, 81, 82, 86
ethnographic displays   171, 187-9, 190, 191
  at Calcutta 1883   188
  at Colonial and Indian Exhibition 1886   20-1, 174, 188
  at Liverpool 1886   22, 188-9
ethnomusicology   177, 213
executive commissions *see* commissioners
exhibition buildings   30, 52-4, 111, 128, 209
  acoustics   40, 41, 42, 44, 47

  layout   31, 49, 53, 151, 154, 172
Exhibition of Musical Art *see under* London International Exhibition 1871
exoticism   170, 187-88, 191
experimental instruments *see under* musical instruments
Exposition Universelle 1889 *see* Paris Exposition Universelle 1889
Ezold, William (piano manufacturer)   65-7, **66**, 74

Fétis, François-Joseph   199 n.85
Fincham, George   146
fine arts *see* art objects
Fisheries Exhibition, *see* International Fisheries Exhibition 1883
Fitz-Stubbs, Maud   75
flauti dolci   103-4
food   17, 18, 28, 107, 186, 196, 198, 199, 208
Ford, Thomas   98
France   5-6, 35, 36, 74, 86, 117, 129-30, 152, 172, 191, 192, 212
Frederick II of Prussia   94
Frescobaldi, Girolamo   99
Fuller-Maitland, John   10, 213

Gagliano, Januarius (violin maker)   89, 184
Garden Palace *see* Sydney International Exhibition 1879
Gemünder, George (violin maker)   72
gender   82, 105-6, 154, 164-7
George IV, King of the United Kingdom   94
Germany   35, 36, 66, 67, 117, 118, 155, 212
Gilbert, Jeffrey James (violin maker)   72
Giorza, Paolo   6, 14-15, 74, 75, 79, 80, 113-14, 115, 116, 168
Glasgow Choral Union   120, 124, 125
Glasgow International Exhibition of Science, Art, and Industry 1888   12, 24, **54**, 60, 132, 135, **136**, 142, 148, 154 n.18, 155, 209-10
  piano manufacturers at   62, 69
  see also bands (brass and military), *see also under* organ recitals
Gluck, Christoph Willibald   95
Godfrey, Charles *see under* bands (brass and military)
Godfrey, Dan *see under* bands (brass and military)
Goebel (piano manufacturer)   74
Gounod, Charles   35-6, 38, 73, 138
Granville, Earl *see* Leveson-Gower, George

Great Exhibition of the Works of Industry of All Nations 1851   1, 2, 3, 6, 7–8, 31, 34, 35, 40–2, 45, 51, 53, 54, 58, 59, 85, 129, 145, 151, 172, 199, 212
   Crystal Palace   28, 32, 34, 40, 42, 43, 172
   legacy   28–9, 49, 209–11
   musical exhibits at   6, 31–2, 40, 42, **43**
   Royal Commission   12, 210
   see also bands (brass and military), classification systems, juries and awards, see also under organ recitals
Greenock Choral Union   124, 125
Grenadier Guards see under bands (brass and military)
Grove, George   109
Gung'l, Joseph   73, 139, 163
Gunther (piano manufacturer)   74

Hallé, Charles   75, 77, 80
Hamilton, James, 2nd Duke of Abercorn   9, 89
Hamilton, Marquis of see Hamilton, James, 2nd Duke of Abercorn
Handel, Georg Frideric   38, 46, 69, 88, 89, 94, 99, 101, 117, 120, 145–6, 149, 158
   Israel in Egypt   121, 123
   Judas Maccabaeus   121, 123, 124
   Messiah   34, 53, 90, 121, 122, 123, 124, 126
   Samson   124
   Ode for St Cecilia's Day   124, 125
Hart, Alice (née Rowland)   140
Hart, Ernest   128, 129, 140
Hart, Robert   195–6, 198, 200
Haydn, Joseph   38, 95, 116, 120
   The Creation   121, 122, 124, 125
Health Exhibition, see International Health Exhibition 1884
Heine, Heinrich   33
Herz, Julius   124
Herz & Co. (piano manufacturer)   75, 81
Hesse, Adolf   46
high art music   39, 45, 48, 61–2, 76, 106–7, 109, 110, 112, 113–17, 119, 121, 123, 126–7, 128–9, 135, 144–5, 148–9, 150, 157, 164, 168, 209
Hiller, Ferdinand   35–6
Hipkins, Alfred   64, 180, 213
historical musical instruments see ancient instruments
historical concerts see ancient music
history of music   2, 18, 30, 87, 90–2, 100, 171, 183–4, 213

Hitchcock, John (spinet maker)   96, **97**
Hoffmann, Ernst Theodor Amadeus   33
Horsley, William   98, 102
Howson, Richard   68
Hoyte, William Stevenson   146
Huenerbein, Charles   74, 75, 79
human exhibits see ethnographic displays
Hungarian 'Blue' National Band see under bands (brass and military)
Huxley, Thomas Henry   54
Hyam, Lottie   75, 81–2

imperialism   2, 20, 172–3, 175–7, 180–1, 189–90
India   9, 12, 16–17, 20–1, 76, 171, 172, 173, 174, 177, 178, 180, 181, 182, 188–9, 193–4 see also Indian musical instruments under non-Western musical instruments
Indigenous Australia   23, 189–91
Indonesia see Java
Industrial Revolution   2, 50, 84, 91, 92, 111
instruments see musical instruments
International Fisheries Exhibition 1883   3, 9, 17, 86, 131, 143, 154, 210
   see also bands (brass and military), see also under organ recitals
International Health Exhibition 1884   3, 9, 18, 59, 86, 128, 131, **133**, 137, 140, 143, 148, 154–5, 178, 186, 195–201, 211, 213
   Old London Street   18, 21, 86
   see also bands (brass and military), Chinese music (Health Exhibition), food, see also under organ recitals
International Inventions Exhibition 1885   3, 9, 18–20, **19**, 26, 59, 61, 69, 70, 72, 84–5, 87–9, 90, 92–105, **97**, **98**, **99**, 100–8, 109, 130–2, 131, **131**, **132**, 138, 148–9, 153, 155–61, 170, 179–84, 186, 202–6, 207, 211
   music room   75, 100, 101–3, 105
   piano manufacturers at   62–4, 68–9, 75
   see also ancient instruments, ancient music, bands (brass and military), curiosities, Oriental Room (Inventions Exhibition), period rooms, Siamese Band (Inventions Exhibition), Strauss Orchestra, see also under organ recitals, piano recitals, see also museum displays under non-Western musical instruments
internationalism   35, 151, 172

Inventions Exhibitions, *see* International Inventions Exhibition 1885
Ireland   181, 212
Irving, Henry   3, **4**
Isawa Shūji   178–9
Italian Opera Company (Calcutta)   16, 76
Italy   35, 36, 105, 211, 212

Japan   171, 174–5, 178–9, 180, 212 *see also* Tokyo Institute of Music
Java   6, 180, 191, 203 n.110
Jeffreys, John   148
Johor   175–6, 178
Joubert, Jules   16, 137
jubilee exhibitions   13 *see also* Adelaide Jubilee International Exhibition 1887
juries and awards   6, 14, 44–5, 51, 67, 175, 176, 177, 178, 179, 211
juvenile exhibitions   13

Kaps (piano manufacturer)   66, 75
Kastner, Frederic *see* pyrophone
Keats, John   94
Kelvingrove Art Gallery and Museum (Glasgow)   210
Ketten, Henri *see under* Austrian Strauss Band
Kierkegaard, Søren   33
King, Blanche   76
Kinsey Vale, William Mountford   9
Kopff, Arnold Theodore *see under* bands (brass and military)
Kowalski, Henri   75, 81

Lachenal & Co. *see* concertina
ladies' orchestras   165–7 *see also* Viennese Ladies' Orchestra
Lamal, Léontine   74, 80
Landon, Letitia Elizabeth   27
Lange, Daniel de   103
Lapland *see* Sámi people
Lassus, Orlande de   103, 105
Lavery, John   135–6
Lee, Elizabeth, Diary of   140
Lefébure-Wely, Louis   69
leisure   29, 45–8, 111, 128–9, 130–4, 144, 145, 209
Lemare, Edwin   146
Leveson-Gower, George, 2nd Earl of Granville   34
Liszt, Franz   39, 95, 117
Liverpool International Exhibition of Navigation, Commerce, and Industry 1886   12, 22, **23**, 59, 132, 134, 135, 140, 142, 154, 164–7, 187–9 *see also* bands (brass and military), Viennese Ladies' Orchestra, *see also under* ethnographic displays
living ethnological exhibits *see* ethnographic displays
Lloyd, Lieutenant-Colonel John   32
London, England   3–4, 9, 12, 28, 29, 58, 74, 119, 130, 140, 156, 168, 171, 198, 203, 209, 211–12
London International Exhibition 1862   18, 28, 34, 41–2, 44–5, 46, 47, 59, 129
London International Exhibition 1871   28, 47, 59
   Exhibition of Musical Art   35–7, 46
London International Exhibition 1872   28, 45, 47, 59, 86
   Special Exhibitions of Ancient Musical Instruments   86–7
London International Exhibition 1873   28, 32, 37–9, 59
London International Exhibition 1874   28, 48, 59
Lunn, Henry C.   34, 36, 161

Macfarren, George   36
Machell, Thomas   69
Mahillon, Victor   88, 98, 100–1, 181
Malay Peninsula *see* Straits Settlements *see also* Johor
manuscripts (historic)   84, 87, 88, 89–90, 92, 95
Maria Theresa, Holy Roman Empress   94
Marr, Robert A.   87
Marshall, Julian   95
Martin, Lizzie   76
Marx, Karl   52, 55, 83
masculinity   105–6, 165
material culture   49, 56–7, 209
Mattei, Tito   75
Meilhan, Jules   74, 79, 80
Melbourne Centennial International Exhibition 1888   6, 9, 12, 13, 24–6, **25**, 60, 73, 76, 114, 121, 124, 132, 134, 136–8, 141, 146, 168, 209, 210, 213–4
   Centennial Exhibition Choir   121, **122**
   orchestral music at   110, 113, 114, 115–19, 141, 213 *see also* Cowen, Frederic
piano manufacturers at   50, 62, 67–8
plebiscite concert   117–19

see also bands (brass and military), *see also under* oratorio, organ recitals, piano recitals
Melbourne International Exhibition 1880   6, 9, 12, 15–16, 51, 59, 73, 77–8, 134, 135, 141, 146, 153, 161–4, 168, 170, 172, 175, 176–178, 209, 210, 212
   piano manufacturers at   58, 60–1, **61**, 63, 67, 75–6, 81
   see also Australian Band, Austrian Strauss Band, bands (brass and military), *see also under* organ recitals, piano recitals
Melbourne Philharmonic Society   120, 123
Mendelssohn, Felix   38, 69, 79, 94, 95, 120, 145, 146
   Athalie   138, 148–9, 158
   Elijah   121, 122
Metzler & Co. (instrument manufacturer)   69, 72
Meyerbeer, Giacomo   35, 73, 146, 154
   Le Prophète   80, 162–3
Miranda, Lalla   76
modernity   18, 84–5, 93, 107–8, 134, 151
Monier-Williams, Monier   188, 193–4
Morgan, George Washbourne   46
Moscheles, Felix   95
Moscheles, Ignaz   95
Mozart, Wolfgang Amadeus   38, 81, 90, 95, 104, 115, 116, 146
Munro, James   9
museums, public   29–30, 95–6
musical commodities *see under* commodity culture
musical instruments   6, 18, 27–30, 31–2, 40–1, 42–5, 49, 50–1, 55–6, 57–60, 72–4, 77, 78–80, 84–5
   as aesthetic objects   51, 56–8, 60, 61–4
   as museum objects   60, 64–5, 72, 87–98, **88**, 209
   as national objects   65–8, 153
   Australian-made   65–7
   experimental   42, 51, 68–70, 89, 182
   see also pyrophone, vocalion
   see also ancient instruments, demonstration recitals, non-Western musical instruments, *see also* musical commodities *under* commodity culture
musical museum concept   28, 33–4, 37–9
music
   definition of   31, 33
   ephemerality   27, 30, 31–3, 37, 39, 48, 148–9, 209

   representation   27, 31–2, 34, 36, 37, 48, 49, 57–8, 214
Myanmar *see* Burma

national musics   34–7
native villages *see* ethnographic displays
Netherlands, the   212
   Dutch Singers (Inventions Exhibition)   99, 103, 105–6, 167
New Zealand   13, 191 n.31, 212
Nicholson, James   78, **79**
non-Western musical instruments   170, 174, 179, 186, 192
   at Adelaide 1887   170, 175
   at Calcutta 1883   170, 176
   at Colonial and Indian Exhibition 1886   170, 173–4, 175, 176
   at Melbourne 1880   170, 175, 176–7
   at Sydney 1879   170, 175
   Indian instruments   174, 176–7, 180, 181–2, 183, 184
   Malay instruments   174–6
   museum displays   87, 88, 92, 170–1, 179–85 *see also* Oriental Room (Inventions Exhibition)
non-Western music   184–5, 186–7, 208, 209, 213
   at Chicago World's Columbian Exhibition 1893   6, 191–2
   at Paris Exposition Universelle 1889   6, 191–2
   comparisons with Scottish music   207–8
   tropes in Western reception of   191–5, 199–201
   see also Burmese Music *under* Burma, *see also* Chinese Music (Health Exhibition), *see also* Siamese Band (Inventions Exhibition)
Norman, Barak (luthier)   89
North, Emilie   75
nostalgia *see* romanticism
Novello   37, 95

Oakley, Herbert   180
ocarina   73
oratorio   110, 112–3, 119–20, 126–7
   at Adelaide 1887   110, 119, 121, 123
   at Edinburgh 1890   26, 110, 119, 124–6
   at Melbourne 1888   110, 119, 121–24
   at Sydney 1879   15, 110, 119, 121, 123, 126
   in Australian culture   120, 124
   in England   119
   in Scotland   120, 124–6

orchestral music   110, 113–19, 213
    see also under Melbourne Centennial
        International Exhibition 1888,
        Sydney International Exhibition
        1879
organisers *see* commissioners
organology   170, 177, 180–1, 183, 184–5,
    192, 199, 203
organ recitals   28, 47, 48, 69, 145–50
    amateur players   146–8
    at Edinburgh 1886   21, 146–7
    at Edinburgh 1890   26, 147–8
    at Fisheries Exhibition 1883   17
    at Glasgow 1888   24, 148
    at Great Exhibition 1851   34, 45–6, 145
    at Health Exhibition 1884   18, 148
    at Inventions Exhibition 1885   20, 99,
        105, 145, 148, 149–50
    at Melbourne 1880   16, 146, **147**,
    at Melbourne 1888   146
    repertoire in relation to band
        music   45, 128, 146, 148
    secular recitals   45–6, 47, 130, 145–6,
        213
organs   47, 78, 128, 145, 178, 199
orientalism   171–5, 179, 180–85, 188,
    191–3, 204, 206–8
    auto-orientalism   174–5
Oriental Room (Inventions
    Exhibition)   87, 170, 180, 181–2
Ortori, Ercole   75

Packer, Charles   121, 123
Paisley Choral Union   124
Palestrina, Giovanni Pierluigi da   99,
    102, 104, 105–6
Paris Exposition Universelle 1889   6,
    86, 152–3, 191 *see also under* non-
    Western music
Pater, Walter   33
Pauer, Ernst   44, 45, 75
Pauer, Max von   75
Peake, George   114
People's Concert Society   112
period rooms   87, 94, 95–7, **97**, **98**, **99**,
    170, 180
phantasmagoria   49, 52, 53, 55, 57
piano recitals   42–5, 73–83, 213
    at Calcutta 1883   73, 76
    at London 1885   44, 73, 75, 77, 78
    at Melbourne 1880   16, 73, 75–6, 77–8,
        81
    at Melbourne 1888   73, 76
    at Sydney 1879   15, 73, 74–5, 77, 78, **79**,
        79–80, 81, **82**

    see also demonstration recitals
pianos   50, 60, 62–8, 70–1
    British manufacturers   64, 67–8
    French manufacturers   58, **60**, 64–5,
        67, 74
    German manufacturers   66–8, 76, 79
    in Australia   50, 51, 65–8
    social significance   50–1, 63, 68, 70
    see also musical instruments
Pigdon, John   9
Pinsuti, Ciro   35–6
Playfair, Lyon   58
pleasure gardens   3, 45, 47, 128, 129–34,
    140–1, 145
Pleyel (piano manufacturer)   62, 64–5,
    74, 75–6
Pomeranian or Blücher Hussars *see under*
    bands (brass and military)
popular music   45, 47–8, 81, 106, 107,
    110, 112, 115, 116, 128–9, 130, 135,
    143–4, 145–6, 148, 150, 153–4, 156,
    157, 160, 187, 198, 209 *see also* bands
    (brass and military), *see also* organ
    recitals, *see also* Strauss Orchestra
Portman, Maurice Vidal   188
Portobello Choral Society   124, 125
press, musical   10–11, 14, 31
    critical priorities   10, 31, 39, 45, 74,
        107, 123, 142–3, 150, 160
    racism in   11, 192–3, 195–6, 199–200
    relationship with general daily
        press   10–11, 39
progressivism   8, 45, 68, 84, 85–6, 91–3,
    170, 171, 183–5, 191 *see also* cultural
    progress
public health   128–9, 130, 134, 139–40,
    209
Pugin, Augustus Welby Northmore   85
Punch Magazine   3, **4**, **5**, 131–2, 137, 155,
    186, 201
Purcell, Henry   104–5
pyrophone   70

race   20, 187, 206–8
racism   170, 174, 180–1, 187, 190–1, 199
    developmentalist racism   92 171,
        177–8, 183–5, 191
Raffles, Stamford   180, 203 n.110
Ramayana (Sanskrit epic)   193–4
Rameau, Jean-Philippe   101, 104
rational recreation   29, 45, 110, 111–13,
    115, 126–7, 129, 130, 134, 139–41, 143,
    145, 150, 178
reception studies   10–11
Reid, Vernon   75

Reid, Colonel William   31
religion   34, 53–4, 61, 128, 140, 145, 204
Reynolds, Thomas   156–7
Rockstro, William Smith   99, 102, 104
Roger-Miclos, Marie-Aimée   75
romanticism   64–5, 84, 85, 87, 91–5, 96, 101, 103, 107
Rose, John (luthier)   94
Rossini, Gioachino   35, 38, 73, 138, 154
    William Tell Overture   117, 143, 162, 163
Round, Catch, and Canon Club   98, 99–100
Rousseau, Jean-Jacques   207
Royal Albert Hall   29, **30**, 37, 45, 48, 84, 87, **88**, 100, 130, 132, 143, 149, 157, 159, 186, 202, 210
Royal Artillery Band *see under* bands (brass and military)
Royal College of Music   88, 181–2, 210
Royal Horse Artillery Band *see under* bands (brass and military)
Royal Horse Guards (Blues) Band *see under* bands (brass and military)
Royal Horticultural Society Gardens   3, 130, **131**, 157
Royal Marines Band *see under* bands (brass and military)
Royal Swedish Värmland Grenadiers *see under* bands (brass and military)
Rubinstein, Anton   95
Rummel, Franz   75
Ruskin, John   91

sacred music   89–90, 99, 102, 104–5, 106, 145
Sámi people   188
Sarasate, Pablo de   95
Sargood, Frederick   213
Scherek, Benno   76
Schipek, Marie *see under* Viennese Ladies' Orchestra
Schlegel, August Wilhelm   91
school bands   40–2
Schubert, Franz   73, 116, 117, 158, 159
Schumann, Clara   95
Schumann, Robert   116, 150
Scotland, United Kingdom   9, 89, 90, 120, 124–5, 126, 135, 137, 142, 146, 155–6, 207–8, 210
Shakespeare, William   31, 94, 143
Shaw, George Bernard   69–70, 72, 94, 104, 105, 106, 131, 143, 145, 149–50, 157, 160, 204, 205, 206, 207–8

Shean, Christian (harpsichord and spinet maker)   89
Shedlock, John South   100, 104
sheet music   210–11
Siam   171, 202–3
    king *see* Chulalongkorn, Rama V
    musical instruments   202, 203, 204
    Siamese Legation in London   203, 205 *see also* Verney, Frederick
Siamese Band (Inventions Exhibition)   20, 186–7, 202, 203
    performance of Western music   205
    reception in London   204–5, 206–8
Smart, George   34
Smith, Alexander Kennedy   9
Smith, Hermann   93–4
Smith, Robert Murray   9
Somers Vine, John   3, **5**, 9
South Kensington   3, **19**, 20, 144, 205, 209
    Albertopolis   29, **30**, 210
    'Gang'   9
    Museum   29, 86–7, 89
Spark, William   146
Special Exhibitions of Ancient Musical Instruments *see under* London International Exhibition 1872
spectacle   29, 49, 52–3, 55, 128, 130
Spohr, Louis   95
Stainer, John   178
Steinway (piano manufacturer)   74, 75, 78, 79–80, 104
Stephen, James (piano manufacturer)   12
Stonyhurst College   180
Stradivarius   72, 87, 89
Straits Settlements   171, 172, 175–6
Strauss, Eduard   20, 153, 154, 157, 158, 159–60, **160**, 165
Strauss I, Johann   150, 157
Strauss II, Johann   116, 138, 157, 158, 162, 163, 164
Strauss, Josef   157
Strauss Orchestra   20, 153, 154, 156, 157–61, 167
Stuart, Prince Charles Edward   94
Sullivan, Arthur   73, 100, 138, 139, 154
    Golden Legend   122
    The Lost Chord   143
    The Mikado   143, 187 n.5
    On Shore and Sea   35–6
'Sumer is icumen in'   90, 100, 102
Summerhayes, Cecilia   74, 80, 81, **82**
Svensson, Axel *see under* bands (brass and military)

Sweelinck, Jan Pieterszoon 103, 105–6
Sydney International Exhibition 1879 2, 6, 12, 14–15, **15**, 59, 73, 77, 79–82, 111, 121, 123, 126–7, 135, 141, 153, 167–8, 170, 175
   orchestral music at 110, 113, 115, 116–17 *see also* Giorza, Paolo
   piano manufacturers at 65–7, **66**, 74–5, 78, **79**, 82
   see also bands (brass and military), *see also under* non-Western musical instruments, oratorio, piano recitals

Tagore, Sourindro Mohun 16, 170, 174, 176–8, 179, 180, 181–2, 183, 210
Tallis, Thomas 90, 102
Tasca, Carlotta 75–6
taste 107, 111–13, 114–16, 117–19, 121, 123–4, 128, 135, 144, 146, 148
Taverner, John 89
taxonomy *see* classification systems
Thailand *see* Siam
Thalberg, Sigismund 51, 79, 80
theatre 3–4, 31, 211–12
Thuringian Regiment (German Infantry) Band *see under* bands (brass and military)
Thürmer (piano manufacturer) 63
Tielke, Joachim (viola maker) 89
Tilley, Arthur *see* banjo
Tokyo Institute of Music 170, 174, 178–9, 180
Tollemache Family 94–5
Toms, Reginald 74
tonic sol-fa 112, 212
Tonking, Henry Charles 146
Toole, John Lawrence 3
Trevor, Lieutenant William 32
Turpin, James 146

Ure, James *see under* Australian Band
United States 6, 14, 42, 74, 111, 129, 172, 195, 212
universalism 92, 151, 168, 172, 183, 208

Valenza, Michele Angelo 76
Varariddhi, Prince Nares 203
Veitch, James 180
Verdi, Giuseppe 35, 73, 95, 138

Verney, Frederick 203–4, 206
Verney, Harry 180, 203 n.110
Victoria, Queen 9, 13, 20, 22, 42, 175
Victoria & Albert Museum 12, 29, 95 n.64, 209
Victorian Orchestra (Melbourne) 210
Viennese Ladies' Orchestra 22, 153–4, 164–7, **165**
   Schipek, Marie 164
Vinaccia, Antonius (mandoline maker) 89
Vinton, Justus Brainerd 188
vocalion 69–70, 149, 202

Waldteufel, Emile 73, 115, 138, 164
Wales, United Kingdom 40–1
Wales, Prince of *see* Albert Edward, Prince of Wales (later Edward VII)
Wagner, Richard 38, 95, 117, 138, 146, 154, 159
   Australian reception 115 n.38, 117–19
   comparisons to non-Western music 200
   Tannhäuser overture 117, 138, 139, 143
Webbe, Samuel 98
Weber, Carl Maria von 35, 146, 158, 163
Weelkes, Thomas 98, 102
Wesley, Samuel 95
Wheatstone & Co. *see* concertina
Wildner, Alois F. *see under* Austrian Strauss Band
women's orchestras *see* ladies' orchestras
Wood, Henry 146
work concept 6, 28, 33–6, 37–9, 57, 78–81
World's Columbian Exposition, Chicago 1893 6, 191, *see also under* non-Western music
Wulf, Charles de 80
Wylde, Henry 200

Young Australia Band *see under* bands (brass and military)

zat pwe see Burmese music *under* Burma
Zavertal, Ladislao *see under* bands (brass and military)
Zelman, Alberto 75, 114
Zimmermann, Agnes 75

Titles listed here were originally published
under the series title *Music in Britain, 1600–1900*
ISSN 1752-1904

Lectures on Musical Life: William Sterndale Bennett
edited by Nicholas Temperley, with Yunchung Yang

John Stainer: A Life in Music
Jeremy Dibble

*The Pursuit of High Culture: John Ella and
Chamber Music in Victorian London*
Christina Bashford

Thomas Tallis and his Music in Victorian England
Suzanne Cole

The Consort Music of William Lawes, 1602–1645
John Cunningham

Life After Death: The Viola da Gamba in Britain from Purcell to Dolmetsch
Peter Holman

*The Musical Salvationist: The World of Richard Slater (1854–1939)
'Father of Salvation Army Music'*
Gordon Cox

*British Music and Literary Context
Artistic Connections in the Long Nineteenth Century*
Michael Allis

New titles published under the series title *Music in Britain, 1600–2000*
ISSN 2053-3217

Hamilton Harty: Musical Polymath
Jeremy Dibble

Thomas Morley: Elizabethan Music Publisher
Tessa Murray

*The Advancement of Music in Enlightenment England:
Benjamin Cooke and the Academy of Ancient Music*
Tim Eggington

George Smart and Nineteenth-Century London Concert Life
John Carnelley

The Lives of George Frideric Handel
David Hunter

Musicians of Bath and Beyond: Edward Loder (1809–1865) and his Family
edited by Nicholas Temperley

Conductors in Britain, 1870–1914: Wielding the Baton at the Height of Empire
Fiona M. Palmer

Ernest Newman: A Critical Biography
Paul Watt

*The Well-Travelled Musician: John Sigismond Cousser and Musical Exchange in
Baroque Europe*
Samantha Owens

Music in the West Country: Social and Cultural History Across an English Region
Stephen Banfield

British Musical Criticism and Intellectual Thought, 1850–1950
edited by Jeremy Dibble and Julian Horton

*Composing History: National Identities and the
English Masque Revival, 1860–1920*
Deborah Heckert

With Mornefull Musique: Funeral Elegies in Early Modern England
K. Dawn Grapes

Music for St Cecilia's Day: From Purcell to Handel
Bryan White

*Before the Baton: Musical Direction and Conducting
in Stuart and Georgian Britain*
Peter Holman

*Organ-building in Georgian and Victorian England:
The Work of Gray & Davison, 1772–1890*
Nicholas Thistlethwaite

*Musical Exchange between Britain and Europe, 1500–1800:
Essays in Honour of Peter Holman*
edited by John Cunningham and Bryan White

The Symphonic Poem in Britain, 1850–1950
edited by Michael Allis and Paul Watt

*British Music, Musicians and Institutions, c. 1630–1800:
Essays in Honour of Harry Diack Johnstone*
Edited by Peter Lynan and Julian Rushton

John Gunn: Musician Scholar in Enlightenment Britain
George Kennaway